History of Cambridge, Massachusetts. 1630-1877

HISTORY

OF

CAMBRIDGE,

MASSACHUSETTS.

1630—1877.

WITH A

GENEALOGICAL REGISTER.

BY

LUCIUS R. PAIGE.

BOSTON:
PUBLISHED BY H. O. HOUGHTON AND COMPANY.
NEW YORK: HURD AND HOUGHTON.
Cambridge: The Riverside Press.
1877.

Lucius R. Paige.

CAMBRIDGE,
AS BOUNDED IN
1644 – 1655.
Extending from
Dedham to the Merrimack River.

Billerica.

Bedford.

Lexington.

Arlington.

Cambridge.

Brighton.

Newton.

The Riverside Press, Cambridge:
Printed by H. O. Houghton and Company.

To

THE MEMBERS OF THE

MASSACHUSETTS HISTORICAL SOCIETY,

AND OF THE

NEW ENGLAND HISTORIC GENEALOGICAL SOCIETY,

This Volume

IS DEDICATED BY ITS AUTHOR,

THEIR ASSOCIATE.

PREFACE.

In collecting materials for a History of Cambridge, I examined first its Municipal Records, which are continuous from the beginning, but generally brief, and its Registry of Births and Deaths, which, during the second hundred years after the foundation of the town, is very defective. To supply what was lacking, I consulted such printed authorities as were accessible, together with the manuscript Records and Archives of the Commonwealth, of the judicial courts, and of several counties, cities, towns, churches, and libraries. My thanks are due to all the custodians of such books, and records, and archives, for their uniform courtesy and kindness. I have also obtained many genealogical details from the Church Record of Baptisms and Burials, from Probate Records and Files, from inscriptions on gravestones, and from funeral sermons, and newspapers. After the expenditure of much time and labor, however, I am conscious of many deficiencies.

It will be seen that the Genealogical Register is chiefly confined to the families who dwelt in Cambridge before the year 1700, — the descendants of such as remained here being traced down to a recent period. A very few families are included who became residents at a later date; but these form the exception, not the rule. So also in regard to the History, comparatively few recent events are mentioned. It would be impracticable, in a single volume, to include with our ancient annals everything which those who are now living have witnessed, and to trace the genealogy of all our nearly fifty thousand inhabitants. A line must be drawn somewhere; but whether I have drawn it in the most proper place, there may be various opinions.

Moreover, the reader may be disappointed because he finds so little concerning Harvard College, and the military occupation of Cambridge, at the commencement of the Revolutionary War; but the facts stated on pages 365 (*note*) and 408 are believed to justify the omission. The almost entire absence of legendary lore may be regretted; but it should be considered, that while it may have been my misfortune, it was not my fault, that I was not born in Cambridge, and that I had no opportunity in the first thirty years of my life to gather the local traditions, which so deeply impress the youthful mind, and which tinge the facts of history with such a brilliant, though often a deceptive light. If lack of vigor and sprightliness be regarded as a serious fault of style, I may plead in extenuation, that although many of my materials were gathered long ago, I was obliged by other engagements, literary as well as secular, to postpone their final arrangement for publication, until impaired health and the infirmities of age became uncomfortably manifest.

LUCIUS R. PAIGE.

CAMBRIDGE, *March*, 1877.

CONTENTS.

CHAPTER I.

General description of the town, its several additions and diminutions of territory. 1–5

CHAPTER II.

The New Town selected as fit for a fortified place. General agreement to erect houses. Several Assistants fail to do so. Controversy between Dudley and Winthrop. Earliest inhabitants. Canal. Palisade. Arrival of the Braintree Company. Common Pales. Division of lands. Highways. 6–16

CHAPTER III.

First Constable appointed. Deputies to the first General Court. Monthly meeting. No houses to be erected without permission, nor outside of the town. All houses to be covered with slate or boards, not with thatch, and to "range even." Trees not to be cut down and left in the highways. Cartway. Windmill-hill. Timber not to be sold out of the town. First Constable elected. Surveyor of highways. Lots not improved to revert to the town. First Townsmen or Selectmen. Surveyors of lands. 17–22

CHAPTER IV.

Prosperity of the New Town. Magistrates. Courts. Dissatisfaction. John Pratt. Straitness for want of land. Exploration of other places. Debates and division in the General Court. The town accepts enlargement offered by Boston and Watertown. Removal to Hartford. Supposed personal rivalry. Names of early inhabitants. . 23–33

CHAPTER V.

Arrival of Shepard's Company, and some of their names. New Municipal Officers. New division of lands. Monthly meetings. Ferry. Lectures. Cow Common. Goats. Herd of cows. Weir for taking alewives. Herd on the south side of the river. Herd of swine. Fowls not permitted to enter gardens. Cartway to the weir. Pound. Stumps. Neither houses nor lands to be sold or let, without consent of the Townsmen. Strangers not to be harbored. Grant of land to the Drummer. Fort Hill. Grant of land at Vine Brook. Swine to be yoked and ringed. Apple trees and other quickset to be preserved from damage by goats. Births, marriages, and burials to be recorded. Farms granted. Grant of money by the General Court for a College. Organization of the militia. The College to be at New Town. Marshal General. The New Town named Cambridge. Printing-press. Bond of Stephen Daye to Jose Glover. . . . . . . 34—45

CHAPTER VI.

Contemplated removal to Weathersfield, Conn. Letter from Winthrop to Hooker. Letter from Hooker to Shepard. Depreciation in the value of property. Danger of general bankruptcy. Reasons for removing. Sir Henry Vane. Grant of Shawshine to Cambridge. Removal of John Haynes. Death of Roger Harlakenden. Arrival of Herbert Pelham. Town Spring. Restrictions on the cutting of trees. Field-drivers, Commissioners to end small causes, Clerk of the Market, and Sealer of Leather, first elected. Calves impounded. Eight-penny ordinary for Townsmen. Penalty for absence from monthly meetings. Prosecution for trespass in the Great Swamp. Fence-viewers first elected. Remission of tax on account of sickness. Chimneys to be swept every month and ladders to be kept ready for reaching the roofs of houses. Orchard. Wharf. Division of Shawshine lands. Incorporation of Billerica. . . . . 46—62

CHAPTER VII.

Change of Government in England. Cromwell desires to colonize Jamaica, and employs Daniel Gookin as special agent. Letters from Gookin to Secretary Thurloe. Death of Cromwell. Whalley and Goffe, two of the late King's judges, visit Cambridge. Fragment of Goffe's Journal. The General Court appoints a Committee, to report concerning "The due observance of obedience and fidelity unto the authority of England, and our own just privileges." Report of Committee. Instructions to the "Messengers" sent to England. Qualified oath of allegiance offered by Gookin and Danforth. The Messengers to England return with a letter from the King, promising to confirm the privileges of the people, but requiring sundry changes in their laws. Day of thanksgiving appointed. Reply of the General Court to the King's letter. Commissioners appointed by the King to enforce obedience. Cambridge sustains the General Court in their controversy with the Commissioners. Edward Randolph, the "arch-enemy of the colony." The Charter abrogated, and Sir Edmund Andros appointed Governor of New England. . . . . 63—78

CHAPTER VIII.

The inhabitants on the south side of the river obtain parochial privileges. Their petition for incorporation as a separate town. Elaborate and vigorous protest by the Selectmen of Cambridge. After long delay, Newton is incorporated, under the administration of Andros. Ship-building in Cambridge. Unruly dogs. Wolf. Drain-

CAMBRIDGE,
AS BOUNDED IN
1644 – 1655.
*Extending from
Dedham to the Merrimack River.*

Billerica

Bedford

Lexington

Arlington

Cambridge

Brighton

Newton

COPYRIGHT, 1877,
BY LUCIUS R. PAIGE.

The Riverside Press, Cambridge:
Printed by H. O. Houghton and Company.

men. Blue Anchor. Samuel Gibson fined for unlawfully entertaining Students. Innholders and Retailers during a century. Petitions of Edmund Angier and John Stedman. Memorial of President Dunster on behalf of Mrs. Bradish. Prices established. Market Places. Market house. Burial places. Common; contest concerning its enclosure. Town House. Athenæum, converted into a City Hall. Sectional rivalry and jealousy. Petition for a division of the town; rejected by the General Court. Unsuccessful attempt to remove difficulties. Petition for a City Charter. A new petition for division interposed, which, like another presented nine years later, was unsuccessful. City Charter granted and accepted. 210-246

CHAPTER XV.

First Meeting-house. Rev. Thomas Hooker and Rev. Samuel Stone. First Church organized. Removal to Hartford. Rev. Thomas Shepard. Another "First Church" organized. Newell's "Church Gathering." McKenzie's "Historical Lectures." Roger Harlakenden. Shepard's reasons for removing to New England. Mrs. Shepard's admission to the Church, and her death. Confessions of candidates for Church membership. Contributions and expenditures. Rev. John Phillips. Death of Mr. Shepard. Synods at Cambridge. Second Meeting-house. Rev. Jonathan Mitchell; in many respects "Matchless." Sibley's "Harvard Graduates." Financial records. Salary. Seating of the Meeting-house. Reputed heresy of President Dunster. Death of Mr. Mitchell, and the place of his burial. Care of the youth. Parsonage erected, and bill of expenses. Rev. Urian Oakes; expense of his ordination. Almsdeeds of the Church. Labors, trials, and death of Mr. Oakes. Intense political and religious excitement. Address by the "Freemen of Cambridge" to the General Court, against universal toleration. Sermon of Mr. Oakes on the same subject. Rev. Nathaniel Gookin and Elders Clark and Stone ordained, with bill of expenses. Quiet ministry and death of Mr. Gookin. Salary of Pastors at different periods. Church organized at the Farms. Ordination of Rev. William Brattle; his ministry and death. Third Meeting-house. Extraordinary snow-storm. Election of Rev. Nathaniel Appleton. Parsonage rebuilt. Enlargement of Meeting-house. Church organized at Menotomy. Fourth Meeting-house. Rev. George Whitefield. Church organized on the south side of the river. The prolonged and valuable services of Dr. Appleton recognized by Harvard College; his death. Installation of Rev. Timothy Hilliard, and his death, after a short ministry. Installation of Rev. Abiel Holmes. Theological controversy, resulting in the disruption of the Church. Results of Councils. Shepard Congregational Society organized. Ordination of Rev. Nehemiah Adams as Colleague Pastor. Dismission and death of Dr. Holmes. Meeting-house. Dismission of Mr. Adams. Rev. John A. Albro, D. D., and Rev. Alexander McKenzie. New Meeting-house. Ordination of Rev. William Newell; his long and peaceful ministry and resignation. Meeting-house. Ordination of Rev. Francis G. Peabody. Ruling Elders. Deacons. 247-306

CHAPTER XVI.

Christ Church, Cambridgeport Parish. University Church. First Baptist. First Universalist. Second Universalist. First Methodist. Third Congregational. Second Baptist. First Evangelical Congregational. Second Evangelical Congregational. Evangelical (East Cambridge). St. Peter's (Episcopal). St. John's. Harvard Street Methodist. Old Cambridge Baptist. Lee Street. St. Peter's (Catholic). Third Universalist. North Cambridge Baptist. North Avenue Congregational. Pilgrim Congregational. Broadway Baptist. Free Church of St. James. Methodist Episcopal (Old Cambridge). St. Mary's. St. John's Memorial. Chapel Congregational. Cottage Street Methodist. St. Paul's. Church of the Sacred Heart. Ascension Church. Charles River Baptist 307–343

CHAPTER XVII.

Antinomians. Baptists. Quakers. Elizabeth Hooton and other disturbers of the peace. Benanuel Bowers, and his family. Witchcraft. Rebecca Jacobs. Petition of Rebecca Fox. Mrs. Kendall. A man troubled by cats or the devil. Winifred Holman, and her daughter Mary Holman. Testimony. Verdict. 344–364

CHAPTER XVIII.

Education. Harvard College. Grammar School. Elijah Corlett. Indian Students. Corlett's letter of thanks to the County Court. Nicholas Fessenden, Jr. William Fessenden, Jr. Samuel Danforth. Veterans now in service. Agreement for erecting a school-house. Allowance to Mr. Dunster and his heirs. Schools of lower grade. Schools established in Cambridgeport and East Cambridge. School-houses in 1845, 1850, and 1876. School Committee. School districts. Graded schools. Hopkins school. Salaries of teachers at different periods. 365–381

CHAPTER XIX.

Indians. Squa Sachem. Tribe near Mystic Pond. Indian titles purchased. Fence to secure the Indians' corn. Cutshamakin. Waban, and Indians at Nonantum. The apostle Eliot's labors ; assisted by his son, Rev. John Eliot, Jr., and by Rev. Daniel Gookin, Jr. Town of Natick. Eliot's mission extended to other tribes. Missions to the heathen emphatically commenced in Cambridge. Partial successes. Attempts to educate the Indians. Dunster's account of expenses for one year. Daniel Gookin actively engaged in the Indian work from the beginning ; appointed Ruler and Superintendent of all the friendly Indians ; record of one of his courts. Philip's War. Prejudice against all the Indians ; many imprisoned on Deer Island. Gookin and Danforth friendly to the Indians ; savage attacks on them, and on the Rev. Mr. Eliot. 382–395

CHAPTER XX.

Military organization. Expedition against Gorton. Narragansett War. Energetic services of Major Gookin. Reasons why old men of sixty years are not to train. Long service of Capt. Samuel Green. Soldiers in the Wars from 1690 to 1740; Old French War, 1744 to 1748; French War, 1753 to 1763. Memorial of Capt. William Angier. Gen. William Brattle. Troop of Cavalry. War of the Revolution. Rolls of Cambridge soldiers in the Battle of Lexington. Some events during that conflict. More persons killed in Cambridge than elsewhere. Monument in memory of the slain. Capt. Samuel Whittemore desperately wounded. Damage to property. Troops stationed in Cambridge. College buildings used for barracks. Hospitals established. Battle of Bunker Hill. Col. Thomas Gardner. Arrival of General Washington. Head-quarters. Military Works in Cambridge. Disposition of the troops. Military operations. Evacuation of Boston. Difficulty in obtaining military stores. Gen. Burgoyne's troops. Cambridge Officers and Soldiers engaged in the Revolutionary War. War of 1812. Cambridge not enthusiastic in its favor. Light Infantry. War of the Rebellion. Cambridge organizes the first military company for the defence of the Union; Roll of that company. Richmond surrendered to a Cambridge Officer. Officers and Soldiers furnished by Cambridge during the War. Soldiers' Monument erected by the City; names inscribed thereon. Nearly forty-six hundred men, about one sixth part of the entire population of Cambridge, rendered active service in this internecine conflict. . . . . 396—438

CHAPTER XXI.

Valuation in 1647. Rate list in 1688. Census in 1777. Valuation in 1781. List of Voters in 1822. Census at intervals from 1765 to 1875. Number of Polls, Valuation, rate and amount of Tax, and amount of the City Debt, in each year from the incorporation of the City in 1846 to 1875. Census in 1875. Vice-president of the United States. Governors. Deputy or Lieutenant-governors. Assistants. Councillors. Senators. Representatives. Selectmen. Assessors. Town Clerks. Town Treasurers. Mayors. Aldermen. Presidents of the Common Council. Members of the Common Council. City Clerks. City Treasurers. Clerks of the Common Council. . . . . 439—475

GENEALOGIES. 477

KEY TO THE PLAN OF "CAMBRIDGE IN 1635,"

Indicating the owners and occupants of the several lots, in 1635, and in 1642. All are supposed to have been homesteads, unless otherwise designated.

No.	In 1635.	In 1642.
1	William Westwood.[1]	Public Lot.
2	James Olmstead.	Edward Goffe.
3	William Pantry.	Harvard College.[2]
4	Rev. Thomas Hooker.	Rev. Thomas Shepard.
5	John White.[2]	Richard Champney.[3]
6	John Clark.[3]	Thomas Beal.[3]
7	William Wadsworth.[2]	Samuel Shepard.[3]
8	John White.	Thomas Danforth.
9	John Hopkins.[3]	Mark Pierce.
10	John White.[3]	Edward Collins.
11	William Goodwin.	Samuel Shepard.
12	John Steele.	Robert Bradish.
13	William Wadsworth.	Richard Champney.
14	Widow Esther Muzzey.	Henry Dunster.[4]
15	Daniel Abbott.	Francis Moore.
16	Daniel Abbott.	John Russell.
17	Thomas Heate.	Thomas Marrett.
18	Christopher Cane.	William Towne.
19	Nathaniel Hancock.	Nathaniel Hancock.
20	George Steele.	Edward Goffe.[4]
21	Edward Stebbins.	Nathan Aldus.
22	Timothy Stanley.	William French.
23	Jonas Austin.	Katherine Haddon.
24	John Hopkins.	Edmund Angier.
25	Thomas Beale.	Thomas Beale.
26	Rev. Samuel Stone.	Nathaniel Sparhawk.
27	Simon Bradstreet, Esq.	Herbert Pelham, Esq.[4]
28	Abraham Morrill.	Thomas Skidmore.
29	Samuel Greenhill.	—— Turges.
30	John Pratt.	Widow Elizabeth Isaac.
31	William Spencer.	John Stedman.
32	Thomas Spencer.	William Dickson.
33	John Haynes, Esq.	Henry Dunster.

[1] " Forfeited ; " afterwards called " Watch-house Hill; " site of the Meeting-house from 1650 to 1833.

[2] Uncertain whether then occupied by a house or not.

[3] Vacant lot.

[4] House, but apparently not a homestead.

No.	In 1635.	In 1642.
34	" Market Place." [1]	" Market Place."
35	James Ensign.	Edward Goffe.[2]
36	Rev. Samuel Stone.[3]	Nathaniel Sparhawk.[3]
37	Widow Isabel Sackett.	Robert Stedman.
38	Matthew Allen.	Thomas Chesholme.
39	Meeting-house.	Meeting-house.
40	Samuel Dudley.	Robert Sanders.
41	William Andrews.	Hezekiah Usher.
42	William Lewis.	John Bridge.
43	George Stocking.	William Manning.
44	Nicholas Olmstead.[3]	John French.
45	Joseph Reading.	Joseph Cooke.
46	Stephen Hart.	Joseph Cooke.
47	Nathaniel Richards.	Joseph Cooke.
48	William Westwood.	John Betts.
49	Dolor Davis.[3]	Edward Mitchelson.
50	John Bridge.	William Andrews.
51	Thomas Fisher.	Edward Shepard.
52	John Benjamin.[2]	John Betts.[2]
53	John Benjamin.[3]	Edward Shepard.[3]
54	John Benjamin.[3]	Moses Payne.
55	Thomas Dudley, Esq.	Herbert Pelham, Esq.
56	Matthew Allen.[3]	William Cutter.
57	Humphrey Vincent.	John Moore.
58	Daniel Patrick.	Joseph Cooke.[3]
59	Richard Lord.[3]	Herbert Pelham, Esq.
60	Matthew Allen.[3]	George Cooke.
61	Edmund Gearner.	Mrs. Eliz. Sherborne.
62	John Arnold.	Thomas Hosmer.
63	William Kelsey.	John Sill.
64	Andrew Warner.	George Cooke.

[1] Now called Winthrop Square.
[2] House, but apparently not homestead.
[3] Vacant lot.

HISTORY OF CAMBRIDGE.

CHAPTER I.

CIVIL HISTORY.

CAMBRIDGE, the original shire town of Middlesex County, in the Commonwealth of Massachusetts, is situated in 42° 22' north latitude, and 71° 6' west longitude from Greenwich.[1] It is bounded on the east by Charles River, which separates it from Boston; on the south by Charles River, which separates it from Brookline and Brighton;[2] on the west by Watertown, Belmont, and Arlington; on the north by Somerville, and by Miller's River, which separates it from Charlestown. Though now small in territorial extent, embracing not more than about four and a half square miles, it is divided into four principal districts, each having a post-office, namely: Cambridge (often called Old Cambridge), Cambridgeport, East Cambridge, and North Cambridge.

Like most ancient townships, Cambridge has had great enlargement and diminution in its boundary lines. At first, it seems to have been designed merely as a fortified place, very small in extent, and apparently without definite bounds. Charlestown and Watertown, on the northerly side of Charles River, had already been settled; but it is doubtful whether a distinct line of separation had been established. Between these two towns a spot was selected as "a fit place for a fortified town," about six months after the arrival of Winthrop with the fleet of emigrants in 1630.[3] Houses were erected here in 1631 by Thomas Dudley, Deputy Governor, and by a few others. It was ordered by the

---

[1] The City Hall, at the corner of Main and Pleasant streets, in Cambridgeport, stands exactly upon the longitudinal line, and about a hundred yards south of the parallel of latitude indicated.

[2] Brighton and Charlestown have re-

cently been annexed to Boston; but they have not yet ceased to be designated by their former names.

[3] The selection was partially made Dec. 21, 1630, and definitely determined Dec. 28, 1630.

Governor and Assistants, Feb. 8, 1631-2, that "there should be three scoore pounds levyed out of the several plantations within the lymitts of this pattent towards the makeing of a pallysadoe aboute the newe towne." [1]   But no definite line of division between the New Town and Charlestown appears to have been established until March 6, 1632-3, when "it was agreed by the parties appointed by the Court, &c., that all the land impaled by the newe towne men, with the neck whereon Mr. Graves his house standeth, shall belong to Newe-town, and that the bounds of Charlestowne shall end at a tree marked by the pale, and to passe along from thence by a straight line unto the midway betwixt the westermost part of the Governor's great lot and the nearest part thereto of the bounds of Watertowne." [2]   The line, thus established, was substantially the same as that which now divides Cambridge from Somerville. The "neck whereon Mr. Graves his house standeth," was the upland included in East Cambridge. The line between Cambridge and Watertown was not definitely established until April 7, 1635. [3] In the mean time, on complaint of "straitness for want of land," at the Court held May 14, 1634, leave was "granted to the inhabitants of Newe Towne to seek out some convenient place for them, with promise that it shalbe confirmed unto them, to which they may remove their habitations, or have as an addition to that which already they have, provided they doe not take it in any place to prejudice a plantation already settled." [4]   After examining several places, "the congregation of Newtown came and accepted of such enlargement as had formerly been offered them by Boston and Watertown." [5]   This "enlargement" embraced Brookline, Brighton, and Newton. Brookline, then called Muddy River, was granted on condition that Mr. Hooker and his congregation should not remove. They did remove; and thus this grant was forfeited. But the grant of what was afterwards Brighton and Newton held good.

[1] *Mass. Col. Rec.*, i. 93. Dr. Holmes, writing in 1800 (*Coll. Mass. Hist. Soc.*, vii. 9), says : " This fortification was actually made ; and the fosse which was then dug around the town is, in some places, visible to this day. It commenced at Brick Wharf (originally called Windmill Hill) and ran along the northern side of the present Common in Cambridge, and through what was then a thicket, but now constitutes a part of the cultivated grounds of Mr. Nathaniel Jarvis ; beyond which it cannot be distinctly traced."

Cambridge was at first called " The New Towne," and afterwards New Town or Newtown, until May 2, 1638, when the General Court " Ordered, That Newetowne shall henceforward be called Cambridge." *Mass. Col. Rec.*, i. 228. No other act of incorporation is found on record.

[2] *Mass. Col. Rec.*, i. 102.
[3] *Ibid.*, p. 144.
[4] *Ibid.*, p. 119.
[5] Savage's *Winthrop*, i. 132, 142.

In the settlement of the line between Cambridge and Charlestown, no indication is given how far the bounds of either extended into the country beyond the line drawn from "the Governor's great lot," or the Ten Hills Farm, to the "nearest part" of Watertown. But the Court, March 3, 1635–6, agreed that "Newe Towne bounds shall run eight myles into the country, from their meeteing house."[1] This grant secured to Cambridge, on its northern border, the territory now embraced in Arlington and the principal part of Lexington; and, as the measurements of that day were very elastic, perhaps the whole of Lexington was included. But even this did not satisfy the craving for land. Accordingly a conditional grant of Shawshine was made, June 2, 1641, and renewed June 14, 1642: "All the land lying upon Saweshin Ryver, and between that and Concord Ryver, and between that and Merrimack Ryver, not formerly granted by this Court, are granted to Cambridge, so as they erect a village there within five years, and so as it shall not extend to prejudice Charlestowne village, or the village of Cochitawit," etc.[2] This grant was confirmed absolutely, March 7, 1643–4,[3] and included the present town of Billerica, parts of Bedford and Carlisle, and a part of Tewksbury, or of Chelmsford, or of both. The terms of the grant — all the land lying between Concord and Merrimac rivers — would seem to include Lowell; yet an Indian village then occupied that territory, and such villages were generally protected.

The township had now attained its full size. In shape somewhat like an hour-glass, about thirty-five miles in length, and wide at each extremity, it was not much more than one mile in width in the central part, where the original settlement was made, and where most of the inhabitants then resided. Such was its shape when Johnson described it in 1651. "This Town is compact closely within itselfe, till of late yeares some few stragling houses have been built: the Liberties of this Town have been inlarged of late in length, reaching from the most Northerly part of Charles River to the most Southerly part of Merrimack River."[4] This description, however, does not comprehend the

[1] *Mass. Col. Rec.*, i. 166.

[2] *Ibid.*, i. 330, ii. 17.

[3] *Ibid.*, ii. 62. The description in this grant is somewhat different from the former: "Shawshin is granted to Cambridg, without any condition of makeing a village there; and the land between them and Concord is granted them, all save what is formerly granted to the military company or others, provided the church and present elders continue at Cambridge."

[4] *Coll. Mass. Hist. Soc.*, xiii. 137.

whole territory then belonging to Cambridge; for both Brighton and Newton are wholly on the southerly side of Charles River. The portion of Dedham, which now constitutes the town of Needham, was the southerly bound.

But Cambridge soon lost a part of its enormous length. In 1655, an amicable arrangement was made between the town and those of its inhabitants who had erected houses at Shawshine, for a separation; this arrangement was confirmed by the General Court, and Shawshine was incorporated as a town, under the name of Billerica.[1] Soon afterwards the inhabitants on the south side of the river, in what is now Newton, where a church was organized July 20, 1664, petitioned for incorporation as a separate town. Cambridge objected; and a long and earnest controversy ensued. The Newton people triumphed at last, as will be fully related in another place, and in 1688 became a separate township.

The northwesterly portion of the territory remaining in Cambridge was for many years called "The Farms," and a church was organized there Oct. 21, 1696. The Farmers, as they were styled, subsequently agreed with the town upon terms of separation, and by an "order passed in Council and concurred by the Representatives," March 20, 1713, they were incorporated as "a separate and distinct town by the name of Lexington, upon the articles and terms already agreed on with the town of Cambridge."[2]

From this period Cambridge was not curtailed of its proportions for nearly a century. Indeed, it obtained some additions. The present southwesterly portion of the city, lying west of Sparks Street and south of Vassall Lane, was set off from Watertown and annexed to Cambridge, April 19, 1754,[3] except the "Cambridge Cemetery" and a few acres between that and the former line, which were annexed April 27, 1855.[4] The line of Watertown was thus carried about a half a mile further westward; and the tract thus acquired embraces some of the most desirable land in the city for dwelling-houses. From Charlestown (now Somerville), the dwellings and a portion of the estates of Nathaniel Prentiss, Josiah Wellington, Stephen Goddard, Benjamin Goddard, and Nathaniel Goddard, including most of the tract bounded by North Avenue, Russell, Elm, and White streets, were annexed

[1] Mass. Col. Rec., iii. 387.
[2] Mass. Prov. Rec., ix. 256.
[3] Ibid., xx. 228. Dr. Bond conjectured that the first meeting-house in Watertown stood on this tract of land, not far from the present residence of James Russell Lowell. — Hist. Watertown, p. 1048.
[4] Mass. Spec. Laws, x. 360.

to Cambridge, March 6, 1802;[1] the estate of William Hunne-
well, Feb. 12, 1818;[2] and a portion of Professor Ware's estate,
now the Norton homestead, June 17, 1820.[3] These three annex-
ations are indicated by the sharp angles on the map. The line
at White Street was somewhat changed April 30, 1856, and
the line between Cambridge and Belmont and Arlington, was
straightened Feb. 25, 1862.

The northwesterly part of the town was made a separate precinct Dec. 27, 1732, and was afterwards styled the Second
Parish, or more generally Menotomy. The line of division was
"Menotomy River from Charlestown till it comes to Spy Pond
Brook; then on said brook till it comes to a water-course or
ditch in Whiting's meadow, so called: the ditch to be the boundary till it comes to Hamblett's Brook, following the course of
the Brook to the Bridge; thence on a straight line to the northwest corner of Mr. Isaac Holden's orchard, and continuing the
same course to Watertown line."[4] This tract, with the addition
of the remaining territory on the westerly side of Menotomy
River, was incorporated, Feb. 27, 1807, under the name of West
Cambridge,[5] which name was changed to Arlington, April 20,
1867.[6]

The inhabitants of the territory left on the south side of
Charles River petitioned to be made a separate precinct, as early
as 1748, and renewed their petition, from time to time, until
April 2, 1779, when they were authorized to bring in a bill to
incorporate them as an ecclesiastical parish, "excepting Samuel
Sparhawk, John Gardner, Joanna Gardner, and Moses Griggs,
and their estates."[7] This was styled the Third Parish, or Little
Cambridge. The whole territory south of Charles River was
incorporated, under the name of Brighton, Feb. 24, 1837.[8]

By the incorporation of West Cambridge and Brighton, which
was the result of an amicable agreement between the several
parties, Cambridge was reduced substantially to its present limits. Several attempts have since been made for a further division; but its incorporation as a city has removed most of the
difficulties which previously existed, and it may be reasonably
expected that no more attempts of the kind will be made during
the present century.

1 *Mass. Spec. Laws*, ii. 520.
2 *Ibid.*, v. 220.
3 *Ibid.*, v. 385.
4 *Mass. Prov. Rec.*, xii. 351.
5 *Mass. Spec. Laws*, iv. 88.
6 *Ibid.*, xii. 244.

7 *Mass. Prov. Rec.*, xxxix. 213.
8 *Mass. Spec. Laws*, iv. 70. By an
act approved May 21, 1873, Brighton was
annexed to Boston, — the annexation to
take full effect on the first Monday in
January, 1874.

CHAPTER II.

CIVIL HISTORY.

THE purpose for which Cambridge was originally established as a town is stated by two of its projectors, Winthrop and Dudley. "The governor and most of the assistants," had "agreed to build a town fortified upon the neck," between Roxbury and Boston, Dec. 6, 1630; but, for several reasons, they abandoned that project, eight days afterwards, and agreed to examine other places. On the twenty-first day of the same month: "We met again at Watertown, and there, upon view of a place a mile beneath the town, all agreed it a fit place for a fortified town, and we took time to consider further about it."[1] Dudley, describing the events of 1630, in his letter to the Countess of Lincoln, says, "We began again in December to consult about a fit place to build a town upon, leaving all thoughts of a fort, because upon any invasion we were necessarily to lose our houses when we should retire thereinto. So after divers meetings at Boston, Roxbury, and Watertown, on the twenty-eighth of December, we grew to this resolution, to bind all the assistants[2] (Mr. Endicott and Mr. Sharpe excepted, which last purposeth to return by the next ship into England), to build houses at a place a mile east from Watertown, near Charles River, the next spring, and to winter there the next year; that so by our examples, and by removing the ordnance and munition thither, all who were able might be drawn thither, and such as shall come to us hereafter, to their advantage, be compelled so to do; and so, if God would, a fortified town might there grow up, the place fitting reasonably well thereto." Johnson describes the original design and its partial accomplishment, in his characteristic manner: "At this time, those who were in place of civil government, having some

---

[1] Savage's *Winthrop*, i. 45, 46.
[2] Winthrop was then Governor, and Dudley Deputy Governor; the Assistants were Sir Richard Saltonstall, John Endi-cott, Increase Nowell, William Pynchon, Thomas Sharp, Roger Ludlow, William Coddington, and Simon Bradstreet.

additional pillars to underprop the building, began to think of a place of more safety in the eyes of man than the two frontier towns of Charles Towne and Boston were, for the habitation of such as the Lord had prepared to govern this pilgrim people. Wherefore they rather made choice to enter further among the Indians than hazard the fury of malignant adversaries who in a rage might pursue them, and therefore chose a place situate on Charles River, between Charles Towne and Water Towne, where they erected a town called New Town, now named Cambridge, being in form like a list cut off from the broad-cloth of the two fore-named towns, where this wandering race of Jacobites gathered the eighth church of Christ." [1]

Notwithstanding it was agreed that "all the assistants" should build at the New Town in the spring of 1631, it does not appear that any of them fulfilled the agreement, except Dudley and Bradstreet. Governor Winthrop indeed erected a house; [2] but he subsequently took it down again and removed it to Boston. This led to a sharp controversy between Dudley and Winthrop, which was at length decided by the elders in favor of Dudley. [3] There may have been good and sufficient reasons why Winthrop should prefer to remain in Boston rather than to remove to the New Town. But it is much to be regretted that he should claim to have substantially fulfilled his obligation, or "performed the words of the promise," by erecting a house; though he immediately removed it. This is scarcely consistent with his otherwise fair fame as a gentleman of singular ingenuousness. It would seem that Sir Richard Saltonstall intended to build a house, and

[1] Coll. Mass. Hist. Soc., xiii. 136.

[2] It has been said that Winthrop erected only the *frame* of a house; but he says it was a house inhabited by servants. See next note.

[3] Savage's *Winthrop*, i. 82, 83. Winthrop says Dudley "complained of the breach of promise, both in the governor and others, in not building at Newtown. The governor answered, that he had performed the words of the promise; for he had a house up, and seven or eight servants abiding in it, by the day appointed; and for the removing his house, he alleged that, seeing that the rest of the assistants went not about to build, and that his neighbors of Boston had been discouraged from removing thither by Mr. Deputy himself, and thereupon had (under all their hands) petitioned him, that (accord-

ing to the promise he made to them when they first sat down with him at Boston, namely, that he would not remove, except they went with him), he would not leave them:—this was the occasion that he removed his house. Upon these and other speeches to this purpose, the ministers went apart for one hour; then returning, they delivered their opinions, that the governor was in fault for removing of his house so suddenly, without conferring with the deputy and the rest of the assistants; but if the deputy were the occasion of discouraging Boston men from removing, it would excuse the governor a *tote*, but not a *tote*. The governor, professing himself willing to submit his own opinion to the judgment of so many wise and godly friends, acknowledged himself faulty."

a lot was assigned to him for that purpose;[1] but he went to England in the spring of 1631, and did not return. Nowell remained at Charlestown; Pynchon, at Roxbury; Ludlow, at Dorchester; and Coddington, at Boston. Endicott and Sharpe were originally free from engagement.

Dr. Holmes says, " the Deputy Governor (Dudley), Secretary Bradstreet, and other principal gentlemen, in the spring of 1631, commenced the execution of the plan." [2]   No list of inhabitants is found until after the " Braintree Company " arrived in the summer of 1632, except this memorandum on the title-page of the Town Records: " The Towne Book of Newtowne. Inhabitants there — Mr. Tho. Dudly Esq., Mr. Symon Bradstreet, Mr. Edmond Lockwood, Mr. Daniell Patricke, John Poole, William Spencer, John Kirman, Symon Sackett." [3]   But this Book

---

[1] The Proprietors' Records show that what is now called Winthrop Square was allotted to Sir Richard Saltonstall; but when it was ascertained that he would not return from England, the lot was assigned for a "Market Place," by which name it was known for more than two centuries, though no market-house was ever erected there. Probably like the old Market Place in Boston, it was used for traffic, in the open air, between the inhabitants and such as brought commodities for sale.

[2] Coll. Mass. Hist. Soc., vii. 7.

[3] Of these eight persons who laid the foundation of the New Town, Thomas Dudley was the most eminent. He was elected Deputy Governor in 1630, became Governor in 1634, and was either Governor, Deputy Governor, or Assistant, during the remainder of his life. He removed to Ipswich, perhaps before May, 1636, when he and Bradstreet were named as magistrates to hold the court there, while others were appointed for the court at New Town. Soon afterwards he removed to Roxbury, were he died July 31, 1653. Simon Bradstreet was an Assistant from 1630 to 1678; Deputy Governor, 1678; Governor, 1679–86, 1689–92. He also removed to Ipswich, probably with Dudley, whose daughter was his wife; was afterwards in Andover for a short time; then in Boston until Sept. 18, 1695, when he removed to Salem, and died there, March 27, 1697. Edmund Lockwood, having the prefix of "Mr.," was appointed by

the General Court, Constable of the New Town, at its organization, May, 1632; and at the same session was selected as one of the two inhabitants of the town " to confer with the Court about raising of a public stock." He died before March, 1635. Daniel Patrick, also styled " Mr.," was one of the two captains appointed by the Court, to command the militia of the Colony. Except as a military man, his character does not appear to have been very reputable. In 1637 he had liberty to remove to Ipswich, but seems rather to have gone to Watertown, where he was Selectman, in 1638. He afterwards removed to Connecticut, and was killed by a Dutchman, at Stamford, in 1643. John Poole probably remained here only a few months, as he is not named in the list of proprietors, in 1633. He was of Lynn, 1638, and afterwards of Reading, where he died April 1, 1667. William Spencer, uniformly styled "Mr." on the court records, was one of the "principal gentlemen." He was associated with Mr. Lockwood, May, 1632, "to confer with the Court about raising of a public stock;" was Deputy or Representative of the New Town, 1634–1637; one of the first Board of Townsmen, 1635; lieutenant of the trainband, 1637, and a member of the Ancient and Honorable Artillery Company, at its organization in 1639; he probably removed to Hartford in 1639, where he was Selectman and Deputy, and died in 1640. John Kirman removed to Lynn, 1632, and was a Deputy, 1635. Simon Sack-of Records was not commenced until 1632, several months after Dudley and Bradstreet performed their promise " to build houses at the New Town." Whether more than the before named eight persons, and indeed whether all these resided in the New Town before the end of 1631, I have not found any certain proof. The number of inhabitants in that year was doubtless small; yet there were enough able-bodied men to be specially included in an order of court passed July 26, 1631, requiring a general training of soldiers in all the plantations.[1]

Although the Governor and Assistants generally did not perform their agreement to make the New Town the place of their permanent residence, they seem to have regarded it as the prospective seat of government, and not long afterwards, as will appear, commenced holding the general and particular courts there. Several orders, passed during the year, indicate such an expectation and intention. For example : June 14, 1631, " Mr. John Maisters hath undertaken to make a passage from Charles River to the New Town, twelve foot broad and seven foot deep ; for which the Court promiseth him satisfaction, according as the charges thereof shall amount unto."[2] On the fifth of the following July, provision was made for the payment of Mr. Masters, when it was " Ordered, That there shall be levied out of the several plantations the sum of thirty pounds, for the making of the creek at the New Town," — but no portion of this sum was assessed upon the New Town. Again, Feb. 3, 1631-2, " It was ordered, That there should be three score pounds levied out of the several plantations within the limits of this patent, towards the making of a pallysadoe about the New Town ; viz. Watertown, viii.*l.* the New Town, iii.*l.* Charlton, vii.*l.* Meadford, iii.*l.* Saugus and Marble Harbor, vi.*l.* Salem, iv.*l.* x.*s.* Boston, viii.*l.* Rocksbury, vii.*l.* Dorchester, vii.*l.* Wessaguscus, v.*l.* Winettsemet, xxx.*s.*"[3]

ett died here before 3d November, 1635, when administration was granted to his widow Isabell Sackett.

[1] *Mass. Coll. Rec.,* i. 90.

[2] *Ibid.,* i. 88. This canal still exists on the westerly side of College Wharf, from Charles River nearly to South Street. It was a natural creek, enlarged and deepened thus far, from which point, turning westerly, it extended along the southerly and westerly sides of South and Eliot streets, and crossed Brattle Street, where the town ordered a causeway and footbridge to be constructed, Jan. 4, 1635-36.

[3] *Mass. Col. Rec.,* i. 98. Winthrop says that Watertown objected against the validity and justice of this assessment : and his learned editor says : " To the agitation of this subject we may refer the origin of that committee of two from each town to advise with the court about raising public moneys ' so as what they should agree upon should bind all,' under date of May of this year. This led to the

Six months later, there was a considerable accession of inhabitants, by order of the General Court. The order does not appear on the records of the Court; but Winthrop says, under date of Aug. 14, 1632, "The Braintree [1] Company (which had begun to sit down at Mount Wollaston), by order of court, removed to Newtown. There were Mr. Hooker's Company." [2] Before their arrival an order was adopted by the inhabitants, in regard to the paling around the common lands; the contemplated assignment of proportions, however, was not made until several months afterwards, when new inhabitants had arrived and had received grants of the common property. The date of this order, which is the first recorded in the town records, is March 29, 1632 : —

"An agreement by the inhabitants of the New Town, about paling [3] in the neck of land. Imprimis, That every one who hath any part therein shall hereafter keep the same in good and sufficient repair; and if it happen to have any defect, he shall mend the same within three days after notice given, or else pay ten shillings a rod for every rod so repaired for him. Further, It is agreed that the said impaled ground shall be divided according to every man's proportion in said pales. Further, It is agreed, that if any man shall desire to sell his part of impaled ground, he shall first tender the sale thereof to the town inhabitants interested, who shall either give him the charge he hath been at, or else to have liberty to sell it to whom he can."

In the list which follows, evidently according to the preceding order, though not immediately succeeding it on the record, I preserve the original orthography, together with the number of rods, indicating the relative shares in the impaled ground.

representative body, having the full powers of all the freemen, except that of elections." — Savage's *Winthrop*, i. 71, note.

[1] Supposed to be so called because they came from Braintree, a town in Essex, about forty miles from London.

[2] Savage's *Winthrop*, i. 87. Mr. Hooker did not arrive until more than a year later; but the members of his flock, who preceded him, in due time again enjoyed his pastoral care.

[3] The location of the greater part of this fence, or "pale" is designated with tolerable accuracy by the ancient records of possessions and conveyances. Commencing in the present College yard, near the northwesterly angle of Gore Hall, and extending eastwardly, it passed very near the junction of Ellsworth Avenue with Cambridge Street, to the line between Cambridge and Charlestown (now Somerville), at its angle on Line Street near Cambridge Street, and thence followed that line to the creek, a few rods easterly from the track of the Grand Junction Railroad. Commencing again at the point first mentioned, the fence extended southwardly to the marsh near the junction of Holyoke Place with Mount Auburn Street. The kind of fence then erected is indicated in an order passed Dec. 5, 1636 : "That the common pales in all places, to be made after this day, shall be done with sufficient posts and rails, and not with crotches."

COMMON PALES DIVIDED AS FOLLOWS:—

John Haynes, Esq. . .	70 rods.	Steven Hart	8 rods.
Thomas Dudly, Esq. .	40 "	William Wadsworth . .	7 "
Mr. Symon Bradstreet .	20 "	George Steele	6 "
John Benjamin . . .	50 "	Richard Goodman . .	6 "
John Talcott	86 "	John Bridg	6 "
Mathew Allen . . .	45 "	Symon Sackett . . .	6 "
William Westwood . .	30 "	Richard Butler . . .	6 "
James Omstead . . .	25 "	Capt. Patrike	5 "
Daniell Denison . . .	25 "	Richard Web	5 "
Samuell Dudly . . .	25 "	John Masters	4 "
Andrew Warner . . .	20 "	Antho. Colby	4 "
William Goodwine . .	16 "	John Clark	3 "
John White	15 "	Nath. Richards . . .	3 "
John Steele	14 "	Richard Lord . . .	3 "
Edward Stebinge . . .	12 "	Abraham Morrill . . .	3 "
William Spencer . . .	12 "	William Kelse	3 "
Thomas Hosmer . . .	10 "	Jonath. Bosworth . .	2 "
William Lewis . . .	10 "	Tho. Spencer	2 "
Hester Musse	10 "	Garrad Hadon . . .	2 "
Joseph Readinge . . .	2 "	Edward Elmer . . .	2 "
Thomas Heate	2 "	Jeremy Addams . . .	2 "

Of these forty-two persons, it is certain that at least one half were not of the Braintree Company, as many have supposed.[1] Precisely how many of the other half were of that company, I have no means to determine; but from whatever place they may have come, the number of inhabitants so increased that in about a year there were nearly a hundred families in the New Town.

The division of lands and the establishment of highways were among the first necessities. . The house-lots were laid out compactly in the "Town," and in the "West End," the tract bounded by Sparks, Wyeth, and Garden streets, Harvard and Brattle squares, and Charles River. For cultivation, lands were assigned in the impaled "Neck," and afterwards elsewhere.

[1] Thomas Dudley, Simon Bradstreet, Daniel Patrick, Simon Sackett, and William Spencer were here before August, 1632, when the "Braintree Company" removed. Samuel Dudley was doubtless here also. Daniel Denison came here from Roxbury. Anthony Colby, Garrad Haddon, and Joseph Reading, were of Boston in 1630; and John Masters of Watertown, in 1631. John Benjamin, Edward Elmer, William Goodwin, William Lewis, James Olmstead, Nathaniel Richards, John Talcott, William Wadsworth, and John White, arrived at Boston, in the *Lion*, Sept. 16, 1632, a month after the Braintree Company removed; and John Haynes did not arrive until Sept. 3, 1633. The name of Simon Oakes is erroneously given in *Col. Mass. Hist. Soc.*, vii. 10, instead of Simon Sackett.

The original assignment is not found; but the work was commenced before the "Braintree Company" arrived; for Winthrop alleged, as early as August 8, 1632, that Dudley "had empaled, at Newtown, above one thousand acres, and had assigned lands to some there."[1] So much of the impaled land as lies northerly of Main Street was so divided, that the divisions are easily traced. The westerly part of what was denominated "the Neck," was allotted in small portions. First came the "planting field," afterwards called the "Old field," which was bounded westerly and northerly by the common pales, easterly by Dana Street, and southerly by Main and Arrow streets; this contained about sixty-three acres, and was assigned in small portions for separate use. Next to this field was the "Small-lot hill," which was bounded southerly by Main Street, westerly by Dana Street, northerly by the common pales, and easterly by a line extended from Somerville, near the northern termination of Fayette Street, to a point on Main Street about one hundred and thirty feet east of Hancock Street. This tract contained about forty-six acres, and was divided into eighteen narrow lots extending from Dana Street to the easterly line. Eastwardly from "Small-lot hill" the land was divided into large lots, which were assigned in the following order and quantity : Samuel Dudley, 22½ acres; Thomas Dudley, Esq., 63 acres ; Richard Goodman, 6 acres ; William Westwood, 27 acres ; John Talcott, 82 acres; Daniel Denison, 22½ acres ; John Haynes, Esq., 63 acres ; (these lots severally extended from what is now Main Street to Somerville line ; the following lots bordered southerly on the Great Marsh) : Widow Hester Mussey, 9 acres ; Matthew Allen, 27 acres ; John Talcott, 45 acres, bordering eastwardly on the marsh, and another lot, wholly marsh, 50 acres ; Atherton Hough, 130 acres of marsh and upland, embracing "Graves his neck," or East Cambridge.

At a later period, another planting field was enclosed by a common fence, and was called the "West field," and sometimes "West-end field." It was bounded northerly by Garden Street, easterly by Wyeth Street, southerly by Vassall Lane, and westerly by the Great Swamp, or Fresh Pond meadows. There was also the Pine Swamp field, whose bounds I cannot trace ; but it was in the vicinity of the intersection of Oxford Street with Everett and Mellen streets.

Such were the principal planting fields in early use. The marshes and meadows were in like manner assigned in severalty.

[1] Savage's *Winthrop*, i. 84.

The principal fresh meadows at first divided were those which adjoin Fresh Pond, called the "Fresh Pond meadows." The marshes on the northerly side of Charles River received distinctive names. The tract lying westerly of Ash Street was called Windmill-hill-marsh "; between Ash Street and College Wharf was "Ox-marsh"; the name of "Ship-marsh" was applied to the tract extending from College Wharf to the point where the river sweeps around to the south; and the narrow strip between this point and Riverside was called "Common-marsh." "Long-marsh" extended from Green Street between Bay and Vernon streets to the river below Riverside, and probably to "Captain's Island," at the south end of Magazine Street. The marsh between Captain's Island and East Cambridge was called the "Great Marsh." Its name will appear the more appropriate, when it is considered that almost the entire territory easterly of a line drawn from the junction of Pearl and Allston streets to the point where the Grand Junction Railroad crosses Miller's River (excepting the high land in East Cambridge), was then one continuous unbroken marsh. A small tract, indeed, lying southeastwardly from the junction of Main and Front streets, was upland, and was an island at high water, afterwards called "Pelham's Island"; and a few other small parcels of dry land appeared on the easterly side of the line before mentioned, but they were more than counterbalanced by tracts of marsh on the westerly side.

The grazing lands were not divided at first; but the herds of cows, goats, and swine were driven forth, under care of their several keepers, to range over the undivided lands, styled "commons." The tract embraced between Garden and Linnæan streets and North Avenue was early set apart for the security of the cows at night. It was called the "Cow-common," and remained undivided nearly a century after it was first so used. Provision was also made for oxen, and the tract lying between the "Common Pales" and Kirkland Street, extending from the Common to Somerville line, was devoted as an "ox-pasture;" to which was subsequently added a corresponding tract on the northerly side of Kirkland Street.

The "Path from Charlestown to Watertown" was probably travelled before the New Town was selected as a place for residence; and it may properly be regarded as the most ancient highway in Cambridge. Its general direction was through Kirkland, Mason, and Brattle streets, Elmwood Avenue, and Mount

Auburn Street. The " Town " and all the grounds originally
impaled were on the southeasterly side of this path. The " common pales," so called, were about a quarter of a mile south of the
path, at the present Somerville line, and about two hundred
yards from it at Gore Hall. Among the earliest of the streets
laid out for the use of the Town were four, running easterly and
westerly, crossed by four others at right angles. These eight
streets, with a single exception, remain substantially in their
original location ; but many of them have been made wider, and
the names of all have been changed.

ANCIENT NAMES.	PRESENT NAMES.
Braintree Street	Harvard Street and Harvard Square.
Spring Street	Mount Auburn Street.
Long Street	Winthrop Street.
Marsh Lane	South Street, and part of Eliot Street.
Creek Lane	Brattle Square and part of Eliot Street.
Wood Street	Brighton Street.
Water Street	Dunster Street.
Crooked Street	Holyoke Street.

Besides these principal streets were sundry highways. The
" highway to Watertown " extended from Brattle Square through
Brattle Street to Mason Street ; and thence was identical with
the " Path from Charlestown to Watertown." From this highway three others diverged southerly : one, to the ox-marsh,
passing near the site of the Brattle Mansion-house ; one to Windmill-hill, now Ash Street ; and one to Watertown marsh, not far
westerly from the residence of Samuel Batchelder, Esq. The
first and last of these three highways were long ago closed.
Mason Street was early distinguished as the " highway from
Charlestown to Watertown." The original " highway to the
Fresh Pond " followed the track of the present Garden Street,
Wyeth Street, and Vassall Lane, except that it passed across the
common from Harvard Square to its northwesterly corner. As
far as to Wyeth Street, Garden Street was called both the
" highway to the Fresh Pond," and the " highway to the Great
Swamp ; " northwesterly from Wyeth Street, it had the latter
name exclusively. An old range-way on the easterly side of the
Botanic Garden, now made wider and called Raymond Street,
was " the other highway to the Great Swamp." The " highway to the Common " indicated that portion of North Avenue
which led from Harvard Square to the point where the Old

Charlestown Path crossed the Common. The other portion of North Avenue was the "highway to Menotomy." The "highway to Charlestown," or the "Charlestown Path," as before stated, was the present Kirkland Street. In the impaled land, the principal highway was the "highway to the Oyster Bank," or the "highway into the neck," extending through Arrow Street, Main Street, and Pleasant Street, to a point near Cottage Street, and thence diagonally across the present streets towards Washington Square. From Pleasant Street a path diverged westerly, and followed the border of the upland, next to the marsh, and was called the "highway to Captain's Island."[1] From the junction of Pleasant and Main streets, the highway extended easterly, nearly in the track of Main Street, and at a later day was called the "highway to Pelham's Island." Between the "old field" and "small-lot hill," was the "highway to the common pales," now called Dana Street, the direction of which, however, is somewhat changed, the northerly termination now being several rods more westerly than it was at first. Another branch extended southerly from Main Street to Riverside, originally called the "highway into the little neck," now Putnam Avenue. From the "town" into the "highway to the oyster-bank" there were two principal entrances: one being a continuation of Braintree (now Harvard) Street, from Holyoke Street easterly, through Harvard Street and the northerly portion of Bow Street to Arrow Street, and indifferently called "Field Lane" and the "highway to the oyster-bank;" the other being a continuation of Spring (now Mount Auburn) Street, or rather branching from a sharp angle in Crooked (now Holyoke) Street, opposite to the site of the printing office, and winding along the higher land above the westerly portion of Bow Street, until it intersected Field Lane at the present junction of Bow and Arrow streets; this was indifferently called "Back Lane," and "Cow-yard Row." "Cow-yard Lane," separating the house-lots from the yards in the rear, extended across the College enclosure, from the Common to the "Old Field," at the distance of about a hundred feet from Harvard Street, having an outlet into Harvard Street about a hundred feet easterly from the present Holyoke Street; this, like that into which it entered, was called "Field Lane." Cow-yard Lane and Field Lane north of Har-

[1] The upland, where the Powder Magazine was erected, an island at high water, was granted to Captain Daniel Patrick, at a very early period, since which time it has always been styled Captain's Island.

vard Street were discontinued and enclosed with the adjoini
lands immediately after "Mr. Hooker's Company" remov
The foregoing are all the highways of which I find any trace
the present bounds of Cambridge, prior to 1636. On the sou
side of the river, however, a highway was early establish
called the "highway to Roxbury," from a point opposite to t
College Wharf, in the general direction of the road from Ca
bridge Great Bridge, through the easterly portion of Bright
to Brookline. Frequent reference is also made, in the ear
records, to the "highway from Watertown to Roxbury."

CHAPTER III.

CIVIL HISTORY.

THE New Town seems never to have been incorporated by specific act. It was originally set apart by the government for public use; and it was from the beginning recognized as a distinct town. As early as June 14, 1631, the Court provided for the making of a canal or "passage from Charles River to the New Town," and, in ordering a tax of thirty pounds, Feb. 3, 1631-2, to defray the expense of a "pallysadoe about the New Town," assessed one tenth part thereof on that town, as related in Chapter II. There is no recorded evidence, however, of any municipal transactions by the New Town until March 29, 1632, when the Town Book of Records was opened; since which time a continuous record has been preserved. The first transaction recorded was the "agreement by the inhabitants of the New Town, about paling in the neck of land." Six weeks later, the Court appointed a constable for the New Town, and selected two of its inhabitants, with a like number from other towns, "to confer with the Court about raising of a public stock."[1] The first named record, March 29, 1632, has been fully quoted in the preceding chapter. The next in order, Dec. 24, 1632, provided for regular meetings of the inhabitants for the transaction of business. The record is mutilated somewhat, and the words supposed to have been worn off are here inserted in brackets:—

"An agreement made by a general consent, for a monthly meeting.

"Imprimis, That every person undersubscribed shall [meet] every first Monday in every month, within [the] meeting house, in the afternoon, within half [an hour] after the ringing of the bell;[2] and that every [one] that makes not his personal appear-

[1] *Mass. Col. Rec.*, i. 95, 96, May 9, 1632: "Mr. Edmond Lockwood was chosen constable of New Towne for this yeare next ensueing, and till a newe be chosen." On the same day, "It was ordered that there should be two of every plantacōn appointed to conferre with the Court about raiseing of a pablique stocks;" — "Mr. Lockwood and Mr. Spencer for Newe Towne."

[2] It is observable that the hour of meeting was thus early announced by "the

2

ance there [and] continues there, without leave from the [   ]
until the meeting be ended, shall forfeit [for each] default xii.
pence: and if it be not paid [before the next] meeting, then to
double it, and so until [it be paid]."

Although a general subscription seems to have been contemplated, only two signatures are appended, namely, Thomas Dudley and John Haynes; and Mr. Haynes must have subscribed his
name several months after the order was adopted, as he did not
arrive until Sept. 3, 1633. At the first meeting holden in pursuance of this "agreement," several municipal arrangements were
made, to secure the beauty and safety of the town, to wit:—

Jan. 7, 1632–3. "It is ordered, that no person whatever
[shall set] up any house in the bounds of this town [without]
leave from the major part.

"Further, it is agreed, by a joint consent, [that the] town
shall not be enlarged until all [the vacant] places be filled with
houses.[1]

"Further, it is agreed, that all the houses [within] the bounds
of the town shall be covered [with] slate or board, and not with
thatch.[2]

"Further, it is ordered, that all [the houses shall] range even,
and stand just six [feet on each man's] own ground from the
street."

ringing of the bell." Johnson represents
that, in 1636, a drum was used, because
the town "had as yet no bell to call men
to meeting." — *Coll. Mass. Hist. Soc.*, xiv.
18. It seems unlikely that "Mr. Hooker's company" transported their bell,
across the wilderness, to Connecticut, and
the story perhaps was inaccurately reported to Johnson. The day of meeting
was changed to the second Monday in
the month, Oct. 1, 1639, because "it was
ordered" by the General Court, "to prevent the hindrance of the military company upon the first Monday in the month,
that no other meetings should be appointed upon that day."

[1] "The town," technically so-called,
was embraced in the district bounded
northerly by Harvard Street and Square,
westerly by Brattle Square and Eliot
Street, southerly by Eliot and South
streets, and easterly by Holyoke Street,
which was then very crooked.

[2] This was a reaffirmation of an agreement made by the original projectors of
the town, nearly two years earlier. In
his letter to the Countess of Lincoln,
dated March 28, 1631, Dudley speaks of
recent disasters by fire, and adds: "For
the prevention whereof in our new town,
intended this summer to be builded, we
have ordered that no man there shall build
his chimney with wood, nor cover his
house with thatch." As an additiona
prevention, the townsmen ordered, Oct
3, 1636, "That no child, under the ag
of ten years, shall carry any fire fro
one house to another, nor any other per
son unless it be covered, upon the forfe
ture of xii. pence a time for every suc
fault: the one half to the person that se
it, the other to the Constable." In the
days of lucifer matches, such an ord
may seem unnecessary; but even with
the last fifty years, it was not unusual
send from house to house for fire.

Next follows the division of the common pales, apparently at the same meeting.

The prohibition against erecting houses outside of " the town " may have been merely a precaution against danger from enemies; yet it is not unlikely to have been occasioned, in part at least, by the continued desire to make this the seat of government, and the most desirable place of residence in the colony. The regularity required in the position of the houses indicates a disposition to make the town symmetrical as well as compact. This orderly arrangement, which had doubtless been observed from the beginning, is referred to by Wood, in his " New England's Prospect," written in this year (1633), as one of the characteristic features of the new town : " This place was first intended for a city; but, upon more serious considerations, it was thought not so fit, being too far from the sea, being the greatest inconvenience it hath. This is one of the neatest and best compacted towns in New England, having many fair structures, with many handsome contrived streets. The inhabitants, most of them, are very rich, and well stored with cattle of all sorts, having many hundred acres of land paled in with general fence, which is about a mile and a half long, which secures all their weaker cattle from the wild beasts." [1]

After this meeting on the seventh of January, no other is recorded until Aug. 5, 1633; from which date there is a consecutive record of the " monthly meetings." A selection from the orders adopted at these meetings may serve to illustrate the primitive condition of the town.

Aug. 5, 1633. Sundry lots were granted for " cow-yards."

Sept. 2, 1633. " It is ordered, that whosoever hath any tree lying across a highway, and doth not remove it within seven days, or whosoever shall hereafter fall any tree and let it lie cross a highway one day, shall forfeit the tree."

Dec. 2, 1633. " It is ordered, that no person whatever shall fell any tree near the town, within the path which goeth from Watertowne to Charlestowne, upon the forfeiture of five shillings for every tree so felled."

---

[1] Boston edition, p. 45. The prosperity of the inhabitants seems not to have been overstated. Of the general tax imposed by the Court, Oct. 1, 1633, Boston, Roxbury, Charlestown, Watertown, and New Town were assessed alike, — forty-eight pounds; Dorchester was the only town in the colony which was required to pay a larger sum, — eighty pounds. In March, 1636, the share of New Town, in a tax of three hundred pounds, was forty-two pounds, when no other town was assessed more than thirty-seven pounds ten shillings.

"Agreed with Mr. Symon Bradstreet, to make a sufficient cartway along by his pales, and keep it in repair seven years; and he is to have ten shillings for the same."

March 2, 1633-4. "Granted John Benjamin all the ground between John Masters his ground and Antho. Couldbyes, provided that the windmill-hill shall be preserved for the town's use, and a cartway of two rods wide unto the same."[1]

April 7, 1634. "Granted John Pratt two acres by the old burying place, without the common pales."[2]

Aug. 4, 1634. "It is ordered, that whosoever shall fall [any] tree for boards, clapboards, or frames of houses, [and] sell them out of the town, shall forfeit for every [tree] so sold twenty shillings."

Nov. 3, 1634. "James Olmsted is chosen Constable for the year following, and till a new be chosen in his room, and presently sworn.[3]

"John White is chosen Surveyor. to see the highways and streets kept clean, and in repair for the year following.

"It is ordered, that every inhabitant in the town shall keep the street clear from wood and all other things against his own ground; and whosoever shall have anything lie in the street above one day after the next meeting-day, shall forfeit five shillings for every such default."

Jan. 5, 1634-5. "It is ordered, that whosoever hath any lot granted by the town, and shall not improve the same, then it is to return to the town; or, if he shall improve the same, he shall first offer it to the town; if they refuse to give him what charges he hath been at, then to have liberty to sell it to whom he can."

Next follows an agreement, accompanied by several orders, whereby the system of municipal government was radically

---

[1] Windmill-hill was at the south end of Ash Street, near the former site of the Cambridge Gas Works. A windmill was there erected for the grinding of corn, as no mill moved by water-power was nearer than Watertown. This mill was removed to Boston in August, 1632, because "it would not grind but with a westerly wind." — Savage's *Winthrop*, i. 87. The hill was afterwards enclosed by Richard Eccles, who owned the adjoining lands, and it so remained until 1684, when the town asserted its rights; and a tract measuring ten rods on the river, six rods and seven feet across the west end, ten rods and four feet on the north line, and seven and a half rods across the east end, was acknowledged by Eccles to be public property, together with a highway to it, two rods wide, through his land; and his acknowledgment was entered on the Proprietors' Records.

[2] See chapter xv.

[3] Edmund Lockwood had been appointed Constable by the Court, May 9, 1632, and John Benjamin, May 29, 1633; but James Olmstead was the first person elected by the inhabitants to fill that office, which was then of great honor and importance.

changed. Hitherto, all the legal voters had met, from month to month, to manage their public affairs. Power was now delegated to a few individuals, at first styled "Townsmen," and afterwards "Selectmen," to transact "the whole business of the town," until the next November, when a new election might be had.[1]

Feb. 3, 1634–5. "At a general meeting of the whole town, it was agreed upon by a joint consent, that seven men should be chosen to do the whole business of the town, and so to continue until the first Monday in November next, and until new be chosen in their room: so there was then elected and chosen John Haynes, Esq., Mr. Symon Bradstreet, John Taylcott, William Westwood, John White, William Wadsworth; James Olmsted, Constable.

"It is further ordered, by a joint consent, [that] whatsoever these Townsmen, thus chosen, shall do, in the compass of their time, shall stand in as full force as if the whole town did the same, either for making of new orders, or altering of old ones.

"Further, it is ordered, that whatsoever person they shall send for, to help in any business, and he shall refuse to come, they shall have power to lay a fine upon him, and to gather [it].

"Further, it is ordered, that they shall have one to attend upon them, to employ about any business, at a public charge.

"Further, it is ordered, that they shall meet every first Monday in a month, at [   ] in the afternoon, according to the former [order]."

Another important board of officers was elected, at the same meeting: —

"Also, there was then chosen, to join [with] James Olmsted, Constable, John Benjamin, Daniell Denison, Andrew Warner, William Spencer; which five, according to the order of Court, [shall] survey the town lands, and enter the [same in] a Book appointed for that purpose.[2]

---

[1] Perhaps the term of service was thus limited in anticipation of the proposed removal of many inhabitants.

[2] *Mass. Col. Rec.*, i. 116. April 1, 1634. "It was further ordered, that the constable and four or more of the chief inhabitants of every town (to be chosen by all the freemen there, at some meeting there), with the advice of some one or more of the next assistants, shall make a surveying of the houses, backside, cornfields, mowing ground, and other lands, im- proved, or enclosed, or granted by special order of the Court, of every free inhabitant there, and shall enter the same in a book (fairly written in words at length and not in figures), with the several bounds and quantities by the nearest estimation, and shall deliver a transcript thereof into the Court within six months now next ensuing; and the same, so entered and recorded, shall be a sufficient assurance to every such free inhabitant, his and their heirs and assigns, of such

" It is further ordered, that these five men [shall] meet every
first Monday in the [month] at the Constable's house, in the
forenoon, at the ringing of the bell."

estate of inheritance, or as they shall have in the New Towne," and, more familiarly,
in any such houses, lands, or frank-tene- the "Proprietors' Records," is still pre-
ments." served in the office of the City Clerk.
    The book thus prepared, called " The The record was not finally closed until
Regestere Booke of the Lands and Houses Feb. 19, 1829.

CHAPTER IV.

CIVIL HISTORY.

THE projectors of the New Town had hitherto suffered two grievous disappointments : the officers of the government had not generally become inhabitants, according to the original agreement; and so great was the disparity in commercial advantages, that it early became manifest that the New Town could not successfully compete with Boston as the great mart of trade. No reasonable hope, therefore, could be entertained that this should become the principal city of the colony. In other respects, the enterprise appears to have been eminently successful. The hope expressed by Dudley, that men of ability might be attracted hither by the advantages offered, had been gratified ; for so early as 1633, Wood wrote concerning them : " the inhabitants, most of them, are very rich and well stored with cattle of all sorts." A reasonable proportion of the rulers resided here. Dudley remained Deputy Governor until May, 1634, when he became Governor, and the next year was an Assistant. Bradstreet was constantly an Assistant ; and Haynes, at the first election after his arrival, was elected as an Assistant, and the next year, 1635, Governor. Moreover, the New Town had become the seat of government ; and, for aught which appears to the contrary, it might have retained that distinction, if the principal inhabitants had not removed.[1]

[1] The first three Courts of Assistants were held at Charlestown in August and September, 1630; after which all the courts were held in Boston until May, 1634. The ' sistants had even voted, Oct. 3, 1632, " It is thought, by general consent, that Boston is the fittest place for public meetings of any place in the Bay." Yet when Dudley was elected Governor, in May, 1634, the courts, both general and particular, were transferred to New Town, and were there held exclusively until May, 1636. Then they returned to Boston ; then to New Town again in April, 1637, until September, 1638, when they became permanently fixed at Boston.

Dr. Holmes, writing in 1800, says, " In some of the first years, the annual election of the Governor and Magistrates of the Colony was holden in this town. The people, on these occasions, assembled under an oak tree, which stood on the northerly side of the Common in Cambridge, a lit-

All these advantages, however, were not satisfactory. The disappointment and uneasiness found vent in words. One memorable example is preserved: "At the court of assistants," says Winthrop, Nov. 3, 1635, "John Pratt of Newtown was questioned about the letter he wrote into England, wherein he affirmed divers things, which were untrue and of ill repute, for the state of the country, as that here was nothing but rocks, and sands, and salt marshes, etc. He desired respite for his answer to the next morning; then he gave it in writing, in which, by making his own interpretation of some passages and acknowledging his error in others, he gave satisfaction."[1] This letter, probably written in the previous year, is not known to exist; but the "answer," which sufficiently indicates its nature, is on record : —

"The answer of me, John Pratt, to such things as I hear and perceive objected against me, as offensive in my letter. First, generally, whatsoever I writ of the improbability or impossibility of subsistence for ourselves or our posterity without tempting God, or without extraordinary means, it was with these two regards: first, I did not mean that which I said in respect of the whole country, or our whole patent in general, but only of that compass of ground wherein these towns are so thick set together; and secondly, I supposed that they intended so to remain, because (upon conference with divers) I found that men did think it unreasonable that they or any should remove or disperse into other parts of the country; and upon this ground I thought I could not subsist myself, nor the plantation, nor posterity. But I do acknowledge that since my letter there have been sundry places newly found out, as Neweberry, Concord, and others (and that within this patent), which will afford good means of subsistence for men and beasts, in which and other such like new plan-

tle west of the road leading to Lexington. The stump of it was dug up not many years since."— *Coll. Mass. Hist. Soc.*, vii. 9. This was probably the tree mentioned in a note to Hutchinson's *Hist. Mass.*, i. 61 : At the election in 1637, the party of Mr. Vane, fearing defeat, refused to proceed, until a certain petition had been read. Mr. Winthrop's party protested against delay. And it is said that "Mr. Wilson, the minister, in his zeal gat up upon the bough of a tree (it was hot weather and the election like that of Parliament men

for the counties in England was carried on in the field), and there made a speech, advising the people to look to their charter and to consider the present work of the day, which was designed for the choosing the governor, deputy governor, and the rest of the assistants for the government of the commonwealth. — His speech was well received by the people, who presently called out, election, election, which turned the scale."

[1] Savage's *Winthrop*, i. 173, 174.

tations, if the towns shall be fewer and the bounds larger than these are, I conceive they may live comfortably. The like I think of Coñecticott, with the plantations there now in hand; and what I conceive so sufficient for myself, I conceive so sufficient also for my posterity. And concerning these towns here so thick planted, I conceive they may subsist in case that, besides the conveniences which they have already near hand, they do improve farms somewhat further off, and do also apply themselves to and do improve the trade of fishing and other trades. As concerning the intimation of the Commonwealth builded upon rocks, sands, and salt marshes, I wish I had not made it, because it is construed contrary to my meaning, which I have before expressed. And whereas my letters do seem to extenuate the judgment of such as came before, as having more honesty than skill, they being scholars, citizens, tradesmen, &c., my meaning was not so general as the words do import; for I had an eye only to those that had made larger reports into England of the country than I found to be true in the sense aforesaid. And whereas I may seem to imply that I had altered the minds or judgments of the body of the people, magistrates, and others, I did not mean this in respect of the goodness or badness of the land in the whole plantation, but only in point of removal and spreading further into other parts, they afterwards conceiving it necessary that some should remove into other places, here and there, of more enlargement; and whereas I seem to speak of all the magistrates and people, I did indeed mean only all those with whom I had any private speéch about those things. And as for the barrenness of the sandy grounds, &c., I spake of them then as I conceived; but now, by experience of mine own, I find that such ground as before I accounted barren, yet, being manured and husbanded, doth bring forth more fruit than I did expect. As for the not prospering of the English grain upon this ground, I do since that time see that rye and oats have prospered better than I expected; but as for the other kinds of grain, I do still question whether they will come to such perfection as in our native country from whence they come. And whereas I am thought generally to charge all that have written into England by way of commendation of this land as if what they had written were generally false, I meant it only of such excessive commendations as I see did exceed and are contrary to that which I have here expressed.

"And as concerning that which I said, that the gospel would

be as dear here as in England, I did it to this end, to put some which intended to come hither only for outward commodity to look for better grounds ere they look this way. As for some grounds of my returning, which I concealed from my friends for fear of doing hurt, I meant only some particular occasions and apprehensions of mine own, not intending to lay any secret blemish upon the State. And whereas I did express the danger of decaying here in our first love, &c., I did it only in regard of the manifold occasions and businesses which here at first we meet withal, by which I find in mine own experience (and so, I think, do others also), how hard it is to keep our hearts in that holy frame which sometimes they were in where we had less to do in outward things, but not at all intending to impute it as necessary to our condition, much less as a fruit of our precious liberties which we enjoy, which rather tend to the quickening of us, we improving the same as we ought.

"This my answer (according with the inward consent and meaning of my heart) I do humbly commend to the favorable consideration and acceptance of the Court, desiring in this, as in all things, to approve myself in a conscience void of offence towards God and man.

" JOHN PRATT.

"Of this answer of John Pratt before written, voluntarily by him made, as we are witnesses, so we do also join with him in humble desire unto the Court, that it may be favorably accepted, and whatever failings are in the letter in regard of the manner of expressions (which may seem hardly to suit with these his interpretations), we do desire the indulgence of the Court to pass over without further question.

" PETER BULKELEY.
JOHN WILSON.
THOMAS HOOKER.

" Whereas John Pratt of Newe Towne, being called before us at this present Court, and questioned for a letter which he wrote into England, dated ————, wherein he raised an ill report of this country, did desire respite till the next day to consider of his answer, he hath now delivered in this before written, which, upon his free submission and acknowledgement of his error, the Court hath accepted for satisfaction, and thereupon pardoned his said offence, and given order that it shall be recorded, and such as desire copies thereof may have the same.

" JOHN HAYNES, Govr.,	WILL^x. CODDINGTON,
RICH: BELLINGHAM,	WILL^x. PINCHON,
JOHN WINTHROP,	ATTERTON HOUGHE,
THO: DUDLEY,	INCREASE NOWELL,
JOHN HUMFRY,	SIMON BRADSTREETE." [1]

This Mr. Pratt was a physician in the New Town, or Cambridge, for several years. He and his wife were drowned near the coast of Spain in December, 1646, as related by Winthrop.[2] He was not the only dissatisfied person, though less cautious than others in expressing his feelings. As early as May, 1634, this spirit of dissatisfaction became so general among the inhabitants of the New Town, that they proposed to abandon their comparatively pleasant homes, and to commence anew in the wilderness. The ostensible reason for removal was the lack of sufficient land. The town was indeed narrow, but its length was indefinite. The limit of eight miles northwesterly from the meeting-house was not fixed until March, 1636; and it does not appear how far the land was previously occupied in that direction. But the westerly line of Charlestown was established, March 6, 1632–3; and it seems to have been understood that the whole territory between that line and the easterly bounds of Watertown was reserved for the use of New Town, however far those lines might extend into the country. But the people appeared impatient of such narrow limits. At the General Court, May 14, 1634, "Those of New Town complained of straitness for want of land, especially meadow, and desired leave of the Court to look out either for enlargement or removal, which was granted; whereupon they sent men to see Agawam and Merrimack, and gave out that they would remove, etc."[3] Early in July, 1634, "Six of New Town went in the Blessing (being bound to the Dutch plantation,) to discover Connecticut River, intending to remove their town thither."[4] In the following September, the same subject was again brought before the General Court. The record is very brief; but the particulars related by Winthrop are of so much interest that they may well be quoted in full: —

Sept. 4, 1634. "The General Court began at New Town, and continued a week, and was then adjourned fourteen days. —

[1] *Mass. Rec.*, i. 358–360.   [2] Savage's *Winthrop*, i. 122.
[3] Savage's *Winthrop*, ii. 239.   [4] *Ibid.*, i. 136.

The main business, which spent the most time and caused the adjourning of the Court, was about the removal of New Town. They had leave, the last General Court, to look out some place for enlargement or removal, with promise of having it confirmed to them, if it were not prejudicial to any other plantation ; and now they moved that they might have leave to remove to Connecticut. This matter was debated divers days, and many reasons alleged pro and con.

" The principal reasons for their removal were, 1. Their want of accommodation for their cattle, so as they were not able to maintain their ministers, nor could receive any more of their friends to help them ; and here it was alleged by Mr. Hooker, as a fundamental error, that towns were set so near each to other. 2. The fruitfulness and commodiousness of Connecticut, and the danger of having it possessed by others, Dutch or English. 3. The strong bent of their spirits to remove thither.

"Against these it was said, 1. That, in point of conscience, they ought not to depart from us, being knit to us in one body and bound by oath to seek the welfare of this commonwealth. 2. That, in point of state and civil polity, we ought not to give them leave to depart : — being we were now weak and in danger to be assailed ; the departure of Mr. Hooker would not only draw many from us, but also divert other friends that would come to us ; we should expose them to evident peril, both from the Dutch, (who made claim to the same river and had already built a fort there,) and from the Indians, and also from our own state at home, who would not endure they should sit down without a patent in any place which our king lays claim unto. 3. They might be accommodated at home by some enlargement which other towns offered. 4. They might remove to Merimack or any other place within our patent. 5. The removing of a candlestick is a great judgment, which is to be avoided.

" Upon these and other arguments the Court being divided, it was put to vote ; and, of the Deputies, fifteen were for their departure, and ten against it. The Governor and two Assistants were for it, and the Deputy and all the rest of the Assistants were against it, (except the Secretary, who gave no vote ;) whereupon no record was entered, because there were not six Assistants in the vote, as the patent requires. Upon this there grew a great difference between the Governor and Assistants and the Deputies. They would not yield the Assistants a negative voice, and the others (considering how dangerous it might be to the commonwealth if they should not keep that strength to balance the greater number of the Deputies) thought it safe to stand upon it. So when they could proceed no farther, the whole Court agreed to keep a day of humiliation to seek the Lord, which was accordingly done, in all the congregations, the 18th day of this month: and the 24th the Court met again. Before they began, Mr. Cotton preached, (being desired by all the Court upon Mr. Hooker's instant excuse of his unfitness for that occasion.) He took his text out of Hag. ii. 4, etc., out of which he laid down the nature or strength (as he termed it) of the magistracy, ministry, and people, viz. — the strength of the magistracy to be their authority ; of the people, their liberty ; and of the ministry, their purity ; and showed how all of these had a negative voice, etc., and that yet the ultimate resolution, etc., ought to be in the whole body of the people, etc., with answer to all objections, and a declaration of the people's duty and right to maintain their true liberties against any unjust violence, etc., which gave great satisfaction to the company. And it pleased the Lord so to assist him and to bless his own ordinance, that the affairs of the Court went on cheerfully; and although all were not satisfied about the negative voice to be left to the magistrates, yet no man moved aught about it, and the congregation of New Town came and accepted of such enlargement as had formerly been offered them by Boston and Watertown ; and so the fear of their removal to Connecticut was removed." [1]

This " enlargement," however, was not permanently satisfactory. The inhabitants of New Town again manifested "the strong bent of their spirits to remove." It does not appear when they received permission of the General Court. Perhaps the liberty granted in general terms, May 14, 1634, was held to be sufficient. It seems certain that a considerable number of them went to Connecticut before Sept. 3, 1635 ; for on that day William Westwood, a New Town man, was "sworn Constable of the plantations at Connecticut till some other be chosen." [2] But the general exodus was several months later. Under date of May 31, 1636, Winthrop says: " Mr. Hooker, pastor of the church of New Town, and the most of his congregation, went to Connecticut. His wife was carried in a horse-litter ; and they drove one hundred and sixty cattle, and fed of their milk by the way." [3] Their possessions in New Town were purchased by Mr. Shepard

<hr>

[1] Savage's *Winthrop*, i. 140–142.   [3] Savage's *Winthrop*, i. 187.
[2] *Mass. Col. Rec.*, i. 159.

and his friends, who opportunely arrived in the autumn of 1635 and the following spring and summer.

The reasons assigned for this removal seem insufficient to justify it; or, at the least, insufficient to require it. As to their inability to maintain their ministers, it should be observed that at the same session when this reason was alleged, New Town was rated as high as any other town in the colony.[1] The real want of accommodation for cattle and for an additional population may be estimated from the facts that, at this time there were probably less than one hundred families here, containing from five hundred to six hundred persons; and, supposing them to have sold one half of their cattle to their successors, their herd may have consisted of about three hundred. Including the land then offered by others and accepted by them, their territory embraced Cambridge, Arlington, Brookline, Brighton, and Newton. After making all needful allowance for improvements in agriculture, one might suppose here was sufficient room for somewhat more than a hundred families, with their flocks and herds.

Another reason is mentioned by Winthrop, namely, "the strong bent of their spirits to remove." The particular pressure which occasioned this "strong bent" he does not describe. But Hubbard, writing before 1682, when many were living who heard the discussion, intimates what that pressure was: "The impulsive cause, as wise men deemed and themselves did not altogether conceal, was the strong bent of their spirits to remove out of the place where they were. Two such eminent stars, such as were Mr. Cotton and Mr. Hooker, both of the first magnitude, though of different influence, could not well continue in one and the same orb."[2] Again he says: "A great number of the planters of the old towns, viz., Dorchester, Roxbury, Watertown, and Cambridge, were easily induced to attempt a removal of themselves and families upon the first opportunity offered; which was not a little advanced by the fame and interest of Mr. Hooker, whose worth and abilities had no small influence upon the people of the towns forementioned."[3] The opinion thus expressed by Hubbard, was adopted by Hutchinson, nearly a hundred years later: "Mr. Hooker and Mr. Cotton were deservedly in high esteem; some of the principal persons were strongly attached to the one of them, and some to the other. The great influence which Mr. Cotton had in the colony inclined Mr. Hooker and his

---

[1] *Mass. Col. Rec.*, i. 129.　　　　　　[3] *Ibid.*, xvi. 305, 306.
[2] *Coll. Mass. Hist. Soc.*, xv. 173.

friends to remove to some place more remote from Boston than New Town. Besides, they alleged, as a reason for their removal, that they were straitened for room, and thereupon viewed divers places on the sea-coast, but were not satisfied with them." [1] Trumbull suggests that political rivalry was mingled with clerical jealousy. Of John Haynes he says : " In 1635 he was chosen Governor of Massachusetts. He was not considered in any respect inferior to Governor Winthrop. His growing popularity, and the fame of Mr. Hooker, who, as to strength of genius and his lively and powerful manner of preaching, rivalled Mr. Cotton, were supposed to have had no small influence upon the General Court in their granting liberty to Mr. Hooker and his company to remove to Connecticut. There it was judged they would not so much eclipse the fame, nor stand in the way of the promotion and honor of themselves or their friends." [2]

Very probably such jealousies and rivalries had some influence upon the removal of Mr. Hooker and his friends. It is known that Winthrop and Haynes differed in judgment upon public policy, the former advocating a mild administration of justice, and the latter insisting on " more strictness in civil government and military discipline," as Winthrop relates at large, i. 177–179. The Antinomian controversy, which did not indeed culminate until a year or two later, had commenced as early as 1635 ; in which Hooker and Cotton espoused opposite sides, and were among the most prominent clerical antagonists. Up to the period of the removal, it seemed doubtful which party would prevail. Both parties were zealous ; both lauded their own clergymen, and spoke harshly of their opponents. It is not surprising, therefore, that Cotton and Hooker should feel that their close proximity was irritating rather than refreshing. On the whole, I think, " the strong bent of their spirits to remove " was not altogether caused by lack of sufficient land or by straitness of accommodations.

However doubtful the cause, the fact is certain, that the greater part of the First Church and Congregation removed from New Town ; more than fifty families went to Hartford, and others elsewhere. Of the families residing here before January, 1635, not more than eleven are known to have remained. The following list of inhabitants is compiled from the Records of the Town, under the dates when they first appear. It should be observed, however, that perhaps many of them were here earlier than the

[1] *Hist. Mass.,* i. 43.   [2] *Hist. Conn.,* i. 234.

dates would indicate. For example, Dudley and Bradstreet, and probably others, under date of 1632, were here in 1631; many of those who are entered under date of 1633 were certainly here in 1632; and some of those whose names first appear in 1634 had perhaps been residents one or two years previously. It may also be observed, that of those who removed, many did not permanently remain in the town first selected, but subsequently went elsewhere; yet it does not properly fall within my province to trace their various emigrations.

1632.

Thomas Dudley, Esq.[1]
Simon Bradstreet.[1]
Edmund Lockwood.[2]
Daniel Patrick.[3]
John Poole.[4]
William Spencer.[5]
John Kirman.[4]
Simon Sackett.[2]

1633.

Jeremy Adams.[6]
Matthew Allen.[5]
John Benjamin.[6]
Jonathan Bosworth.[7]
John Bridge.[6]
Richard Butler.[5]
William Butler.[5]
John Clark.[5]
Anthony Colby.[1]
Daniel Denison.[1]
Samuel Dudley.[9]
Edward Elmer.[5]
Richard Goodman.[5]
William Goodwin.[5]
Garrad Haddon.[3]

Stephen Hart.[6]
John Haynes, Esq.[5]
Thomas Heate.[7]
Rev. Thomas Hooker.[5]
John Hopkins.[5]
Thomas Hosmer.[5]
William Kelsey.[5]
William Lewis.[4]
Richard Lord.[5]
John Masters.[6]
Abraham Morrill.
Hester Mussey.[5]
James Olmstead.[5]
William Pantry.[5]
John Pratt.[5]

Joseph Reading.[1]
Nathaniel Richards.[5]
Thomas Spencer.[5]
Edward Stebbins.[5]
George Steele.[5]
John Steele.[5]
Rev. Samuel Stone.[5]
John Talcott.[5]
Wm. Wadsworth.[5]
Andrew Warner.[5]
Richard Webb.[5]
William Westwood.[5]
John White.[5]

1634.

Daniel Abbott.[10]
William Andrews.[5]
John Arnold.[5]
Guy Banbridge.[6]
John Barnard.[5]

Thomas Beale.[6]
Christopher Cane.[6]
Mrs. Chester.[6]
Nicholas Clark.[5]
Dolor Davis.[11]

Robert Day.[5]
Joseph Easton.[5]
Nathaniel Ely.[5]
James Ensign.[5]
Thomas Fisher.[12]

[1] Removed to Ipswich.
[2] Died here; family removed to Connecticut.
[3] Removed to Watertown.
[4] Removed to Lynn.
[5] Removed to Hartford.
[6] Remained here.
[7] Removed to Hingham.
[8] Removed to Salisbury.
[9] Removed to Boston.
[10] Removed to Providence.
[11] Removed to Concord.
[12] Removed to Dedham.

Edmund Gearner.[1]	Thomas Judd.[8]	Michael Spencer.[7]
John Gibson.[2]	William Mann.[2]	Timothy Stanley.[8]
Seth Grant.[8]	John Maynard.[8]	George Stocking.[8]
Bartholomew Green.[8]	Joseph Mygate.[9]	Timothy Tomlins.[7]
Samuel Green.[9]	Stephen Post.[8]	Humphrey Vincent.[8]
Samuel Greenhill.[8]	John Prince.[5]	Samuel Wakeman.[8]
Nathaniel Hancock.[2]	Thomas Scott.[8]	Samuel Whitehead.[8]
Edmund Hunt.[4]	Garrad Spencer.[7]	Simon Willard.[8]

[1] Perhaps the Edmund Gardner, who was in Ipswich, 1638.
[2] Remained here.
[8] Removed to Hartford.
[4] Removed to Duxbary.
[5] Removed to Hull.
[6] Removed to Ipswich.
[7] Removed to Lynn.
[8] Removed to Concord.

CHAPTER V.

CIVIL HISTORY.

It has already been mentioned in the preceding chapter, that Mr. Hooker and a large proportion of his church removed from New Town in 1635 and 1636; and that Mr. Shepard with another company purchased their houses and lands. Among "the reasons which swayed him to come to New England," Mr. Shepard says in his Autobiography, "Divers people in Old England of my dear friends desired me to go to New England there to live together, and some went before and writ to me of providing a place for a company of us, one of which was John Bridge, and I saw divers families of my Christian friends, who were resolved thither to go with me." Accordingly "in the year 1634, about the beginning of the winter," he embarked at Harwich, having with him "brother Champney, Frost, Goffe, and divers others, most dear saints," who afterwards were inhabitants of Cambridge. They were driven back by stress of weather, and the voyage was abandoned. But "about the 10th of August, 1635," he again embarked; "and so the Lord. after many sad storms and wearisome days and many longings to see the shore, brought us to the sight of it upon Oct. 2, 1635, and upon Oct. the 8d, we arrived with my wife, child, brother Samuel, Mr. Harlakenden, Mr. Cooke, &c., at Boston. — When we had been here two days, upon Monday Oct. 5, we came (being sent for by friends at Newtown) to them, to my brother Mr. Stone's house; and that congregation being upon their removal to Hartford at Connecticut, myself and those that came with me found many houses empty and many persons willing to sell, and here our company bought off their houses to dwell in until we should see another place fit to remove into; but having been here some time, divers of our brethren did desire to sit still and not to remove farther, partly because of the fellowship of the churches, partly because they thought their lives were short and removals to near plantations full of troubles, partly because they foun sufficient for themselves and their company,"[1] Besides those who are here named by Mr. Shepard, another Mr. Cooke and William French came in the same ship (*The Defence*) with him; and the larger portion of those whose names first appear in 1635 and 1636 may safely be regarded as members of his company, to wit: —

1635.

Jonas Austin.[2]
Thomas Blodgett.[3]
Thomas Blower.[3]
William Blumfield.[4]
Robert Bradish.[3]
Thomas Brigham.[3]
William Buck.[2]
William Butler.[4]
Clement Chaplin.[4]
Thomas Chesholme.[3]
George Cooke.[3]
Joseph Cooke.[3]
Simon Crosby.[3]
Nicholas Danforth.[3]
William French.[3]
Edmund Frost.[3]
Richard Girling.[3]
Edward Goffe.[3]
Percival Green.[3]

Roger Harlakenden, Esq.[3]
Atherton Haugh.[3]
William Holman.[3]
John Jackson.[3]
William Jones.[3]
Barnabas Lamson.[3]
Thomas Marrett.[3]
John Meane.[3]
Nicholas Olmstead.[4]
Thomas Parish.[3]
Robert Parker.[3]
John Pratt.[3]
William Ruscoe.[4]
John Russell.[3]
Samuel Shepard.[3]
Rev. Thomas Shepard.[3]
Edward Winship.[3]
William Witherell.[7]

1636.

William Adams.[9]
Edmund Angier.[3]
James Bennett.[9]
Thomas Besbeech.[10]
Richard Betts.[3]
Peter Bulkeley.[9]
Benjamin Burr.[4]
John Champney.[3]
Richard Champney.[3]

Josiah Cobbett.[3]
Edward Collins.[3]
John Cooper.[3]
Gilbert Crackbone.[3]
Francis Griswold.[3]
Thomas Hayward.[11]
Ralph Hudson.[12]
Joseph Isaac.[3]
Richard Jackson.[3]

[1] *Life of Shepard*, edition of 1832, pp. 42–58.
[2] Removed to Hingham.
[3] Remained here.
[4] Removed to Hartford.
[5] Removed to Charlestown.
[6] Removed to Hartford. Two of the same name were here.

[7] Afterwards settled in the ministry at Scituate.
[8] Removed to Ipswich.
[9] Removed to Concord.
[10] Removed to Scituate or Duxbury; afterwards to Sudbury.
[11] Removed to Duxbury.
[12] A proprietor; but resided in Boston.

John King.[1]	John Santley.[1]
John Moore.[2]	Nathaniel Sparhawk.[2]
Walter Nichols.[3]	Comfort Starr.[5]
Richard Parke.[2]	Gregory Stone.[2]
William Patten.[2]	William Towne.[2]
Richard Rice.[4]	Thomas Welles.[5]
Nicholas Roberts.[1]	John Woolcott.[7]

Immediately after the arrival of Mr. Shepard's company, they became prominent in municipal affairs, although the larger part of Mr. Hooker's company did not remove until six months afterwards. I quote again from the Town Records : —

Nov. 23, 1635. "At a general meeting of the whole town, there was then chosen, to order the business of the whole town for the year following, and until new be chosen in their room, Mr. Roger Harlakenden, William Spencer, Andrew Warner, Joseph Cooke, John Bridge, Clement Chaplin, Nicholas Danforth, Thomas Hosmer, William Andrews: which nine men are to have the power of the Town as those formerly chosen had, as may appear in the order made the 3d Feb. 1634. (1634–5.)

" Further, there was chosen and sworn William Andrews, constable for the year following, and until a new be chosen.

" Further, there was then chosen for the year following Barnabas Lambson to be surveyor of the highways.

" It is further ordered, That the Town Book shall be at William Spencer's house."

With a change of government came a change of customs. Some of the common planting fields became private property. Thus the Old Field, containing about sixty-three acres, was divided between Edward Goffe, Samuel Shepard, and Joseph Cooke. Small-lot-Hill, in like manner, passed into fewer hands. Farms were granted to such as desired them, both on the south side of the River, and in the territory now embraced in Arlington and Lexington. Much the larger portion of the inhabitants continued to reside in the "town," and "West End," very few venturing beyond the line of Sparks, Wyeth, and Garden Streets; but provision was made for the suitable care of their cattle, on the commons, by keepers specially appointed. Rules were adopted to promote the comfort and convenience of the inhabitants, and to protect them against annoyance by undesirable

[1] Names soon disappeared.
[2] Remained here.
[3] Removed to Charlestown.
[4] Removed to Concord.
[5] Removed to Duxbury.
[6] Removed to Hartford.
[7] A proprietor; but resided in Watertown.

associates. A few extracts from the Records may help to exhibit their condition.

Dec. 7, 1685. "It is ordered, That the monthly meeting, every first Monday [in the month], according to the first order, shall [be continued;] and whosoever appears not within half an hour after the ringing of the bell, shall pay for the first day vi^d., and [for the second] day xii^d., and so to double it every day, [unless he have] a just excuse, such as may give satisfaction to the rest of the company.[1]

"It is further ordered, That there shall be a sufficient bridge made down to low-water mark on this side the River, and a broad ladder [set up] on the farther side the River, for convenience [of] landing; and Mr. Chaplin, Mr. Danforth and Mr. Cooke to see it made."[2]

Jan. 4, 1635–6, "It is ordered, That Mr. Joseph Cooke shall keep the ferry, and have a penny over, and a half a penny on Lecture days.[3]

"It is further ordered, That there shall be a double rail set up from the Pine Swamp fence to West-end Field fence, for the milch cows to lie in, on nights, and that no other cattle whatever to go there, either swine, goats, mares, or the like."[4]

Feb. 8, 1635–6, "Agreed with Mr. Chapline, that his man

---

[1] This order would seem to require a monthly meeting of all the inhabitants; but the records indicate that only the Townsmen thus met. A general town meeting was seldom held, except annually in November, for the election of officers.

[2] This bridge, or causeway, was at the southerly end of Dunster Street. Traces of the old road on the south side of the river were not long ago (and perhaps still remain), several rods east of the present road leading from the Great Bridge to Brighton. Connected with this causeway was the ferry, named in the next order.

[3] Although there were then few, if any, inhabitants of the New Town residing on the south side of the River, yet many persons crossed the ferry, in going from town to town, especially on Lecture-days. Winthrop tells us, in 1634, — "It being found that the four Lectures did spend too much time, and proved overburdensome to the ministers and people, the ministers, with the advice of the magistrates, and with the consent of their con-

gregations, did agree to reduce them to two days, viz.: Mr. Cotton one Thursday, or the 5th day of the week, and Mr. Hooker at New Town the next 5th day; and Mr. Warham at Dorchester one 4th day of the week, and Mr. Welde at Roxbury, the next 4th day." This arrangement was not effectual; for Winthrop adds five years later, in 1639, "there were so many Lectures now in the country, and many poor persons would usually resort to two or three in the week, to the great neglect of their affairs, and the damage of the public," etc. The General Court attempted to correct the evil; but the Elders, or Pastors of Churches, manifested such a keen jealousy of their rights, that the attempt was abandoned, and all evidence of it was suppressed, or excluded from the records. Savage's *Winthrop*, I. 144, 324–326.

[4] This fence was where Linnaean Street now is, and was the northern boundary of the cow-common; the other sides were bounded by the present Garden Street and North Avenue.

shall keep the goats, and to have three half pence a week for one
goat, and a penny a week for wethers or kids; to begin next
Monday."

March 1, 1635–6, "Agreed with Richard Rice to keep 100
cows for the space of three months, to begin when he shall be
appointed; and is to have ten pounds paid him within ten days
after the ships be come in, or in June. Also he is to have 2 men
to help him keep them the first 14 days, and one man the next 7
days; also to have them kept 2 sabbath days, and he one, during
the time. Also he is to fetch the cows into the town every morning out of the common, half an hour after the sun is up, at the
farthest, and to bring them into the town half an hour before the
sun goeth down, and to pay iii^d. a cow for every night he
leaveth out any. Also he is not to keep any cattle for any man
except he have leave from the Townsmen, upon the forfeiture of
v^s. a cow he shall so keep. Also he hath liberty to keep his own
heifer without pay."

"Agreed with John Clarke to make a sufficient weir to catch
alewives upon Menotomies River in the bounds of this town, before the 12th of April next, and shall sell and deliver unto the
inhabitants of the town and no other, except for bait, all the alewives he shall take at iii^s., 6^d. per thousand, and shall at all
times give such notice to the persons that shall be appointed to
fetch them away as he shall be directed, who shall discharge the
said John Clarke of them within 24 hours after notice, or else he
to have liberty to sell them to whom he can. Provided, and it is
the meaning of the Townsmen, that if any shall desire to have
some to eat before the great quantity cometh, then he is to have
ii^d. a score and fetch them there, or iii^d. a score and he bring
them home. Further the Townsmen do promise in the behalf
of the town to make good all those fish that he shall be damnified
by the Indians, that is, shall himself deliver unto them, being
appointed before by the Townsmen how many he shall deliver.
Also to save him harmless from any damage he shall sustain by
Wattertowne, provided it be not his own fault. He is to have
his money within 14 days after he hath done fishing."

March 13, 1635–6, "Agreed with William Patten to keep
100 cattle on the other side the River for the space of seven
months, to begin when the Town shall appoint him, and to have
twenty pounds, the one half paid him in money when he hath
keep half his time, and the other half in corn when he hath done
keeping, at the price which the common rate of corn goeth when

he is to be paid. And he is to have a man to help him the first 14 days, he paying him for one week, the Town for the other; also he is to lodge there except once a week, and to have a man to keep them every other sabbath day; and he to pay x⁵. a beast for every beast he shall lose; and to keep no cattle of any man, except the Townsmen give leave, upon the forfeiture of 5⁵. a head for every head he shall so keep."

"The hog-keeper began to keep on the first of April, being the fifth day of the week, at 10⁵. per week so long as the Townsmen please to have him keep them; and he is to keep them at Rocky Meadow."

April 4, 1636. "Agreed with John Talcott and William Wadsworth to have their house at Rocky Meadow this year, for the hog-keeper to abide in; and they are to have their cattle go free from paying towards the pound for dry cattle this year."

"It is ordered, That Richard Rice shall begin to keep the cows the 11th of April, 1636."

"It is ordered, That William Pattine shall begin to keep the dry cattle the 14th of April."

"Ordered, That whosoever finds a cock, hen, or turkey, in a garden, it shall be lawful for them to require three pence of the owner; and if they refuse to pay, then to kill the same."

"Andrew Warner and Joseph Cooke to make a rate for the division of the alewives." [1]

April 23, 1636. "Agreed with Andrew Warner to fetch home the alewives from the weir; and he is to have xvi⁴. a thousand, and load them himself, for carriage; and to have power to take any man to help him, he paying of him for his work.

"Andrew Warner appointed to see a cartway made to the weir."

"William Reskie appointed to make a pound."

Oct. 3, 1636. "Agreed with Mr. Cooke to take up all the stubs that are within the bounds of the town, that is, within the town gates;[2] and he is to have ix⁴. apiece for taking up the same,

---

[1] It was customary to put one or more alewives in each hill of corn, and to use them otherwise for the enrichment of the soil. They were considered of so much value for this purpose as to be divided ratably. As late as June 10, 1649, it was "ordered, by the Townsmen, that all persons provide that their dogs may do no harm in corn or gardens, by scraping up the fish, upon the penalty of 3⁴. for every dog that shall be taken *damage feasant*, with all other just damages."

[2] "Town gates" then stood across Harvard Street, near Linden Street; across Brattle Street, probably near Ash Street; and across the street between the College yard and the Burial-place. Besides these, there were other gates to protect the cow-common; one across Kirkland Street, near Oxford Street; one

and filling up the holes, all above iii. inches [deep], which he is
to do before the first of December, or else to forfeit 5*l.*"

Dec. 5, 1636. " Ordered, That no man inhabiting or not inhabiting within the bounds of the town shall let or sell any house)
or land unto any, without the consent of the Townsmen then in
place, unless it be to a member of the congregation ; and lest any
one shall sustain loss thereby, they shall come and proffer the
same unto them, upon a day of the monthly meeting, and at
such a rate as he shall not sell or let for a lesser price unto any
than he offereth unto them, and to leave the same in their hands,
in liking, until the next meeting day in the next month, when, if
they shall not take it, paying the price within some convenient
time, or provide him a chapman, he shall then be free to sell or
let the same unto any other, provided the Townsmen think them
fit to be received in."

" Ordered, That whosoever entertains any stranger into the
town, if the congregation desire it, he shall set the town free
of them again within one month after warning given them, or
else he shall pay 19*s*. 8*d*. unto the townsmen as a fine for his
default, and as much for every month they shall there remain.

" There is granted unto Frances Gresbold, the Drummer, 2
acres of land, lying at the end of Barnebe Lambson's pale towards Charlestowne, in regard of his service amongst the soldiers
upon all occasions, as long as he stayeth, with condition, if he
depart the town and leave off that service within two years, he
shall leave it unto the town at the charge it hath cost him in
building and enclosing."

Jan. 2, 1636-7. " It is granted unto Joseph Cooke to have the
hill by his house, which have been hitherto preserved for a place
to build a fort upon for defence, with all the lane leading thereunto ; provided if the town shall ever make use of it for that
end, he shall yield it again ; or else to remain to him and his
heirs forever.[1]

" Granted to Mr. Richard Harlakingden six hundred acres of
upland and meadow, at the place called Vine Brook, in the midway between Newtowne and Concord, upon condition he sendeth
over his man, or ordereth that some other may build upon it and

across Garden Street, at the west end of
Linnæan Street, and probably another at
its east end, across North Avenue.

[1] The house of Joseph Cooke stood at
the northeasterly corner of Holyoke Street
and Holyoke Place ; and it is believed by

some that a portion of it still remains.
The hill reserved for a fort is the high
land at the southeasterly angle of Holyoke
Place. Mr. Cooke's lot contained five
acres, lying east of Holyoke Street, and
south of Mount Auburn Street.

improve it for him the next summer after this next ensuing, and now, this spring, [give] certain intelligence he will do so; and upon condition likewise that he cometh himself the next summer after being the third from this time; and if he shall fail in all or any one of these three conditions, then this grant to be void." [1]

Jan. 14, 1638–9. " Ordered, there being found much damage done by swine in this town, since the order of the General Court was repealed, and they left at liberty for each town to order, — it is therefore ordered, at a general meeting of the Townsmen, with a general consent of the inhabitants then present, that is to say, that none, either rich or poor, shall keep above two swine abroad on the common, one sow hog and a barrow, or 2 barrows; and these to be sufficiently yoked and ringed, after the judgment of the two brethren that are appointed to see to the execution of this order, and to bring in a note of such defaults as they find. And if any be found defective, to break this order, either by keeping more than 2 hogs, and such hogs, so let abroad, if not sufficiently [yoked and ringed] after the order, shall pay for every breach of this order 2s., unless in case there should be any failing by unexpected providence, and can be so proved by sufficient evidence; in that case there may be mitigation of this fine, otherwise to take place without all excuses, to the end that each man and this commonweal may be preserved from damage by that creature in this our town."

Oct. 1, 1639. " Ordered, for the preservation of apple-trees and all other kind of quick-set, in men's yards or elsewhere, and for preventing all other damage by them and harm to themselves by skipping over pales, That no goats shall be suffered to go out of the owner's yard without a keeper; but if it appeareth to be willingly, they shall pay unto any one that will put them to pound two pence for every goat, beside damage and poundage. And because the charge would be too great if only a part of them be kept, it is therefore also ordered, that whosoever shall not put forth their goats shall notwithstanding pay to the keeper within one third part as much for every goat as they that do put them out, until the first of March; and after that day, to the full as much as any do for those that are with the herd."

March, 1639–40. " Ordered, That William Towne shall regis-

---

[1] Richard Harlakenden was elder brother to Roger Harlakenden, and had been very kind to Mr. Shepard in England. He did not comply with the conditions of this grant; and the same land was assigned, April 2, 1638, to Roger Harlakenden, in lieu of five hundred acres previously granted to him on the south side of the river. Vine Brook passes through the central portion of Lexington.

ter every birth, marriage, and burial, according to the order of
Court in that case provided, and give it in, once every year, to be
delivered by the Deputies to the Recorder; and shall gather for
every particular entrance 1 penny for the Recorder's fees, and
xii⁴. for himself."

—— 1640. "Granted unto Joseph Cooke a farm of 400
acres of the nearest upland adjoining to his meadow lying beyond Cheesecake Brook[1] and between that and Charles River;
and also liberty to go with a straight line, (on the hithermost
side of his meadow on this side Cheesecake Brook), down by the
edge of the highland, to Charles River.".

At the same meeting grants of farms were made to other persons, to wit: to Samuel Shepard 400 acres adjoining and beyond the farm of Joseph Cooke; to Capt. George Cooke, 600
acres; to Edward Goffe, 600 acres; to John Bridge, 350 acres;
severally "about the outside of the bounds between Watertowne,
Concord, and Charlestowne."

During this period, the General Court passed several orders,
affecting the comfort and prosperity of the people dwelling
here : —

Oct. 28, 1636. "The Court agreed to give 400l. towards a
school or college, whereof 200l. to be paid the next year, and
200l. when the work is finished, and the next Court to appoint
where and what building."[2]

Dec. 13, 1636. "It is ordered, That all military men in this
jurisdiction shall be ranked into three regiments, viz., Boston,
Roxberry, Dorchester, Weimoth, Hingham, to be one regiment,
whereof John Winthrope, senior, Esquire, shall be colonel, and
Tho. Dudley, Esquire, lieftenant colonel :

"Charlestowne, Newetowne, Watertowne, Concord, and Ded-
dam, to be another regiment, whereof John Haynes, Esq'. shall
be colonel, and Roger Herlakenden Esq'. lieftenant colonel :

[1] Cheesecake Brook is in the westerly
part of Newton.

[2] Mass. Col. Rec., i. 183. President
Quincy (Hist. Harv. Coll., i. 1), states
that this foundation of the College was
laid Sept. 8, 1636, overlooking the fact
that the General Court, which met on
that day, adjourned until October, and
made this grant on the 28th day of that
month. The College was ordered to be
established at Newtown, Nov. 15, 1637,
and the town granted "to the Professor"
2⅔ acres of land, on which Holworthy,
Stoughton, and Hollis Halls are supposed to stand. This grant to the Professor, made May 11, 1638, is defined on
the record to be "to the Town's use forever, for a public school or college; and
to the use of Mr. Nathaniel Eaton as
long as he shall be employed in that
work; so that at his death, or ceasing
from that work, he or his shall be allowed
according to the charges he hath been at,
in building or fencing."

" Saugust, Salem, Ipswich, and Neweberry, to be another regiment, whereof John Endecot Esq'. shall be colonel, and John Winthrope, junior, leiftenant colonel:

" And the Governor for the time being shall be chief general."[1]

" March 9, 1636–7. " For Newetowne, Mr. George Cooke chosen captain; Mr. Willi: Spencer, leiftenant; Mr. Sam: Shepard, ensign."[2]

Nov. 15, 1637. " The College is ordered to be at Newetowne."[3]

Nov. 20, 1637. " For the College, the Governor, Mr. Winthrope, the Deputy, Mr. Dudley, the Treasurer, Mr. Bellingham, Mr. Humfrey, Mr. Herlakenden, Mr. Staughton, Mr. Cotton, Mr. Wilson, Mr. Damport, Mr. Wells, Mr. Sheopard, and Mr. Peters, these or the greater part of them, whereof Mr. Winthrope, Mr. Dudley, or Mr. Bellingham, to be alway one, to take order for a College at Newetowne.

" Edward Michelson, being appointed marshall of the Court, is appointed to have for any execution 12d. in the pound for the first ten pounds, and 6d. in the pound to 40l., and after, 3d. in the pound to a hundred pounds, and 1d. in the pound for all above 100l., to be paid out of the estate which the execution is served upon. For every attachment of goods or persons the marshall is to have 2s. 6d.; and if he goeth any way, he is to have 12d. a mile beside. And the marshall is to have 2s. 6d. for every commitment in Court, and 10l. stipend for this year to come."[4]

May 2, 1638. " It is ordered, That Newetowne shall henceforward be called Cambridge."[5]

Dec. 4, 1638. " The town of Cambridge was fined 10s. for want of a watch-house, pound, and stocks; and time was given them till the next Court."[6]

---

[1] Mass. Coll. Rec., i. 186, 187.

[2] Ibid., i. 190.

[3] Ibid., i. 208. In his Wonder-Working Procidence, Johnson says concerning the College: " To make the whole world understand that spiritual learning was the thing they chiefly desired, to sanctify the other and make the whole lump holy, and that learning being set upon its right object, might not contend for error instead of truth, they chose this place, being then under the orthodox and soul-flourishing ministry of Mr. Thomas Shepheard, of whom it may be said, without any wrong to others, the Lord by his ministry hath saved many hundred souls." Coll. Mass. Hist. Soc., xvii. 27, 28.

[4] Mass. Col. Rec., i. 217. Mr. Michelson held this office, equivalent to that of High Sheriff, until 1681, when he died and was succeeded by his son-in-law, John Green.

[5] Ibid., i. 228. This name is supposed to have been selected, because a place of the same name is the seat of a university in England, where several of the Magistrates and Elders had been educated.

[6] Ibid., i. 247.

March 18, 1688–9. "It is ordered, That the College agreed upon formerly to be built at Cambridge shall be called Harvard College." [1]

Under date of March, 1639, Winthrop says, "a printing-house was begun at Cambridge by one Daye, at the charge of Mr. Glover, who died on sea hitherward. The first thing which was printed was the freeman's oath; the next was an almanac made for New England by Mr. William Peirce, mariner; the next was the Psalms newly turned into metre." [2] Many years ago, the late Thaddeus William Harris, M. D., then Librarian of Harvard College, gave me a copy of an ancient document preserved in the archives of that institution, which manifestly relates to this affair, though, perhaps for prudential reasons, no mention is made in it concerning printing. It is a bond in the usual form, given by Stephen Day [3] of Cambridge, county of Cambridge, locksmith [4] to Josse Glover, [5] clerk, in the penal sum of one hundred pounds, and dated June 7, 1638. The condition is thus stated: "The condition of this obligation is such, that, whereas the above named Josse Glover hath undertaken and promised to bear the charges of and for the transportation of the above bounden Stephen Day and Rebecca his wife, and of Matthew [6] and Stephen Day, their children, and of William Bordman, [7] and three menservants, which are to be transported with him the said Stephen to New England in America, in the ship called the John of London; and whereas the transportation of all the said parties will cost the sum of forty and four pounds, which is to be disbursed by the said Joos Glover; and whereas the said Joos Glover hath delivered to the said Stephen Day kettles and other iron tools to the value of seven pounds, both which sums amount to the sum of fifty and one pounds; If,

---

[1] *Mass. Col. Rec.*, i. 253. So called in honor of Rev. John Harvard, who endowed the college with half of his estate together with the whole of his library.

[2] Savages' *Winthrop*, i. 289.

[3] He wrote his name Daye.

[4] Although Daye was recognized by the General Court, Dec. 10, 1641, as "the first that set upon printing," he was a locksmith, and not a printer, by trade. Perhaps his son Matthew had already received some instruction as a printer. It is not probable that his successor, Samuel Green, had much knowledge of the printer's mystery, at the time of his appointment. I think that Marmaduke Johnson, who came to assist in printing the Indian Bible, was the first thoroughly instructed printer in New England.

[5] The true name of Mr. Glover was Joss.

[6] Matthew Daye was a printer, and the first known Steward of Harvard College. He died 10th May, 1649.

[7] William Boardman was son of Stephen Daye's wife by a former husband, and was both Steward of the College and the progenitor of at least four stewards. He died 25th March, 1685, aged 71.

therefore, the said Stephen Day do and shall with all speed[1] ship himself and his said wife and children and servants, and the said William Bordman in the same ship, and cause him and themselves to be transported in the said ship to New England aforesaid, with as much speed as wind and weather will permit; and also if the said Stephen Day, his executors, administrators or assigns do truly pay or cause to be paid to the said Josse Glover his executors or assigns the sum of [fifty] and one pounds, of lawful [money of] England within twenty and four months next after the arrival of the said Stephen Day the father in New England aforesaid, or within thirty days next after the decease of the said Stephen Day the father, which of the said times shall first and next happen to come or be after the date above written; and also if the said Stephen Day the father and his servants and every of them do and shall from time to time labor and work with and for the said Josse Glover and his assigns in the trade which the said Stephen the father now useth in New England aforesaid, at such rates and prices as is usually paid and allowed for the like work in the country there; and also if the said Stephen the father, his executors or administrators, do and shall, with the said sum of fifty and one pounds, pay and allow unto the said Joos Glover, his executors or assigns, for the loan, adventure and forbearance of the same sum, such recompense, damage and consideration as two indifferent men in New England aforesaid, to be chosen for that purpose, shall think fit, set down, and appoint; and lastly, if the said Joos Glover, his executors and assigns shall and may from time to time detain and take to his and their own uses, towards the payment of the said sum of money, and allowances aforesaid, all such part and so much of the wages and earnings which shall be earned by the works and labors aforesaid, (not exceeding the principal sum aforesaid) as the said Joos, his executors or assignes shall think fit; that then this obligation to be void, or else it to stand in force and virtue."

[1] He appears to have arrived in New England with the printing-press, about four months after the date of this bond. In a letter, dated at Salem, Oct. 10, 1638, Hugh Peter says: " We have a printery here, and think to go to work with some special things."— *Coll. Mass. Hist. Soc.*, xxxvi. 99.

The business of printing was conducted exclusively at Cambridge for nearly half a century, during which time the Indian Bible was printed; after about the year 1700, very little if any work of this kind was performed here (except by Samuel Hall in 1775-76), until 1800, when a printing press was established by William Hilliard. — *Coll. Mass. Hist. Soc.*, vii. 19.

During the present century, the printers of Cambridge have constantly held a very high comparative rank, for both the quantity and the quality of their work.

CHAPTER VI.

CIVIL HISTORY.

NOTWITHSTANDING Mr. Shepard and his associates here "found sufficient for themselves and their company," and appear by the Records to have enjoyed temporal prosperity, as indicated in the foregoing chapter, they were not fully satisfied, but seriously contemplated a removal to Connecticut. To such removal they were advised and encouraged by Mr. Hooker, whose eldest daughter had become the second wife of Mr. Shepard in 1637. How far Mr. Hooker may have been influenced by family considerations, or how far by that spirit of emulation, or perhaps of jealousy, which naturally enough existed between the rival colonies, — or whether his advice was altogether disinterested, — does not distinctly appear; but that he gave such advice, even with urgency, his own letters to Mr. Shepard afford conclusive evidence. Very probably Gov. Winthrop intended that Mr. Hooker should make a personal application of his general remarks contained in a letter addressed to him as early as 1638: "If you could show us the men that reproached you, we should teach them better manners than to speak evil of this good land God hath brought us to, and to discourage the hearts of their brethren; only you may bear a little with the more moderate of them, in regard that one of yours opened the door to all that have followed, and for that they may conceive it as lawful for them to discourage some with us from forsaking us to go to you, as for yours to plott by encouragements &c., to draw Mr. Shephard and his whole church from us, *Sic fama est.*"[1] Two years later, Mr. Hooker wrote an earnest letter to Mr. Shepard, which was long preserved in the library of the Massachusetts Historical Society, but which is now in the Massachusetts Archives: —

"DEAR SON, Since the first intimation I had from my cousin Sam: when you was here with us, touching the number and

[1] *Life and Letters of John Winthrop, Esq.,* vol. ii., p. 421.

nature of your debts, I conceived and concluded the consequents to be marvellous desperate in the view of reason, in truth unavoidable and yet unsupportable, and as were likely to ruinate the whole: for why should any send commodities, much less come themselves to the place, when there is no justice amongst men to pay what they take, or the place is so forlorn and helpless that men cannot support themselves in a way of justice; and *ergo* there is neither sending nor coming, unless they will make themselves and substance a prey.

"And hence to weary a man's self to wrestle out an inconvenience, when it is beyond all possibilities which are laid before a man in a rational course, is altogether bootless and fruitless, and is to increase a man's misery, not to ease it. Such be the mazes of mischievous hazards, that our sinful departures from the right and righteous ways of God bring upon us, that as birds taken in an evil net, the more they stir, the faster they are tied. If there was any sufficiency to make satisfaction in time, then respite might send and procure relief; but when that is awanting, delay is to make many deaths of one, and to make them all more deadly. The first and safest way for peace and comfort is to quit a man's hand of the sin, and so of the sting of the plague. Happy is he that hath none of the guilt in the commission of evils sticking to him. But he that is faulty, it will be his happiness to recover himself by repentance, both sudden and seasonably serious; and when that is done, in such hopeless occasions, it is good to sit down under the wisdom of some word: That which is crooked nobody can make strait, and that which is awanting none can supply: 1 Eccl. 15; and then seek a way in heaven for escape, when there is no way on earth that appears.

"You say that which I long since supposed; the magistrates are at their wits end, and I do not marvel at it. But is there, then, nothing to be done, but to sink in our sorrows? I confess here to apply, and that upon the sudden, is wholly beyond all my skill. Yet I must needs say something, if it be but to breathe out our thoughts, and so our sorrows. I say ours, because the evil will reach us really more than by bare sympathising. Taking my former ground for granted, that the weakness of the body is such that it is not able to bear the disease longer, but is like to grow worse and more unfit for cure, which I suppose is the case in hand, then I cannot see but of necessity this course must be taken : —

[1.] "The debtors must freely and fully tender themselves

and all they have into the hands, and be at the mercy and devotion of the creditors. And this must be done nakedly and really. It is too much that men have rashly and unjustly taken more than they were able to repay and satisfy: *ergo* they must not add falseness and dissimulation when they come to pay, and so not only break their estate but their consciences finally. I am afraid there be old arrearages of this nature that lie yet in the deck.

"2. The Churches and the Commonwealth, by joint consent and serious consideration, must make a privy search what have been the courses and sinful carriages which have brought in and increased this epidemical evil; pride and idleness, excess in apparel, building, diet, unsuitable to our beginnings or abilities; what toleration and connivance at extortion, and injustice, and oppression; the tradesman willing the workman may take what he will for his work, that he may ask what he will for his commodity.

"3. When they have humbled themselves unfeignedly before the Lord, then set up a real reformation, not out of politick respects, attending our own devices, but out of plainness, looking at the rule and following that, leave the rest to the Lord, who will ever go with those who go his own way.

"*Has premisses:* I cannot see in reason but if you can sell, and the Lord afford any comfortable chapman, but you should remove. For why should a man stay until the house fall on his head? and why continue his being there where in reason he shall destroy his substance? For were men merchants, how can they hold it, when men either want money to buy withal, or else want honesty, and will not pay? The more honest and able any persons or plantations be, their rates will increase, stocks grow low, and their increase little or nothing. And if remove, why not to Mattabeseck?[1] For may be either the gentlemen[2] will not come, and that's most likely; or if they do, they will not come

---

[1] Now Middletown, Connecticut.

[2] The reference here is not to the "gentlemen" in Cambridge with Mr. Shepard, but to certain others in England, for whom Mr. Fenwick, the proprietor of Mattabesick, desired to provide, as appears by another letter from Hooker to Shepard, without date: "Touching your business at Matabesick, this is the compass of it: Mr. Fenwick is willing that you and your company should come thither upon these terms; Provided that you will reserve three double lots for three of the gentlemen, if they come; that is, those three lots must carry a double proportion to that which yours take. If they take twenty acres of meadow, you must reserve forty for them; if thirty, three score for them. This is all we could obtain, because he stays one year longer in expectation of his company, at the least some of them; and the like hath been done in Quinipiack, and hath been usual in such beginnings. Therefore, we were silent in such a grant, for the while."

all; or if all, is it not probable but they may be entreated to abate one of the lots? or, if not abate, if they take double lots, they must bear double rates; and I see not but all plantations find this a main wound; they want men of abilities and parts to manage their affairs, and men of estate, to bear charges. I will tell thee mine whole heart; considering, as I conceive, your company must break, and considering things *ut supra*, if you can sell you should remove. If I were in your places, I should let those that must and will transport themselves as they see fit, in a way of providence and prudence. I would reserve a special company, but not many, and I would remove hither. For I do verily think, either the gentlemen will not come, or if they do, they may be over-intreated not to prejudice the plantation by taking too much. And yet if I had but a convenient spare number, I do believe that would not prove prejudicial to any comfortable subsistence: for able men are most fit to carry on occasions by their persons and estates with most success. These are all my thoughts; but they are *inter nos;* use them as you see meet.

" I know, to begin plantations is a hard work; and I think I have seen as much difficulty, and came to such a business with as much disadvantage as almost men could do, and therefore, I would not press men against their spirits: when persons do not choose a work, they will be ready to quarrel with the hardness of it. This only is to me beyond exception. If you do remove, considering the correspondence you have here of hearts, and hands, and helps, you shall never remove to any place with the like advantage. The pillar of fire and cloud go before you, and the Father of mercies be the God of all the changes that pass over your heads.

" News with us here is not much, since the death of my brother Stone's wife and James Homstead; the former smoaked out her days in the darkness of melancholy ; the other died of a bloody flux, and slept sweetly in the Lord, having carried himself graciously in his sickness.

" I have of late had intelligence from Plymouth. Mr. Chancy and the Church are to part; he to provide for himself, and they for themselves.

" At a day of fast, when a full conclusion of the business should have been made, he openly professed he did as verily believe the truth of his opinions as that there was a God in heaven, and that he was settled in it as the earth was upon the centre. If ever such confidence find good success, I miss of my mark.

" Since then he hath sent to Mr. Prydden to come to them,

4

being invited by some of the Brethren by private letters: I gave
warning to Mr. Prydden to bethink himself what he did; and I
know he is sensible and watchful. I profess, how it is possible
to keep peace with a man so adventurous and so pertinacious,
who will vent what he list and maintain what he vents, its beyond all the skill I have to conceive. Mr. Umphrey, I hear, in-
vites him to Providence, and that coast is most meet for his
opinion and practice. The Lord says he will teach the humble
his way; but where are those men? The Lord make us such,
that he may shew us such mercy.

" Totus tuus,   T. HOOKER.

"*Nov.* 2th. 1640.

"I writ another letter, because happily [1] some of the brethren
would be ready to desire the sight of what is writ; that you may
shew; this you ∧ shew or conceal, as you see meet.

" Sunt mutua preces in perpetuum.
" All here salute you and yours." [2]

The Town Records give no intimation of this financial distress.
But from other sources we learn that in the year 1640, not only
Cambridge but the whole Colony was in imminent danger of
bankruptcy. Hutchinson says that, in this year, " the importation of settlers now ceased. The motive to transportation to
America was over, by the change in the affairs of England. —
This sudden stop had a surprising effect upon the price of cattle.
They had lost the greatest part of what was intended for the
first supply, in the passage from Europe. As the inhabitants
multiplied, the demand for the cattle increased, and the price of
a milch cow had kept from 25 to 30*l*, but fell at once this year
to 5 or 6*l*. A farmer, who could spare but one cow in a year
out of his stock, used to clothe his family with the price of it, at
the expense of the new comers; when this failed they were put
to difficulties. Although they judged they had 12,000 neat cattle,
yet they had but about 3,000 sheep in the Colony." [3] Winthrop
says, " This year there came over great store of provisions, both
out of England and Ireland, and but few passengers (and those
brought very little money), which was occasioned by the store of
money and quick markets which the merchants found here the
two or three years before, so as now all our money was drained

[1] Haply.
[2] A part of Mr. Hooker's letter was
published in Albro's *Life of Thomas
Shepard*, 1847; but his copy contained
several mistakes which are here corrected,
and the missing portions are inserted:—
[3] *Hist. Mass.*, i. 93.

from us, and cattle and all commodities grew very cheap, which enforced us at the next General Court, in the eighth month, to make an order, that corn should pass in payments of new debts; Indian, at 4s. the bushel; rye, at 5s., and wheat, at 6s.; and that upon all executions for former debts, the creditor might take what goods he pleased (or, if he had no goods, then his lands), to be appraised by three men, one chosen by the creditor, one by the debtor, and the third by the Marshall." [1]

To this state of things Mr. Hooker probably referred when he renewed his efforts, in the letter already quoted, to persuade Mr. Shepard and his congregation to remove. But why they should remove to Connecticut rather than to some other part of Massachusetts does not very plainly appear. There were large tracts of unappropriated lands here. There is no evidence that Mr. Shepard or his people had any jealousy, such as some have supposed to operate on their predecessors. On the contrary, Mr. Shepard was a prominent member of the religious party which had recently triumphed in the Antinomian controversy, and his own congregation had been preserved from all taint of the great heresy. Concerning the " Antinomian and Familistic opinions " which then distracted the churches, Cotton Mather says, " a synod [2] assembled at Cambridge, whereof Mr. Shepard was no small part, most happily crushed them all. The vigilancy of Mr. Shepard was blessed, not only for the preservation of his own congregation from the rot of these opinions, but also for the deliverance of all the flocks which our Lord had in the wilderness. And it was with a respect unto this vigilancy, and the enlightening and powerful ministry of Mr. Shepard, that, when the foundation of a college was to be laid, Cambridge rather than any other place was pitched upon to be the seat of that happy seminary : out of which there proceeded many notable preachers, who were made such by their sitting under Mr. Shepard's ministry." [3] Possibly, however, this " vigilancy " of Mr. Shepard, and this faithfulness of his congregation, throughout one of the most violent conflicts of religious opinion ever known in this country, may have stimulated the subsequent desire to remove beyond the limits of Massachusetts. This seems to be indicated in the fifth

[1] Savage's *Winthrop*, ii. 7.
[2] This Synod met at Cambridge, Aug. 30, 1637, and " began with prayer made by Mr. Shepard." Mr. Bulkeley of Concord, and Mr. Hooker, of Hartford, were the Moderators. Having condemned "about eighty opinions, some blasphemous, others erroneous, and all unsafe, —. the assembly brake up," Sept. 22, 1637. — Savage's *Winthrop*, i. 237-240.
[3] *Magnalia*, B. III., ch. v., § 12.

"Reason for removing," entered by Mr. Shepard on the fly-leaf of one of his manuscript books,[1] namely : —

" Reas. for removing.

" 1. You say some brethren cannot live comfortably with so little.

" 2. We put all the rest upon a temptation. Lots being but little, and estates will increase or live in beggary. For to lay land out far off is intolerable to men ; near by, you kill your cattle.

" 3. Because if another minister come, he will not have room for his company. — Religion. —

" 4. Because now if ever is the most fit season ; for if gate be opened, many will come in among us, and fill all places, and no room in time to come ; at least, not such good room as now. And now you may best sell.

" 5. Because Mr. Vane will be upon our skirts."

Mr. Vane was elected Governor of Massachusetts in 1636, and was an active associate of Mrs. Hutchinson in the Antinomian party. Chiefly, it would seem, on account of his religious opinions, he was superseded in 1637, and soon returned to England. It was probably feared that he would use his great interest at court in opposition to the Colony which had thus denounced him as a heretic and disappointed his political hopes. Mr. Shepard and his congregation may have considered themselves in peculiar danger on account of their very energetic opposition to him, and have thought that Connecticut would afford a more secure shelter from his wrath. Subsequent events, however, showed that all such fears were groundless. Mr. Vane manifested his friendship to the colonists, through life, by many kind offices in their behalf.

This temptation to remove was not kept secret, though no direct reference to it appears on record.[2] It was discussed in a

---

[1] This book contains " The confessions of diverse propounded to be received and were entertayned as members " of the Church, together with sketches of sermons.

[2] In addition to the before named discouragements, which tempted Mr. Shepard and his company to abandon Cambridge, may be mentioned the loss of two most valuable associates, namely John Haynes, who removed to Hartford in 1637, and Roger Harlakenden, who died November 17, 1638, aged 27 years. The

former had been Assistant, 1634 ; Governor, 1635 ; and Assistant again, 1636, and remained in office up to the time of his removal in the spring of 1637 ; — the latter was elected Assistant in 1636, at the first election after his arrival, and re-elected in 1637 and 1638. One was colonel, and the other lieutenant-colonel, of the military force. Both were conspicuous for moral excellence and mental ability, and each bore a large share of the pecuniary burdens of the public. The death of Mr. Harlakenden was pecul-

Church meeting at Cambridge, Feb. 14, 1640-1, as appears by Mr. Shepard's Diary, at which time the project passes out of sight, probably in consequence of a grant then recently made by the General Court, to wit: Oct. 7, 1640. "The town of Cambridge is granted a month to consider of Shawshin for a village for them, and if they like it not, the town of Roxberry hath liberty to consider of it for a village for them till the next General Court." The examination was satisfactory; for the grant was conditionally made June 2, 1641: "Shawshin is granted to Cambridge, provided they make it a village, to have ten families there settled within three years; otherwise the Court to dispose of it." About a year later this grant was renewed, with slight change of condition; and a final disposition was made of the affair, March 7, 1643-4: "Shawshin is granted to Cambridge, without any condition of making a village there; and the land between them and Concord is granted them, all save what is formerly granted to the military company or others, provided the church and present elders continue at Cambridge."[1] The church and elders did remain; lands at Shawshine were soon afterwards assigned to individuals, thus relieving the supposed deficiency of accommodations; a competent number became resident proprietors and cultivators; and in 1655, Shawshine was incorporated as a separate town, called Billerica, which has since been shorn of its original dimensions by the incorporation of other towns.

iarly grievous to Mr. Shepard, who had been protected by him in England, when pursued by the emissaries of the established Church. Describing his sufferings during the last few months of his residence in his native land, Mr. Shepard says, in his autobiography: "Being in great sadness and not knowing where to go, nor what to do, the Lord sent Mr. Roger Harlakenden and my brother Samuel Shepard to visit me after they had heard of our escape at sea, who much refreshed us and clave to me in my sorrows." Again, in a house at Bastwick, freely offered by Mrs. Corbett, "an aged eminent godly gentlewoman," he says: "I lived for half a year all the winter long among and with my friends (Mr. Harlakenden dwelling with me, bearing all the charge of housekeeping), and far from the notice of my enemies, where we enjoyed sweet fellowship one with another and also with God, in a house which was fit to entertain any prince for fairness, greatness, and pleasantness. Here the Lord hid us all the winter long, and when it was fit to travel in the spring, we went up to London, Mr. Harlakenden not forsaking me all this while, for he was a father and mother to me," etc. (Boston Ed., 1832, pp. 54, 55). Mr. Shepard was accompanied to New England by this "most precious servant of Jesus Christ," and bitterly lamented his early death; This loss was partially repaired by the accession of Herbert Pelham, Esq., in 1638 or 1639. He married the widow of Mr. Harlakenden, and was successively Treasurer of Harvard College, 1643, Assistant, 1645-49, and Commissioner of the United Colonies, 1645-46. He brought with him his daughter Penelope, who afterwards became the wife of Governor Josiah Winslow, and died at Marshfield, 7 Dec., 1703, aged 72. Mr. Pelham was an active citizen and officer, but returned to England about 1649, was a member of Parliament, and a steadfast friend of this Colony. He died in 1673.

[1] Mass. Coll. Rec., i. 305, 330; ii. 62.

The grant of the Shawshine lands removed all reasonable doubt of sufficient "accommodation," and the Mattabeseck project seems to have been utterly abandoned. These lands were not immediately divided, but were held in reservation for future use. Meanwhile, measures were adopted for the improvement of the present abode, as the records indicate.

Dec. 13, 1641. "Agreed that Robert Holmes and John Stedman shall take care for the making of the town-spring, against Mr. Dunster's barn, a sufficient well, with timber and stone, fit for the use of man and watering of cattle. Also Richard Jackson is to be an assistant to them by way of advice, if they shall require it." [1]

Nov. 5, 1646. "Ordered by the Townsmen, that there shall be fifty shillings paid unto Tho. Longhorne, for his service to the town in beating the drum this two years last past."

Jan. 11, 1646–7. "Ordered, That whatever person or persons shall cut down, or cause to be cut down, any tree or trees whatsoever, whether living or dead, in swamp or upland, on this side Menottime River (the great swamp only exempted), shall forfeit for every tree so felled ten shillings. This order to continue until further order be taken by the Townsmen.

"It is also further ordered, That whatsoever person or persons who hath any land at Menottime laid out unto himself or his house wherein he dwelleth shall, after the 12th day of this present month, cut out or take away directly or indirectly any wood or timber on this side the path which goeth from the mill [2] to Watertowne, every such person shall forfeit for every such load, if it be timber, five shillings per load, and if wood, two shillings per load. Provided, that there is liberty granted, until the 20th day of this present month, for the fetching home of what is already cut out; and after that whatever is found to be forfeit."

Field-drivers were first elected in 1647: Gilbert Crackbone for the West field, Thomas Hall for the Pine-swamp field, Thomas Beale for the Town within the pales, and —— Russell for the Neck of land. Commissioners "to end small causes," Sealer of Leather, and Clerk of the Market, first elected in 1648.

June 12, 1648. "Upon the complaint of Edward Goffe against Richard Cutter for wrongful detaining of calves impounded by

---

[1] This spring may still be seen a few feet westerly from the University Press between Brattle and Mount Auburn Streets. Mr. Dunster's barn stood on the northerly side of Brattle Street, near Church Street, where he owned a lot containing six acres.

[2] Cooke's Mill, afterwards known as Rolfe's Mill, or Cutter's Mill, near the Town House in Arlington.

him of the said Edward Goffe's, wherein Samuell Eldred witnesseth : — Edward Goffe desired his calves of Richard Cutter, promising to pay all damages and cost as two men should apprehend to be right; but the said Richard Cutter denied to let him have them except he would take a course with his boy and promise they should never come there again ; and a second time, being desired to let Edward Goffe have the calves, he answered, No. The Townsmen, having considered the business, they thus order, — that Edward Goffe shall pay fourteen pence damage to Richard Cutter, and Richard Cutter shall pay for the costs of the same witnesses, four shillings and seven pence."

Nov. 20, 1648. "Ordered, That there shall be an eight-penny ordinary provided for the Townsmen every second Monday of the month, upon their meeting day ; and that whoever of the Townsmen fail to be present within half an hour of the ringing of the Bell (which shall be half an hour after eleven of the clock), he shall both lose his dinner and pay a pint of sack, or the value, to the present Townsmen ; and the like penalty shall be paid by any that shall depart from the rest, without leave. The charges of the dinner shall be paid by the Constable out of the town stock." The practice, thus inaugurated, of dining or partaking of other refreshments at the public expense, seems to have been generally observed by the selectmen for nearly two hundred years, until the municipal form of goverment was changed ; not indeed at every meeting, nor was the expense always limited to eight pence each.

Feb. 16, 1648–9. Voted, by the Town, "That the Townsmen should prosecute suit in law against such of the inhabitants of Watertowne as have trespassed in our Great Swamp."[1]

[1] At this time Sparks Street and Vassal Lane formed part of the boundary line between Cambridge and Watertown ; and the Great Swamp extended northerly from Vassal Lane on both sides of Menotomy River. It would seem that the Townsmen immediately commenced suit against one of the trespassers. In the Court Files of Middlesex County, 1649–50, is still preserved "The Reply of Richard Jackson and Thomas Danforth, plaint., in the behalf of the town of Cambridge, against Samuel Thatcher, of Watertown, def., unto his several answers in the action of the cause for taking away wood out of their bounds." In answer to the allegation that the swamp was common property, it is declared that, "The present inhabitants of Cambridge purchased the whole dimensions of the town (this legally settled their bounds by order of Court) of the Harford Company about fourteen years since, at which time the chiefest and best parts of this swamp for wood was allotted into particular propriety and fenced in with their planting land by a general fence." If the trespass continue, "It would then be a groundwork of endless contention, if not the desolating of our poor straitened town, and that for these reasons. (1.) The branches of the swamp so runeth over all our bounds, which is for five miles together not much

Fence-viewers were first elected March 12, 1648-9, for the Neck, Pine-swamp fields, Menotomy fields, and West field; a Sealer of Weights and Measures, Jan. 14, 1649-50; and a Gauger, "to size cask," Nov. 10, 1651.

Feb. 11, 1649-50. "The request of Richard ffrances for re-mitting the present town rate, in regard of God's visitation by sickness on himself and family, is granted."

Dec. 9, 1650. "Whereas dreadful experience shows the inevi-table danger and great loss, not only to particular persons, but also to the whole town, by the careless neglect of keeping chim-neys clean from soot, and want of ladders in time of need, the select Townsmen, taking the same into their serious considera-tion, do therefore order that every person inhabiting within the bounds of this town, before the 10th of the next month provide one or more sufficient ladders at all times in a readiness to reach up to the top of his or their house; and forthwith and at all times hereafter see that their chimneys be kept clean swept at least once every month, upon the penalty of 2s. 6d. for every month's neglect herein."

March 10, 1650-1. "Mr. Joseph Cooke hath liberty granted to fell timber on the common for to fence in his orchard."

Jan. 7, 1651-2. "William Manning is granted liberty by the inhabitants of the town, at a general meeting, to make a wharf out of the head of the creek,[1] towards Mr. Pelham's barn, and build a house on it, to come as high as the great pine stump, and range with Mr. Pelham's fence next the high street into town."

Besides the foregoing transactions of a general character, the Records show that, during this period, a new meeting-house was erected, and provisions made for the support of the Grammar school; both which subjects will be mentioned in another place. Measures were also adopted to convert the Shawshine territory to profitable use. No general division of the land was made before 1652; yet the Records indicate some grants to individuals,

if any above a mile broad, so that hereby no man can peaceably enjoy his own propriety. (2.) It is the chief supply of the town for wood, being near to us, and many having none elsewhere within the compass of four miles and a half of the town, which cost them two shillings a load more than they can have it for in the swamp. Besides the expense of the in-habitants, it is not unknown the great ex-pense of wood in our town by the College, which we cannot estimate much less than 350 load a year, the chief supply whereof if it be not out of the swamp, it will be costly, as every load must be fetched above five miles." It is added that the wood from the swamp costs four shillings per load in Cambridge; the cost of cutting and hauling being twenty pence.

[1] At the foot of Dunster Street.

and the appropriation of one thousand acres " for the good of the church." I quote again from the Town Records : —

April 9, 1648. "It was agreed at a general meeting, when the whole town had special warning to meet for the disposing of Shawshine, that there should be a farm laid out, of a thousand acres, to be for a public stock, and improved for the good of the church and that part of the church that here shall continue ; and every person or persons that shall from time to time remove from the church do hereby resign up their interest therein to the remaining part of the church of Cambridge. This thousand acres of land, given to the use aforesaid, shall be laid out either all together, or else severally part in one place and part elsewhere, according to the discretion of the men that are appointed to lay out the land."

" Also there was granted to several brethren that had no house-right in the town, if they did desire it," farms at Shawshine : —

" Imprimis, Capt. Googine a farm, if he buy a house in the town ; also to Bro. Edward Oakes, Tho. Oakes, and Richard Hildreth, each of them a farm for their encouragement, if they see it may make for their support and desire it.

" Further, it is granted to Mr. Henry Dunster and Mr. Edward Collins liberty to have their small farms at Shawshine, and to be considered in their quantity more than others in regard of their work and place."

April 1649. Agreed, " that Mr. Henry Dunster, President of Harvard College, should have 500 acres, whereof 400 is granted by the town to his own person and heirs, to enjoy freely forever, and the other 100 acres for the use of Harvard College.

" Item, unto Mr. Daniell Googine 500 acres.

" Item, unto Mr. Edward Collins, in lieu of his small farm within the town bounds, with some addition in respect of his place in the Deacon's office, it was agreed that he should have 500 acres."

June 9, 1652. " It was agreed by the Church that Shawshine should be divided as followeth : —

" To Mr. Michell, five hundred acres.

" To Edw. Okes, three hundred acres.

" To Thomas Okes, one hundred and fifty acres.

" It was agreed that these three above named should have their lots laid out by a committee with as little prejudice to any lot as may be, and so not to draw any lot.

" Also, the Church doth agree that although the land be, by
grant of the General Court, peculiar to the Church only, yet the
whole town, viz., such as are owners of house and land in the
town, shall come into the division thereof.

" Also, it is agreed, that every man shall have a proportion of
land, more or less, according to the proportion now allotted him.

" Also, that every man shall have a part of the meadow in
proportion with his upland, to be laid out after the same rule
that the upland is, both by lot and quantity.

" Also, it is agreed, that, after the farms formerly granted are
laid out, the remainder of the land shall· be divided into three
breadths, viz., two of the said breadths to lie between the rivers,
and the third on this side Shawshine River. The first lot to
begin upon a line continued over Shawshine River, the same that
is between Woburn and us, running towards Concord until it
meet with Mr. Wintrop's farm : and so the said first lot to butt
south upon that line, and on Shawshine River, and Mr. Wintrop's farm ; and so each lot to proceed one after another, by
due parallels, until they come clear of the farms already laid out,
and then to extend in two divisions between the Rivers, and a
third division on the east side Shawshine River, and so every
man's lot to follow one another, taking all the three breadths at
once, the nearest land to the first centre being still always the
next lot in order.

" The number of every man's lot and quantity of acres is as
followeth on the other side.

Lot.		Acres.	Lot.		Acres.
1.	Daniell Cheaver	20	17.	Wᵐ. Homan	50
2.	William Clemmance, senʳ.	30	18.	Nath. Greene and Mother	80
3.	Daniell Kempster	80	19.	Richard ffrench	20
4.	William Bull	15	20.	John Watson	80
5.	Roger Bucke	10	21.	Richard Woodes	10
6.	Thomas ffox	80	22.	John Taylor	60
7.	Humphery Bradshew	15	23.	Wid: Wilkerson	60
8.	Mr. Boman	20	24.	Lieft. William ffrench	150
9.	William Clemmance	30	25.	Joseph Miller	15
10.	Richard Cutter	80	26.	Jonath. Hide	20
11.	Thomas Longhorne	60	27.	David ffiske	60
12.	Daniell Blogget	40	28.	Wid: Hancocke	10
13.	Robert Holmes	150	29.	And. Stevenson	60
14.	Th. Hall	20	30.	Mr. Elijath Corlet —.	100
15.	Widow Banbricke	40	31.	David Stone	50
16.	John Jacson	50	32.	Tho. Danforth	220

Lot.		Acres.	Lot.		Acres.
33.	Rich. ffrances	60	78.	Richard Parke	100
34.	John Parker	10	79.	ffranc. Whitmore . .	50
35.	Jonath. Padlefoote . .	15	80.	Jonas Clearke	60
36.	Edw. Hall	70	81.	John Hasteings . . .	80
37.	Ri. Oldam	60	82.	Henry Prentise . . .	80
38.	Gilbert Cracbone . . .	90	83.	Elder Champnis . . .	350
39.	Robert Stedman . . .	90	84.	Nath. Sparhauke . . .	140
40.	Tho. Swœtman . . .	70	85.	John Stedman	300
41.	Wᵐ. Bordman . . .	60	86.	Willᵐ. Russell . . .	60
42.	John Betts	90	87.	William Patten . . .	90
43.	John Shepard	60	88.	Ben. Bower	20
44.	Daniell Stone	50	89.	Tho. Briggam	180
45.	John ffrenches children .	30	90.	John Russell	80
46.	John ffownell	100	91.	Will. Bucke	20
47.	Samⁿ. Hides	80	92.	Richard Ecles	70
48.	Tho. Marret	200	93.	Mrs. Sarah Simes . .	50
49.	Edw. Winship . . .	200	94.	Mr. Jacson	400
50.	Goodm. Hammond . .	15	95.	Mr. Andrews	150
51.	Steven Day	50	96.	Abra. Errington . . .	70
52.	John Gibson	80	97.	Widd: Cutter	40
53.	Edw. Goffe	450	98.	ffr. Moore, senʳ. . . .	50
54.	William Man	70	99.	Mr. Josseph Cooke . .	300
55.	Ri. Jacson	200	100.	Wᵐ. Wilcocke . . .	90
56.	Willᵐ. Dixon	80	101.	Christopher Cane . . .	80
57.	George Willowes . . .	60	102.	Rich. Dana	20
58.	Tho. Chesholme . . .	100	103.	Mr. Angier	300
59.	Mr. Edmund ffrost . .	200	104.	Vincet Druse	15
60.	John Hall	20	105.	Rogʳ. Bancroft . . .	100
61.	Edw. Michelson . . .	150	106.	John Cooper	140
62.	And. Belcher	50	107.	Edw. Shepard	80
63.	John Swan	20	108.	Tho. Bridge	50
64.	Phil. Cooke	80	109.	Ranold Bush	10
65.	ffr. Moore, junior . . .	50	110.	Tho. Prentise	150
66.	Widd: Sill	40	111.	Math. Bridge	80
67.	Robert Parker	60	112.	Golden Moore	100
68.	Willᵐ. Manning . . .	60	113.	Robert Brodish . . .	30
69.	Richard Hassull . . .	60	Memᵒ. There is these two per-		
70.	Nicho. Withe	90	sons overslipped, viz.		
71.	Willᵐ. Hamlet	60	28.	Richard Robbins . . .	80
72.	Willᵐ. Towne	70	91.	Daniell Wines	10
73.	Samᴴ. Greene	80	These two lots must come		
74.	Robert Browne . . .	40	in their due order.		
75.	John Boutell	20	The town do give to Greg-		
76.	John Bridge	250	ory Stone, adjoining to his		
77.	Tho. Beal	100	farm, one hundred acres.	. 100 "	

Although, by the generosity of the Church, all the inhabitants received allotments of the Shawshine lands, comparatively few of them established a residence upon that territory. As early, however, as 1655, there were so many householders in Shawshine, gathered from Cambridge and elsewhere, that they were incorporated as a distinct town, named Billerica, and an amicable arrangement was made by them with the inhabitants of Cambridge, in regard to their respective territorial rights and liabilities.

The Town Records, Jan. 29, 1654–5, show that " In answer to a letter sent to the town from our neighbors of Shawshine, alias Bilracie, wherein they desire that whole tract of land may be disengaged from this place and be one entire body of itself, — the town consented to choose five persons a Committee to treat and conclude with them concerning their request therein; at which time there was chosen Mr. Henry Dunster, Elder Champney, John Bridge, Edward Goffe, and Edward Winship." The result appears in the Record of the General Court, under date of May 23, 1655: —

" In answer to the desire of our brethren and neighbors, the inhabitants of Shawshin, requesting immunities and freedom from all public rates and charges at Cambridge, and that all the land of that place, as well those appertaining to the present inhabitants of Cambridge as those granted them by the Court, might belong entirely to that place, for the better encouragement and carrying on of public charges that will necessarily there fall out, —

" We, whose names are underwritten, being empowered by the inhabitants of Cambridge, at a public meeting of the town, the 29th of January, 1654, to make such propositions and conclusions therein as to us might seem most meet and equal, do make these following propositions with reference to the compliance of the above named our beloved brethren and neighbors, the inhabitants of Shawshin, and the approbation of the General Court for the full conclusion thereof.

1. " That all the lands belonging to that place called by the name of Shawshin, with its appurtenances or latter grants made by the General Court, as well those the propriety and peculiar right whereof belongeth to any particular person, as those granted by the town or church of Cambridge to that place for a township, as also those given by the inhabitants of Cambridge for the fur-

therance and encouragement of a plantation there, shall be one
entire township or plantation, always freed and acquitted from
all manner of common charges or rates, of what nature or kind
soever, due or belonging of right to be paid unto Cambridge by
virtue of any grant of that place unto them by the General Court.

"2. That whensoever any of the inhabitants of Cambridge,
their heirs or assigns, whether in that place or elsewhere, shall
make any improvement of their lands above premised, more or
less, by fencing, building or breaking up, or mowing of the meadows, every such person shall pay to the common charges of that
place, *i. e.*, Shawshin, suitable to his or their improvement of
the aforesaid kind, in due proportion with the rest of the inhabitants in that place, the whole estate and improvements of the
place being laid at an equal and proportionable rate.

"3. That the inhabitants of Shawshin shall, at all time and
times hereafter forever, acquit and discharge the inhabitants of
Cambridge from all common charges, rates, dues, duties, and in-
cumbrances by any manner of ways or means due by them to be
paid, executed, or performed, by virtue of their interest in that
place, given unto them by the grant of the General Court.

"4. That whensoever any of the inhabitants of Cambridge
shall alienate their present interest in any of the above named
lands from themselves and heirs, then the said lands shall, in all
respects, be liable to common charges of that place, as though
those particular persons had their grants thereof made them from
the said town or plantation of Shawshin.

"5. That no person or persons which either have had or hereafter shall have any lot or allotment granted them in the above
named township of Shawshin, in case they make not improvement thereof by building and fencing, especially the houselot,
shall have any power to make any sale or gift thereof to any
other person, but such land and allotments shall return again to
the town, *i. e.*, Shawshin; and in case, after such like improvement, any person shall then remove, to the deserting and leaving
their brethren and neighbors that have adventured by their encouragement to settle there with them, no such person or persons,
for seven years next ensuing the confirmation hereof, shall have
power to make either sale, or gift, or alienation thereof to any
person or persons whatsoever, save only unto such as the greater
part of the inhabitants then resident at Shawshin shall consent
unto and approve of.

"6. That in case any grievance shall hereafter happen to arise,

which for the present neither side foresee, nor is hereby clearly
determined, that then all such matter of grievance or difference
shall be from time to time heard and determined by meet persons,
three or five, indifferently chosen by the prudential men of Cambridge and Shawshin.

"And these aforementioned propositions to be subscribed by
all the present inhabitants of Shawshin, and by all such as
hereafter shall have any allotments granted them there, and return hereof made to the inhabitants of Cambridge within ten
days after the end of the first session of the next General Court.
Given under our hands this 17th 12ᵐ 1654, by us,

> "HENRY DUNSTER,·
> RICHARD CHAMPNEY,
> EDWARD GOFFE,
> JOHN BRIDGE.

"These propositions are accepted of and consented unto by us
the present inhabitants of Shawshin; and we do humbly crave
this honored Court to confirm and record the same.

"Your humble servants,

"RALPH HILL, Sen'.	JAMES PARKER,
WILLIAM FRENCH,	JONATHAN DANFORTH,
JOHN STERNE,	HENRY JEFTES,
WILLIAM PATTIN,	WILLIAM CHAMBERLYN,
GEORGE FARLEY,	JOHN PARKER,
RALPH HILL, Jun'.,	ROBERT PARKER.
JOHN CROE,	

"Their request was granted by the Court."

On the same day, May 28, 1655, "in answer to the petition of
several proprietors and inhabitants of Shawshin, humbly desiring a tract of land lying near the line of the farms of John and
Robert Blood, and so along by the side of Concord River, &c.,
the Court grants their request in that respect, so as it hinder no
former grants, and grant the name of the plantation to be called
Billirikey." [1]

Thus was this first dismemberment of the extensive township
of Cambridge amicably accomplished. No reasonable objection
could be urged against granting an independent ecclesiastical
and civil organization to those persons who resided at such a
great distance from the centre of the town, as soon as they were
able to defray their necessary expenses.

[1] *Mass. Col. Rec.*, iv. (i.), 237-240.

CHAPTER VII.

CIVIL HISTORY.

DURING the period embraced in the preceding chapter, very important events occurred in England. The ecclesiastical yoke which the Fathers of New England were unable to bear was broken, and the people enjoyed comparative religious freedom. The civil government also was overturned and established on new foundations. King Charles the First was beheaded Jan. 30, 1649, and the House of Lords was soon afterwards suppressed. For a few years, a Parliament consisting of a single House, and the army under the command of Cromwell, as chief general, exercised a joint, or perhaps rather antagonistic, supremacy, until Dec. 16, 1653, when Cromwell, with the title of Protector, grasped the reins of government, which he held with a firm hand so long as he lived. After this Revolution in England, and as one of its consequences, the inhabitants of Cambridge were once more tempted to remove. "Cromwell had been very desirous of drawing off the New Englanders to people Ireland after his successes there, and the inhabitants of New Haven had serious thoughts of removing, but did not carry their design into execution. Jamaica being conquered, Cromwell renewed his invitation to the colony of the Massachusetts to remove and to go and people that island, and it appears by Mr. Leverett's letters and a letter from the General Court to Cromwell, that he had it much at heart. Cromwell foresaw that the West India planters would raise estates far superior to those of the inhabitants of the northern colonies, and though a mere worldly consideration was not proper for him to urge, yet accompanied with the fulfillment of a divine promise, that God's people should be the head and not the tail, it was in character, and he artfully enough joined it with the other consideration. But all was insufficient to induce the people of New England to quit a country where they could live tolerably, and were indulged with all the privileges they desired, and we have no account of many families having removed."[1] Although this temptation was offered to the people of the whole Colony, the inhabitants of Cambridge may be supposed to have been peculiarly sensitive to its force, inasmuch as it was presented by one of their most honored and trusted townsmen. Captain Gookin was in England in 1655, and was selected by Cromwell as a special agent to manage this affair. Having received his instructions, he returned to New England and devoted himself earnestly to his appointed task. Several of his letters to Secretary Thurloe concerning this mission are printed in Thurloe's State Papers. In the first, dated Jan. 21, 1655–6, he announces his recent arrival at Boston, "after ten weekes of an exercising passage from the Isle of Wight."[2] At a later period, he mentions in detail some of his labors, and hopes, and discouragements, reminding the secretary that he undertook the work with some misgivings. This letter may deserve insertion : —

"RIGHT HONORABLE. Since my arrival in New England, which was the 20th of January last, I wrote two letters by way of Barbadoes, and this 3d also the same way being destitute of a direct conveyance from hence. The sum of the 2 first were to inform your honour of my arrivall here, and of a little motion that I had then made in his highnesse's affayres ; but the sharpness of the winter prevented my travill into other colonies. But I procured a meeting of the council of this colony March the 7th being the soonest they mett, although the governour called them a month before ; but in the interval between my arrival and the counsel's meeting, I endeavoured to make knowne, as far as I could, the sum of his highness desires ; but there was little done during th... season for the forementioned reson, but after the counsell of this colony mett, and I had delivered his highness letters, and declared the cause of my coming, they thankfully accepted and readily made an order for the promotion thereof, requiring their officers to attend my motions in the publishing the same. Whereupon I did forthwith cause a short declaration to be printed and published unto all the towns and plantations of the English, not only in this, but other colonys, (the copie of which printed paper and order I have enclosed,) and together therewith I procured and imployed persons of trust in severall parts (where I could not be in person) to promote the business and take subscriptions. Shortly after this was done in mid Aprill

[1] Hutchinson's *Hist. Mass.*, i. 190–192.   [2] Vol. iv., p. 440.

For p 64 turn back to p 81.

(as soone as the waies were well passable) I tooke my journey to the colonies of Conecticut and New Haven (about 150 miles, for the most part through the woods) and unto the magistrates of those colonies declared my busines, delivering his highness letters to Mr. Eaton, &c. They all thankfully accepted his great love, manefesting themselves very ready to further the worke in the West Indies, which they trust is of God. But as for this place of Jamiaca now tendred, the minds of most were averse at present, for as much as at that very season their came divers letters from thence, signifieing the sore afflicting hand of God in the mortalitie of the English upon the Island, in so much that of 8,000 and upward, that landed there, there was not living above one halfe; and those very weake, and lowe, and many of them dieing daily, wherein also was related the death of major general Fortescue, Mr. Gage, and divers others. These tydings are a very great discouragement unto the most and best persons, which otherwise would have ingaged to remove; only some few families have subscribed, but not considerable. If the Lord please to give the state either Hispaniola, Cuba, or any other helthful place, I have good reason to beeleve, that sundry persons of worth, yea and some whole churches would remove from hence into those parts. But as for this Island (though through God's mercy late intelligence of 7th of March from the commissioners give great hope, that the good lord is returneing to visit the remnant, that is left, with health and cure; and also they give great incouradgment of the fertilitie of the said island, all which tidings I have endevored to publish with my best skill, and what the effects may be towards the drawing in of more persons, I canot yet determine; but this island, through many bad reports of it, is not of such esteme here, as in several respects I conceive it deserves. For the present their are some few godly discrete persons, that intend to pass theither in a ship of the states called the Hope, whereof one Martin is comander, which is now here ladeing masts for the fleet. These persons leave their familie here; and if it shall please God to cary them safe, and that the island be liked by them (as I hope it may) then upon their returne and inteligence, 't is probable, that many will remove, and in the interim if the Lord's purposes be to plant the said island with any people from hence, 't is possible upon this last newes I may heare of greater motion than formerly among the people. There is one thing, that I desire to mention to your honour, that is, an objection I mett with from some principal

5

persons, that incline to transplant, and indeed the motions of such will draw or hinder many. If his highness see cause to remove it, 't is probable it may further the work. They say, there is no incouradgment in the propositions for ministers or men of place, but what is equall with other men. Now if a minister and people remove, the people wil not be in a capacity, untill they are settled, to maintayne their ministers, for as much as they cannot cary their estates from hence, being it principally consists in land and cattle. Now if there were some annual allowance made unto such persons for a few yeares, until the people recruite, or other waies be contrived, it would then take of that hinderance.

"Thus I have, as breefly as I may, perticulerly signified unto your honour, the sume of what is hetherto done. I am hartily sorry, that my service hath beene hetherunto so unprofitable to his highness and the state, whome I desire, through the strength of God, to serve with a faithfull hart and diligent hand. But I trust your wisdomes wil consider the providences of God, that have occurred; and also remember some litle mention I made of my feares this way, before I undertooke the service; but yet I am not out of hope, that his highness pious intentions and motions in this great worke both in the West Indies, and elsewhere, shal be owned and crowned with the Lord's blessing in his best season.

"Thus with my most humble service presented, and earnest prairs to him, on whose shoulders the government is, to give his gracious presence and assistance to his highness and your honer in all emergencies, I remaine desirous to be, sir, his highness and your honer's most humble and faithful servant,

DANIEL GOOKIN.

"*Cambridge in New England, May* 10th, 1656."[1]

Captain Gookin wrote again, Oct. 23, 1656, announcing the probable failure of the project, inasmuch as "the great difficulties and discouragement the English have grapled with in that place, being fully known here, have made the most considerable persons slow to appeare or ingage to transplant for present, lest they should bring themselves and families into great inconveniences; only there was about three hundred souls that subscribed, who for the most part are young persons under family government, and many of them females, and for quality of low estates, but divers personally godly."[2]

---

[1] *State Papers,* v. 6, 7.   [2] *Ibid.,* v. 502.

While the Protectorate of Cromwell continued, Massachusetts was a favored colony, and the inhabitants of Cambridge shared the general benefit of political and ecclesiastical privileges. But his death, and the incompetency of his son Richard, prepared the way for the accession (or Restoration, as it was styled) of Charles the Second, who, on the twenty-ninth day of May, 1660, the anniversary of his birth, entered London in triumph. From this time a constant struggle for chartered rights was maintained for many years, resulting in the forcible abrogation of the old charter. In this struggle, Cambridge men were active participants.

It is related by Hutchinson, under date of 1660, that, "in the ship which arrived from London the 27th of July there came passengers Col. Whaley and Col. Goffe, two of the late King's judges. . . . . They did not attempt to conceal their persons or characters when they arrived at Boston, but immediately went to the governor, Mr. Endicot, who received them very courteously. They were visited by the principal persons of the town, and among others they take notice of Col. Crown's coming to see them. He was a noted royalist. Although they did not disguise themselves yet they chose to reside at Cambridge, a village about four miles distant from the town, where they went the first day they arrived. . . . . The 22d of February the Governor summoned a court of assistants to consult about securing them, but the court did not agree to it. Finding it unsafe to remain any longer, they left Cambridge the 26th following and arrived at New Haven the 7th of March." [1] The particular reason why they selected Cambridge for their residence does not distinctly appear. A principal inhabitant of the town, Edward Goffe, was the namesake of one of the regicides, and may have been his brother or cousin ; but I have found no proof of such relationship. Perhaps their acquaintance with Captain Gookin may have induced them to reside here. In a "Narrative of the Commissioners from England about New England," published by Hutchinson in his "Collection of Papers," [2] it is alleged that "Col. Whaley and Goffe were entertained by the magistrates with great solemnity and feasted

---

[1] *Hist. Mass.*, i. 213–215. From New Haven the regicides retreated to Hadley, where they found shelter in the house of Rev. John Russell. Whalley is supposed to have died there about 1670, and to have been buried in Mr. Russell's cellar. Goffe survived several years ; but the time and place of his death are not known. A chapter relative to their romantic adven-

tures and fate in New England, may be found in Judd's *History of Hadley*, pp. 214–223.

It should be added, that although Hutchinson and others style Whalley and Goffe "Colonels," both were actually Major-generals under Cromwell.

[2] Pages 419, 420.

in every place, after they were told they were traytors and ought
to be apprehended; they made their abode at Cambridge untill
they were furnished with horses and a guide and sent away to
Newhaven; for their more security Capt. Daniell Gookin is reported to have brought over and to manage their estates; and
the commissioners being informed that he had many cattle at his
farm in the King's Province which were supposed to be Whalyes
or Goughs, caused them to be seazed for his Majestyes use till
further order, but Capt. Gookin, standing upon the privilege of
their charter and refusing to answer before the commissioners, as
soe, there was no more done in it; Capt. Peirce, who transported
Whaly and Gough into New England, may probably say something to their estate." It has been said that Gookin had made
a second visit to England, and that he returned in the same ship
with Whalley and Goffe.

A fragment of General Goffe's journal, descriptive of his residence in Cambridge, has been printed in the " Proceedings of
the Massachusetts Historical Society," 1863, 1864.[1] Among other
things he says : —

" 27 d. 5 m. Wee came to anchor betwen Boston and Charlestown betwen 8. and 9. in ye morning: all in good health thro:
ye good hand of God! upon us: oh! yt men would praise the
Lord for his goodness, — as ps. 107. 21 &c."

" 29 d. 5 m.— Lds day; wee had opportunity of waiting upon
God in his publick ordinances, wch wer solemnly performed by
Mr. Mitchel."

" 9 d. 6 m. — At night Majr Gookins shewed us a printed
paper yt was brought in ye Scotch ship, wherein ye Lords do
order 66 members of ye High court of Justice to be secured, wth
yr estates, — its dated 18 d. May, 1660. But I will meditate on
Hebr. 13. 5, 6."

" 15 d. 6 m. — Sup't at Mr. Chancey's; the good old servant
of ye Lord, still expressing much affection, & telling us, he was
perswaded ye Ld had brought us to this country for good both to
them and or selves."

" 28 d. 6 m. — In ye evening wee vissited Elder Frost, who
recd us with great kindness & love esteeming it a favour yt we
would come into yr mean habitation; assured us of his fervent
prayers to ye Lord for us: — A glorious saint makes a mean cottage a stately palace; were I to make my choyce, I would rather
abide wth ye saint in his poor cottage then wth any one of ye
princes yt I know of at ye day in ye world."

[1] Pages 281-282.

" 24 d. 6 m. — Wee visited G.[1] Beale, sorely afflicted with ye stone. He complained yt he could not in ye extremity of ye pain submitt with cheerfullness to ye will of God; & told us yt God spake many things to him under this exercise."

" 26 d. 6 m. — Mr. Mitchell wth diverse came to visit us; or discourse tended to provoke to give up or selves wholly to Jesus Christ and make him ye whole delight of or souls."

Within a few days after Whalley and Goffe left Cambridge, orders arrived from England for their arrest; and there was at least a show of earnest exertion, on the part of the magistrates, to overtake them; but the effort was in vain. Knowing that dissatisfaction existed in the English government, not only on account of their friendly reception of the regicides, but also for their persistent disregard of the navigation laws, and many other acts of insubordination, the General Court which assembled May 22, 1661, attempted to remove some of the causes of offence. They rebuked the apostle Eliot for publishing a book advocating a " Christian Commonwealth " rather than a monarchy; they modified their laws concerning Quakers, and soon afterwards expressed their intention to comply with the laws concerning navigation. On the last day of the session, which had extended into June, they adopted a vote which clearly indicates their conception of the grave difficulties which surrounded them, and their anxiety to devise means of escape: —

" For as much as the present condition of our affairs in highest concernments call for a diligent and speedy use of the best means seriously to discuss and rightly to understand our liberty and duty, thereby to beget unity amongst ourselves in the due observance of obedience and fidelity unto the authority of England and our own just privileges, for the effecting whereof it is ordered by this Court, that Mr. Symon Bradstreet, Mr. Samuell Symonds, Major General Denison, Mr. Danforth, Major Wm. Hauthorne, Capt. Tho. Savage, Capt. Edward Johnson, Capt. Eliazer Lusher, Mr. Mather, Mr. Norton, Mr. Cobbet, and Mr. Michell, be and hereby are appointed a committee, immediately after the dissolution or adjournment of the Court, to meet together in Boston on second day next, at twelve of the clock, to consider and debate such matter or thing of public concernment touching our patent, laws, privileges, and duty to his Majesty, as they in their wisdom shall judge most expedient, and draw up the result of their apprehensions, and present the same to the next session for consideration

[1] Goodman.

and approbation, that so (if the will of God be) we may speak
and act the same thing, becoming prudent, honest, conscientious,
and faithful men."

This important committee consisted of four Assistants, four
Deputies, and four clergymen, of whom Danforth and Mitchell
were of Cambridge. The report was signed by Danforth, and
was probably written by him; it is here inserted, as it indicates
the skill and firmness with which encroachments on their chartered rights were resisted by the party of which he was the acknowledged leader. Immediately after the appointment of this
committee, the Court adjourned. It met again on the tenth of
June, after a recess of probably less than a week. The first business presented was this Report: —

" The answers of the Committee unto the matters proposed to
their consideration by the honored General Court:

" 1. Concerning our liberties.

" 1. We conceive the patent (under God) to be the first and
main foundation of our civil polity here, by a Governor and Company, according as is therein expressed.

" 2. The Governor and Company are, by the patent, a body
politic, in fact and name.

" 3. This body politic is vested with power to make freemen.

" 4. These freemen have power to choose annually a Governor,
Deputy Governor, Assistants, and their select representatives or
deputies.

" 5. This government hath also [power] to set up all sorts of
officers, as well superior as inferior, and point out their power
and places.

" 6. The Governor, Deputy Governor, Assistants, and select
representatives or deputies have full power and authority, both
legislative and executive, for the government of all the people
here, whether inhabitants or strangers, both concerning ecclesias-
tics and in civils, without appeal, excepting law, or laws repugnant to the laws of England.

" 7. The government is privileged by all fitting means (yea,
and if need be, by force of arms), to defend themselves, both by
land and sea, against all such person or persons as shall at any
time attempt or enterprise the destruction, invasion, detriment, or
annoyance of this plantation or the inhabitants therein, besides
other privileges mentioned in the patent, not here expressed.

" 8. We conceive any imposition prejudicial to the country contrary to any just law of ours, not repugnant to the laws of England, to be an infringement of our right.

" 2. Concerning our duties of allegiance to our sovereign lord the King.

" 1. We ought to uphold and to our power maintain this place, as of right belonging to our sovereign lord the King, as holden of his majesty's manor of East Greenwich, and not to subject the same to any foreign prince or potentate whatsoever.

" 2. We ought to endeavor the preservation of his majesty's royal person, realms, and dominions, and so far as lieth in us, to discover and prevent all plots and conspiracies against the same.

" 3. We ought to seek the peace and prosperity of our king and nation, by a faithful discharge in the governing of this people committed to our care. (1.) By punishing all such crimes (being breaches of the first or second table) as are committed against the peace of our sovereign lord the King, his royal crown and dignity. (2.) In propagating the gospel, defending and upholding the true Christian or Protestant religion according to the faith given by our Lord Christ in his word; our dread sovereign being styled 'Defender of the faith.'

" The premises considered, it may well stand with the loyalty and obedience of such subjects as are thus privileged by their rightful sovereign (for himself, his heirs and successors forever), as cause shall require, to plead with their prince against all such as shall at any time endeavor the violation of their privileges.

" We further judge that the warrant and letter from the King's majesty, for the apprehending of Col. Whalley and Col. Goffe, ought to be diligently and faithfully executed by the authority of this country.

" And, also, that the General Court may do safely to declare, that in case (for the future) any legally obnoxious, and flying from the civil justice of the state of England, shall come over to these parts, they may not here expect shelter.

" Boston 10. 4m. 1661. By order and consent of the Committee.   " THO. DANFORTH.

" The Court allows and approves of the return of the Committee." [1]

On the last day of the year 1661, the General Court determined to send " Mr. Symon Bradstreet and Mr. John Norton "

[1] *Mass. Col. Rec.*, iv. (ii.) 34-36.

to England, as special agents. Among their instructions were these: "1. You shall present us to his majesty as his loyal and obedient subjects." "(4.) You shall not engage us by any act of yours to anything which may be prejudicial to our present standing according to patent." [1] The agents were received more favorably than they expected, and returned with a gracious letter from the King. This letter was read in Court, Oct. 8, 1662. In consequence of the King's declaration therein, "We will preserve and do hereby confirm the patent and charter heretofore granted unto them by our royal father of blessed memory, and they shall fully enjoy all the privileges and liberties granted to them in and by the same," — the Court appointed a special thanksgiving, making mention of "the safe and speedy return of our public messengers sent for England, together with the continuance of the mercies of peace, liberties, and the gospel;" and on the same day it was further ordered, "that henceforth all writs, process, with indictments, shall by all magistrates, the secretary, clerk of the several courts and writs, be made and sent forth in his Majesty's name, i. e., you are hereby required in his Majesty's name, etc., any usage or custom to the contrary notwithstanding." Some of the other requisitions, especially those interfering with their ecclesiastical polity, were very unwelcome, and the Court was not ready to comply. "The Court, having duly considered of his Majesty's letters now in Court, and the contents thereof, do hereby order the publication thereof. And forasmuch as the said letter hath influence upon the churches as well as the civil state, it is further ordered, that all manner of actings in relation thereunto be suspended until the next General Court, that so all persons concerned may have time and opportunity to consider of what is necessary to be done, in order to his Majesty's pleasure therein." [2]

In their answer to the King's letter, after expressing thankfulness for his confirmation of the charter, the Court say: "As

. [1] *Mass. Col. Rec.*, iv. (ii.) 37. Loyalty to the king was held to be qualified or modified by the provisions of the charter; two examples are preserved in the *Mass. Archives*, cvi. 132, 133. "Daniel Gookin, before he took the oath of allegiance in Court, May 24th, 1665, did openly and plainly declare that in taking that oath he would be so understood as not to infringe the liberty and privileges granted in his Majesty's royal charter to the Governor and Company of Massachusetts,

whereof he is a member, and unto which he is sworn formerly. Boston the 24th of May, 1665. DANIEL GOOKIN."

"Before I take the oath of allegiance to his Majesty, which I am ready to do, I do declare that I will be so understood as not to infringe the liberty and privileges granted in his Majesty's royal charter to this Colony of the Massachusetts. THOMAS DANFORTH. 26 (2) 1665."

[2] *Mass. Col. Rec.*, iv. (ii.) 56.

touching the further purport of the letter, we have this particular account to give, viz: for the repealing of all laws here established since the late changes, contrary and derogatory to his Majesty's authority and government, we having considered thereof, are not conscious to any of that tendency. Concerning the oath of allegiance, we are readily to attend to it as formerly, according to the charter. Touching the administration of justice in his Majesties name, hath been done, the practice whereof, which was discontinued in the late changes, is now reassumed. Concerning liberty to use the common Prayer Book, none as yet among us have appeared to desire it. Touching administration of the sacraments, this matter hath been under consideration of a synod, orderly called, the result whereof our last General Court commended to the several congregations, and we hope will have a tendency to general satisfaction. In reference to our elections of magistrates, we humbly answer, that it hath always been, and is, great care and endeavor, that men of wisdom, virtue and integrity be chosen to places of trust; and to that end, that such as vote in elections should be orthodox in religion, virtuous (and not vicious) in conversation, and all those that according to the orders and customs of the colony here established, agreeable to the provisions of our charter, having proved themselves to be such in their places where they live, have from time to time been admitted in our elections; and if anything yet remain to be acted by us respecting the premises, it is under consideration among us to that end. We humbly desire your honor will be pleased to assure his Majesty of the loyalty and good affection of his subjects here, they resting secure in their charter and his Majesty's gracious aspect towards them." [1]

This letter, manifesting the same spirit which was exhibited a hundred years afterwards, — personal loyalty to the King, but an unwillingness to submit to the arbitrary government of a Council or Parliament in which they were not represented, — was not satisfactory to the English Government; and after some further correspondence, a board of commissioners, consisting of Col. Richard Nichols, Sir Robert Carr, George Cartwright, Esq., and Samuel Maverick, Esq., was appointed in 1664, to visit the New England Colonies and enforce their subjection. A long controversy, shrewdly managed on the part of the Court, resulted in the departure of the commissioners without having accomplished their object. The inhabitants of Cambridge were not

[1] Danforth Papers, in *Coll. Mass. Hist. Soc.*, xviii. 47, 48.

backward in rendering encouragement to their magistrates. At a special session, commencing Oct. 19, 1664, — "The Court being met together and informed that several persons, inhabitants of Cambridge, were at the door and desiring liberty to make known their errand, were called in, and Mr. Edward Jackson, Mr. Richard Jackson, Mr. Edward Oakes, and Deacon Stone, coming before the Court, presented a petition from the inhabitants of Cambridge, which was subscribed by very many hands, in which they testified and declared their good content and satisfaction they took and had in the present government in church and commonwealth, with their resolution to be assisting to and encouraging the same, and humbly desiring all means might be used for the continuance and preservation thereof: and at the same time and the next day several petitions of like nature from Wooborne, Dorchester, Redding, Chelmsford, Concord, Billirrikey, Boston, Dedham, and Meadfield, and also one from several inhabitants of Roxbury, all which are on file." [1] The Cambridge petition is here inserted, partly on account of its patriotic spirit, and partly to preserve the list of names appended to it : —

"To the honoured Generall Court of Massachusetts Colonie. The humble representation of the inhabitants of the towne of Cambridg.

"For as much as we have heard that theire have beene representations made unto his Maiesty conserning divisions among us and dissatisfactions about the present goverment of this colonie; we whose names are under written, the inhabitants and householders of the towne above mentioned, doe hearby testify our unanimous satisfaction in and adhearing to the present government so long and orderly estableshed, and our earnest desire of the continuance theirof and of all the liberties and privileges pertaining theirunto which are contained in the charter granted by King James and King Charles the First of famous memory, under the encouredgment and security of which charter we or our fathers ventered over the ocean into this wildernesse through great hazards, charges, and difficulties; and we humbly desire our honored General Court would addresse themselves by humble petition to his Maiesty for his royall favour in the continuance of the pres-

---

[1] *Mass. Col. Rec.*, iv. (ii) 136, 137. Archives to the Judicial Court Files for The Cambridge petition, for some reason, Suffolk County, in the Court House, has been removed from the Massachusetts Boston.

ent estableshment and of all the previleges theirof, and that we may not be subjected to the arbitrary power of any who are not chosen by this people according to theire patent,

"Cambridg the 17th of the 8. 1664.

"CHARLES CHAUNCY.
EDWARD OAKES.
SAM^LL ANDREWE.
JONATHAN MITCHELL.
ELIJAH CORLETT.
RICHARD CHAMPNY.
EDMUND FROST.
GREGORY STONE.
JOHN BRIDGE.
JOHN STEDMAN.
FFRANCIS WHITMOR.
RICHARD JACKSON.
EDWARD SHEPHARD.
GILBERT X CRACBON.
JOHN FISENDEN.
JOHN COOPER.
ABRAHAM ERRINGTOON.
HUMFRY BRADSHA.
JOHN GIBSON.
RICHARD HASSELL.
DANILL KEMPSTER.
THOMAS X FOX.
GEORGE X WILLIS.
THOMAS X HALL.
RICHARD DANA.
NICOLAS X WYTHE.
THOMAS CHESHOLM.
SAMUEL GREEN.
THO. SWETMAN.
RICHARD ROBINS.
WILLIAM DIKSONE.
RICHARD ECCLES.
THOMAS LONGHORNE.
JOHN WATSONN.
ROGER X BUKK.
ANDREW X STEVENSON.
JOHN X PARENTS.
JAMES HUBBARD.
ROBERT X WILSON.
ROB. X PARKER.
JOHN X BOUTTELL.

ROBERT STEDMAN.
THOMAS CHENY.
WILLYAM X HEALLY.
JOHN PALFRAY.
FFRANCIS MOORE, sen^r.
JOHN GOVE.
WILL X MICHELSON.
EDWARD HALL.
WILLIAM BARRETT.
JOHN HOLMAN.
WILL. BORDMAN.
ZACHARYE HICKS.
SAM^LL MANNING.
RICHARD CUTTER.
JOHN GREEN.
FFRA. MOORE, jun^r.
JOHN X ADAMS.
BEINIMAN CRACKBONE.
JOHN MARRITT.
NATHANELL HANCOCKE.
WILLYAM TOWN.
ABRAHAM HOLMAN.
JOHN SHEPHARD.
SAMUELL FROST.
WALTER HASTING.
NATH. GREEN.
ESTER GOSSOM.
PETER TOWNE.
EDWARD MITCHELLSON.
ANDREW BELCHER.
EDMUND ANGIER.
RICHARD PARK.
JOSEPH COOKE.
JERMIE FISMAN.
JOHN TALLER.
DANIEL CHEKAVER.
JOHN ELIOT.
EDWARD JACKSON.
SAMUELL HADEN.
JOHN JACKSON.
GREGORY COOKE.

John ✕ Parker.
Mathew ✕ Boone.
Thomas Hammond, senyor.
Thomas Hammond, junyor.
Vincent ✕ Druse, junyor.
John ✕ Hanchet.
Job ✕ Hides.
Samuell ✕ Hydes.
Rebeccah ✕ Daniell.
Jonathan Hides.
David Stone.
Samuell Stone.
Jeames ✕ Cutler.

John Wintor.
John Collar.
Joseph Miriam.
Isack Starnes.
David Fiske.
Solomon Prentes.
Joseph Sill.
Samuell Hasting.
Richard ✕ Frances.
Robart ✕ Brown.
Thomas ✕ Brown.
John Swan."

" We, whose names are subscribed, being of the traine band and singell men in the above sayd town, doe also desire to manifest ourselves to be of the same mynd with our parents, masters, and the aged men and housholders of the place.

" Thomas Oliver.
Jonathan Jackson.
John Jackson.
Sebres Jackson.
Steven Cooke.
Jacob Goble.
Joseph ✕ Stevenes.
Daniel Champnes.
John Steadman.
Thomas Gates.
Arther ✕ Henbury.
Robart ✕ Shepard.
Daniell ✕ Prat.
Philip Eastman.
Arthur Call.
Thomas Marritt.
Joseph Pratt.
Thomas Ffledg.

John Hastins.
John More.
John Holis.
Gershom Frost.
Abraham ✕ Howell.
Beniaman ✕ Russell.
Sameuel Bucke.
Joseph Ffrost.
William Reyle.
Samuell ✕ Garry.
Nath. Patten.
Stephen Frances.
Reuben Luxfford.
Samuell ✕ Robines.
Benony ✕ Eaton.
Rudger Chandler.
Joseph Holme."

It does not appear that Cambridge, in its corporate capacity, was actively engaged in the political contest which continued, with scarcely any intermission, for more than twenty years ; but there is the best evidence that its representative men were among the most active leaders in opposition to the arbitrary measures of the English court. Edward Randolph, " the arch enemy of the Colony," addressing the Lords of Trade in 1676, says: " Amongst the Magistrates, some are good men and well affected to his Majesty, and would be well satisfied to have his Majesty's authority in a better manner established; but the major part are of different principles, having been in the government from the time they formed themselves into a Commonwealth. These direct and manage all affairs as they please, of which number are Mr. Leverett, Governor, — Mr. Symons, Deputy Governor, — Mr. Danforth, Mr. Ting, Major Clarke, and Major Hathorn, still continued a magistrate, though commanded by his Majesty upon his allegiance to come into England, yet refused, being encouraged in his disobedience by a vote of the Court not to appear, upon some reasons best known to themselves. These, with some few others of the same faction, keep the country in subjection and slavery, backed with the authority of a pretended charter." [1]

To the Bishop of London he writes, May 29, 1682, "I think I have so clearly layd downe the matter of fact, sent over their lawes and orders to confirme what I have wrote, that they cannot deny them : however, if commanded, I will readily pass the seas to attend at Whitehall, especially if Danford, Goggin, and Newell, magistrates, and Cooke, Hutchinson and Fisher, members of their late General Court and great opposers of the honest Governor and majestrates, be sent for to appeare before his Majesty ; till which time this country will always be a shame as well as inconveniency to the government at home." [2] Soon afterwards, June 14, 1682, he writes to the Earl of Clarendon, "His Majesties quo warranto against their charter, and sending for Thomas Danforth, Samuel Nowell, a late factious preacher and now a magistrate, and Daniel Fisher and Elisha Cooke, deputies, to attend and answer the articles of high misdemeanures I have now exhibited against them in my papers sent Mr. Blaithwait per Capt. Foy, will make the whole faction tremble." [3]

"During these distresses of the colony," says Hutchinson in 1681, " there were two parties subsisting in the government, both of them agreed in the importance of the charter privileges, but differing in opinion upon the extent of them, and upon the proper measures to preserve them. The governor, Mr. Bradstreet, was at the head of the moderate party. Randolph in all his letters takes notice of it. . . . . Mr. Stoughton, Mr. Dudley, and William Brown of Salem, these fell in with the Governor. The deputy governor, Mr. Danforth, was at the head of the other party : the principal members of the court with him were Major Gookins of Cambridge, Peter Tilton of Hadley, Elisha Cooke and Elisha

[1] *Hutch. Coll.,* p 499.　　　[2] *Ibid.,* 532.　　　[3] *Ibid.,* 535.

Hutchinson of Boston. This party opposed the sending over agents, the submitting to acts of trade, &c., and were for adhering to their charter according to their construction of it, and leaving the event. Gookins, being aged, desired a paper he drew up as his dying testimony, might be lodged with the court, containing the reasons of his opinion." [1]

Through the whole of this protracted controversy, Danforth and Gookin, together with the Deputies from Cambridge, continued firm in their resistance to the arbitrary measures of the English government. They were at last overpowered, however, and the Colony was reduced to a state little better than slavery. On the 25th day of May, 1686, Joseph Dudley, the newly appointed President, with his Council, assumed the government of the Colony, the charter having been abrogated. A few months later, Dec. 20, 1686, he was superseded by Sir Edmund Andros, who had been appointed Governor of New England.

[1] *Hist. Mass.*, i. 331.

CHAPTER VIII.

CIVIL HISTORY.

As early as 1654, some of the inhabitants upon the south side of the River commenced a movement, which resulted, seven years afterwards, in an order of the General Court, that all who resided more than four miles from the meeting-house should "be freed from contributing towards the ministry on the north side the river," so long "as the south side the river shall maintain an able ministry."[1] This was not wholly satisfactory, and a petition for more extensive privileges was presented to the General Court, Oct. 18, 1672, but action thereon was postponed until the next session, May 7, 1673, at which time this record is found: "In answer to the petition of Mr. Edward Jackson and John Jackson in behalf of the inhabitants of Cambridge Village, on the south side of Charles River, this Court doth judge meet to grant the inhabitants of the said village annually to elect one constable and three selectmen, dwelling among themselves, to order their prudential affairs of the inhabitants there according to law, only continuing a part of Cambridge in paying country and county rates, as also town rates so far as refers to the grammar school and bridge, and also pay their proportion of the charges of the deputies of Cambridge, and this to be an issue to the controversy between Cambridge and them."[2] But the people were not content to be a precinct. Accordingly at the session of the General Court, commencing May 8, 1678, a petition was presented for incorporation as a town: —

"To the honored Governor, Deputy Governor, together with the honored Magistrates and Deputies of the General Court, now sitting in Boston.

"The humble petition of us, the inhabitants of Cambridge Village, on the south side of Charles River, showeth, that the

---

[1] *Mass. Col. Rec.*, iv. (ii.) 16.   [2] *Ibid.*, 555.

late war, as it hath been a great charge to the whole Colony, so
to us in particular, both in our estates and persons, by loss of life
to some, and others wounded and disabled for their livelihood,
besides all our other great charges in building of our meeting-
house and of late enlargement to it, as also our charge to the
minister's house.   And, as you know, the Lord took that worthy
person from us in a little time, and now in great mercy hath
raised up another in the place, who hath a house in building for
him, which requires assistance : As also we are now, by the great
mercy of God, so many families that a school is required for the
education of our children according to law, besides our public
charge of the place.   Yet, notwithstanding, this last year, the
Townsmen of Cambridge have imposed a tax upon us, amounting to the sum of three country Rates, without our knowledge or
consent, which we humbly conceive is very harsh proceeding for
any Townsmen of their own will and power to impose upon the
inhabitants what taxes they please, and to what end, without
ever calling the inhabitants to consider about such charge.
Nevertheless, for peace sake, the inhabitants of our place did
meet together and jointly consent to give the town of Cambridge
the sum of one hundred pounds, and to pay it in three years,
without desiring any profit or benefit from them of wood, timber,
or common lands, but only our freedom, being content with our
own proprieties, which some of us had before Cambridge had any
right there : which tender of ours they having rejected, as also
to grant to us our freedom from them, we do most humbly commend our distressed condition to the justice and mercy of this
honored Court, that you will please to grant us our freedom from
Cambridge and that we may be a township of ourselves, without
any more dependence upon Cambridge, which hath been a great
charge and burden to us ; and also that you would please to give
the place a name, and if there should be any objection against us
that the honored Court will admit our reply and defence.   So
hoping the Almighty will assist you in all your concerns, we rest
your humble petitioners.

" MR. EDWARD JACKSON.	THOMAS PRENTICE, jun'.
CAPT. THOMAS PRENTICE.	JOHN KENRICK, jun'.
JOHN FULLER, sen'.	JOHN MASON.
JOHN KENRICK, sen'.	WM. ROBINSON.
ISAAC WILLIAMS.	THOMAS GREENWOOD.
JOHN WARD.	JOHN PARKER (south).
JOSEPH MILLER.	HUMPHREY OSLAND. —

For p. 65 see after p. 88?

JOSEPH BARTLETT.	SAMUEL HIDES, jun'.
ISAAC BACON.	NOAH McDANIEL.
JACOB BACON.	JOHN FULLER, jun'.
SAMUEL TRUSDALE.	JOSHUA FULLER.
SIMON ONGE.	JOHN ALEXANDER.
JONATHAN FULLER.	JOHN PRENTICE.
JONATHAN HIDES, sen'.	NATH^L. HAMMOND.
THOMAS PARKES, sen'.	JOB HIDES.
JAMES TROWBRIDGE.	JOHN PARKER (east).
NOAH WISWALL.	WIDOW JACKSON.
THOMAS HAMMOND.	EDW^D. JACKSON, jun'.
JONATHAN HIDES, jun'.	DANIEL KEY.
JAMES PRENTICE, sen'.	THOS. PRENTICE, jun'.
DAVID MEADS.	ABRAHAM JACKSON.
VINCENT DRUSSE.	STEPHEN COOKE.
JOHN HIDES.	RICHARD PARKS.
EBEN^R. WISWALL.	JOSEPH FULLER.
ELIAH KENRICK.	ISAAC BEACH.
SEBEAS JACKSON.	PETER HANCHET." [1]

The historian of Newton says this petition " was no doubt drawn up by Mr. Edward Jackson, senior." He adds a list of " Freemen in the Village who did not sign this petition," [2] namely : —

" Rev. Nehemiah Hobart.	Daniel Bacon.
Elder Thomas Wiswall.	John Spring.
Dea. Samuel Hyde.	Daniel McCoy.
John Woodward.	John Park.
Henry Segar.	Samuel Hyde, Son of Jona.
Thomas Park, jun'.	James Prentice, jun'."

" In answer to the petition of the inhabitants of Cambridge Village, on the south side of the river, the Court judgeth it meet to grant them a hearing of the case mentioned on the first Tuesday of the next session in October, and all parties concerned are ordered to have timely notice." [3]

At the time appointed, a long protest was presented by the Selectmen of Cambridge, a part of which was printed in Jackson's " History of Newton," pp. 58–60. Notwithstanding its length, it is here inserted in full, on account of the historical facts mentioned in it, and the picture it presents of the general condition of affairs : —

[1] Mass. Arch., cxii. 250.   [2] Mass. Col. Rec., v. 188, 189.
[3] Jackson's Hist. of Newton, 50, 52.

6

" The answer of the Selectmen of Cambridge to the petition exhibited against them by their Brethren and Neighbors of the Village on the South Side of Charles River.

" To omit what they express by way of narration, declaring ' the loss of lives and estates to them sustained by the late war, the death of their former minister and their having now got another for whom a house is building,' &c. — the impertinency and absurdity of their argument therein being obvious to all intelligent minds, — we shall only concern ourselves with what they make the main of their petition, which may be divided into these two parts:

" I. The cause on our part, viz. the hard usage by the Townsmen of Cambridge, *i. e.* imposing upon them a tax of their own will and power, and what they please, and to what end they please.

" For answer hereunto, the Cambridge Townsmen have imposed a tax (as they call it) if they intend no more than the making of a rate for the paying of the charges of the whole town, and putting upon them their just proportion of the charge of those things, properly belonging to them to bear their part of, according to the order of the General Court with reference to them, made May 7th, 1673, and then declared to be the issue of the controversy between the town and the petitioners, thus far we own to be a truth. But whereas they charge us that we have thus done, 1, of our own will, 2, of our own power, 3, what we please, 4, to what end we please, — these are high and sad accusations which we cannot own to be true: for 1st it was not by our will that any taxes have been imposed on them or any other of the inhabitants, but their own will, so declared in orderly town-meetings, legally warned, whereat themselves either were or might have been present and had their votes. 2. Nor was it of our own power, but by the authority of the General Court, committing to us by the law, as we are Selectmen of the town, power for the ordering of the prudentials of the town and levying what is necessary for the payment of the annual disbursements regularly made for the town's occasions. 3. Nor have we imposed upon the town in general, or the petitioners, what we please. The rule that we have observed in raising our rates being to make them no greater than is of absolute necessity for the payment of the town's debts, and most an end falling considerably short by reason of the town's poverty, and upon each inhabitant in particular according to a list of their persons and

rateable estates. 4. Nor hav we improved the moneys raised
to what end we please, but have faithfully disposed of the same
for the end for which we raised it, namely, the payment of the
town's just debts. If herein we have transgressed the line of our
power, we beg pardon (and direction for the future) of this honored Court. If our accusers shall deny the truth of what we
assert, either in general or any one article, we crave liberty to
put in our further defence and evidence.

" II. That which is the 'main of their petition they thus express, viz., ' that we may be a township of ourselves, without any
more dependence on Cambridge.' And this their petition they
strengthen with two arguments; the 1ˢᵗ is prefatory to their petition, wherein they say ' they plead only for their freedom, being
content with their own propriety ; ' the 2ᵈ is subsequent ' because
their dependence on Cambridge hath been a great charge and
burthen to them.'

" We shall begin with their arguments why they would be
freed from Cambridge. To the 1ˢᵗ, whereas they say that they
plead only for their freedom, being content with their own proprieties, we answer, 1. That the inhabitants of Cambridge now
dwelling on the north side of Charles River have well nigh three
thousand acres of land that is laid out into several lots, some ten,
some twenty, some forty, acres, more or less, that they are at this
time seised of, and by them kept for herbage, timber, wood, and
planting lands, as they shall have occasion for to use the same,
all which is by the petitioners included within the line of division
between the town and them ; and therefore they do not say words
of truth when they say they are content with their own proprieties. 2. Nor is it true that they plead only for freedom ; for they
having obtained these our lands and proprieties to be within the
line of that division and payable to the ministry, they would become our masters and charge us for our lands and cattle that we
shall put thereon to all their common charges, if they may obtain
to be a distinct township.

" To their 2ᵈ argument, viz. that their dependence on Cambridge hath been a great charge and burden to them. For answer hereto, 1ˢᵗ we shall say something that hath reference to
them more generally, and 2ᵈ, we shall distinguish between the
persons that are petitioners, and speak something more particularly. 1. More generally. They well know, before their settlement in that place, that all those lands that they now petition
for did belong to Cambridge, and were the grant of the General

Court to them, for their enabling to maintain the ordinances of God among them, and all other common charges inevitably arising in a township; so that what they call a burden will appear to be no more than their duty which they owe to the town; and if, in that sense, charge and burden may be admitted as a just plea, may not the servant as well petition the Court to be freed from his master, the tenant from his landlord, or any single town petition his Majesty to have their freedom, and be a distinct Colony, and plead that the annual charges for maintenance of government and the peace of the commonwealth is to them a great charge and burden? 2. Their charge and burden hath not been greater than their brethren and neighbors; for we have not, by burdening or charging them, eased ourselves of our just dues and proportion in any kind; and although their accommodations for enabling them to bear and discharge their dues are far better than those of the town, yet it seems that what they call great (and we may without wronging our case freely concede to the truth thereof, that when all our shoulders bear, and hands and hearts join together, we find it so by daily experience) they are content that we should bear it alone, not pitying us, though we sink and break under it; for they know full well that their withdrawing will not abate the weight of our burden; for the bridge must be maintained, the school must be kept up, the Deputies must be sent to the General Court: and they have no other charge or burden imposed upon them by us than their just proportion of that which these do ordinarily require. 3. They know full well that such hath been the tenderness of the town towards them at all times, that they have evermore chosen a Constable that hath been resident among them, and for the Selectmen also they have desired that they might constantly have some of them joined with those of the town, partly for their help, and partly that they might more easily have help from them, and be satisfied in the equity and justice of their proceedings in all respects; so that we know they cannot and dare not to plead that we have at any time been unwilling to execute the power of the Selectmen for gathering the rates due to their minister or otherwise more properly belonging to them, nor that we have carried crossly, proudly, or perversely towards them. If we have, let us be accused to our faces, and not backbitten and slandered as we have been in the other particulars whereof they accuse us.

"Thus far in answer to the petitioners' 2^d argument in general. We shall now make answer thereto more particularly.

And here we must divide the petitioners into two sorts: 1. Those that were dwellers in the town before they went to inhabit on that side. 2. Another sort are those that came from other towns.

1. "Those that proceeded from the town, who knowing the straitness and want of accommodation to be had among their brethren there, and the lands on that side the water being then of small value, procured to themselves large and comfortable accommodation for a small matter. We have confidence that these dare not to say that their being in Cambridge hath been any charge or burden to them. They must and will own that God hath there greatly blessed them : that whereas we on the town side, of £1,000 that we or our parents brought to this place, and laid out in the town, for the purchasing at dear rates what we now enjoy, can not, divers of us, show £100, they may speak just contrary or in proportion. We could, if need were, instance some,* whose parents lived and died here, who, when they came to this town had no estate, and some were helped by the charity of the church, and others yet living that well know they may say truly, with good Jacob, — over this Jordan came I with this staff, — and so may they say, over this River went I, with this spade, hoe, or other tool, and now, through God's blessing, am greatly increased. Yet here we would not be understood to include every particular person ; for we acknowledge that Mr. Jackson brought a good estate to the town, as some others did, and hath not been wanting to the ministry or any good work among us ; and therefore we would not reflect upon him in the least.

"2. There are another sort of persons that did not proceed from the town, but came from other towns, where there had been much division and contention among them, who, though they knew the distance of the place from the public meeting-house, the dependency thereof on Cambridge, which they now call a great charge and burden, yet this they then did choose, and we are assured will own, generally at least, that they have there increased their estates far beyond what those of the town have or are capable to do. We might instance also in the Inventories of some of them, whose purchase at the first cost them a very small matter, and their stock and household stuff we judge to be proportionable, and yet when they deceased, an in-

* John Jackson's Invent., £1,230. Rich. Park's Invent., £972.

ventory † amounting to more than 1,100 pounds is given into
the Court; and others that are yet living have advanced in some
measure suitable. But poor Cambridge quickly felt the sad
effect of their coming among us; for though some of them came
from their dwellings very near the meeting-houses in other
towns, and these beforehand knew the distance of their now
dwellings from Cambridge, yet this did not obstruct them in
their settlement there; but before they were well warm in their
nests, they must divide from the town. And though such was
the endeared love of our brethren and neighbors that went from
us to this Church and the ministry thereof, that it was long before they could get them (at least with any considerable unan-
imity) to join with them, yet they would petition, some few of
them in the name of the rest, to the honored General Court, for
their release from the town. And when the Court, being tired
out with their eager pursuit and more private fawnings and in-
sinuations, granted them Committee upon Committee to hear
and examine the ground of their so great complaints, at last all
issued in a declaration of the unreasonableness of their desire
with reference to the town and unseasonableness on their part,
as may appear by the return of the Committee made to the General Court, October 14, 1657, the Worshipful Richard Russell
Esq., Major Lusher and Mr. Ephraim Child subscribing the
same, and was accepted by the Court.

"Yet here they rested not; but in the year 1661 petitioned
the Court, and then obtained freedom from rates to the ministry
for all lands and estates more than four miles from Cambridge
meeting-house; and this being all that they desired, although
we were not at that time advantaged with an opportunity to
send any one to speak in the town's behalf, yet considering the
impetuousness of their spirits, and their good words, pretending
only the spiritual good of their families that could not travel
(women and children) to the meeting-house at Cambridge, we
rested therein, hoping now they would be at rest. But all this
did not satisfy them; but the very next year ‡ they petition the
Court again. And then as a full and final issue of all things in
controversy between Cambridge town and the petitioners, there
is another Committee appointed to come upon the place and determine the bounds or dividing line between the town and them;
the result whereof was such that, whereas their grant was for all
the lands that were above four miles from the town, they now

"† Old Hammond's Invent., £1,159.   "‡ Octob. '62.

obtain the stating of a line that for the generalty is (by exact measure) tried and proved to be very little above three miles from Cambridge meeting-house. Yet did not Cambridge (thus pilled and bereaved of more than half the lands accommodable to their town at once) resist, or so much as complain, but rested therein,'— the Court having declared their pleasure and given them their sanction, that this, as abovesaid, should be a final issue of all things between the town and the petitioners.

" All this notwithstanding, these long-breathed petitioners, finding that they had such good success that they could never cast their lines into the sea but something was catched, they resolve to bait their hook again ; and as they had been wont some of them for twenty years together to attend constantly the meetings of the town and selectmen, whilst there was any lands, wood, or timber, that they could get by begging, so now they pursue the Court for obtaining what they would from them, not sparing time or cost to insinuate their matters, with reproaches and clamors against poor Cambridge, and have the confidence in the year 1672 again to petition the Court for the same thing, and in the same words that they now do, viz. 'that they may be à township of themselves, distinct from Cambridge '; and then the Court grants them further liberty than before they had, viz. to choose their own Constable and three selectmen amongst themselves, to order the prudential affairs of the inhabitants there, only continuing a part of Cambridge in paying Country and County rates, as also Town Rates so far as refers to the Grammar School, Bridge, and Deputy's charges, they to pay still their proportion with the town ; and this the Court declares, once more, to be a final issue of the controversy between Cambridge and them.

" Cambridge no sooner understands the pleasure of this honored Court, but they quietly submitted thereunto ; and we hope our brethren neither can nor dare in the least to accuse us (first or last) of refusing to acquiesce in the Court's issue, although we may and must truly say we have been not a little grieved when by the more private intimations and reproachful backbitings of our neighbors, we have, in the minds and lips of those whom we honor and love, been rendered either too straitlaced to our own interest, or unequally-minded towards our brethren. And did not this honored Court, as well as we, conclude that the petitioners, having exercised the patience of the Court by their so often petitioning, as well as giving trouble to the town by causing them to dance after their pipes, from time to time, for twenty-four years, as will appear by the Court Records, in which time they have petitioned the Court near if not altogether ten times, putting the town to great charges in meeting together to consider and provide their answers, and to appoint men to attend the Court, and the Committees that have been from time to time appointed by the Court, as also the charges of entertaining them all, which hath been no small disturbance to their more necessary employments for their livelihood, and expense of their time and estates ; — yet all this notwithstanding, we are summoned now again to appear before this honored Court to answer their petition exhibited for the very same thing, nothing being added save only sundry falsehoods and clamorous accusations of us : § so that now it is not so much Cambridge as the arbitrary and irregular acting of them and their Townsmen that they plead to be delivered from, as being their bondage and burden.

"It now remains that we speak something as to the main of their petition, which they thus express, *i. e.*, 'that we may be a township of ourselves, without any more dependence on Cambridge.' The reasons why we apprehend they may not have this their petition granted them may be taken from —

"I. The injustice of this their request, which may thus appear: — 1. If it would be accounted injustice for any neighboring towns, or other persons, to endeavor the compassing so great a part or any part of our town limits from us, it is the same (and in some sense far worse) for those that belong to us so to do. This we conceive is plain from God's Word, that styles the child that robs his father to be the companion of a destroyer, or, as some render the word, a murderer ; although the child may plead interest in his father's estate, yet he is in God's account a murderer if he takes away that whereby his father's or mother's life should be preserved ; and this, we apprehend not to be far unlike the case now before this honored Court. 2. All practices of this nature are condemned by the light of nature, Judges xi. 24. They who had their grants from the heathen idolaters did not account it just that they should be dispossessed by others. And idolatrous Ahab, although he was a king, and a very wicked king also, and wanted not power to effect what he desired, and was so burdened for the want of Naboth's vineyard that he could neither eat nor sleep, and when denied by his own subject tendered a full price for the same, yet he had so much conscience left that he did

"§ A Machiavellian practice.

For 81. See after p. 64.
-88

not dare to seize the same presently, as the petitioners would so great a part of our possession as this is, were it in their power. 8. The liberty and property of a Colony, so likewise (in its degree) of a township, is far more to be insisted upon than the right of any particular person ; the concerns thereof being eminently far greater in all respects, both civil and ecclesiastical. 4. The General Court having forty-five years since (or more) made a grant of the land petitioned for to Cambridge town, the Court's grant to each town and person as his Majesty's royal charter is to this honored Assembly and the whole Colony, we have confidence that such is their wisdom and integrity that they will not deem it to be in their power * to take away from us, or any other town or person, any part of what they have so orderly granted and confirmed to them. 5. Had we no grant upon Record (which is indubitably clear that we have, none in the least questioning the same), yet by the law of possession it is ours, and may not, without violation of the law and faith of the honored Court be taken from us.

"II. Could the petitioners obtain what they ask, without crossing the law of justice, yet we apprehend it would be very unequal ; and that may thus appear : — Because Cambridge town is the womb out of which the petitioners have sprung, and therefore ought, in the first place, to be provided for ; and the question in equity ought to be, not what do the petitioners crave, and might be convenient for them, but what may Cambridge spare ? Now that Cambridge can not spare what they desire we shall thus prove: — 1. From the situation of our town, being planted on a neck of land, hemmed about by neighboring towns, Watertown coming on the one side within half a mile of our meeting-house, and Charlestown as near on the other side ; so that our bounds is not much above a mile in breadth for near three miles together ; and, on the south side the River, the petitioners have gained their line (as we before related) to come very near within three miles of our meeting-house. 2. The most considerable part of the best and most accommodable lands of these near lands to the town are belonging to Mr. Pelham and others that live not in the town ; so that the far greater number of those that live in the town are put to hire grass for their cattle to feed upon in the summer time, which costs them the least twelve shillings and some

---

"* It was no dishonor to Paul, that had all church power, that he could do nothing against the truth ; nor diminutive to the power of God Himself, that He is a God that cannot lie.

fifteen shillings a head in money, for one cow, the summer feed; and corn-land they have not sufficient to find the town with bread. 3. Cambridge is not a town of trade or merchandize, as the seaport towns be; but what they do must be in a way of husbandry, although upon never so hard terms, they having no other way for a supply. 4. By the same reason that the petitioners plead immunity and freedom, our neighbors that live far nearer to Concord than to us may plead the like, and with far greater reason; and should they have a township granted them also, there would be nothing left for Cambridge, no, not so much commonage as to feed a small flock of sheep.

"That our town is thus situated, narrow and long. on each wing, Watertown and Charlestown nipping us up close on each side, there needs no proof; it is sufficiently known to sundry of the members of this honored Court. And that we are in other respects circumstanced as we have related, so as that we must be no town nor have no church of Christ nor ministry among us, in case we be clipped and mangled as the petitioners would have, we conceive there needs not further evidence than our testimony. We know not why we should not be believed. We conceive that the honor of God and of this Court is more concerned in providing against the laying waste an ancient town and church of Christ, settled in this place for more than forty years, than any of us can be to our personal interest;—nothing that we here enjoy as to our outward accommodation being so attractive as that we should be forced here to continue, if we be disabled to maintain God's ordinances. Yet for evidence of the truth of what we thus assert we might allege the removing of Mr. Hooker and the whole church with him to Hartford, and that for this very reason, because they foresaw the narrowness of the place was such that they could not live here. Also the endeavor of Mr. Shepherd and the church with him, before his death, to remove in like manner, and that for no other reason but this, because they saw, after many years hard labor and expense of their estates that they brought with them from England, that they could not live in this place. Also we may add, that the Committee, which the honored General Court appointed to inquire into the estate of the town, 14th. 8mo. 57, made their return that they found the state of Cambridge to be as we have declared.

"We do freely own that, as our place is straitened so the charges are great for the maintenance of our Great Bridge and schools, &c., besides all other charges common to other places.

Shall this be an argument therefore to countenance any to seek
to pluck from us our right, and to pull away their shoulders, to
whom of right it appertains to bear a part with us, and have far
the greatest part of the accommodation that should uphold the
same? We would not speak passionately; but let not this honored Court be offended if we speak a little affectionately. We
know not wherein we have offended this honored Court, or why
poor Cambridge above all other towns in the country must be
thus harassed from Court to Court, and never can have an end
in twenty-four years time, although the Court have declared and
given in their sanction that this and the other determination
should be a final issue, never to be troubled more with the petitioners; yet still their petitions and clamors are received, and we
compelled to make answer thereto. If we have transgressed in
any kind, and this Court or any the members thereof have a prejudice against us, we humbly entreat that our offence may be
declared. And if we have been such arbitrary taxmasters as the
petitioners render us, that we may either be convicted, or recompense given us for our cost and damage by their unjust molestation of us from time to time, for the just vindication of our
innocency against their unjust calumnies.

" Also we do humbly entreat of this honored Court that,
whereas the petitioners at the time of their first grant which
they obtained from this Court then pleaded that, for and towards
the maintenance of the ministry in that place, they might have
the lands and estates on that side the River that were more than
four miles from the town, that we might have the line stated
accordingly; the whole being our own, as we have before pleaded
and proved, and we having need thereof, we conceive we can not
in justice be denied the same.

" Also, whereas they have not submitted unto nor rested in
the Court's last grant made them for the choice of a Constable
and three Selectmen among themselves, but have carried it fro-
wardly one towards another, and in like manner towards the
town from whom they proceeded and unto whom they of right
belong, we humbly entreat that the said order may be reversed,
and that we being all one body politic may have a joint choice
in the Selectmen and Constables of the town, according as the
law doth determine the right and privilege of each town.

" Finally, we humbly entreat that this our defence may be
entered in the Court's register, there to remain, for the vindication of our just right, *in perpetuam rei memoriam.* Praying ·

that the God of wisdom and truth may direct and guide this
honored Court in their issuing of this and all other their more
weighty concerns, we subscribe ourselves, honorable Sirs, your
humble and dutiful servants and suppliants,

Cambridge,   JOHN COOPER,
    23 (8) 78.   WILLIAM MANNING,
                              JOHN STONE,
                              WALTER HASTING,
                              FFR. MOORE,
                              NATHANIELL SPARHAWK." [1]

In Jackson's "History of Newton," it is stated that "the result was that the Court granted the prayer of the petition, and
Cambridge Village was set off from Cambridge, and made an
independent township. The doings of the Court in this case are
missing, and have not as yet been found, and therefore we do
not know the precise conditions upon which the separation took
place. But the Town record is quite sufficient to establish the
fact of separation. The very first entry upon the new Town
Book records the doings of the first Town-meeting, held '27, 6,
1679, by virtue of an order of the General Court,' at which meeting the first board of Selectmen were duly elected, namely, Captain Thomas Prentice, John Ward, and James Trowbridge; and
Thomas Greenwood was chosen Constable." [2] "1691. December 8. 'In answer to the petition of the inhabitants of Cambridge Village, lying on the south side of Charles River, sometimes called New Cambridge, being granted to be a township,
praying that a name may be given to said town, it is ordered,
that it be henceforth called New Town.' This order of the General Court, for a name only, has been mistaken by historians for
the incorporation of the town, whereas the petitioners had been
an independent town for twelve years. The child was born on
the 27th August, 1679, but was not duly christened until the 8th
of December, 1691." [3]

It is evident that the township was incorporated before Dec. 8,
1691 (or rather Dec. 18; the session of the Court commenced
Dec. 8, but the order granting a name was adopted ten days
later). This order plainly enough recognizes the village as already a distinct "township." Moreover, in 1689, when a General Court assembled after Andros was deposed and imprisoned,

1 Mass. Arch., cxii. 253-264.   3 Ibid., page 63.
2 Hist. of Newton, page 60.

Ensign John Ward appeared as a Deputy from New Cambridge, and was admitted to a seat, apparently without objection. So far, Mr. Jackson has a good case. But other facts of public notoriety would justify grave doubts whether the town was incorporated so early as 1679. It is a very suspicious circumstance, scarcely reconcilable with such an early date of incorporation, that for the seven years following 1679, until the charter government was overturned in 1686, the Village, or New Cambridge, never assumed, as a town distinct from Cambridge, to send a Deputy to the General Court; but did not miss representation a single year for half a century after the government was established under the new charter. People as tenacious of their rights as the inhabitants of the Village manifestly were, both before and after incorporation, would not be likely to let the newly-acquired right of representation lie dormant for seven years, during a period of intense political excitement. The election of a Constable and three Selectmen in 1679 by no means furnishes countervailing proof of incorporation; for this is precisely what the inhabitants were authorized to do by the order passed May 7, 1673, which was never understood to confer full town privileges, and which, for aught that appears to the contrary, was the order mentioned in the Town Record dated 27.6. 1679.[1]

But the evidence in the case is not wholly of this negative character. One of the documents published by Mr. Jackson[2] indicates with some distinctness a different day (Jan. 11, 1687–8) as the true date of incorporation into a distinct town: —

"Articles of agreement, made September 17, 1688, between the Selectmen of Cambridge and the Selectmen of the Village, in behalf of their respective towns: That, whereas Cambridge Village, by order of the General Court in the late government, was enjoined to bear their proportion in the charges in the upholding and maintaining of the Great Bridge and School, with some other things of a public nature in the town of Cambridge; also there having been some difference between the Selectmen of said

---

[1] At the close of their elaborate "answer" the Selectmen of Cambridge allege that the petitioners "have not submitted unto nor rested in the Court's last grant made to them for the choice of a constable and three Selectmen," etc. It seems highly probable that, having again failed in their efforts to obtain incorporation in 1678, and despairing of present success, the petitioners determined to exercise the power granted in 1673, and accordingly elected a Constable and three Selectmen, Aug. 27, 1679. Such action would sufficiently account for the record bearing that date in what Jackson styles the "New Town Book."

[2] *Hist. of Newton*, p. 62.

towns, concerning the laying of rates for the end above said, that
the Village shall pay to the town of Cambridge the sum of £5,
in merchantable corn, at the former prices, at or before the first
day of May next ensuing the date above, in full satisfaction of
all dues and demands by the said town from the said Village, on
the account above said, from the beginning of the world to the
11ᵗʰ January, 1687.   Provided, always, and it is to be hereby
understood, that the town of Cambridge on consideration of £4,
in current county pay, already in hand paid to the Village above
said, shall have free use of the highway laid out from the Village Meeting-house to the Falls, forever, without any let, molestation, or denial; also, that the Constable of the Village shall
pay to the town of Cambridge or [all?] that is in their hands un-
paid of their former rates due to the town of Cambridge above
said.   In witness whereof, the Selectmen above said hereunto set
their hands, the day and year first above written.

		JOHN COOPER,	
JOHN SPRING,	Selectmen	SAMUEL ANDREW,	Selectmen
EDWARD JACKSON,	of New	WALTER HASTING,	of
JAMES PRENTICE,	Cambridge.	DAVID FISKE,	Cam-
		SAMUEL STONE,	bridge."
		JONATHAN REMINGTON.	

What seems probable by the reference to Jan. 11, 1687–8, in
the foregoing agreement, is rendered certain by two documents,
which Mr. Jackson probably never saw, but which are yet in
existence.   One is an order of notice, preserved in the Massachusetts Archives, cxxviii. 7 : " To the Constables of the town
of Cambridge, or either of them.   You are hereby required to
give notice to the inhabitants of the said town, that they or some
of them be and appear before his Excellency in Council on
Wednesday next, being the 11th of this instant, to show cause
why Cambridge Village may not be declared a place distinct by
itself, and not longer be a part of the said town, as hath been
formerly petitioned for and now desired: and thereof to make
due return.   Dated at Boston the sixth day of January in the
third year of his Majesty's reign, annoque Domini, 1687.   By
order, &c., J. WEST, D. Sec'."   What was the result of this
process does not appear on record ; for the records of the Council
during the administration of Andros were carried away, and no
copy of the portion embracing this date has been obtained.   For-
tunately, however, a certified copy of the order, which is equiv-

alent to an act of incorporation, is on file in the office of the clerk of the Judicial Courts in Middlesex County : —

"At a Council held at the Council Chamber in Boston on Wednesday the eleventh day of January, 1687 ; Present,

"His Exc". S". Edmund Andros, Kt., &c.

"William Stoughton,
Robert Mason,
Peter Buckley,
Wait Winthrop,
} Esqs.

John Usher,
Edward Randolph,
Francis Nicholson,
} Esqs.

"Upon reading this day in Council the petition of the inhabitants of Cambridge Village in the County of Middlesex, being sixty families or upwards, that they may be a village and place distinct of themselves and freed from the town of Cambridge to which at the first settlement they were annexed; they being in every respect capable thereof, and by the late authority made distinct in all things saving paying towards their school and other town charges, for which they are still rated as a part of that town; and also the answer of the town of Cambridge thereto; and hearing what could be alleged on either part, and mature consideration had thereupon; those who appeared on the behalf of the town of Cambridge being contented that the said Village be wholly separated from them as desired, and praying that they may be ordered to contribute towards the maintenance of Cambridge Bridge, and that other provision be made as formerly usual to ease the town therein: — Ordered, that the said village from henceforth be and is hereby declared a distinct village and place of itself, wholly freed and separated from the town of Cambridge, and from all future rates, payments, or duties to them whatsoever. And that, for the time to come, the charge of keeping, amending, and repairing the said bridge, called Cambridge Bridge, shall be defrayed and borne as followeth (that is to say), two sixth parts thereof by the town of Cambridge, one sixth part by the said Village, and three sixth parts at the public charge of the County of Middlesex.

"By order in Council, &c.   JOHN WEST, D". Sec".

"This is a true copy, taken out of the original, 4th day of Decem. 88.

"As attests,   LAUR. HAMMOND, Cler."

There remains no reasonable doubt, that "Newtown," which received its name December, 1691, was "separated from the town of Cambridge," and was declared to be " a distinct village and place of itself," or, in other words, was incorporated as a town, by the order passed Jan. 11, 1687, old style, or Jan. 11, 1688, according to the present style of reckoning.[1]

A few matters of less public nature, belonging to this period, should not be entirely overlooked. I quote from the Town Records.

Dec. 14, 1657. " Liberty is granted unto Mr. Stedman, Mr. Angier, &c., the owners of the Ketch Triall, to fell some timber on the common for a ware-house."

Nov. 14, 1670. " Granted to the owners of the Ketches that are to [be] builded in the town liberty to fell timber upon the common for the building of the said Ketches."

By the County Court Records, it appears that in April, 1672, Daniel Gookin, Walter Hastings, and Samuel Champney, recovered ten pounds damage and costs of court, against William Carr for the unworkmanlike finishing of two ketches, or vessels, of thirty-five tons and twenty-eight tons. Among the papers in this case, remaining on file, is a deposition, to wit : " John Jackson, aged about 25 years, testifieth that, being hired to work upon the two vessels (whereof William Carr was master-builder) in Cambridge, I wrought upon the said vessels about four months in the winter 1670," etc. Sworn April 2, 1672. These were probably the vessels mentioned in the Town Order, Nov. 14, 1670. They were small in size ; but it appears from Randolph's narrative,[2] written in 1676, that more than two thirds of all the vessels then owned in Massachusetts ranged from six tons to fifty tons.

Feb. 18, 1658. The Town voted, " That the Great Swamp lying within the bounds of this town, on the east side of Fresh Pond meadow and Winottomie Brook, shall be divided into particular allotments and propriety."

March 23, 1662-3. " Ordered, that if any man be convicted that his dog is used to pull off the tails of any beasts, and do not

---

[1] The orders in council are dated Jan. 1687; but that this was in the Old Style, calling March 25th the first day of the year, and thus equivalent to Jan. 1688, commencing the year, as we now do with the first day of January, is certain, because (1) according to the present style, Wednesday was not the eleventh day of January in 1687, but it was in 1688 ; and (2) King Charles II., died Feb. 6, 1684-5, and consequently the third year of the reign of James II. did not commence until Feb. 6, 1686-7, and the only January in that "third year" was in 1687-8, that is, in 1688, by the present style of reckoning.

[2] Hutchinson's *Coll. Papers*, 496.

effectually restrain him, he shall pay for every offence of that kind twenty shillings, in case that further complaint be made."

Feb. 13, 1664–5. "The Constables are ordered to allow Justinian Holden ten shillings towards a wolf, killed partly in Watertowne and partly in this."

May 8, 1671. "Granted to William Barrit and Nathaniell Hancock, to dig a sluice, to drain the pond by their houses, in the town's land, provided they secure it from doing damage as soon as may be: and in case the Townsmen see reason for it, they are to stop it up again." This pond was on the easterly side of Dunster Street, about midway between Mount Auburn and Harvard Streets.

May 29, 1671. A committee was appointed "to make a covenant with Phillip Jones, or any other able person, to make a sufficient fence of stone of four foot high, — between Watertowne bounds and ours," as far as to Rocky Meadow; with gates to the highways from Concord to Watertown and from Cambridge to Watertown.

Feb. 14, 1675–6. "William Maning, and Nathaniell Hancocke, and John Jackson, and John Gove, are appointed by the Selectmen, to have inspection into families, that there be no bye drinking, or any misdemeanour, whereby sin is committed, and persons from their houses unseasonably."

"The selectmen of Cambridge plaintiffs against Capt. Lawrence Hammond and John Cutler, jun., defendants, do humbly declare as followeth, &c. In the year 1634 the General Court granted them liberty to erect a ware upon Minottomy River, and they accordingly so did, and have had quiet possession of the same from that time until now, without any disturbance of their neighbors of Charlestown or any other; and hath been in a manner the stay and support of the town by fishing their Indian corn, which is the principal part of their husbandry and livelihood. But this last spring the defendants, to the great damage of the plaintiffs, have interrupted their fishing by crossing said River below the wares granted to Cambridge by the Court, whereby the grant of the Court is made null and void, and they are put out of the possession of that which they have peaceably enjoyed forty-six years, contrary to law and equity. And after that the plaintiffs had obtained a writ of nuisance to bring the case to a legal trial, the defendants have both violently and contemptuously proceeded to obstruct the passage of the fish to the wares, which they so long possessed as above said, to their great damage

7

and loss of two hundred thousand fish, which we judge will be a hundred pounds damage to the town in their crop, and tending to the inevitable impoverishing of divers poor families. The justice of this honored Court for their relief from this great wrong done them by the defendants is the favor they beg.

" JOHN COOPER.
WILLIAM MANNING.
WALTER HASTING.
FFR. MOORE."

The jury rendered a special verdict : " If the General Court's grant to Cambridge — for the erecting a ware in Menottimyes River, within their own bounds, be a legal and perpetual title, they find for the plaintiffs five pounds and costs of Court; if not, for the defendants, costs of court." The Court considered the title good. This case is entered in the County Court Records, under date of June 21, 1681, and the papers are on file. The practice of "fishing their Indian corn" was long ago abandoned by cultivators in Cambridge; but the privilege of taking fish in Menotomy River remains valuable. It has been subject to occasional controversies and litigations since 1681, in all which Cambridge has preserved the rights originally granted; and to the present day " Fish Officers " are annually appointed by the City Council, to take care that those rights suffer no infringement.

CHAPTER IX.

CIVIL HISTORY.

On the 17th day of May, 1686, Joseph Dudley and his associates communicated to the General Court a copy of the King's commission authorizing them to assume the government of the Colony. The Court replied, under date of May 20, 1686, addressed, "These for Joseph Dudley, Esq. and the rest of the gentlemen named in his Majesties commission," as follows:—[1]

"Gent": We have perused what you left with us as a true coppy of his majesties commission, shewed to us the 17th instant, impowring you for the governing of his majesties subjects inhabitting this colony and other places therein mentioned. You then applied yourselves to us, not as a Governor and Company, but (as you were pleased to terme us) some of the principall gentlemen and cheife of the inhabitants of the severall townes of the Massachusetts, amongst other discourse saying it concerned us to consider what there might be thought hard and uneasy. 1. Upon perusall whereof wce finde, as wee conceive, first, that there is no certaine determinate rule for your administration of justice, and that which is seemes to be too arbitrary. 2. That the subjects are abridged of their liberty as Englishmen, both in the matter of legislation and in the laying of taxes, and indeed the whole unquæstioned priviledge of the subject transferred upon yourselves, there being not the least mention of an assembly in the commission. And therefore wee thinke it highly concernes you to consider whither such a commission be safe, either for you or us: but if you are so satisfied therein as that you hold yourselves obleidged thereby, and do take upon you the government of this people, although wee cannot give our assent thereto, yet hope shall demeane ourselves as true and loyall subjects to his Majesty, and humbly make our addresses unto God, and, in due time, to our gracious prince, for our releife. Past by the whole Court, nemine contradicentes. By order,

"Edward Rawson, Secretary."

[1] *Mass. Col. Rec.*, v. 515, 516.

Dudley was superseded in the government by Sir Edmund
Andros, who "landed at Boston Dec. 20, 1686, and his commission was published the same day."[1]   During his administration,
the people were in a condition little better than slavery.   In the
"Massachusetts Archives"[2] is a statement by Thomas Danforth,
that, "Our rulers are those that hate us and the churches of
Christ and his servants in the ministry; they are their daily
scorn, taunt, and reproach; and yet are we, our lives, and liberties, civil and ecclesiastical, in their hands, to do with us as they
please; some of the chief of them have said, — no better than
slaves, only they had not power to sell us for slaves.   We are
deprived of privileges of Englishmen, of the benefit of the great
Charter of our nation; our lands and possessions seized and
granted to strangers, contrary to the Stat. Car. I. Cap. 10, and
contrary to the assurance given to his Majesty's subjects here,
by the declaration of his late Majesty and of his present Majesty,
copies whereof I herewith send you."

A tract was published at London, in 1689, entitled "A Sixth
Collection of Papers relating to the present juncture of affairs in
England."   The tenth and last paper in the collection is "'A
narrative of the miseries of New England, by reason of an Arbitrary Government erected there."   It was evidently prepared
by a person well acquainted with the facts, perhaps by Increase
Mather, who was at that time in London.   The case is so well
stated that I shall quote freely: —

"Before these changes happened, New England was of all the
foreign plantations (their enemies themselves being judges) the
most flourishing and desirable.   But their Charters being all (one
way or other) declared to be void and insignificant, it was an easy
matter to erect a French Government in that part of the King's
dominions, (no doubt intended by the evil counsellors) as a specimen of what was designed to be here in England as soon as the
times would bear it.   Accordingly Sir Edmond Andross (a
Gernsey man) was pitched on as a fit instrument to be made use
of; and a most illegal commission given him, bearing date June
3, 1686, by which he, with four of his Council (perhaps all of
them his absolute devotees) are empowered to make laws, and
raise moneys on the King's subjects without any Parliament,
Assembly, or consent of the people. . . . . Laws are made by a
few of them, and indeed what they please: nor are they printed,
as was the custom in the former governments, so that the people

¹ Hutchinson's *Hist. Mass.*, i. 358.   ² *Mass. Arch.*, cxxviii. 142, 148.

pologies.

are at a great loss to know what is law, and what not. Only one law they are sensible of, which doth prohibit all Town-meetings, excepting on a certain day once a year: whereas the inhabitants have occasion to meet once a month, sometimes every week, for relief of the poor, or other Town-affairs. But it is easy to penetrate into the design of this law, which was (no question) to keep them in every town from complaining to England of the oppression they are under. And as laws have been established so moneys have been raised by the government in a most illegal and arbitrary way, without any consent of the people."[1] "Several gentlemen in the country were imprisoned and bound to their good behavior, upon mere suspicion that they did encourage their neighbors not to comply with these arbitrary proceedings, and that so they might be sure to effect their pernicious designs, they have caused juries to be picked of men who are not of the vicinity, and some of them mere strangers in the country and no freeholders, which actings are highly illegal. One of the former magistrates was committed to prison without any crimes laid to his charge, and there kept half a year without any fault; and though he petitioned for a Habeas Corpus, it was denied him. Also inferior officers have extorted what fees they please to demand, contrary to all rules of reason and justice. They make poor widows and fatherless pay 50s. for the probate of a will, which under the former easy government would not have been a tenth part so much. Six persons, who had been illegally imprisoned, were forced to give the officers 117l., whereas upon computation they found that here in England their fees would not have amounted to 10l. in all. And yet these things (though bad enough) are but a very small part of the misery which that poor people have been groaning under, since they have been governed by a despotic and absolute power. For their new masters tell them that, their Charter being gone, their title to their lands and estates is gone therewith, and that all is the King's; and that they represent the King; and that therefore all persons must take patents from them, and give what they see meet to impose, that so they may enjoy the houses which their own hands have built, and the lands which, at vast charges in subduing a wilderness, they have for many years had a rightful possession of as ever any people in the world had or can have."[2] "These were the miserable effects of New England's being deprived of their Charters,

[1] The case of Ipswich is related. [2] Seizures of land in Charlestown and Plymouth are specified.

and with them of their English liberties. They have not been altogether negligent, as to endeavors to obtain some relief in their sorrowful bondage; for several gentlemen desired Increase Mather, the Rector of the College at Cambridge in New England, to undertake a voyage for England, to see what might be done for his distressed country, which motion he complied with; and in June the 1st, 1688, he had the favor to wait on the King, and privately to acquaint him with the enslaved and perishing estate of his subjects in New England. The King was very gracious and kind in his expressions; then and often after promising to give them ease as to their complaints and fears. Amongst other things the said Mather caused a petition from the town of Cambridge in New England to be humbly presented to his Majesty; which, because it doth express the deplorable condition of that people, it shall be here inserted.

" To the King's most excellent Majesty.

" The petition and address of John Gibson, aged about 87, and George Willow, aged about 86 years; as also on behalf of their neighbors the inhabitants of Cambridge in New England, in most humble wise sheweth :

" That your Majesty's good subjects, with much hard labor and great disbursements, have subdued a wilderness, built our houses, and planted orchards, being encouraged by our indubitable right to the soil by the Royal Charter granted unto the first planters, together with our purchase of the Natives : as also by sundry letters and declarations sent to the late Governor and Company from his late Majesty, your royal Brother, assuring us of the full enjoyment of our properties and possessions, as is more especially contained in the declaration sent when the Quo Warranto was issued out against our Charter.

" But we are necessitated to make this our moan and complaint to your excellent Majesty, for that our title is now questioned to our lands, by us quietly possessed for near sixty years, and without which we cannot subsist. Our humble address to our governor, Sir Edmond Andross, shewing our just title, long and peaceable possession, together with our claim of the benefit of your Majesty's letters and declarations, assuring all your good subjects that they shall not be molested in their properties and possessions, not availing.

" Royal Sir, we are a poor people, and have no way to procure money to defend our cause in the law; nor know we of friends at Court; and therefore unto your royal Majesty, as the public Father of all your subjects, do we make this our humble address for relief, beseeching your Majesty graciously to pass your royal Act for the confirmation of your Majesty's subjects here in our possessions to us derived from our late Governor and Company of this your Majesty's Colony. We now humbly cast ourselves and distressed condition of our wives and children at your Majesty's feet, and conclude with the saying of Queen Esther, — If we perish, we perish."

In the Massachusetts Archives [1] is a manuscript by Thomas Danforth, so nearly identical with this petition that it may properly be regarded as its first draught. It is highly probable that Danforth prepared it, and sent it to Mather, who made a few verbal alterations before presenting it to the king. It seems to have been written in 1688, while Randolph was endeavoring to obtain possession of seven hundred acres of land near Spy Pond. This was one of his many attempts, of a similar kind, to enrich himself at the public expense. Besides asking for free grants in divers other places, he " petitioned for half an acre of land, to be taken out of the common in Boston, for a house lot." [2] Several documents relating to the Cambridge case are here inserted, as a specimen of the wrongs and indignities to which the inhabitants were subjected under the arbitrary government of Sir Edmund Andros. Other communities suffered like evils; and other persons were only less rapacious than Edward Randolph.

" At a Council held at the Council Chamber in Boston on Wednesday the nine and twentieth of February, 1687. Present,
" His Excellency Sir Edmund Andros, Knt., &c.

" Joseph Dudley,		John Green,	
John Winthrop,	Esqrs.	Edward Randolph,	Esqrs.
Wait Winthrop,		ffrancis Nicholson,	
John Usher,		Samuell Shrimpton,	

" Upon reading this day in Council the petition of Edward Randolph Esq., praying his Majesty's grant of a certain tract of vacant and unappropriated land, containing about seven hundred acres, lying between Spy Pond and Saunders Brook, near Watertown in the County of Middlesex, — Ordered, That the Sheriff of said County do forthwith after receipt hereof, give public notice both in Cambridge and Watertown, that if any person or persons have any claim or pretence to the said land, that they appear before his Excellency the Governor in Council, on

---

[1] Mass. Arch., cxxviii. 300.   [2] Hutchinson's Hist. Mass., i. 360.

Wednesday the 7th of March next, then and there to show forth the same, and why the said land may not be granted to the petitioner as desired; of which he is not to fail, and to make due return. By order in Council, &c.

" JOHN WEST. D. Sec[y]."

" Per virtue of this order, notice is given to the persons concerned. 5 March 87–8, pr. Sam[u]. Gookin Shff." [1]

" March 4, 1687–8. Mem°. This warrant was sent up from Boston to Cambridge on the Sabbath day morning by a boat, which was an unusual thing in that place to see the Sabbath day so profaned and a warrant posted on the meeting house to give notice." [2]

At the time appointed, the inhabitants of Cambridge asserted their claims, to wit : —

" To his Excellency Sir Edmund Andros, Knt., Captain General and Governor in chief of his Majesty's territory and dominion of New England, and his Majesty's Council. The petition and address of his Majesty's most loyal subjects, the inhabitants of Cambridge, in most humble wise showeth:

" In observance of the Council's order sent unto us referring unto those lands petitioned for by Edward Randolph, Esq., — we humbly inform and certify your Excellency and the Council, that they are neither vacant nor unappropriated lands, but are a part of those lands granted by his Majesty's royal Charter, under the great seal of England, to the persons therein mentioned, and by the Governor and Company of the Massachusetts Bay to this town of Cambridge, as the Records of the General Court will show, and have been quietly possessed and improved by this town of Cambridge for more than fifty years; and was also purchased of the Indian Natives that claimed title thereto. And more particularly as to those mentioned by the petitioner situate and lying between Spy Pond and Sanders Brook, they were by allotment granted and measured out, more than forty years now past, to sundry of the inhabitants of this town; and they have accordingly peaceably possessed and improved the same, and are at this day lawfully seized thereof. And for that other part, lying near to Watertown line, the town hath hitherto improved those lands in common, for timber, firewood, and pasture for all

---

[1] *Mass. Arch.*, cxxviii. 56.
[2] *Ibid.*, p. 68. This memorandum, endorsed on a copy of the order of notice, is in the handwriting of Thomas Danforth.

sorts of cattle, the just interests of each person therein having been legally settled more than forty years; and the proprietors have accordingly respectively bought and sold their interests, as they have seen meet; and for the securing said lands from damage to ourselves by our neighbors of Watertown, the proprietors of the said lands have, at their great charge, erected a stone wall, more than one mile in length, and made provision of gates upon the highways as was needful.

"We do also humbly inform your Excellency and Council, that the lands above petitioned for are of so great concernment to the inhabitants of this town for their necessary supplies of timber, firewood, and pasture, that, should we be deprived thereof, it would be the inevitable ruin of more than eighty families of his Majesty's subjects here settled, who have spent their strength and estates in confidence of their indubitable right and peaceable enjoyment thereof, by virtue of his Majesty's royal Charter, and to them legally derived in manner as is above recited.

"We do therefore humbly render to your Excellency and honorable Council our humble and thankful acknowledgement of your respect to our welfare (as well as to justice and equity) in giving us this opportunity to inform your Excellency and Honors of our claim and just title to those lands petitioned for, as above said, and do humbly pray that the royal authority wherewith his Majesty have invested your Excellency for the government of this part of his dominion may put a check upon the abovesaid information and unreasonable request of the petitioner for said lands, and that your petitioners may not be thence illegally ejected or disturbed in their peaceable enjoyment thereof, contrary to his late Majesty's declaration of the 26 July 1683, published upon the issuing a Quo Warranto against the late charter of this Colony, and to his present Majesty's gracious declaration to all his loving subjects for liberty of conscience and maintaining them in all their properties and possessions in any their lands and properties whatsoever; the benefit whereof we humbly claim.

"Your petitioners are his Majesty's most loyal subjects and your Excellency's humble servants, in the name and by the order of the inhabitants of Cambridge. JOHN COOPER,
WALTER HASTING,
FFRANCIS MOORE,
JOHN JACKSON,
SAMUELL ANDREW."[1]

[1] *Mass. Arch.*, cxxviii. 397.

In his rejoinder, Randolph gives an abstract of his petition and the order thereon, together with the objections urged by the inhabitants of Cambridge, and then proceeds thus:—

"To which the Petitioner answereth, that, in case the inhabitants of Cambridge do produce to your Excellency and the Council the royal grant to any person or persons of the said land petitioned for, and from such person or persons a legal conveyance to the inhabitants of the said town, and that the said town were by that name, or by what other name the same hath been to them granted, able and sufficient in the law to receive a grant of such lands, then the petitioner will cease any further prosecution of his said prayer: otherwise the petitioner humbly conceives the right still to remain in his Majesty, and humbly prays a grant for the same. ED. RANDOLPH. Boston March ye 17th 1687-8."[1]

Subsequently, another order of notice was issued:—

"Boston 22^d June 1688. Mr. Sheriff, You may give notice to any persons that lay claim to the land in Cambridge petitioned for by Edward Randolph Esq., that on Thursday next, in the forenoon, they appear before his Excellency in Council, and give their full answer therein. I am, sir, your servant,

                 JOHN WEST, D. Sec."

Superscribed, "To Samuell Gookin Esq. High Sheriff of Middlesex, at Cambridge."[2]

At the time appointed, the proprietors of the lands in controversy presented their case more fully:—

"The Reply of the proprietors of those lands lying between Sanders Brook and Spy Pond near unto Watertown, in the County of Middlesex, to an answer made to their address presented to your Excellency and the honorable Council, referring to the petition of Edward Randolph Esq., he praying a grant of seven hundred acres, part of the abovesaid tract of land, as vacant and unappropriated.

"Your humble suppliants do crave leave to remind your Excellency and the honorable Council, that, in our former address, we have briefly declared and asserted our just title and claim to said lands, deriving the same from his Majesty's royal grant by his letters patent under the great seal, under the security whereof the first planters of this Colony adventured themselves into this then waste and desolate wilderness, and have here wasted and

---

[1] *Mass. Arch.*, cxxviii. 111, 112.   [2] *Ibid.*, p. 281.

spent great estates and many lives, for the planting, peopling, and defending themselves and his Majesty's right therein. The abovesaid royal grant being made not enly to the gentlemen named in said letters patent, but also to all such others as they shall admit and make free of their society, making them one body politic by the name of the Governor and Company of the Massachusetts Bay in New England, and under that name are empowered to make laws and ordinances for the good and welfare of said company and for the government and ordering of the said lands and plantation, and the people that shall inhabit therein, as to them shall seem meet. We further declared that, by the said Governor and Company, the lands petitioned for by Edward Randolph Esq. are granted to Cambridge, then called Newtown, and by the said town have been orderly distributed among their inhabitants, the grants and settlement whereof upon the several proprietors and their names as they stand entered upon the Town Book we do hereby exhibit to your Excellency and the Council. If further evidence be required of the same, or of our possession and improvement thereof, plainly evincing that those lands are neither vacant nor unappropriated, as the petitioner' hath most untruly represented, we are ready to present the same, if your Excellency shall please to appoint us a time for so doing.

"Your Excellency have not required of us to show or demonstrate that the formalities of the law have been, in all the circumstances thereof, exactly observed, nor do we judge it can rationally be expected of a people circumstanced as the first planters were, by whom those matters were acted in the infancy of these plantations; they not having council in the law to repair unto, nor would the emergencies that then inevitably happened admit thereof; and, as we humbly conceive, nor doth the law of England require the same of a people so circumstanced as they then were. But from the beginning of this plantation [they] have approved themselves loyal to his Majesty, and in all respects have intended the true ends of his Majesty's royal grant, and, through God's great blessing on their endeavors, raised here a plantation that redounds greatly (as is now well known in the world) to the honor and profit of the crown. And his late Majesty, by his letters sent to the Governor and Company, accordingly declared his royal acceptance thereof, with promise of protection in our long and orderly settlement of this Colony, as his Majesty was graciously pleased to term the same:

the further security whereof, given us by the declaration of his late Majesty, when the Quo Warranto was issued forth against this Colony, as also by his present Majesty in his declaration, as in our address so we do hereby again humbly claim. If any thing be yet behind on our part, necessary for the evincing our claim, we humbly pray that we may be informed what those things are, and time given us to bring in our further answer to your Excellency and the Council. In the name and by the order of the proprietors, together with ourselves of those lands petitioned for by Edward Randolph Esq.

" Sam^{ll}. Andrew.

Walter Hasting.

Zachariah Hicks.

John Gove."[1]

On the same day, June 28, 1688, the Council passed the following order : —

" Upon further hearing of the petition of Edward Randolph Esq., praying his Majesty's grant for a certain parcel or tract of vacant and unappropriated land, containing about seven hundred acres, lying between Spy Pond and Sanders Brook near Watertown in the County of Middlesex, as also a certain writing presented by Samuell Andrews and others of Cambridge, termed the reply of the proprietors of the lands lying between Saunders Brook and Spy Pond to an answer made to their address : but they declaring they had no authority to speak in behalf of others but only for themselves [2] and by reason of the general description of the land petitioned for not knowing whether the lands claimed by them be within the quantity desired or not : It is ordered, that a survey and draught be forthwith made of the said land and returned into the Secretary's office accordingly.

" By order of Council, &c.,   John West, D. Sec." [3]

Nothing further is found in the Archives concerning this transaction, and the Records of the Council are not accessible. A the title to the lands in controversy was not afterwards disputed it seems probable that the act of robbery was not consummated or, if it was, such arbitrary proceedings were held to be utterl void, after the Revolution which soon followed.[4]

1 *Mass. Arch.*, cxxviii. 115, 116.   3 *Mass. Arch.*, cxxix. 3.

2 They could not speak by the authority   4 About two years before this Revol of the town, because the town was pro-   tion, Cambridge lost one of her mo hibited from holding meetings, except   eminent citizens, Maj.-gen. Daniel Go once in each year for the choice of officers.   kin, more familiarly known as Maj

Early in 1689, much excitement was produced by a rumor that the Prince of Orange had landed in England, with an armed force, and that a Revolution in the English Government was probable. This rumor took a more definite form, April 4, when " one Mr. Winslow came from Virginia and brought a printed copy of the Prince of Orange's declaration. Upon his arrival, he was imprisoned by Justice Foxcroft and others, for bringing a traitorous and treasonable libel into the country, as the mittimus expressed it. Winslow offered two thousand pounds bail, but it could not be accepted. A proclamation was issued, charging all officers and people to be in readiness to hinder the landing of any forces which the Prince of Orange might send into those parts of the world. The old magistrates and heads of the people silently wished, and secretly prayed, for success to the glorious undertaking, and determined quietly to wait the event. The body of the people were more impatient. The flame, which had been long smothered in their breasts, burst forth with violence Thursday, the 18th day of April, when the Governor and such of the Council as had been most active, and other obnoxious persons, about fifty in the whole, were seized and confined, and the old magistrates were reinstated." [1] Several accounts of this Revolution appeared within a few months after it occurred, in which there is a substantial agreement in regard to the most important circumstances. Among others, a pamphlet of twenty pages, written by Judge Nathaniel Byfield, was published at London in 1689, entitled " An account of the late Revolution in New England, together with the Declaration of the Gentlemen, Merchants, and Inhabitants, of Boston, and the country adjacent, April 18, 1689." He describes the outbreak thus : " Upon the eighteenth instant, about eight of the clock in the morning, it was reported at the south end of the town that at the north end they were all

Gookin. Sad and disheartened at the loss of the Old Charter, yet cheered by the consciousness that he had faithfully and earnestly labored for its preservation, he survived the catastrophe not quite a year. He found rest from his labors and deliverance from oppression, March 19, 1686–7, at the ripe age of 75 years; and a large horizontal slab marks the spot of his sepulture in the old burial-place. In his will, dated Aug. 13, 1685, he says, — " I desire no ostentation or much cost to be expended at my funeral, because it is a time of great tribulation, and my estate but little and weak." Hence it has been supposed that he was quite poor. On the contrary, while he was not rich, the number of houses, and the quantity of silver plate and other goods bequeathed by him, in his will, denote that his estate was at least equal to the average at that period. His character is described very tersely by Judge Sewall, in his Journal : "March 19, Satterday, about 5 or 6 in the morn, Major Daniel Gookin dies. A right good man."

[1] Hutchinson's Hist. Mass., i. 373.

in arms; and the like report was at the north end respecting the south end: whereupon Capt. John George[1] was immediately seized, and about nine of the clock the drums beat through the town, and an ensign was set up upon the beacon. Then Mr. Bradstreet, Mr. Danforth, Major Richards, Dr. Cooke, and Mr. Addington, &c., were brought to the Council-house by a company of soldiers under the command of Capt. Hill. The mean while, the people in arms did take up and put into goal Justice Bullivant, Justice Foxcraft, Mr. Randolf, Sheriff Sherlock, Capt. Ravenscroft, Capt. White, Farewel, Broadbent, Crafford, Larkin, Smith, and many more, as also Mercey, then goal-keeper, and put Scates, the bricklayer, in his place. About noon, in the gallery at the Council-house, was read the Declaration here inclosed," etc.[2] Under eleven heads, this Declaration sets forth the grievances which had become intolerable, and which justified armed resistance. It is scarcely possible that a document of such length and character could have been prepared in the four hours of intense excitement and confusion, between eight o'clock and noon. In all probability, it had been previously written in anticipation of some such occasion for its use. The twelfth article in this Declaration announces the conclusion: "We do therefore seize upon the persons of those few ill men, which have been (next to our sins) the grand authors of our miseries; resolving to secure them for what justice, orders from his Highness, with the English Parliament, shall direct; lest, ere we are aware, we find (what we may fear, being on all sides in danger) ourselves to be by them given away to a foreign Power, before such orders can reach unto us: for which orders we now humbly wait. In the mean time, firmly believing that we have endeavored nothing but what mere duty to God and our country calls for at our hands, we commit our enterprise unto the blessing of him who hears the cry of the oppressed, and advise all our neighbors, for whom we have thus ventured ourselves, to join with us in prayers and all just actions for the defence of the land."[3] As a fitting result of this Declaration, Judge Byfield inserts the summons sent by the magistrates and others to Sir Edmond Andros, who had retired to the fortification on Fort Hill: —

"At the Town House in Boston, April 18, 1689. Sir, Ourselves and many others, the inhabitants of this town and the places adjacent, being surprised with the people's sudden taking

---

[1] Captain of the Frigate *Rose*, then at anchor in Boston harbor.

[2] *Revolution*, etc., pp. 3, 4.

[3] *Ibid.*, p. 19.

of arms, in the first motions whereof we were wholly ignorant, being driven by the present accident, are necessitated to acquaint your Excellency that for the quieting and securing of the people inhabiting this country from the imminent dangers they many ways lie open and exposed to, and tendering your own safety, we judge it necessary you forthwith surrender and deliver up the government and fortification, to be preserved and disposed according to order and direction from the Crown of England, which suddenly is expected may arrive; promising all security from violence to yourself or any of your gentlemen or soldiers, in person and estate; otherwise we are assured they will endeavor the taking of the fortification by storm, if any opposition be made.

"To Sir Edmond Andross, Knight.

"WAIT WINTHROP. ELISHA COOK.
SIMON BRADSTREET. ISAAC ADDINGTON.
WILLIAM STOUGHTON. JOHN NELSON.
SAMUEL SHRIMPTON. ADAM WINTHROP.
BARTHOLOMEW GIDNEY. PETER SERGEANT.
WILLIAM BROWN. JOHN FOSTER.
THOMAS DANFORTH. DAVID WATERHOUSE." [1]
JOHN RICHARDS.

Unable to resist the force arrayed against him, the Governor obeyed this summons, surrendered the fort, and with his associates went to the town-house, whence he was sent under guard to the house of Col. John Usher, who had been Treasurer under his administration, but, like Stoughton and other members of his Council,[2] united with the patriotic party in this revolutionary movement. But this kind of duress did not satisfy the people; and on the following day, at their urgent demand, he was imprisoned in the fort. Some of his associates shared his confinement, while others were committed to close jail. The day after the Governor was thus securely confined, some of the old magistrates, together with several other persons who had been active in overturning the former government, organized a "Council for the Safety of the People and Conservation of the Peace," of which the old Governor, Bradstreet, was elected President and Isaac Addington, Clerk. The authority of this Council needed the support of a body more directly representing the people. "On the second of May, they recommended to the several towns in the

[1] *Revolution*, etc., p. 20. Gedney), and Brown, had been members
[2] Winthrop, Shrimpton, Gidney (or of the Council.

colony to meet and depute persons, not exceeding two for each town, except Boston four, to form an assembly, to sit the ninth of the same month. Sixty-six persons met and presented a declaration to the president and former magistrates in particular, taking no notice of such as had associated with them, but upon receiving an answer in writing, they desired the whole council to continue in their station until the twenty-second instant, at which time it was agreed there should be a meeting of the representatives of all the towns in the colony, at Boston, who were to be specially instructed by their towns." [1] A large majority of the towns instructed their representatives to vote in favor of reassuming the old Charter. The magistrates hesitated to adopt such a decisive measure; but at length, when a new House of Representatives, which assembled on the fifth of June, " urged the council to take upon them the part they ought to bear in the government, according to the charter, until orders should be received from England, and declared ' they could not proceed to act in any thing of public concerns until this was conceded,' an acceptance was voted, this declaration being given as the reason of the vote. By these steps the change was made from the unlimited power of Sir Edmund and four of his council, to the old government, which had continued above fifty years; but the weight and authority did not return with the form." [2] This form of government, by consent of the King, was administered about three years, until Sir William Phips arrived, in 1692, with the new Charter.

In this change of government, the inhabitants of Cambridge were actively engaged, and took their full share of the responsibility. Their delegate to the Convention which assembled on the ninth of May, presented the following declaration : [3] —

" Cambridge, May 6, 1689. We, the freeholders and inhabitants of the town of Cambridge, being very sensible of and thankful unto God for his mercy in our late deliverance from the oppression and tyranny of those persons under whose injustice and cruelty we have so long groaned; and withal desirous heartily to express our gratitude to those worthy gentlemen who have been engaged in conserving of our peace since the Revolution; yet withal being apprehensive that the present unsettlement may expose us to many hazards and dangers, and may give occasion to ill-minded persons to make disturbance : — do declare that we expect that our honored Governor, Deputy Governor, and assis-

---

[1] Hutchinson's *Hist. Mass.*, i. 382, 383.   [3] *Mass. Arch.*, cvii. 20.
[2] *Ibid.*, pp. 387, 388.

tants, elected by the freemen of this Colony, in May, 1686, together with the Deputies then sent down by the several respective towns to the Court then holden, which was never legally
dissolved, shall convene, and re-assume and exercise the Government as a General Court, according to our Charter, on the ninth
of this instant May, or as soon as possible. And in so doing,
we do engage that, to the utmost of our power, with persons and
estates, we will contribute to their help and assistance, as in duty
and equity we are bound, praying that God would direct them
in this difficult juncture; and do hope that all that are concerned for the peace and good of this land will readily join with
us herein.

"Memorandum. It is here to be understood that what we
expect to be done, as above, is only for a present settlement
until we may have an opportunity to make our address unto,
or shall be otherwise settled by, the supreme power in England.

"These lines above written, as they are worded, was agreed
upon by the inhabitants of the town of Cambridge, this 6th of
May, 1689, as attests Samuel Andrew, Clerk, in the name of the
town."

This revolutionary movement was full of danger. It was not
yet known here whether the Prince of Orange would be successful in his attempt to dethrone King James the Second. If he
should fail, those who had resisted and imprisoned the king's
Governor might well expect the direst vengeance. But this peril
did not prevent the inhabitants of Cambridge from pledging
their "persons and estates" to the support of the principal actors; nor did it prevent their favorite and trusted leader, Thomas
Danforth, from taking a conspicuous position in the front rank
of those actors. The venerable Bradstreet, indeed, was made
President of the Council of Safety, and reinstated as Governor,
when it was decided to organize the government according to
the old Charter; but he was now eighty-seven years of age,
and however desirable and important it may have been to connect his name and his presence with the enterprise, he was
incapable of energetic action. Moreover, he was timid and yielding in disposition, and counselled submission rather than resistance during the controversy which preceded the abrogation of
the Charter. On the contrary, Danforth had been recognized as
a skilful and resolute leader through the former struggle; and
now, at the age of sixty-seven, he retained the full possession of

his faculties, and bated not one jot in his hatred of tyranny. He was reinstated as Deputy-governor,[1] ostensibly the second office, but, under the circumstances, the chief position of labor and responsibility. What Palfrey says of their respective capacity, when originally elected Governor and Deputy-governor in 1679, had become even more manifestly true at this later period: — Bradstreet "can scarcely be pronounced to have been equal, either in ability of mind or in force of character, to the task of steering the straining vessel of state in those stormy times. More than any other man then living in Massachusetts, Thomas Danforth was competent to the stern occasion."[2] Danforth did not hesitate to act, though fully conscious that his head was in danger, if King James succeeded in retaining the throne, — the more because he had so long been the leader in opposition to arbitrary authority, — and, even if the Prince of Orange became King, that this seizure of the government, in opposition to the constituted authority, might be regarded and punished as an act of treasonable rebellion.[3] Yet he took the prominent position assigned to him, and manfully performed its duties for the space of three years, until Sir William Phips became Governor under the new Charter in 1692. For some reason he was not one of the Councillors appointed under the new Charter; but his fellow citizens manifested their regard for him and their approbation of his long and faithful services, by placing him in the Council, at the first general election, 1693, and kept him there by successive elections as long as he lived. They could not reinstate him in his former position, nor promote him to a higher, because, under the new charter, both the Governor and Lieutenant-governor were appointed by

---

[1] Also, as President of Maine, June 28, 1693.

[2] *Hist. New Eng.*, ii. 332.

[3] In a letter to Governor Hinkley of Plymouth, dated April 20, two days after Sir Edmund Andros was deposed, he says, "I yet fear what the consequences thereof may be. I heartily pray that no bitter fruits may spring forth from this root. We have need of God's pity and pardon; and some do apprehend it will be wisdom to hasten our address to those that are now supreme in England for pardon of so great an irruption, and for a favorable settlement under the sanction of royal authority." — *Coll. Mass. Hist. Soc.*, xxxv. 192.

Three months later, writing to Rev. Increase Mather, then in London, he says: — "I am deeply sensible that we have a wolf by the ears. This one thing being circumstanced with much difficulty, — the people will not permit any enlargement, they having accused them of treason against their king and country; and those restrained, they threaten at a high rate for being denied a *habeas corpus.* I do therefore earnestly entreat of you to procure the best advice you can in this matter, that, if possible, the good intents of the people and their loyalty to the Crown of England may not turn to their prejudice." — Hutchinson's *Coll. Papers*, 568, 569.

the King. Before his election to the new Council, he had been appointed one of the judges of the Superior Court. His associate, Judge Sewall, in his Journal, thus refers to his appointment: "Tuesday Dec. 6, [1692.] A very dark cold day; is the day appointed for chusing of Judges. W^m. Stoughton Esq. is chosen Chief Justice, 15 votes (all then present): Tho. Danforth Esq., 12: Major Richards, 7: Major-Genl. Winthrop, 7: S. S.,[1] 7. . . . . This was in Col. Page's[2] rooms, by papers on Wednesday, Xr. 7th, 1692."[3] "Dec. 8, Mr. Danforth is invited to dinner, and after pressed to accept his place." This place, which he seems to have accepted with some hesitation, he retained through life, and presided in a court at Bristol, less than two months before his death.

It is due to the reputation of Danforth, to state emphatically, that he was not a member of the court which tried and condemned the unhappy persons accused of witchcraft. That special Court of Oyer and Terminer, appointed by Governor Phips and his Council, May 27, 1692, consisted of William Stoughton, John Richards, Nathanael Saltonstall, Wait Winthrop, Bartholomew Gedney, Samuel Sewall, John Hathorne, Jonathan Corwin, and Peter Sargeant;[4] and it completed its bloody work before the next December, when the Superior Court was organized, of which Danforth was a member. Notwithstanding he held no judicial office during this period (except that he was one of the first Justices of the Peace and Quorum), the name of Danforth has often been very improperly associated with the witchcraft tragedy. Even Savage, familiarly acquainted as he was with the history of that period, was so forgetful as to say that he was appointed "in 1692, judge of Sup. Court for the horrible proceedings against witches."[5] The only connection he had with those proceedings, so far as I have ascertained, is mentioned by Hutchinson.[6] Before the arrival of Governor Phips, he presided as Deputy-governor, over a Court of Assistants at Salem, April 11, 1692, for the examination of accused persons, — not for their trial. There is no evidence that he was satisfied with the result of that examination, which, according to Hutchinson's account, seems to have been conducted chiefly if not entirely by Rev. Samuel Parris.[7] On the

[1] Samuel Sewall.
[2] Col. Nicholas Paige.
[3] Two days, it seems, were devoted to this selection of judges.
[4] Council Records. It is said that Sal-

tonstall left the court, being dissatisfied with its proceedings.
[5] Genea. Dict.
[6] Hist. Mass., II. 27–30.
[7] Mr. Poole says, — "Mr. Parris on no

contrary, perhaps partly in consequence of this examination, he declared his dissatisfaction, and dislike of the judicial proceedings. In a letter dated Oct. 8, 1692, Thomas Brattle, one of the most intelligent and persistent opposers of the witchcraft infatuation, says: "But although the chief judge, and some of the other judges, be very zealous in these proceedings, yet this you may take for a truth, that there are several about the Bay, men for understanding, judgment, and piety, inferior to few, if any, in N. E., that do utterly condemn the said proceedings, and do freely deliver their judgment in the case to be this, viz., that these methods will utterly ruin and undo poor N. E. I shall nominate some of these to you, viz., the Hon. Simon Bradstreet, Esq. [our late governor]; the Hon. Thomas Danforth, Esq. [our late deputy-governor]; the Rev. Mr. Increase Mather, and the Rev. Mr. Samuel Willard. Major N. Saltonstall Esq., who was one of the judges, has left the Court, and is very much dissatisfied with the proceedings of it. Excepting Mr. Hale, Mr. Noyes, and Mr. Parris, the Rev. Elders, almost throughout the whole country, are very much dissatisfied. Several of the late justices, viz., Thomas Graves Esq., N. Byfield Esq., Francis Foxcroft Esq.,[1] are much dissatisfied; also several of the present justices: and in particular, some of the Boston justices were resolved rather to throw up their commissions than be active in disturbing the liberty of their majesties' subjects, merely on the accusations of these afflicted, possessed children."[2] That Danforth, in common with almost all his contemporaries, believed in witchcraft, and considered witches justly obnoxious to

occasion was employed to examine the accused. At the request of the magistrates, he took down the evidence, he being a rapid and accurate penman. On the occasion mentioned in the next paragraph, Danforth put the questions, and the record is, 'Mr. Parris being desired and appointed to write out the examination, did take the same, and also read it before the council in public.'" — Gen. Reg., xxiv. 395. Mr. Upham also says, — "The deputy-governor first called to the stand John Indian, and plied him, as was the course pursued on all these occasions, with leading questions." — Salem Witchcraft, ii. 102. But, after quoting from Hutchinson a part of the examination, Mr. Upham adds, — "I would call attention to the form of the foregoing ques-

tions. Hutchinson says that 'Mr. Parris was over-officious: most of the examinations, although in the presence of one or more magistrates, were taken by him.' He put the questions. They show, on this occasion, a minute knowledge beforehand of what the witnesses are to say, which it cannot be supposed Danforth, Russell, Addington, Appleton, and Sewall, strangers, as they were, to the place and the details of the affair, could have had." — Ibid., p. 104. For this reason, even if there were not many others, it seems most probable that the "leading questions" were put by Parris, and not by Danforth.

[1] Son-in-law of Thomas Danforth.
[2] Coll. Mass. Hist. Soc., v. 74, 75.

punishment, is probably true; but it is not true, that he was a member of that special court which held such bloody assizes, nor, if we may believe Brattle, his personal friend, did he approve its proceedings. The Superior Court, of which he was a member, held a session at Salem in January, 1693, at which twenty persons were tried, and three convicted; but "spectral evidence" was not admitted;[1] moreover, there is no proof that he concurred with his associates, all of whom had been members of the Commission of Oyer and Terminer.

The latter years of Danforth's life seem to have been peaceful. Doubtless he lamented the loss of the old Charter, for whose preservation he had struggled so long and so manfully. His strong opposition to some of the provisions of the new Charter is said to have induced Mather to omit his name from the list of Councillors; yet he finally accepted it as the best which could be obtained, and faithfully labored, both as Councillor and Judge, to administer its provisions in such a manner as to secure the benefit of the people.[2]

In the long and perilous conflict on behalf of chartered rights, Gookin and Danforth were supported by their brethren the Deputies from Cambridge, all good men and true. Deacon Edward Collins was Deputy from 1654 to 1670, without intermission; Edward Oakes, 1659, 1660, 1669–1681; Richard Jack-

---

[1] Upham's *Witchcraft*, ii. 349.

[2] The closing scene is thus described by Judge Sewall in his Journal: 1699. "Oct. 28. I visit Mr. Danforth who is very sick; his daughter Foxcroft tells me he is much troubled with the palsy. Was much indisposed the 22d instant, which was the beginning of his sickness; yet would go to meeting, which did him hurt, especially going out in the afternoon. I wished him refreshings from God under his fainting sickness." — "Lord's day, Nov. 5. Tho. Danforth Esq., dies, about 3 past merid., of a fever. Has been a magistrate forty years. Was a very good husbandman, and a very good Christian, and a good councillor; was about 76 years old." "Third day, Nov. 7. Mr. Stoughton, in his speech to the grand jury, takes great notice of Judge Danforth's death; saith he was a lover of religion and religious men; the oldest servant the country had; zealous against vice; and if [he] had any detractors, yet [there] was so

much on the other as to erect him a monument among this people. Mr. Willard, in his prayer, mentioned God's displeasure in his removal, and desired the Judges might act on the Bench as those who must also shortly go to give their account. Indeed it is awful, that while we are sitting on the bench, at the same time the ancientest Judge should be lying by the wall, dead, in his house. I can't tell how it came about, but I told Mr. Danforth at Bristow I thought he would never come thither again; which made him take a more particular leave than otherwise he would have done." "Sixth day, Nov. 10, 1699. Mr. Danforth is entombed about ½ of an hour before 4 P. M. Very fair and pleasant day; much company. Bearers: on the right side, Lt-Governor, Mr. Russell, Sewall; left side, Mr. W. Winthrop, Mr. Cook, Col. Phillips. I helped lift the corpse into the tomb, carrying the feet."

son, 1661, 1662; Edward Winship, 1663, 1664, 1681–1686; Edward Jackson, 1665–1668, 1675, 1676; Joseph Cooke, 1671, 1676–1680; Thomas Prentice, 1672–1674; Samuel Champney, 1686, and again, after the Revolution, from 1689 to 1695, when he died in office. Their names should be in perpetual remembrance.

CHAPTER X.

CIVIL HISTORY.

It has already been stated, that the General Court, March 3, 1635–6, "Agreed, that Newe Towne bounds should run eight myles into the country from their meeteing howse," and that large farms, near the eight mile line were soon afterwards granted by the town; among which grants was one to Richard Harlakenden of "six hundred acres of upland and meadow, at the place called Vine Brook, in the midway between Newtowne and Concord," on certain conditions, Jan. 2, 1636–7. This tract of land was in the central portion of the present town of Lexington. The conditions of the grant not being performed by Richard Harlakenden, the land was subsequently granted to his brother, Roger Harlakenden, who died in 1638. Herbert Pelham married the widow of Harlakenden, and became the owner of his real estate; he bequeathed this property to his son Edward Pelham, who conveyed by deeds, Oct. 28, 1693, to Benjamin Muzzey 206 acres in Cambridge, towards Concord, being a part of " Mr. Pelham's farm," and to John Poulter 212 acres of the same farm. Precisely when the first houses were erected and actual settlements commenced at the " Farms," so called, does not appear on record; but as early as 1682, about thirty families were there, generally styled " Farmers." They had then become so numerous and so strong, that they desired a separation from the parent town; but they petitioned at first to be made a distinct parish. Although they were unsuccessful for nine years, and did not fully accomplish their purpose for more than thirty years, their petition and the reply to it are inserted, as they indicate the condition of the people at that period.

" To the honorable the General Court now assembled in Boston, October 11th, 1682.
" The petition of several of the inhabitants within the bounds of the town of Cambridge humbly showeth : That by the providence of God, who hath determined the times before appointed

and the bounds of the habitations of all men, your petitioners are
seated at a great distance, the nearest of them above five miles
(some of them six, some seven, some eight, some nine if not ten
miles) from the public place of meeting to worship God, in the
town that we appertain unto: that your petitioners, by reason
thereof, have now (many of us) for a long time conflicted with
very great difficulties in respect of themselves, who have been
forced to be absent at some seasons of the year, and especially
their children, for whose spiritual good and the means leading
thereunto they desire to be solicitous as well as for themselves:
that there are now about thirty families, in which are contained
at least one hundred and eighty souls, within the circumstances
and condition abovementioned: that your petitioners have humbly and affectionately represented the premises to the Townsmen
at Cambridge, at their meetings, withal signifying their desire of
liberty from them to call a minister to preach amongst them and
catechise their children, they being willing to build a meeting-
house which may be situated so as to be within two miles and an
half near thirty families, and to advance for the present forty
pounds per annum for his maintenance: that the premises notwithstanding, they have as yet obtained no relief or encouragement from the town of Cambridge in this affair. Your petitioners, therefore, who are the heads of families, fearing the sad effects
of this remoteness from the public worship of God and particularly in respect of their children and those that* shall come after
them, lest they should grow weary of attendance upon the public
means of grace, and think it too much (as Jeroboam tells Israel it
was to go up to Jerusalem) to travel so many miles for such an
end, and so should cease to worship the Lord God of their fathers, think it their bounden duty humbly to address to this honored
Court, praying that you will please to take the case of your petitioners into your serious consideration, that by your favor they
may be licensed to provide for themselves a person that may be
meet and able to dispense unto them the word of God; and
that in order thereunto they may be freed from payments to
the town of Cambridge, from whom, as their dear and beloved
brethren, they no ways desire separation for any other but the
forementioned cause alone ; declaring it to have been their standing affliction and cause of grief that, by reason of their remoteness, they have not been in a capacity, according to their desires,
to enjoy more fellowship and communion with them.   And your
petitioners shall pray, as in duty bound, &c.   James Cutler,
Matthew Bridge Senr., David Fiske Senr., Samuel Stone, Senr.,

Francis Whitmore, John Tedd, Ephraim Winship, John Winter, in the behalf of the rest of the families." [1]

The petitioners presented a strong case. To travel so far, every week, for the purpose of attending public worship would now be regarded as a grievous burden: and the burden was greater two hundred years ago, when travelling was almost exclusively accomplished on horseback or on foot. But the petition was presented in a time of general distress and alarm. The Charter, regarded as the palladium of liberty, was in imminent peril, and there were fearful apprehensions of calamities which might result from its loss. Financial embarrassment was already felt, and general bankruptcy was feared. Under such circumstances, the town opposed the petition of the "Farmers" and action thereupon was "respited" until the next General Court, at which time the town presented an earnest remonstrance against the proposed dismemberment : —

"To the honorable the General Court assembled in Boston, October the 16th, 1688.

"Your humble supplicants, the selectmen of Cambridge, in obedience to a warrant sent to us, and the concerns of our town, do humbly present unto your Honors' consideration, in answer to a petition of the remote farms of our town. Some of your Honors may yet remember the unsettled condition of this church when it was about to remove to Mattabesick,[2] for the prevention of which the honored General Court, held at Boston, in March 1643–4, was pleased to grant to this Church a tract of land at Shawshine, and another parcel adjoining to Concord line, for the enlargement of our boundaries, and to enable this church and towne (with the rest of our accommodations) to maintain the ministry in this place, provided the then Church and Elders did continue in this place ; which condition was accordingly performed, though this Church and town (as may be demonstrated) was abler to maintain the ministry and defray public charges then than it now is, by reason most of our principal men are now removed from us, some by death and others into England and other countries. We also humbly present unto your Honors' consideration the great disenablement of our church and town by the village on the south side of the River breaking off from us,[3] which was so considerable a part of our town, and bare a considerable part of our charge in the maintenance of our ministry,

[1] Mass. Arch., xi. 24.   [3] See chap. viii.
[2] See chap. vi.

and now bears none of that nor several other charges our town
is at; whereby we are greatly disenabled so comfortably to
maintain our ministry and discharge our public charges as we
want and ought to do, by reason one principal arm of our town
is cut off, and our accommodations for husbandry so poor and
small, and our trade so little and inconsiderable, that it is even
a wonder to ourselves how we do subsist and carry on public
charge so well as we do, though we do it not so well as we should.
We therefore present unto this honorable General Court's most
serious consideration the great damage it will be 'to this poor
Church and town, (that have suffered so many diminutions already), if the honored Court should grant our Farmers' petition
to let them have a ministry of their own, and so be wholly taken
off from contributing to ours; but much more should we be damnified if the honored Court should grant any part of our outlands
unto them, we are so exceedingly straitened in the boundaries
of our lands, as we shall plainly demonstrate to the honored
Court. For the distance of place that our brethren at the Farms
are from the public meeting with us, it is but the same it was
when they first settled themselves and families there; and they
have there other conveniences with it, and Concord is not far
from them, which in bad weather they may go unto. If we
should have this arm cut off too, we shall be much disenabled to
carry on God's work amongst us, both in Church and Commonwealth; that as it hath been the care of the honored fathers of
our Commonwealth formerly to take care for the subsistence and
well being of this senior Church of Christ in Cambridge, so we
still crave the continued care of the honored fathers of the Commonwealth now in being, that they would not destroy the parent
for the offspring. We humbly leave our languishing condition to
your Honors' most serious consideration; and your supplicants
shall pray as in duty bound, etc.   William Manning, Sam".
Andrewe, Samuel Chamne, in the name of the town of Cambridge." [1]

The consideration of this petition was further postponed until
the next General Court. Both the Council and the House of
Representatives manifested a willingness, at their session in October, 1684, to establish a village at the Farms; but they could
not agree where the division line should be drawn between the
village and the parent town, and nothing was accomplished.[2]

[1] Mass. Arch., xl. 25.   [2] Mass. Arch., xl. 27, 28.

During the troublous times which succeeded, — the disastrous administration of Andros and the perilous Revolution which followed, — no further effort appears to have been made for a division of the town. Seven years afterwards, a new petition was presented ; it is not found on the files of the Court, but the result is recorded under date of December 15, 1691: —

" Upon reading the petition of the Farmers and inhabitants of the Farms within the precincts and bounds of the town of Cambridge towards Concord, therein setting forth their distance (the nearest of them living above five miles) from Cambridge meeting house, the place of the public worship, praying that, according to former applications by them several years since made unto this Court for the advantage of themselves, families, and posterity, they may have this Court's favor and license in order to the calling of a fit minister for dispensing the gospel among them ; as also that they may be a distinct village for the ends proposed in their said petition : — the selectmen of Cambridge having had a copy of said petition sent them, with a notification of the time for their being heard thereupon this day, and accordingly attending : — After a full hearing and consideration of what was offered by both parties, it is granted and ordered by this Court, that the petitioners be and are hereby permitted and allowed to invite and settle an able and orthodox minister for the dispensing of the gospel among them ; and that all inhabitants being within the line formerly stated by a Committee of this Court, anno 1684, beginning at the first run of water or swampy place over which is a kind of bridge in the way on the southerly side of Francis Whitmore's house, towards the town of Cambridge aforesaid, cross the neck of land lying between Woburn line and that of Watertown side, upon a southwest and northeast course, do pay unto the ministers maintained there ; and are hereby empowered annually to choose three or five meet persons to assess their inhabitants for the support and maintenance of their minister, as also a Constable or Collector, to gather the same by warrant from the said Assessors. The said Farmers not being hereby discharged from paying their proportion as formerly unto all public charges in the town, except what refers to the ministry, so long as they maintain an able minister among themselves." [1]

In the remonstrance against this division, in 1688, it was represented that the town would be grievously " damnified " if the

[1] *Mass. Prov. Rec.*, vi. 208.

"outlands," or common lands not yet divided, should be granted
to the petitioners. The Court listened thus far to the remonstrance, and preserved to the town the ownership of this public
property, some of which was afterwards sold to the precinct.
Two such sales are entered on the Town Records, under date of
Jan. 16, 1692-3. It should be added, that these financial transactions indicate a friendly spirit in both parties, the separation
having apparently been effected without such sharp controversy
as occurred in the case of Newton. In the same spirit, March
11, 1699–1700, the town "voted, to give the little meeting-house
bell to the Farmers. Voted, that the Selectmen, in the name of
the inhabitants, do give their thanks to Capt. Andrew Belcher
for the bell for their meeting-house he has given them."

Twenty-one years after their establishment as a precinct, the
Farmers, according to their original design, sought to be entirely
separated from the town of Cambridge, and to be a "township by
themselves." This separation was readily obtained on terms satisfactory to both parties. The Cambridge records show that, —
"At a meeting of the inhabitants belonging to the meeting house
in the Body of the town of Cambridge, orderly convened the 1st
December 1712, Capt. Thomas Oliver was chosen Moderator.
And whereas the Farmers, at their public meeting on the 28th of
October last, appointed a committee to petition the town that
they may be dismissed from the town, and be a township by
themselves, as appears by their petition bearing date the 6th
November, 1712, which has been now read; voted, That Capt.
Thomas Oliver, Mr. Jonathan Remington, and Andrew Bordman, be a Committee to treat with the Committee appointed by
the Farmers aforesaid; and that the articles to be proposed to
the said Committee, as terms of their dismission, are their paying a part toward the charge of the Great Bridge, and to the
Town House, and a consideration for some of our Poor." The
meeting was then adjourned until Jan. 12, 1712-3, at which time
it was "Voted, That the Farmers, upon their being dismissed
from the town, shall annually pay to our Town Treasurer such a
proportion of our part of the charge of the Great Bridge over
Charles River in Cambridge as shall fall to them according to
their annual proportion with us in the Province Tax. (2) Voted,
That the said Farmers shall pay their proportion of twenty-five
pounds toward the arrears of our Town House. The aforesaid
articles being complied with by the Farmers, Voted (3) That the
article that has been proposed, referring to their paying their

proportion toward the relief of some of our Poor, (viz. Robert Webber and Richard a negro, and his wife,) be referred to the Committee formerly appointed, (viz. Capt. Oliver, Mr. Remington, and Andrew Bordman,) to debate further upon, who are fully empowered in behalf of the town, either to insist upon the said article or to consent to their being dismissed from the town upon the articles aforementioned which they have complied with." In accordance with this agreement, the Farmers were incorporated March 20, 1712–13, by an act of the General Court, which provided that the "tract of land known by the name of the northern precinct in Cambridge be henceforth made a separate and distinct town, by the name of Lexington, upon the articles and terms already agreed on with the town of Cambridge." [1]

During this period and half a century afterwards, very few public events occurred, materially affecting the welfare of Cambridge. Some facts, however, though of a more private or personal character, should not be entirely overlooked, as they throw light on the state of society and the condition of the people.

By the Town Records it appears that Cullers of Bricks were first elected, Nov. 10, 1684: Town Clerk, as an officer distinct from the Selectmen, March 13, 1692–3: Town Treasurer, March 30, 1694: Assessors, July 16, 1694.

The County Records indicate that Thomas Danforth was Treasurer of Middlesex, before 1657, when he was succeeded by Edward Goffe, who died in 1658, and John Stedman was appointed, who held the office until 1683; Samuel Andrew was his successor and remained in office until 1700, except during the administration of Andros. All these were Cambridge men. In the settlement of the Treasurer's accounts, charges were allowed in 1690, to wit: "52 wolves killed by the English, 20ˢ. per wolf, and one killed by an Indian, 10ˢ, is £52. 10ˢ . . . . Paid one half the charge of Cambridge Great Bridge, £26. 7ˢ· 6ᵈ." And in 1696, the Treasurer was allowed twelve pence in the pound of all collections and disbursements; Grand Jurors were paid two shillings per day for attendance; no allowance was made for travel, but the county paid for their dinners at one shilling each. Seventy-six wolves had been killed, and 13s. 4d. per head was allowed in compensation.

May 22, 1691. "Upon the death of John Green, late Marshal General, in the beginning of the last Court of Assistants, Mr. Samuel Gookin being appointed by said Court to supply that vacancy, and sworn to the faithful discharge of his duty in that place, the said Samuel Gookin is hereby confirmed in the said office of Marshal General of this Colony." [1]

June 17, 1700. The General Court granted five pounds, to aid in repairing the road to Connecticut, "especially betwixt Wooster and Brookfield," which was described as "much incumbered with trees fallen, and many rocky swamps, and other obstructions to travellers, drovers, and others, to the hazarding life or limb of both men and horses." [2] Six years earlier, Rev. Benjamin Wadsworth, afterwards President of Harvard College, accompanied the commissioners appointed to treat with the Maquas or Mohawks, at Albany, and travelled over this road to Brookfield, then generally called Quaboag: "Capt. Sewal and Major Townsend, being commissioned to treat with the Mockways, set out from Boston about half an hour past twelve, Monday, August 6, 1694. Several gentlemen did accompany them to Watertown, and then returned. At Watertown we met with Lieutenant Hammond and thirty troopers, who were appointed for a guard to Springfield. We came to our first stage at Malberough, about half an hour past eight in the evening. We lodged at Abraham How's, [3] and thence set forward the next morning about half an hour past seven of the clock. There was nothing remarkable this day, but only Mr. Dwite, of Hatford, did accidentally fall into our company, and after the same manner, scil. accidentally, he and his horse both together fell into a brook; but both rose again without damage. This day we dined in the woods. Pleasant descants were made upon the dining room: it was said that it was large, high, curiously hung with green; our dining place was also accommodated with the pleasancy of a murmuring rivulet. This day, some of our company saw a bear; but being near a thick swamp, he escaped our pursuit. Towards night we heard (I think) three guns; but we knew not who shot them. Our whole company come this day to Quaboag, about sundown, not long before nor after." [4] The easterly section of this road is mentioned by Pemberton, under date of Sept. 30, 1783, in his manuscript "Chronology," preserved in the library of the Mass. Hist. Society: "A gentleman of this State remarks, 'that soon after the settlement of our Fathers at Boston, the persons appointed to explore the country, and lay out public roads did it as far as the

[1] Mass. Col. Rec., vi. 184.   [3] The "Wayside Inn," celebrated by
[2] Mass. Prov. Rec., vii. 99.   Longfellow.
                                     [4] Coll. Mass. Hist. Soc., xxxi. 102.

bank by Mrs. Biglow in Weston, and reported that they had done it as far as they believed would ever be necessary, it being about seven miles from the College in Cambridge.'" It is proper to add, that I have never seen any contemporary authority for this extraordinary statement.

Col. Shute, the newly appointed Governor of Massachusetts and New Hampshire, arrived in Boston, Oct. 4, 1716, and on the 15th day of the same month commenced a journey to New Hampshire. Instead of crossing the ferry to Charlestown, he passed out of Boston over the neck, through Roxbury and Brookline, to Cambridge Great Bridge. The commencement of his journey, and the manner of his reception in Cambridge, are described in the "Boston News Letter," October 22, 1716: "On Monday last, the 15th current, his Excellency, our Governor, about eight o'clock in the morning, set out from hence by land for his other government of New Hampshire, attended by the honorable the Lieut.-Governor and several of the chief gentlemen of this and that Province, and on this side of the river was met by Spencer Phips Esq., with his Troop of Horse, the Sheriff of Middlesex, and other gentlemen of that County, and by them conducted to Harvard College in Cambridge, where he was received by the President, Fellows, and Students, and entertained in the Hall with a congratulatory Latin Oration, by Mr. Thomas Foxcroft: after which his Excellency was pleased to take a view of the Library, and then proceeded on his journey to Lynn," etc.

Col. Edmund Goffe was elected Representative, June 6, 1721. "Samuel Smith was charged with putting in two votes in the first voting for Representative, made oath that he put in but one vote for Representative. Also Daniel Gookin being charged with putting in two votes at the second voting for a Representative, made oath that he put in but one vote for a Representative: said oaths were administered in the public meeting per Mr. Justice Leverett." [1]

In 1721, the small-pox prevailed more extensively and fatally than ever before in Boston and its vicinity. A statement of results was made officially in the "Boston News Letter": "Boston, Feb. 24, 1721-2. By the Selectmen. The number of persons visited with the small-pox since its coming into town, in April last past, having been inquired into by direction from the Selectmen, amounts to 5,889: — 844 of whom died and were buried in the preceding months, as follows: — May, 1; June, 8; July, 11; Aug.,

1 _Town Records._

26; Sept., 101; Oct., 411; Nov., 249; Dec., 81; Jan., 6." T
extent of the destruction of life in Cambridge, by this scourge
not known with exactness; but references to it are found in t
"New England Courant:" "Cambridge, Thursday, Nov. 80, 17?
This morning died here William Hutchinson, of Boston, Esq.,
the small-pox, in the 38th year of his age." (Dec. 4, 1721
"Last week died one of the Indian hostages (mentioned in c
last) of the small-pox at Cambridge." (Jan. 22, 1721-2.) "(
Friday last, the General Assembly of this Province met at Ca
bridge, there not being a sufficient number of members to ma
a House on Wednesday, to which day they were before p
rogued. They are adjourned till Tuesday next, when they i
to meet a few miles out of town, the small-pox being now in t
heart of that place." (March 5, 1721-2.) The Town Recor
show that a Committee was appointed, Jan. 29, 1721-2, to pi
vide "for the relief of such persons and families as may stand
need thereof, in case the small-pox spread amongst us." Inocu
tion for the small-pox was first introduced in Boston at this til
by Dr. Zabdiel Boylston, who encountered the most violent op|
sition. "Out of 286 persons who were inoculated for the sma
pox, but six died." [1]

In 1730, the small-pox again prevailed in Cambridge wi
alarming violence. Nine town meetings were held betwe
March 20 and April 3, to devise means for its exterminatic
A vote passed at the first of these meetings indicates that inoc
lation had been injudiciously or carelessly practiced: "Where
Samuel Danforth, Esq's late practice of inoculation of small-p
amongst us has greatly endangered the town, and distress
sundry families amongst us, which is very disagreeable to ›
wherefore, voted, that said Samuel Danforth, Esq. be desi-
forthwith to remove such inoculated persons into some conv-
ient place, whereby our town may n't be exposed by them." 7
College studies were broken up for a time; but the students wa
recalled by an advertisement, dated May 2, 1780, and publisl
in the "Weekly Journal:" "The small-pox having been latel1,
Cambridge, which occasioned the dispersion of the scholari-
escape danger; but now, through the Divine goodness, that a-
temper having utterly ceased here; it is agreed and ordered y
the President and Tutors, that the undergraduates forth th
repair to the College, to follow their studies and stated exerois
Benjamin Wadsworth, Pres." The distemper returned ang

[1] Drake's Hist. Boston, pp. 562, 568.   ch

before the end of the year, as appears by a paragraph in the "News Letter," dated Oct. 8, 1730: "We hear from Cambridge, that Mr. William Patten, Representative for the town of Billerica, being taken sick of the small-pox, while the General Assembly was sitting there, is since dead, and was interred on Monday last, the 5th instant." On Saturday, Oct. 3, the Court was adjourned to meet at Roxbury on the next Wednesday.

Again, in 1752, the small-pox caused the cessation of study in College from April 22 until Sept. 2; and the corporation voted, May 4, "that there be no public Commencement this year," and in October voted to have no winter vacation. The town appointed a committee, May 18, to devise measures to prevent the spreading of the disease, and on the 3d of October, "voted that a public contribution be in the three parts of this town, next Lord's-day come seven night, for the speedy raising of money to defray the charges the town have been at in the support, &c., of sundry persons lately visited with the small-pox, belonging to this town. Also voted that the thanks of this town be given to the Selectmen of the town of Charlestown for their great friendship, assistance and civility to us, when visited with the small-pox." I find no record of the number of lives destroyed in Cambridge by this visitation of the small-pox. But its ravages were frightful in Boston during the previous year. Professor Winthrop recorded the fact, in his interleaved Almanac, that while only five persons in Cambridge had the disease in 1751, of whom three died, in Boston, with a total population of 15,734, 5,060 whites had it the natural way, of whom 470 died; also, 485 blacks, of whom 69 died; and by inoculation 1,985 whites and 139 blacks were sick, of whom 24 whites and 6 blacks died.

The town continued, as aforetime, to be watchful against the admission of undesirable associates. "At a meeting of the freeholders and inhabitants of the town of Cambridge, orderly convened 9th Decr. 1723. — Whereas, of late years, sundry persons and families have been received and entertained amongst us, to the great trouble of the Selectmen and damage of the town: for preventing such inconveniences for the future, Voted, that henceforth no freeholder nor inhabitant in said town shall receive or admit any family into our town to reside amongst us for the space of a month, without first having obtained the allowance and approbation of the freeholders and inhabitants of said town, or of the Selectmen for the time being, on penalty of paying to the Treasurer of said town, for the use of the poor, the sum of twenty shillings. Also voted, that no inhabitant in said town shall receive and entertain any person into their family (excepting such as are received by reason of marriage, or such as are sent for education, or men or maid servants upon wages, or purchased servants or slaves), for the space of a month, without having the allowance and approbation of the freeholders and inhabitants, or selectmen, as aforesaid, on penalty of paying the sum of twenty shillings for the use of the poor, as aforesaid."

The meeting-house was equally guarded against improper intrusion, though by a less severe penalty. On the 12th of May, 1729, it was "Voted, that so often as any dog or dogs is or are seen in the meeting house on the Lord's day in the time of public worship, the owner or owners of said dog or dogs shall for every such offence pay one shilling, half to go to the officer appointed to regulate said dogs, the other half part of said fine to be for the use of the poor of the town. And on refusal to pay said fine or fines, the aforesaid officer is hereby obliged, authorized and empowered to prosecute the owners of the above described dogs before any one of his Majesty's Justices of the Peace in said County. This to continue for one year."

March 10, 1728–9. "Put to vote, whether said inhabitants would grant the sum of 50£. for Joseph Hanford, to fit him out in the practice of physic, and it passed in the negative."

In 1736, John Vassall (afterwards Major and Colonel) purchased the large estate at the southwest corner of Brattle and Ash streets, and became a resident in Cambridge. He was born in the West Indies, inherited a princely fortune, married (in 1734) a daughter of Lieut.-gov. Spencer Phips, became at once a very popular citizen, and was elected Selectman and Representative in 1739, and again in 1740. Shortly after his second election, some enthusiastic friend thus exulted in the "Weekly Journal" of May 20, 1740: "Cambridge, May 19. On Monday last came on the choice of a Representative for this town in the approaching General Assembly. The meeting was as full as most that ever were known among us on such an occasion, there being 109 qualified voters present at it. After the Selectmen had put an end to some tedious contests and lingering delays, (which arose on adjusting preliminaries, and which only interrupted and kept off the business of the day,) we at length had the liberty to proceed fairly to the choice; and then it soon appeared that Mr. John Vassall was chosen by the overbearing majority of more than double the number of all those votes which were not for him, viz. by the majority of 75 to 34; a proportion much greater on the side of the person chosen our Representative this year than he [1] had who was our Representative the last. By this it seems a certain person elect has a growing interest." Alas for the fickleness of popular favor. Mr. Vassall was not afterwards elected either Selectman or Representative until a few months before his death in 1747. His "interest" attained its full growth suddenly, like Jonah's gourd, and as suddenly collapsed. He was disturbed by a disparaging remark of a townsman, and sought legal redress with disastrous result. The history of the suit is entered on the Records of the Inferior Court for the County of Middlesex, December term, 1740, page 172. By this it appears that Samuel Whittemore of Cambridge, Deputy Sheriff, on the 13th of March, 1739, declared publicly that though Mr. Vassall had been elected Selectman, he "was no more fit to discharge said trust than the horse that he, the said Samuel, then rode on." On the next day Vassall commenced suit, claiming £1,000 damage for defamation of character; he caused Whittemore to be arrested and imprisoned. On the trial, two months afterwards, the Court adjudged that "the words . . . . spoken by the said Samuel were not actionable." Vassall appealed to the Superior Court, which affirmed the judgment of the Inferior Court. Whittemore then sued Vassall, for false and malicious imprisonment, and recovered £200 damage and costs of court. So much appears on record. Tradition says that the writ was served on Vassall at his own table, when surrounded by a large and fashionable dinner-party.

Mr. Vassall was equally unsuccessful in his appeal to the General Court for protection against what he regarded as a personal insult and an encroachment on his official privileges. John Hovey had recovered judgment against him on two bonds, notwithstanding his "plea of privilege (as on file) which was overruled by the Court," and had levied on his estate. The Records of the General Court show that notice was issued, Dec. 5, 1740, to John Hovey and Samuel Gookin, to make answer to Mr. John Vassall, Representative of Cambridge, who complained of sundry insults received from them. Dec. 10, Mr. Samuel Gookin appeared, and the case was fully examined. "Then the question was put, whether it appears to this House that an attachment being served on Mr. John Vassall's estate on the 18th of Novem-

[1] He was his own predecessor. The increased majority indicated the "growing interest."

ber last is a breach of the privileges of the members of this House. It passed in the negative." But this was not the end. December 18, 1740, "A petition of Mr. John Hovey of Cambridge, praying that this House would order Mr. John Vassall, the member of Cambridge, to refund his expenses occasioned by an unjust and groundless complaint of said Mr. Vassall, particularly mentioned in said petition, for the reasons exhibited, — read, and in answer thereto, ordered, that the said John Vassall pay to the petitioner, the said John Hovey, the sum of ten pounds, in full recompense for his time and expense occasioned by said complaint."

An epidemic occasioned great alarm in 1740. It was called the "throat distemper," and was probably the same "influenza" which Thacher describes: "The amazing rapidity with which it spread through the country resembled more a storm agitating the atmosphere than the natural progress of a disease from any contagious source. Almost a whole city, town, or neighborhood, became affected with its influence in a few days, and as it did not incapacitate people in general from pursuing their ordinary occupations, it was common to observe, in every street and place of resort, a constant coughing, hawking, and wheezing, and, in public assemblies, little else was to be heard or attended to. Although all classes of people experienced the operation of the influenza, it is remarkable that a small number, comparatively speaking, were so ill as to require medical attendance, and instances of its fatal termination were of rare occurrence." [1] It proved so fatal here, however, that the students were dismissed from College by vote passed June 23, 1740: "Whereas, through the holy Providence of God, several families in the town of Cambridge are visited with the throat distemper, and the President's and Steward's families are under very afflicted circumstances by reason of that mortal sickness; and whereas we apprehend that there is great danger of the distemper spreading and prevailing as it hath done formerly in other places, and that the students are much endangered thereby; therefore Voted, that they be immediately dismissed from the College, and that the vacation begin from this time; and that the Commencement for this year be not until the expiration of the vacation." [2]

---

[1] *Medical Biography*, i. 28.

[2] In a private note-book, the steward of the College, Andrew Bordman, Esq., made this record: "Our grandchild, Ruth Bordman, died 23 June 1740: our grandchild Andrew Bordman died 24 June 1740: both of the distemper called the throat distemper." Memorials are found in the burial-place, of "Mrs. Margaret Holyoke, wife to the Revd. Mr. Ed-

In former days, each town was required to pay its own Representatives in the General Court, and was liable to a fine if not duly represented. This town, however, on the 14th of May, 1750, "Voted, that the town will make choice of two Representatives to represent them at the next General Court, or Assembly, provided the same serve the town *gratis*: also voted, that they will proceed to choose two Representatives, upon that condition only, that those who are chosen be not the Representatives of said town unless, upon their choice, they declare that they will serve the town *gratis*, as aforesaid. Then Andrew Bordman and Edmund Trowbridge Esqs. were chosen Representatives," and both accepted the office. The same course was pursued the next year, and the same persons were elected. But, in 1752, Andrew Bordman refused the office on this condition, and Henry Vassall was elected in his stead. This practice was soon afterwards wholly abandoned.

April 19, 1754. The territory lying west of Sparks Street and south of Vassall Lane was transferred from Watertown to Cambridge by the General Court, by a line described thus: "To begin at Charles River, and from thence to run in the line between the lands of Simon Coolidge, Moses Stone, Christopher Grant, and the Thatchers, and the land of Col°. Brinley and Ebenezer Wyeth, to the Fresh Pond, so called." [1] Several acres were subsequently added to Cambridge, bounded westerly on Coolidge Avenue, extending to and including the Cambridge Cemetery.

Some excitement was occasioned as late as 1754, by the appearance of a bear in the easterly part of Cambridge, long after we might suppose this section of the country to have been rid of wild beasts. The "Boston News Letter" of September 19, contained this paragraph. "On Tuesday last, a Bear, that had wandered down to Cambridge, was discovered on Lieut. Gov'. Phips' farm,[2] and being closely pursued took to Charles River; whereupon several boats put off from Charlestown, and one from

ward Holyoke, President of Harvard College," who died June 25, 1740, aged 39; and of "William Holyoke," their "youngest son," who died June 23, 1740, aged nearly three years. Similar memorials are found of two children of Mr. Ebenezer Stedman, — Martha, who died June 23, 1740, aged 4 years; and Sarah, who died June 24, 1740, aged nearly 6 years. The dates indicate that all these were victims of the same disease.

[1] *Mass. Prov. Rec.*, xx. 228.
[2] This farm embraced East Cambridge, and extended westerly nearly to Columbia Street. Five years later, in September, 1759, Dr. Belknap, then a student in Harvard College, made this record: "A great many bears killed at Cambridge and the neighboring towns about this time, and several persons killed by them." — *Life of Belknap*, p. 11.

the west part of this town, which last shot and entered two bul
lets into him ; but not killing him, the Bear made directly toward
the boat and got one paw upon the side, upon which one of th
men struck an adze into his skull, and despatched him in an ir
stant, and brought him ashore. The whole of the body weighe
196 pounds. When he was opened, a great number of the bone
of fowls &c. were found in his belly."

The earliest notice which I have seen of a fire-engine in Can
bridge is dated March 3, 1755, when, "upon the motion of Cap
Ebenezer Stedman and others, referring to the town's agreein
with Henry Vassall Esq., who has an Engine and is willing th
same should be improved for the town's use on certain condition:
the question was put whether the town would act on said motior
and it passed in the negative." In all probability, however, th
town then possessed one or more engines. Boston had one befor
1679, and seven as early as 1733 ;[1] and Cambridge would nc
be likely to remain entirely destitute. Yet the machines then i
use might seem almost worthless, compared with the powerfu
steam-engines recently introduced.

The Town Record of Births and Deaths in the last three qua:
ters of the eighteenth century is very imperfect ; all the death
recorded between 1722 and 1772 are contained on two folio page
Professor Winthrop inserted brief bills of mortality, for a fe
years, in his interleaved almanacs, which afford a glimpse of th
truth : —

"1758.   Bill of mortality in first Parish in Cambridge.[2]

Under 2 years old 12	Between 40 and 50 = 1	
Between 2 and 5 = 2	Between 50 and 60 = 1	
Between 5 and 10 = 0	Between 60 and 70 = 1	Whites, 20
Between 10 and 20 = 1	Between 70 and 80 = 0	Blacks, 5
Between 20 and 30 = 2	Between 80 and 90 = 3	25
Between 30 and 40 = 2	25	

1762.   Causes of death, etc.

"Accidental,	1	Fits,	1	Males, 10
Age,	1	Infancy,	2	Females, 8
Colic,	1	Palsy,	1	18
Consumption,	7	Sore,	1	
Dysentery,	2	Stillborn,	1	Whites, 15
			18	Blacks, 3
				18."

---

[1] Drake's *Hist. Boston*, 431, 593.   [2] The First Parish then embraced wh:
is now the whole city.

1763. Causes of death, etc.

" Accidental,	2	Fit, (suddenly)	2	Males,	10	
Cancer,	2	Infancy,	9	Females,	10 '	
Consumption,	1	Palsy,	1		20	
Dropsy,	3		20			
				Whites,	17	
				Blacks,	3	
					20."	

In the " Boston News Letter," November 30, 1764, is a reference to a custom then recently introduced, but unwisely abandoned afterwards. " On Monday the 19th instant died at Cambridge, in the 78th year of her age Mrs. Hannah Burrill, relict of the late Hon. Theophilus Burrill Esq., and sister to the Rev. Mr. President Holyoke, at whose house she had for some time past resided. She was a gentlewoman of a virtuous disposition, and possessed of many amiable qualities. Her remains were interred the Thursday following, without the expense of mourning apparel, agreeable to the laudable method now practised in Boston. As this is the first example of the kind in that town, and introduced by a gentleman of so worthy and respectable a character, we doubt not it will acquire imitation." [1]

[1] Rev. John Cotton of Newton, in a letter dated Nov. 7, 1717, and preserved in the library of the *Mass. Hist. Soc.*, says that at the funeral of Hon. Andrew Belcher, " All the ministers there had scarves and gloves. They say 50 suits of cloaths were made. All first cousins, Remington, Blowers, &c., put into mourning. John Colman, Caswell, &c., all that had been apprentices to him, were also. 90 dozen of gloves were bought, and none of any figure but what had gloves sent 'em."

A bill of expenses at the funeral of Col. Edmund Goffe, in October, 1740, remains on file in the Probate Office; it was rendered by Edmund Trowbridge, Esq., grand nephew of the deceased. Among the charges are these: —

" To 5 pair of gloves at 7s. 6d., and a mourning weed,	£1	17	6
To a pair of shoe buckles, 6s., knee buckles, 4s. 6d., black stads, 1s. 3d.,	0	11	9
To a hat, 60s., mourning wigg, £5,	8	0	0
To a pair of gloves, black silk, 25s.	1	5	0
To a suit of mourning for the widow, and pair of shoes,	30	0	0
To another pair of black silk gloves, 25s.	1	5	0
To ten rings of Mr. Hurd, as per account,	23	14	0
To mourning for my aunt Barnard,	33	6	0
To the same for my sister Dana,	33	6	0
To a pair of gloves for her husband,	0	5	0
To cash paid the taylors for making the cloaths,	3	19	0
To two gallons of wine, 30s., a dozen of pipes, and 2 papers of tobacco, 5s.	1	15	0
To cash paid for bricks, and bricking the grave,	1	10	0
To stones to cover the grave,	0	10	0 "

This bill was allowed by the judge, though the estate was soon afterwards rendered insolvent. The Belcher estate was large, and might easily afford the outlay. It is to be regretted that the efforts made by President Holyoke and others to abolish such extravagant and useless customs were ineffectual.

CHAPTER XI.

CIVIL HISTORY.

In this history of a single town, it is not proposed to enumerate all the causes of the American Revolution, or the various events which occurred during its accomplishment; but some of those causes and events will be mentioned, with which the town of Cambridge had more or less intimate connection. One very prominent question at issue, in the commencement of the Revolutionary struggle, was whether or not the British Parliament had a legal right to impose taxes on the American provinces (which were not represented therein), without their consent. In the exercise of this pretended right of supremacy, among other methods for raising a revenue from the provinces, Parliament enacted a law, styled the Stamp Act, with a provision that it should take effect Nov. 1, 1765. With special reference to this Act, the American doctrine was affirmed, Oct. 29, 1765, by the Massachusetts House of Representatives, in fourteen resolutions, three of which were these: "III. *Resolved*, That no man can justly take the property of another without his consent; and that upon this original principle the right of representation in the same body which exercises the power of making laws for levying taxes, which is one of the main pillars of the British constitution, is evidently founded." "XII. *Resolved*, as a just conclusion from some of the foregoing resolves, That all acts made by any power whatever, other than the General Assembly of this Province, imposing taxes on the inhabitants, are infringements of our inherent and unalienable rights, as men and British subjects, and render void the most valuable declarations of our Charter. XIII. *Resolved*, that the extension of the powers of the Court of Admiralty within this Province is a most violent infraction of the right of trials by juries, — a right which this House, upon the principles of their British ancestors, hold most dear and sacred, it being the only security of the lives, liberties, and properties of his Majesty's subjects here." [1]

[1] Hutchinson's *Hist. Mass.*, iii. 477, 478.

A distinct opinion had been expressed by Cambridge, a fortnight earlier, at a town meeting held on the 14th day of October, 1765, when it was " Voted, That (with all humility) it is the opinion of the town, that the inhabitants of this Province have a legal claim to all the natural, inherent, constitutional rights of Englishmen, notwithstanding their distance from Great Britain; that the Stamp Act is an infraction upon these rights. (One instance out of many, in our opinion, is this: — the Distributor of Stamps will have a sovereignty over every thing but the lives of the people, since it is in his power to summon every one he pleases to Quebec, Montreal, or Newfoundland, to answer for pretended or real breaches of this Act; and when the faithful subject arrives there, by whom is he to be tried? Not by his peers (the birth-right of every Englishman); no, but by the Judge of Admiralty, without a jury, and it is possible without law. Under these circumstances, the Stamp-Master may unrighteously get more than his Majesty will upon a balance by the stamps; for who would not rather pay the fine than be thus harassed, thus tried? Why are not his Majesty's subjects in Great Britain treated in this manner? Why must we in America, who have in every instance discovered as much loyalty for his Majesty, and obedience to his laws, as any of his British subjects (and whose exertions in some of the provinces during the last war have been greater), be thus discriminated? At this time especially, whilst we are under an almost insupportable load of debt, the consequence of this exertion. We believe it may be truly said that no one in Great Britain pays so great a tax as some in this province, in proportion to their estates. Let this Act but take place, liberty will be no more: trade will languish and die; our medium will be sent into his Majesty's exchequer, and poverty come on us as an armed man. The town, therefore, hereby advise their Representatives by no means whatsoever to do any one thing that may aid said Act in its operation; but that, in conjunction with the friends of liberty, they use their utmost endeavors that the same might be repealed: — That this vote be recorded in the Town Book, that the children yet unborn may see the desire their ancestors had for their freedom and happiness: — and that an attested copy of it be given to said Representatives."

While the inhabitants of Cambridge thus protested against the arbitrary exercise of power by Parliament, and against the enforcement of the Stamp Act in particular, they were not ready to encourage any violent outbreak of popular fury. During the preceding August, by hanging him in effigy, breaking into his house, and destroying part of his furniture, some of the inhabitants of Boston had induced Mr. Secretary Oliver to promise that he would not act as Distributor of Stamps; and on the evening of the 26th of the same month, they attacked the house of Lieutenant-governor Hutchinson, who had rendered himself obnoxious by his subserviency to the British ministry, and " destroyed, carried away, or cast into the street, everything that was in the house; demolished every part of it, except the walls, as far as lay in their power; and had begun to break away the brick-work. The damage was estimated at about twenty-five hundred pounds sterling, without any regard to a great collection of public as well as private papers in the possession and custody of the Lieutenant-governor." [1] At a town meeting in Cambridge three days later (Aug. 29), it was " Voted, that the inhabitants of this town do detest and abhor the riotous proceedings in the town of Boston, in robbing and destroying the dwelling-houses of the Lieutenant-governor and others; and they will, on all occasions, use their utmost endeavors to secure their own inhabitants and their dwelling-houses and property against such ravages." But when the Governor, in his address to the General Court, recommended that compensation should be made to the sufferers, and intimated that, if they did not make it voluntarily, they might soon be required to do so," [2] the town voted, Oct. 14, 1765, that their " Representatives be and are hereby instructed by no means to vote for any moneys being drawn out of the Province treasury to make good the demands of the late sufferers, as mentioned in his Excellency's speech, have sustained." In their reply to the Governor's address, Oct. 25, 1765, the House of Representatives said, " We highly disapprove of the late acts of violence which have been committed; yet till we are convinced that to comply with what your Excellency recommends will not tend to encourage such outrages in time to come, and till some good reason can be assigned why the losses those gentlemen have sustained should be made good rather than any damage which other persons on any different occasions might happen to suffer, we are persuaded we shall not see our way clear to order such a compensation to be made. We are greatly at a loss to know who has any right to require this of us, if we should differ with your Excellency in point of its being an act of justice which concerns the credit of the government." [3] A year later, however, when the odious

[1] Hutchinson's *Hist. Mass.*, iii. 124.   [2] *Ibid.*, iii. 475, 476.
[3] *Ibid.*, iii. 129.

Stamp Act had been repealed, and this subject was again considered, at a town meeting, October 27, 1766, "The inhabitants having taken into consideration the affair now pending in the Great and General Court, relative to the losses sustained by divers persons, by means of the outrage and violence of the mob in Boston, in the month of August, A. D. 1765, — Voted, That it be an instruction to the Representative of this town to use his best endeavors in the General Court that a compensation be made to the Lieutenant-governor and other sufferers (upon proper application by them made for that purpose), by advancing such sum or sums of money out of the public treasury as may be judged adequate to their losses; and that he likewise use his endeavors that such measures may be gone into for replacing such money in the Province treasury as shall appear just and equitable." The General Court, after much discussion, enacted a law, granting compensation to the sufferers, and at the same time a free pardon to all "who had been guilty of any crimes or offences against law, occasioned by the late troubles." The Governor was induced to give his approval, because, "if the act should not be approved in England, all the effect would be the suspending, for three or four months, of prosecutions which, experience had shown, could not be carried on:" "but as to the compensation, the act would have an immediate effect and could not be recalled. The act was disapproved, upon its being laid before the king, merely from the nature of it, and the danger of establishing a precedent; but the money was paid before the news arrived, and nothing further passed upon the subject." [1]

"On the 16th of May, [1766] a copy of the Act of Parliament for the repeal of the Stamp Act was brought to Boston. No rejoicings, since the revolution, had been equal to those on this occasion." [2] But the people were not quite ready to forgive those members of the provincial government who had made themselves obnoxious by their advocacy of those arbitrary measures which threatened the extinction of popular liberty. At the organization of the government, later in the same month, "the Lieutenant-governor, the secretary, one of the judges of the Superior Court, and the attorney-general, were struck off from the council. Another of the judges, apprehensive of this slight, chose to re-

---

[1] Hutchinson's *Hist. Mass.*, iii. 158–160.

[2] *Ibid.*, iii. 147. — "We hear from Cambridge and other neighboring towns, that they have expressed their joy on account of the repeal of the Stamp Act, by illuminations, fireworks, &c., &c." — *Boston Evening Post*, May 26, 1766.

sign before the election came on." [1] The intention to exclude from the Council some of those crown officers who were supposed to be too subservient to the British ministry, is foreshadowed in the instructions given to the Representative of Cambridge, May 26, 1766, two days before the meeting of the General Court. These instructions, reported by a committee consisting of Samuel Whittemore, Ebenezer Stedman, and Eliphalet Robbins, contain the usual protestation of loyalty to the crown, of a general confidence in the good intentions of Parliament, and of a desire for the continuance of friendship and harmony between the British government and the American Colonies. At the same time, they counsel the utmost watchfulness against any possible encroachment of arbitrary power, and contain other suggestions of much importance. Two of the instructions were as follows: —

"With regard to the General Assembly, of which you will be, it is of the greatest importance that each branch should have its due weight and power; and as you are to have a part in the election of one of these branches, we instruct you to avoid giving your suffrage for any gentleman already holding offices incompatible with a seat there, or who, by any sort of dependence or connection, may be under temptations to yield to unreasonable demands of prerogative; and this we esteem of singular importance under the present circumstances of our public affairs."

"There is one thing more which we would enjoin upon you, as a matter of considerable importance; which is, that you endeavor to get a vote passed in the House, that a gallery be provided where as many persons as conveniently can, may be admitted to hear their debates; this is agreeable to the practice in the mother country, and may be attended with very salutary effects here; amongst other advantages which may arise from such an order of the House, we would hope that this would be one, namely, that it would give an opportunity to any person who desires it of seeing that nothing is passed by that assembly that is not of real benefit, and of advantage to their constituents, and that the Representatives of the people are patrons of their rights and privileges." [2]

Soon after the close of this session of the General Court, news

[1] Hutchinson's *Hist. Mass.*, iii. 148.

[2] By the printed Journal of the House of Representatives, it appears that on the 11th of June, 1767, it was ordered, "that the debates in this House be open, and that a gallery be erected on the westerly side of this room for the accommodation of such persons as shall be inclined to attend the same:" — provided, "that no person be admitted to a seat in the gallery, without applying to and being introduced by a member of this House."

arrived from England that the Parliament had by no means relinquished the intention to derive a revenue from the colonies,
but had "determined to lay small duties on paper, glass, and
painters' colors, imported into America; to take off 12ᵈ., which
had been charged in England on every pound of tea exported,
and to lay 3ᵈ. only, payable upon its importation into America."[1]
At the same time commissioners of customs were appointed, and
it was supposed that the collection of this tax was one of their
principal duties. Popular discontent and excitement followed,
as might have been expected. Associations were formed to encourage home manufactures, and to refrain from the use of foreign
articles subject to taxation. At their next winter session, the
House of Representatives prepared letters to several noblemen in
England, praying them to obtain a repeal of the new tax act,
and an address to the king; copies of which they sent to the
Assemblies of the other colonies, asking their coöperation. These
proceedings gave great offence in England. When the next
General Court met, in May, 1768, "the Governor sent a message
to the House, which engaged the whole of their attention. In
pursuance of instructions which he had received, he required
them, in His Majesty's name, to rescind the resolution of the last
House of Representatives, in consequence of which a circular
letter had been sent to the several assemblies upon the continent."[2] A few days afterwards the demand was renewed, with
a threat of dissolution as the penalty of refusal. After due consideration, and after preparing a letter to the English Secretary
for the Colonies, in justification of their proceedings, the House
refused to rescind, by a vote of ninety-two against seventeen.
This decision was communicated to the Governor, who immediately executed his threat and dissolved the House. "It was
thus made known that the vital right of representation was to be
enjoyed only on the condition of a servile compliance with an
arbitrary royal instruction."[3] It was soon afterwards reported
that three regiments of soldiers were to be stationed in Boston,
to enforce submission to the government. The inhabitants thereupon assembled in town meeting, and sent a message to the Governor, inquiring if he expected such a military force, and requesting him to summon a new General Court. On his refusal, the
town "Resolved, that as the people labor under many grievances,
and as the Governor has declared himself unable, at the request

[1] Hutchinson's *Hist. Mass.*, iii. 179.   [3] Frothingham's *Rise of the Republic*,
[2] *Ibid.*, iii. 196.   p. 221.

of the town, to call a General Court, which is the assembly of the states of the province, for the redress of such grievances, the town will make choice of a suitable number of persons, to act for them as a committee in convention, with such as may be sent to join them from the several towns in the province, in order that such measures may be concerted and advised, as his majesty's service and the peace and safety of his subjects in the province may require." [1] The time fixed for the meeting of the Convention was Sept. 22, 1768. For some reason, which does not appear, Cambridge did not elect delegates until Sept. 29: — on which day, it was "put to vote, whether it be the mind of the inhabitants of this town to proceed on the article in the Warrant, relating to the choosing a person to join with the committees of Convention of the other towns in this Province, now sitting in Boston, and it passed in the affirmative. Also voted, that they will now make choice of one or more persons, as a committee . . . . to attend the Convention that may now or hereafter be sitting in Boston in this Province. Also voted that they will make choice of two persons for the purpose aforesaid. Then Andrew Bordman was chosen, who declined the service. Then Deac. Sam^{n}. Whittemore was chosen, who declined the service. Then Capt. Sam^{n}. Whittemore was chosen, who accepted said choice. Then Thomas Gardner was chosen, who accepted said choice." If Cambridge was somewhat late in the election, her delegates were not a whit behind others in patriotism and resolution. Capt. Whittemore was the veteran, who, at the age of seventy-nine years, performed yeoman's service with his musket, on the memorable 19th of April, 1775; and Thomas Gardner, having been successively elected Captain and Colonel, sealed his patriotic devotion with his life-blood on Bunker Hill.

In the succeeding years the conflict between arbitrary power and the rights and privileges of the people became more and more earnest. The British government insisted on its right to bind the colonies in all cases, to impose taxes without their consent, to place over them rulers not of their own choice, to overawe them by the presence of foreign troops, and to supersede established laws and customs by "Royal Instructions." On the other hand, while the people professed loyalty to the crown, they protested against this invasion of their inalienable rights as freeborn Englishmen, and indicated a determination to resist to the last extremity. Among other methods adopted for the accom-

[1] Hutchinson's *Hist. Mass.*, iii. 204, 205.

plishment of this purpose, at a town-meeting in Boston, Nov. 2, 1772, upon the motion of Samuel Adams, it was voted, "that a committee of correspondence be appointed, to consist of twenty-one persons, to state the rights of the colonies, and of this province in particular, as men, as Christians, and as subjects; to communicate and publish the same to the several towns in this province and to the world, as the sense of this town, with the infringements and violations thereof that have been, or from time to time may be, made: also requesting of each town a free communication of their sentiments on this subject." At an adjourned meeting, Nov. 20, the report of this committee was accepted, and ordered to be printed in pamphlet form and distributed agreeably to the original vote. The response of Cambridge was prompt and decisive. The Records show that, at a town-meeting, Dec. 14, 1772, it was "Voted, That the letter and the book sent by order of the town of Boston to the Selectmen of Cambridge, signed in the name and by order of the town, William Cooper, Town Clerk, should be publicly read and acted upon. The Moderator [1] protested against it, as it was not in the warrant; and the same was read accordingly. Voted, That a committee be appointed to write to the committee appointed by the town of Boston, and to acknowledge the vigilance and care, discovered by the metropolis, of the public rights and liberties, acquainting them that this town will heartily concur in all salutary, proper and constitutional measures for the redress of those intolerable grievances which threaten, and if continued must overthrow, the happy civil constitution of this province; and that said committee take under consideration the rights as stated by the committee of correspondence of the town of Boston, and the infringements and violations of the same, and to make report at the adjournment of this meeting." [The Committee was then elected, consisting of Capt. Samuel Whittemore, Capt. Ebenezer Stedman, Capt. Ephraim Frost, Capt. Eliphalet Robbins, Capt. Thomas Gardner, Joseph Wellington, Abraham Watson, Jr., Nathaniel Sparhawk, and Samuel Thatcher, Jr.] "Voted, That said committee prepare instructions to the Representative, and report upon both forthwith, or as soon as may be. The committee retired; the meeting not adjourned: in less than twelve minutes

---

[1] William Brattle, Esq., was the Moderator. In the early part of the struggle he advocated the rights of the people, insomuch that he was negatived as a member of the Council in 1769, by Gov. Barnard. But promotion to the rank of Major-general, in 1771, is generally supposed to have rendered him much more favorable to the Governor and his associates.

returned, and presented their report upon the letter and resolves aforesaid, and also reported instructions for the Representative; ..hich reports were received, and accepted, and voted by a majority of the inhabitants then present.

" The instructions : — To Capt. Thomas Gardner, Representative of the town of Cambridge in General Assembly. Sir, We, his Majesty's .most dutiful and loyal subjects, freeholders and other inhabitants of the town of Cambridge, in town-meeting legally assembled this fourteenth day of December, A. D. 1772, to consult upon such measures as may be thought most proper to be taken at this alarming crisis, and most conducive to the public weal, do therefore with true patriotic spirit declare, that we are and ever have been ready to risk our lives and fortunes in defence of his majesty King George the Third, his crown and dignity, and in the support of constitutional government. So, on the other hand, we are as much concerned to maintain and secure our own invaluable rights and liberties and that glorious inheritance which was not the gift of kings or monarchs, but was purchased at no less price than the precious blood and treasure of our worthy ancestors, the first settlers of this province, who, for the sake of those rights, left their native land, their dearest friends and relations, goodly houses, pleasant gardens and fruitful fields; and in the face of every danger settled a wild and howling wilderness, where they were surrounded with an innumerable multitude of cruel and barbarous enemies, and destitute of the necessaries of life ; yet aided by the smiles of indulgent heaven, by their heroic fortitude (though small in number) they subdued their enemies before them, and by their indefatigable labor and industry cultivated this land, which is now become a fruitful field, which has much enriched our mother country, and greatly assisted in raising Great Britain to that state of opulence that it is now in ; that if any people on earth are entitled to the warmest friendship of a mother country, it is the good people of this Province and its sister colonies. But alas, with what ingratitude are we treated, how cruelly oppressed ! We have been sighing and groaning under oppression for a number of years; our natural and charter rights are violated in too many instances here to enumerate; our money extorted from us, and appropriated to augment our burdens ; we have repeatedly petitioned our most gracious sovereign for a redress of grievances, but no redress has yet been obtained, whereby we have been almost driven to despair. And, in the midst of our distresses, we are still further alarmed with seeing the Governor of the Province made independent of the people, and the shocking report that the Judges of the Superior Court of Judicature and other officers, have salaries affixed to their offices, dependent on the crown and ministry, independent of the grants of the Commons of this Province. By this establishment our lives and properties will be rendered very precarious, as there is the utmost danger that, through an undue influence, the streams of public justice will be poisoned. Can we expect the scales will be held equal between all parties? Will such Judges be unmoved by passion or prejudice, fear or favor? What a miserable situation will the man be in, under a corrupt administration, who shall dare to oppose their vile measures. Must he not expect to feel the keenest resentment of such administration, by Judges thus bribed to pursue the plan of the ministry? In fine, we look upon this last innovation so great a grievance, especially when added to the many other grievances we have been so long groaning under, as to be almost insupportable. We therefore think it seasonable and proper to instruct you, our Representative, in General Assembly, that you use your greatest influence at the next session of the General Court for a speedy redress of all our grievances. And inasmuch as it has been for some years past thought that the Judges of the Superior Court, especially since their circuits have been enlarged, have not had salaries adequate to their important services, we desire you would make due inquiry into this matter, and if you shall find it to be a fact, you would use your utmost endeavors that their salaries may be enlarged and made adequate to their merit and station; and in all our difficulties and distresses, depend upon your prudence and firmness."

The business seems not to have been fully completed at this time, and the meeting was adjourned for three weeks:—

" At an adjournment of the Town-meeting from December the fourteenth, A. D. 1772 to January the fourth 1773, the following report was read and accepted by a great majority: The Committee appointed to take under consideration the rights of the Colonists, and of this Province in particular, as stated by the town of Boston, and also a list of the infringements and violations of those rights, beg leave to report, That, in their opinion, the rights of the Colonists and of this Province in particular, as men, as Christians and as subjects, are properly stated, and that the lists of the infringements and violations of those rights are notorious facts; and as there appears to be the greatest reason to apprehend,

agreeable to the intimation made to us in the said list of grievances, that stipends or salaries are affixed to the offices of Judges of
the Superior Court, whereby they are made not only independent of the people, but absolutely dependent upon the Crown for
their support, it is further the opinion of this Committee, that
such establishment, if made, is in direct repugnancy with the
Charter of the Province, and the invariable usage from the time
the same was granted; that thereby a dangerous connection is
formed, and an undue influence in their decisions introduced, and
therefore tends to the poisoning the streams of justice in the
land; that there will, moreover, be the utmost danger that the
Bar may hereafter be overawed by a corrupt Court, insomuch that
no gentleman of shining genius and abilities in the profession of
the Law will dare to stand up in defence of an injured country.
For these and many other reasons that may be offered, the Committee beg leave further to report the following resolve, viz:
Resolved, as the opinion of this town, that the said establishment
is a dangerous innovation and grievance, especially when added to
the many other grievances we have been so long groaning under,
and that we have the strongest aversion to a measure which is of
so ruinous a tendency, and can never be reconciled to it."

Before this last named town-meeting was held, the Committee
of Correspondence, elected on the 14th of December, executed a
part of the duty assigned to them, by addressing a letter to the
Committee of Boston, which was published in the " Boston
Gazette," Dec. 28, 1772: —

" To the Committee of Communication and Correspondence at
Boston.   The Committee appointed by the town of Cambridge to
write to the Committee of Communication and Correspondence
at Boston, gladly embrace this opportunity.   In the name and
behalf of the said town of Cambridge, and with the most sincere
respect, they acknowledge the vigilance and care discovered by
the town of Boston of the public rights and liberties; acquainting
you that this town will heartily concur in all salutary, proper,
and constitutional measures for the redress of those intolerable
grievances which threaten, and if continued must overthrow, the
happy civil constitution of this Province.   It is with the greatest
pleasure we now inform you that we think the meeting was as
full as it has been for the choice of a Representative, for a number of years, if not fuller; and that the people discovered a glorious spirit, like men determined to be free.   We have here en-

closed you a copy of the votes and proceedings of this town, at their meeting, so far as they have gone. We would add, — May the town of Boston, the capital of this Province, rejoice in perpetual prosperity. May wisdom direct her in all her consultations. May her spirited and prudent conduct render her a terror to tyrants. May every town in this Province, and every other colony upon the Continent, be awakened to a sense of danger, and unite in the glorious cause of liberty. Then shall we be able effectually to disappoint the machinations of our enemies. To conclude: That this land may be purged from those sins which are a reproach to a people, and be exalted by righteousness, that God Almighty may be our God as he was the God of our fathers, and that we may be possessed of the same principles of virtue, religion, and public spirit, which warmed and animated the hearts of our renowned ancestors, is the sincere prayer of your friends in the common cause of our country, the Committee of the town of Cambridge. EBENEZER STEDMAN, per order.

In 1773, the British Ministry adopted another measure to secure the payment of a tax by the colonists. The East India Company, embarrassed by the accumulation of teas which the American merchants did not purchase, were encouraged to export them, on their own account, by an offer of a drawback of the whole duty payable in England on all such as should be exported to the British colonies in America; but the duty of three pence on a pound was still required to be paid at the port of entry. The tax demanded was very small, but it stood as the representative of a great principle ; the right, namely, of Parliament to bind the colonies in all cases whatever, — which right was asserted by the ministry and denied by the colonists. The fire of contention, which had seemed to be smouldering for a time, now burst forth into a fierce blaze. Public meetings were held, and resolutions adopted, indicating a stern spirit of resistance. Cambridge placed on record its determination to maintain its rights:—

"At a very full meeting of the inhabitants of the town of Cambridge, legally assembled, Nov. 26, 1773, Capt. Ebenezer Stedman was chosen Moderator. This town being greatly alarmed at an Act of the British Parliament, passed in the last session of Parliament, whereby the East India Company in London are empowered to export their teas on their own account to the British Plantations in America, and expose the

same to sale, subject to a duty, payable in America, to be collected by a set of worse than Egyptian taskmasters, — which, if
submitted to, we fear will prove fatal to the Colonies : — and as
we apprehend the sense of this town cannot be better expressed
than by adopting the Resolves of the patriotic citizens of Philadelphia ; — Resolved, that the disposal of their own property is
the inherent right of freemen ; that there can be no property
in that which another can of right take from us without our consent ; that the claim of Parliament to tax America is, in other
words, a claim of right to levy contributions on us at pleasure.
2. That the duty imposed by Parliament upon tea landed in
America is a tax on the Americans, or levying contributions on
them without their consent. 3. That the express purpose for
which the tax is levied on the Americans, namely, for the support of government, the administration of justice, and the defence
of his Majesty's dominions in America, has a direct tendency to
render Assemblies useless, and to introduce arbitrary government
and slavery. 4. That a virtuous and steady opposition to this
ministerial plan of governing America is absolutely necessary to
preserve even the shadow of liberty, and is a duty which every
freeman in America owes to his country, to himself, and to his
posterity. 5. That the resolution lately come into by the East
India Company, to send out their tea to America, subject to the
payment of duties on its being landed here, is an open attempt
to enforce the ministerial plan, and a violent attack upon the
liberties of America. 6. That it is the duty of every American
to oppose this attempt. 7. That whoever shall, directly or indirectly, countenance this attempt, or in any wise aid or abet in
unloading, receiving or vending, the tea sent or to be sent out by
the East India Company, while it remains subject to the payment of a duty here, is an enemy to America.

"And whereas the town of Boston have assembled twice on
this alarming occasion, and at each meeting did choose a committee of very respectable gentlemen, to wait upon the persons who
are appointed by the East India Company to receive and sell
said tea, and in a genteel manner requested them to resign their
appointment; notwithstanding the said factors have repeatedly
refused to give them any satisfaction, but, on the contrary, their
answers were evasive and highly affrontive: by such a conduct
they have forfeited all right and title to any respect from their
fellow-countrymen : — Therefore resolved, that this town will by
no means show them any respect whatever, but view them as

enemies to their country. And whereas it is reported that the said factors of the East India Company by their conduct have rendered themselves despicable in the town of Boston, yet they can retire into the country towns, where they are treated with respect, which, if true, is truly scandalous : — Therefore resolved, that any one who shall harbor said factors in their houses, except said factors immediately make full satisfaction to this justly incensed people, are unfriendly to their country. Resolved, That any person or persons, inhabitants of this Province, that shall import any teas subject to the payment of a duty in America, are in an eminent degree enemies to their country, and ought to be treated with equal contempt and detestation with the present supposed factors. And, as it is very apparent that the town of Boston are now struggling for the liberties of their country : Therefore resolved, that this town can no longer stand idle spectators, but are ready, on the shortest notice, to join with the town of Boston and other towns, in any measures that may be thought proper, to deliver ourselves and posterity from Slavery."

Within a month afterwards, the Gordian knot of this controversy was cut, by the destruction of the tea in Boston Harbor, after an earnest and protracted effort to induce the consignees to send it back to Europe. Whether any Cambridge men participated in this final act, or not, it is reasonably certain that they assisted in the preliminary measures. Hutchinson says, " the Committees of Correspondence of the towns of Boston, Roxbury, Dorchester, Brookline, and Cambridge, united, and held their meetings daily, or by short adjournments, in Faneuil Hall, or one of the rooms belonging to it, and gave such directions as they thought proper. Two of the other vessels with tea arriving from London, they were ordered by this new body to the same wharf where the first ships lay, under pretence of the Conveniency of having the whole under one guard. It soon after appeared that a further conveniency accompanied it." [1] The overt act is described in the "Boston Gazette," Monday, December 20, 1773: — " On Tuesday last the body of the people of this and all the adjacent towns, and others from the distance of twenty miles, assembled at the Old South meeting-house," and, after a fruitless negotiation with the parties in the interest of the government, " adjourned to the Thursday following, ten o'clock. They then met ; . . . . and the people, finding all their efforts to preserve the property of the East India Company and return it safely to London, frustrated by the tea consignees, the collector of the cus-

[1] *Hist. Mass.,* iii. 432.

toms, and the Governor of the Province, *dissolved* their meeting. But behold what followed. A number of brave and resolute men, determined to do all in their power to save the country from the ruin which their enemies had plotted, in less than four hours, emptied every chest of tea on board the three ships commanded by the captains Hall, Bruce, and Coffin, amounting to 342 chests, into the sea, without the least damage done to the ships or any other property. The masters and owners are well pleased, that their ships are thus cleared, and the people are almost universally congratulating each other on this happy event."

This destruction of the tea excited the liveliest indignation of the British government. It was construed as an act of open rebellion, demanding condign punishment. "The words, often cited, of the arrogant, insolent, and galling Venn, were then uttered and circulated through the colonies: ' The offence of the Americans is flagitious : the town of Boston ought to be knocked about their ears and destroyed. *Delenda est Carthago.* You will never meet with proper obedience to the laws of this country until you have destroyed that nest of locusts.' These words embodied the feeling of England in an hour of her insolence." [1] The Boston Port Bill followed, which took effect on the first day of June, 1774, enforced by an array of armed vessels, effectually preventing ingress or egress. The sympathy, not only of Massachusetts but of all the American Colonies, was excited on behalf of the oppressed and suffering inhabitants of the devoted town, which sympathy was manifested by material aid. Although Cambridge was to some extent a joint-sufferer with Boston, it was voted, at a town meeting, July 28, 1774, " That the Committee of Correspondence be a Committee to receive the donations that may be given by the inhabitants of this town for the relief of our distressed brethren in the town of Boston, now suffering for the cause of all America under an act of the British Parliament for blocking up the port of Boston ; and that they transmit the same to the Committee appointed by the town of Boston to receive such donations for the purpose abovesaid."

The Port Bill was followed by a more comprehensive measure, abrogating the Charter of Massachusetts, in some important particulars, and changing the character of the government. It provided that the members of the Council should no longer be elected by the General Court, but that they, as well as the Governor and Lieutenant-governor, should be appointed by the King. The Lieutenant-governor (Thomas Oliver), and two members

[1] *Rise of the Republic*, p. 316.

of the Council Samuel Danforth and Joseph Lee), appointed
under the provisions of this act, were inhabitants of Cambridge.
Colonel Oliver was a man of wealth and character, but had not
previously held public station, except military. [1] It was indeed
suggested by some, that his name was inserted in the commission
by mistake, instead of Peter Oliver, the Chief Justice and a
member of the old Council. Judge Lee had been a Representative, but never before a member of the Council; on the contrary,
Judge Danforth was the senior member of that Board, having
held office, by thirty-six successive elections, since May, 1739.
The new Council (styled the Mandamus Council because its
members were appointed by command of the King) consisted of
thirty-six persons, of whom, however, only twenty-four accepted
office; and of that number nine soon afterwards resigned. [2] Its
first meeting was at Salem, on the 8th day of August, 1774.
The Governor had previously (June 17) dissolved the General
Court, so that the sole governing power now vested in himself
and the newly appointed Council. The struggle between arbitrary power and the spirit of liberty became more and more intense. Some of the results, of which Cambridge was the scene
of action, and its inhabitants were among the more prominent
actors and sufferers, are related at large in the " Boston Gazette " of Monday, Sept. 5, 1774: —

" On Wednesday last, the new Divan (consisting of the
wretched fugitives with whom the just indignation of their respective townsmen, by a well-deserved expulsion, have filled this
capital) usurped the seats round the Council Board in Boston.
Their deliberations have not hitherto transpired. And with
equal secresy, on Thursday morning, half after four, about 260
troops embarked on board 13 boats, at the Long Wharf, and
proceeded up Mistic River to Temple's Farm, where they landed
and went to the powder-house,[3] on quarry-hill in Charlestown
bounds, whence they have taken 250 half barrels of powder,
the whole store there, and carried it to the castle. A detach-
ment from this corps went to Cambridge and brought off two field
pieces which had lately been sent there for Col. Brattle's Regiment. The preparation for this scandalous expedition caused

---

[1] Perhaps one exception should be
made: " We hear that Thomas Oliver,
Esq., of Cambridge, is appointed Judge of
the Provincial Courts of Vice-Admiralty
for this Province and New Hampshire."—
Boston Gazette, May 3, 1772.

[2] See *Gen. Register*, xxviii. 61, 62.

[3] This powder-house is still standing in
Somerville, about half a mile southeasterly from Tufts' College.

much speculation, as some who were near the Governor gave out that he had sworn the committee of Salem should recognise or be imprisoned; nay, some said, put on board the Scarborough and sent to England forthwith. The committee of Boston sent off an express after 10, on Wednesday evening, to advise their brethren of Salem of what they apprehended was coming against them, who received their message with great politeness, and returned an answer purporting their readiness to receive any attack they might be exposed to for acting in pursuance to the laws and interests of their country, as became men and Christians.

" From these several hostile appearances, the County of Middlesex took the alarm, and on Thursday evening began to collect in large bodies, with their arms, provisions, and ammunition, determining by some means to give a check to a power which so openly threatened their destruction, and in such a clandestine manner robbed them of the means of their defence. And on Friday morning, some thousands of them had advanced to Cambridge, armed only with sticks, as they had left their fire-arms, &c., at some distance behind them. Some, indeed, had collected on Thursday evening, and surrounded the Attorney-General's house,[1] who is also Judge of Admiralty on the new plan, for Nova Scotia; and being provoked by the firing of a gun from a window, they broke some glass, but did no more mischief. The company, however, concerned in this, were mostly boys and negroes, who soon dispersed.

" On perceiving the concourse on Friday morning, the committee of Cambridge sent express to Charlestown, who communicated the intelligence to Boston, and their respective committees proceeded to Cambridge without delay. When the first of the Boston committee came up, they found some thousands of people assembled round the court-house[2] steps, and Judge Danforth standing upon them, speaking to the body, declaring in substance that having now arrived at a very advanced age,[3] and spent the greater part in the service of the public, it was a great mortification to him to find a step lately taken by him so disagreeable to his country, in which he conscientiously had meaned to serve them; but finding their general sense against his holding a seat at the Council Board on the new establishment, he assured

---

[1] Jonathan Sewall was Attorney-general, and his house still remains at the westerly corner of Brattle and Sparks Streets.

[2] The court-house was on the westerly side of Harvard Square, where the Cambridge Lyceum now stands.

[3] Almost seventy-seven years old.

them that he had resigned said office, and would never henceforth accept or act in any office inconsistent with the charter-rights of his country; and in confirmation of said declaration, he delivered the following certificate drawn up by himself, and signed with his own hand, viz.: —

"'Although I have this day made an open declaration to a great concourse of people, who assembled at Cambridge, that I had resigned my seat at the Council Board, yet for the further satisfaction of all, I do hereby declare under my hand that such resignation has actually been made, and that it is my full purpose not to be any way concerned as a member of the Council at any time hereafter. Sept. 2ᵈ, 1774. S. DANFORTH. A true copy. Attest N. CUDWORTH, *Cl.*'

"Judge Lee was also on the court-house steps, and delivered his mind to the body in terms similar to those used by Judge Danforth, and delivered the following declaration, also drawn up and signed by him, viz.: —

"'Cambridge, 2ᵈ Sept. 1774. As great numbers of the inhabitants of the County are come into this town since my satisfying those who were met, not only by declaration but by reading to them what I wrote to the Governor at my resignation, and being desirous to give the whole County and Province full satisfaction in this matter, I hereby declare my resignation of a seat in the new constituted Council, and my determination to give no further attendance. JOS. LEE. A true copy. Test, NATH. CUDWORTH, *Cl.*' -

"Upon this a vote was called for, to see if the body was satisfied with the declarations and resignations abovesaid, and passed in the affirmative, *nem. con.*

"It was then moved to know whether that body would signify their abhorrence of mobs, riots, and the destruction of private property, and passed in the affirmative, *nem. con.*

"Col. Phips, the High-Sheriff of the County, then came before the Committee of the body, and complained that he had been hardly spoken of, for the part he had acted in delivering the powder in Charlestown Magazine to the soldiery; which the Committee candidly considered and reported to the body that it was their opinion the High-Sheriff was excusable, as he had acted in conformity to his order from the Commander-in-chief. Col. Phips also delivered the following declaration by him subscribed, viz.: —

"'Col. Phips's answer to the honorable body now in meeting

upon the common, viz. : — That I will not execute any precept
that shall be sent me under the new Acts of Parliament for
altering the Constitution of the Province of the Massachusetts
Bay, and that I will recall all the venires that I have sent out
under the new establishment. Cambridge, Sept. 2ᵈ 1774.
DAVID PHIPS. A true copy. Test, NATH. CUDWORTH, *Cl.*'
Which was accepted as satisfactory. [1]

"About 8 o'clock, his Honor Lieut. Governor Oliver set off
from Cambridge to Boston, and informed Governor Gage of the
true state of matters and the business of the people ; — which, as
his Honor told the Admiral, were not a mad mob, but the freeholders of the County, — promising to return in two hours and
confer further with them on his own circumstance as President of
the Council. On Mr. Oliver's return, he came to the Committee
and signified what he had delivered to the body in the morning,
viz. that as the commissions of Lieut. Governor and President of
the Council seemed tacked together, he should undoubtedly incur
his Majesty's displeasure, if he resigned the latter and pretended
to hold the former ; and nobody appeared to have any objection
to his enjoying the place he held constitutionally ; he begged he
might not be pressed to incur that displeasure, at the instance of
a single County, while any other Counsellor held on the new
establishment. Assuring them, however, that in case the mind
of the whole Province, collected in Congress or otherwise, appeared for his resignation, he would by no means act in opposition to it. This seemed satisfactory to the Committee, and they
were preparing to deliver it to the body, when Commissioner
Hallowell came through the town on his way to Boston. The
sight of that obnoxious person so inflamed the people, that in a
few minutes above 160 horsemen were drawn up and proceeding in pursuit of him on the full gallop. Capt. Gardner of Cambridge first began a parley with one of the foremost, which caused
them to halt till he delivered his mind very fully in dissuasion of
the pursuit, and was seconded by Mr. Deavens of Charlestown,
and Dr. Young of Boston. They generally observed that the
object of the Body's attention, that day, seemed to be the resignation of unconstitutional counsellors, and that it might introduce confusion into the proceedings of the day if any thing else
was brought upon the carpet till that important business was fin-

[1] Notwithstanding his satisfactory dec-   He was son of Lieutenant-governor Spen-
laration, Col. Phips adhered to the Royal   cer Phips.
cause, left the country, and never returned.

ished; and in a little time the gentlemen dismounted their horses and returned to the body.

"But Mr. Hallowell did not entirely escape, as one gentleman of a small stature pushed on before the general body, and followed Hallowell, who made the best of his way till he got into Roxbury, where Mr. ——— overtook and stopped him in his chaise. Hallowell snapped his pistols at him, but could not disengage himself from him till he quitted the chaise and mounted his servant's horse, on which he drove into Boston with all the speed he could make; till, the horse failing within the gate, he ran on foot to the camp, through which he spread consternation, telling them he was pursued by some thousands, who would be in town at his heels, and destroy all friends of government before them. A gentleman in Boston, observing the motion in the camp, and concluding they were on the point of marching to Cambridge from both ends of the town, communicated the alarm to Dr. Roberts, then at Charlestown Ferry, who, having a very fleet horse, brought the news in a few minutes to the Committee, then at dinner. The intelligence was instantly diffused, and the people whose arms were nearest, sent persons to bring them, while horsemen were despatched both ways to gain more certain advice of the true state of the soldiery. A greater fervor and resolution probably never appeared among any troops. The despatches soon returning and assuring the body that the soldiers still remained and were likely to remain in their camp, they resumed their business with spirit, and resolved to leave no unconstitutional officer within their reach in possession of his place. On this the Committee assembled again, and drew up the paper of which the following is a copy, and at the head of the body delivered it to Lieut. Governor Oliver, to sign, with which he complied, after obtaining their consent to add the latter clause, implying the force by which he was compelled to do it. Mr. Mason, Clerk of the County of Middlesex, also engaged to do no one thing in obedience to the new Act of Parliament impairing our Charter.

"'Cambridge, Sept. 2, 1774. Thomas Oliver, being appointed by his majesty to a seat at the Council Board, upon and in conformity to the late Act of Parliament, entitled An Act for the better regulation of the Province of Massachusetts Bay, which being a manifest infringement of the Charter rights and privileges of the people, I do hereby, in conformity to the commands of the body of the County now convened, most solemnly renounce

and resign my seat at said unconstitutional Board, and hereby
firmly promise and engage, as a man of honor and a Christian,
that I never will hereafter upon any terms whatsoever accept a
seat at said Board on the present novel and oppressive plan of
government. My house [1] at Cambridge being surrounded by
about four thousand people, in compliance with their command I
sign my name.   THOMAS OLIVER.' "

" The gentlemen from Boston, Charlestown, and Cambridge,
having provided some refreshment for their greatly-fatigued
brethren, they cheerfully accepted it, took leave, and departed
in high good humor and well satisfied."

Such is the account given in the "Boston Gazette" of the
memorable proceedings in Cambridge on the second day of September, 1774, resulting in the compulsory resignation of three
Mandamus Councillors, and the pledge of the Sheriff that he
would not execute any precept sent to him under the new Acts
of Parliament for altering the constitution of the Province. The
importance of the events, and the vivid picture afforded of the
excitement which then filled the public mind, may justify the
reproduction of the history at full length.

In the same paper [2] is published " a true copy of a letter said
to be wrote by General Brattle to the commander-in-chief, and
picked up in this town last week, viz. : —

" Cambridge, August 27, 1774. Mr. Brattle presents his duty
to Governor Gage. He apprehends it his duty to acquaint his
Excellency, from time to time, with every thing he hears and
knows to be true, and is of importance in these troublesome times,
which is the apology Mr. Brattle makes for troubling the General
with this letter.

" Capt. Minot of Concord, a very worthy man, this minute
informed Mr. Brattle that there had been repeatedly made press-
ing applications to him, to warn his company to meet at one
minute's warning, equipt with arms and ammunition, according
to law; he had constantly denied them, adding, if he did not
gratify them, he should be constrained to quit his farms and town:
Mr. Brattle told him he had better do that than lose his life and
be hanged for a rebel: he observed that many captains had done
it, though not in the Regiment to which he belonged, which

---

[1] This house was erected by Mr. Oliver,
about 1767, on the westerly side of Elmwood Avenue. The *Boston Gazette* of
Sept. 12, announced that "Lieut. Gov.
Oliver has removed his family and goods
from Cambridge to this town." He never
returned but died in exile, at Bristol
England, Nov. 29, 1815.
[2] *Boston Gazette*, Sept. 5, 1774.

was and is under Col. Elisha Jones, but in a neighboring Regiment. Mr. Brattle begs leave humbly to query whether it would not be best that there should not be one commission officer of the militia in the Province.

"This morning the selectmen of Medford came and received their town stock of powder, which was in the arsenal on quarryhill, so that there is now therein the King's powder only, which shall remain there as a sacred depositum till ordered out by the Captain-General. To his Excellency General Gage, &c. &c. &c."

This letter of Gen. Brattle had been printed in a hand-bill before it appeared in the "Gazette," and he had prepared an explanation of it, which was already in the hands of the printer; but its publication was postponed until the next week, Sept. 12th. It was characteristic of the writer, manifesting a strong desire to stand well with both parties: —

. "Boston Sept. 2, 1774. I think it but justice to myself to give an account of my conduct, for which I am blamed, and to obviate some mistakes which are believed. His Excellency Governor Gage wrote me in the words following: 'Sir, as I am informed there are several military stores in your charge at Cambridge, I beg the favor of you to send me a return of them as soon as convenient, specifying the different sorts of each. T. GAGE. To Major General Brattle.' Which order I obeyed. I did the like to Governors Pownal, Bernard, and Hutchinson; in doing of which, every soldier will say I did but my duty. But it is affirmed, I advised the Governor to remove the powder : this I positively deny, because it is absolutely false. It never so much as entered into my mind or thought. After I had made my return, I never heard one word about the affair till the night before last, when Sheriff Phipps came to my house with the Governor's order to deliver him the powder and guns ; the keys of the powder-house I then delivered him, and wrote to Mr. Mason, who had the care of the guns under me, to deliver them, which I suppose he did; both I imagine were taken, but where transported I know not. I wrote to the Governor what is contained in the Hand-Bill lately printed. I did not write the Governor the grounds and reasons of the Quere therein contained, but I will now mention them. They proceeded from a real regard both to the Commission-officers and to the Province; first to the Commission-officers; I thought and still think it was best for them; many of whom I thought would be unwilling to issue their warrants, and if they did not, I apprehended they might meet with some difficulty; and those that did, I was not convinced so great good would result therefrom as if another method was taken. Secondly, I thought and still think it would be much better for the Province; for supposing there was not one Commission-officer for the present in it, what danger could the Province sustain? It may be answered, Commission-officers are supposed to be the most understanding in military affairs. I grant it: But supposing their commissions were vacated, supposing the respective companies in the Province were disposed and determined to do any one matter or thing which they imagined to be for its safety, and proper persons were to be employed to lead them, &c., doth their not having commissions in the least unfit them from being employed in the particular services they may be chosen to execute? and in this way can not any one conceive that the Commission-officers leading their respective companies, might in the eyes of the judicious be looked upon more blamable in doing such and such things, than they would be if they were not military officers, and did not act under commission? Might not the difference with respect to the Province be looked upon very great, both at home and here? It was suggested that General Gage demanded the Towns Stocks of Powder; this certainly he did not; the above order speaks for itself. As I would not have delivered the Provincial powder to any one but to his Excellency or order, so the Towns Stocks I would have delivered to none but to the selectmen or their order. Upon the whole, the threatenings I have met with, my banishment from my own home, the place of my nativity, my house being searched, though I am informed it was without damage, and the sense of the people touching my conduct &c. cannot but be grievous, yet this grief is much lessened by the pleasure arising in my mind from a consciousness that I am a friend to my country; and, in the above instances, that I really acted according to my best judgment for its true interest. I am extremely sorry for what has taken place; I hope I may be forgiven, and desire it of all that are offended, since I acted from an honest, friendly principle, though it might be a mistaken one.

" W. BRATTLE."

The Governor having dissolved the House of Representatives in June, writs were issued for the election of a new House, to assemble at Salem on the 5th of October. Meantime, the Council elected by the former House had been superseded by the Mandamus Council. Having already compelled the resignation

of some members of this new council, and knowing that many
others had resigned or declined to accept the office, the inhabitants of Cambridge utterly refused to recognize the official authority of that obnoxious body, and, like most of the towns in
the province, instructed their Representatives, Oct. 8, 1774, to
join only with the Council which had been duly elected by the
General Court: " To Capt. Thomas Gardner and the Honble
John Winthrop Esq. Gentlemen, As you are now chosen to
represent this town in General Assembly, to meet at Salem the
5th of this instant October, you are instructed and empowered
to join with the Honble his Majesty's Council who were chosen
by both Houses legally assembled in May last, and were approved, and are the only constitutional Council in this Province
to act with them as an House of Representatives, or to act with
the Delegates that are or may be chosen by the several towns in
this Province, to form a Provincial Congress : to meet with them
from time to time, and at such time and place as by them, or
either of them, shall be agreed upon ; to consult and determine
(in either capacity) upon such matters and things as may come
before you, and in such a manner as to you may seem most conducive to the real interest of this town and province, and most
proper to deliver ourselves and all America from the iron jaws of
slavery." [1] A firm resolution to maintain their position at all
hazards, and to resist arbitrary authority even unto blood, is indicated by votes adopted at the same town meeting, empowering
the Selectmen to procure a carriage for the cannon belonging to
the town, to purchase another cannon, and to furnish powder and
balls for both; also to draw money from the treasury for the
payment of drummers and fifers, for the instruction of fifers, the
purchase of fifes, and the refreshment of soldiers, till further order. At a subsequent meeting, Nov. 28, 1774, it is recorded
that, " whereas the Provincial Congress did, on the 28th day of
October last, resolve and appoint Henry Gardner Esq. of Stow
to be Receiver General of this Province, for reasons most obvious," etc., the collectors of taxes were directed and required to
pay the province taxes to said Gardner, and the town agreed to
indemnify them ; " and if any person or persons shall refuse to
comply with the true and obvious spirit and design of the said
resolve and this vote, this town will consider them as operating

---

[1] The Governor dissolved this new
House of Representatives before the day
appointed for meeting. The members met,
however, on the 5th of October, and two
days afterwards, having resolved themselves into a Provincial Congress, adjourned to Concord, where sessions were
held during the next two months.

with the enemies of the rights and liberties of this injured and oppressed people."

A few months later, the Revolutionary War commenced, and Cambridge became the head-quarters of the American army. Of the share borne by the inhabitants of the town in the military struggle which continued nearly eight years, a brief sketch will be given in another place. The record of civil proceedings of the town, during that period, is meagre; a few facts, however, may be gleaned.

For many years after the commencement of resistance to the arbitrary measures of the ministry and of Parliament, loyalty to the King, or to the crown was professed. At length, absolute independence appeared to be the only safe and effectual solution of the difficulty. The Continental Congress, before adopting and proclaiming a Declaration of Independence, naturally desired to know whether the people would abide by it, and sought advice from the several colonies. This question was referred to each town by the General Court of Massachusetts. At a town meeting in Cambridge, May 27, 1776, it was " unanimously voted, that whereas in the late House of Representatives of this colony, 10 May 1776, it was resolved, as the opinion of that House, that the inhabitants of each town in this Colony ought, in full town-meeting warned for that purpose, to advise the person or persons who shall be chosen to represent them in the next General Court, whether that, if the honorable Congress should, for the safety of the said Colonies, declare them independent of the Kingdom of Great Britain, they the said inhabitants will solemnly engage with their lives and fortunes to support them in the measure,— We the inhabitants of the town of Cambridge, in full town-meeting assembled and warned for the purpose abovesaid, do solemnly engage with our lives and fortunes to support them in the measure." Most faithfully did they redeem their pledge.

The inhabitants of Cambridge suffered the various privations and inconveniences incident to warfare, from which they sought relief in a quiet and peaceable manner. On the 18th of September, 1776, Edward Marrett, by direction of the town, petitioned the General Court that the hospital at Sewall's Point in Brookline might no longer be used for the treatment of small-pox, as coasters were fearful of passing up the river with fuel; and so much wood in Cambridge and the vicinity had been destroyed by the army, that the inhabitants and students could obtain none except at exorbitant prices. The Court ordered " that the barracks standing within the fort at Sewall's Point be not used for a hospital, and that they be kept clear of infection."[1] August 14, 1777, the General Court granted a parcel of nails ("3300 double tens") to a Committee, for repairing the jail at Cambridge, the Committee not being able to obtain them elsewhere, — the said nails to be paid for by the town.[2] September 10, 1777. "The petition of the selectmen of the town of Cambridge, in behalf of themselves and the inhabitants of said town, humbly sheweth, — That whereas the inhabitants of said town are in great necessity of the article of salt, and it not being in their power to procure the same at any price or to make the same, our wood being at so high a price as twelve dollars a cord, and as we understand the State have supplied most of the towns within the same with some considerable quantity of the article, and are still in possession of a quantity of the same, and therefore pray that we may be supplied with such a quantity as your honors in your wisdom may see fit," etc.[3] Sept. 24, 1777. " On the petition of Isaac Bradish, under-keeper of the gaol in Cambridge, setting forth that he hath in custody a number of Scotch and Hessian prisoners, (28 in all,) and is unable to procure bread-corn sufficient for their sustenance, and therefore praying he may be allowed to draw bread-corn out of the public stores for the support of said prisoners : — Resolved, that the Board of War be, and they hereby are directed to supply the said Bradish with eight barrels of flour for the purpose above mentioned ; he the said Bradish paying for the same."[4]

It has already been stated that Cambridge instructed its Representatives, October 3, 1774, not to recognize the Mandamus Council, so called, but to join with the Council elected in the previous May, under the provisions of the Charter, or, if this were impracticable, " to act with the Delegates that are or may be chosen by the several towns in this Province to form a Provincial Congress." Such a Congress was formed, and was succeeded by others, whose resolves and recommendations, by general consent, had the force of law, — administered chiefly by committees and other officers elected by towns. After the commencement of hostilities, advice was requested of the Continental Congress, respecting a more regular form of government. On the 9th of June, 1775, that Congress "Resolved, That no obedience being due to the act of parliament for altering the Charter of the colony

[1] *Mass. Rec.*, xxxv. 257.
[2] *Mass. Arch.*, ccxv. 46.
[3] *Ibid.*, chxxiii. 134.
[4] *Printed Journal*, Ho. Rep.

of Massachusetts Bay, nor to a governor and lieutenant-governor who will not observe the directions of, but endeavor to subvert, that charter ; the governor and lieutenant-governor are to be considered as absent, and their offices vacant. And as there is no council there, and the inconveniences arising from the suspension of the powers of government are intolerable, especially at a time when General Gage hath actually levied war, and is carrying on hostilities against his majesty's peaceful and loyal subjects of that colony ; that in order to conform, as near as may be, to the spirit and substance of the charter, it be recommended to the Provincial Congress to write letters to the inhabitants of the several places which are entitled to representation in assembly, requesting them to choose such representatives ; and that the assembly, when chosen, should elect counsellors ; which assembly and council should exercise the powers of government, until a governor of his majesty's appointment will consent to govern the colony according to the charter." [1] This advice was accepted, and a General Court was duly organized. Not many months later, Governor Gage fled from the colony, independence was declared, and subjection to British authority and law was utterly renounced. Some new form of government, suitable to a free and independent people, was desired ; and the General Court proposed to frame a constitution. The people of Cambridge manifested their disapprobation of this method, and at a town-meeting, June 16, 1777, " Voted, That the Representative of this town be and hereby is instructed not to agree to any attempt that may be made at present to form a new constitution for this State by the General Court, or any other body of men whatever, but to oppose any such attempt with all his influence." And when the General Court, " acting as a Convention," agreed upon such a Constitution, Feb. 28, 1778, and submitted it to the people for approval, it was unanimously rejected by the inhabitants of Cambridge. At a town meeting, May 25, 1778, " The plan of a constitution and form of Government for the State of the Massachusetts Bay, as proposed by the Convention, was read and fully debated on ; the number of voters present was seventy-nine, all of them being freemen more than twenty-one years of age, and neither 'a negro, indian, or molatto,' among them ; the question was determined by yeas and nays, when there appeared for the proposed form, none : and against it, seventy-nine." This constitution was rejected by a large majority of the voters in the Commonwealth.

---

[1] *Journals of each Provincial Congress*, 350.

On the first day of September, 1779, a Convention of Delegates, elected for that special purpose, assembled at Cambridge,[1] and continued in session by successive adjournments until March 2, 1780. As a result of its labors, it submitted a "Constitution or Frame of Government," which was accepted by the people, and remained in force, without alteration, for the next forty years. The action of Cambridge indicates a watchful regard for popular rights, and at the same time a commendable disposition to yield individual preferences for the sake of having some established government: At a town meeting, May 22, 1780, "Voted, unanimously, in favor of the Declaration of the Bill of Rights in the new frame of government. . . . . Forty-three voted to adopt said frame of government, and with the following amendments, (two against it). By way of instructions to our Delegate for Convention: — We therefore instruct you to use your endeavors to procure an erasement of the clause in the 4th Article of the 1st Section of the 1st Chapter of the Constitution, empowering the General Court to impose and levy duties and excises upon any produce, goods, wares, merchandize, and commodities whatever, brought into, produced, manufactured, or being, within the Commonwealth; because we conceive such a power to be oppressive and dangerous to the subjects of the State. It is oppressive, as employing a great number of persons to collect the revenue, who will swallow up a considerable part of it, and who will have the most favorable opportunities to carry on iniquitous [practices] without being detected. It is likewise oppressive, as the money is raised upon the consumers, and instead of being a tax upon trade, much more considerable sums of money are taken from our consumers and thrown into the hands of the sellers than would otherwise be transferred, because the sellers will put their advance upon the money they pay as excise, in addition to the advance upon the articles of sale. It is also oppressive, as the officers must necessarily be trusted with a right to make a forcible entry into the most retired apartments; for if they have not this power, the widest door will be open for perjury. It is dangerous to the liberty of the subjects, as the government would of course be trusted with unknown sums of money, and sums which from their own nature must be uncertain, and by means of this money they may secure such influence as may subvert the liberty

---

[1] The sessions were held at Cambridge, Sept. 1-7, and Oct. 28 to Nov. 11; at Boston from Jan. 5 to March 2. The delegates from Cambridge were Abraham Watson, Esq., Mr. Benjamin Cooper, and Capt. Stephen Dana.

we have purchased at so dear a rate.   You are also instructed to
obtain an insertion of a clause in the 2ᵈ article of the 6ᵗʰ chapter of the Constitution, whereby settled Teachers of morality, &c.,
and all persons whatever who do not pay taxes shall be excluded
from a seat in the House of Representatives ; because those persons who bear no part of the public burden can not be such competent judges of the ability of the people to pay taxes, as those
who support their part. And as to the exclusion of settled
Teachers of morality, &c., let it suffice to say that we think them
very important officers in the State, and that the community must
suffer much from having so great a number employed in services
so distinct from their particular offices as undoubtedly will be,
provided the insertion be not made. At the same time, we
are not unwilling that gentlemen of this order, of shining abilities, should be introduced into superior departments by the suf-
frages of the people at large.

" However, we do not mean to be so strenuous in our objections
as to decline receiving the whole as it stands, provided in the
opinion of the Convention the amendments ought not to be made.
Accordingly, we, being willing to give up our own opinion in
lesser matters, in order to obtain a government whose authority
may not be disputed, and which we wish may soon be established,
do instruct and direct you in our name and behalf, to ratify and
confirm the proposed form, whether the amendments be made or
not."

Soon after the adoption of the Constitution, uneasiness began
to be manifested in various portions of the Commonwealth, followed by more or less tumultuary assemblages of the people, culminating, in 1786, in armed resistance to the government. From
the name of a prominent leader, this has been called the " Shays
Rebellion," which at one time assumed a formidable aspect. The
wide-spread disaffection which prevailed was not without cause.
" A heavy debt lying on the State, added to burdens of the same
nature, upon almost every incorporation within it ; a relaxation
of manners, and a free use of foreign luxuries ; a decay of trade
and manufactures, with a prevailing scarcity of money ; and,
above all, individuals involved in debt to each other, are evils
which leave us under no necessity of searching further for the
reasons of the insurrections which took place." [1] The nature
of the complaints made by the insurgents, under the name of
" grievances," may be gathered from the printed proceedings of

[1] Minot's Hist. Insurrections, 27, 28.

a convention at Hatfield, Aug. 22, 1786, declaring the following to be some of the "grievances and unnecessary burdens now lying upon the people: — The existence of the Senate; the present mode of representation; the officers of government not being annually dependent on the representatives of the people, in General Court assembled, for their salaries; all the civil officers of government not being annually elected by the representatives of the people, in General Court assembled; the existence of the Courts of Common Pleas and General Sessions of the Peace; the Fee table as it now stands; the present mode of appropriating the impost and excise; the unreasonable grants made to some of the officers of government; the supplementary aid; the present mode of paying the government securities; the present mode adopted for the payment and speedy collection of the last tax; the present mode of taxation, as it operates unequally between the polls and estates, and between landed and mercantile interests; the present method of practice of the attornies at law; the want of a sufficient medium of trade, to remedy the mischiefs arising from the scarcity of money; the General Court sitting in the town of Boston; the present embarrassments on the press; the neglect of the settlement of important matters depending between the Commonwealth and Congress, relating to monies and averages." " It is scarcely possible for a government to be more imperfect, or worse administered, than that of Massachusetts is here represented to be. Essential branches of the legislative and judicial departments were said to be grievous; material proceedings upon national concerns erroneous; obvious measures for paying the debt blindly overlooked; public monies misappropriated; and the constitution itself intolerably defective." [1] " The immediate remedies proposed by this convention were, the issue of paper money which should be made ' a legal tender in all payments, equal to silver and gold;' a revision of the Constitution; and a session of the General Court forthwith, for the redress of the 'grievances' complained of." [2] The first notice of this civil commotion found on the town records is under date of July 24, 1786: —

" A letter to the Selectmen of Cambridge, and signed by John Nutting, purporting to be written by desire of a meeting of committees from the towns of Groton, Pepperell, Shirley, Townsend, and Ashby, and requesting our concurrence in a County Convention to be held at Concord on the 23d of August next, in order to consult upon matters of public grievances, and find out means

[1] Minot's Hist. Insurrections, 34–37.   [2] Ibid., 35.

of redress, having been read, it was Voted, that the Selectmen be desired to answer said letter, and express the attachment of this town to the present constitution and administration of government, and also to express our aversion to use any irregular means for compassing an end which the constitution has already provided for, as we know of no grievances the present system of government is inadequate to redress. Voted, that the above mentioned letter, signed by John Nutting and directed to the Selectmen of this town, be printed, together with their answer, and that the Selectmen cause the same to be done." The letter and reply were accordingly printed in the " Boston Independent Chronicle," July 27, 1786, as follows: —

" To the Selectmen of Cambridge. Gentlemen, We, the committees chose by the several towns hereafter mentioned, viz. Groton, Pepperell, Shirley, Townsend, and Ashby, met at Groton the 29th day of June, 1786, to consult upon matters of public grievances ; and after appointing a chairman for that day, it was thought best to notify all the towns in this county to meet by their committees, at the house of Capt. Brown, innholder in Concord, on the 23d day of August next, to consult upon matters of public grievances and embarrassments that the people of this Commonwealth labor under, and to find out means of redress, &c. By order of the committee: JOHN NUTTING, Chairman. Groton, July 19. 1786. N. B. It is expected that a committee from the Convention that is to set in Worcester County, the 15th of August, will attend."

" To Capt. John Nutting, Pepperell, &c., &c. Cambridge, 24th July, 1786. Sir, Your letter, dated June 29, 1786, desiring the concurrence of this town in a proposed Convention, for the redress of grievances, we have received and laid before the inhabitants at a meeting. Agreeably to their request, we shall give you their sentiments on the subject. The government under which we live, the government which we have expended much blood and treasure to establish, we conceive to be founded on the most free principles which are consistent with the being of any government at all. The constitution has provided for the annual choice of every branch of the Legislature, and that the people in the several towns may assemble to deliberate on public grievances, and to instruct their Representatives. By annual elections there are frequent opportunities to change the Representatives, if their conduct is disapproved. Of what use then a Convention can be, without authority to call for information, and without power to inforce their regulations, is to us inconceivable. If any man in a town is more deserving of confidence than the rest, he should be chosen Representative; but to forbear sending constitutional Representatives, and to send unconstitutional ones, is wrong as well as trifling. It is trifling, because they can do us no good; and it is wrong, not only because it is putting the people to needless expense, but because the constitution, by providing a mode in which the business shall be done, by a very strong implication forbids its being done in any other way. The only case then in which we think Conventions justifiable, is where the legislative or executive powers of the State have been evidently and notoriously applied to unconstitutional purposes, and no constitutional means of redress remains. We have yet heard of no such abuse of power; and no grievances to be redressed being specified in your letter, a proposition of this kind seems wholly unjustifiable. We accordingly, in the name of the town, assure you, not only of our aversion to joining in this measure, but of our perfect attachment and firm adherence to the present excellent constitution and administration of government. It is in our estimation the peculiar happiness of this people to live under a mild and equitable administration, in which the penal laws are few and well executed. We therefore shall use our utmost endeavors to prevent the operations of government from being obstructed to gratify the restless disposition, or to promote the sinister views, of any designing party. By order and in behalf of the Selectmen, WILLIAM WINTHROP, Chairman."

When the Constitution of the United States was submitted to the several States, in 1788, for adoption, although it narrowly escaped rejection, being violently opposed by those who had recently manifested disaffection towards the State government, and by others who imagined that it involved an improper surrender of State rights, the voice of Cambridge was given in its favor by her two delegates, Hon. Francis Dana and Stephen Dana, Esq.

Of the inhabitants of Cambridge, a great majority were true "sons of liberty." Yet there were a few, chiefly office-holders, or citizens of the more wealthy and aristocratic class, who adhered to the British government. Some of this number made their peace and remained unmolested; others retired to Boston, on the commencement of hostilities, and subsequently found refuge in the British Provinces or in England. So many of this class resided on Brattle Street, that it was sometimes denominated

"Tory Row;" indeed they owned and occupied almost every estate bordering on that street, between Brattle Square and Mount Auburn. General William Brattle,[1] Col. John Vassall,[2] Penelope Vassall, widow of Col. Henry Vassall,[3] Richard Lechmere[4] (succeeded by Jonathan Sewall, June 10, 1771), Judge Joseph Lee,[5] Capt. George Ruggles[6] (succeeded by Thomas Fayerweather, Oct. 31, 1774), and Lieut.-gov. Thomas Oliver,[7] owned and resided on contiguous estates; and their families composed a select social circle, to which few others were admitted. Prominent among those few were Judge Samuel Danforth,[8] John Borland,[9] and Col. David Phips.[10] Of this circle of friends Madame Riedesel speaks in her Letters. Her husband was a General, captured with Burgoyne's Army, and was quartered in the Lechmere House, at the corner of Brattle and Sparks streets. She says, — "Never had I chanced upon such an agreeable situation. Seven families,[11] who were connected with each other, partly by the ties of relationship and partly by affection, had here farms, gardens, and magnificent houses, and not far off plantations of fruit. The owners of these were in the habit of daily meeting each other in the afternoons, now at the house of one, and now at another, and making themselves merry with music

---

[1] House, next westerly from the "University Press."

[2] House, afterwards Washington's Headquarters, now the homestead of Prof. Henry W. Longfellow, and famous both as the tent of Mars and as the favorite haunt of the Muses.

[3] House nearly opposite to the Headquarters, now the homestead of the venerable Samuel Batchelder.

[4] House, corner of Brattle and Sparks streets, now the homestead of John Brewster.

[5] House, corner of Brattle and Appleton streets, now the homestead of George Nichols.

[6] House, corner Brattle and Fayerweather Streets, long the homestead of the late William Wells.

[7] House, Elmwood Avenue, the homestead successively of Vice-president Elbridge Gerry, Rev. Charles Lowell, and his son Prof. James Russell Lowell, — each, in his respective sphere of politics, theology, and poetry, more illustrious than the original occupant.

All these houses remain in good condition, though erected more than a hundred years ago; but the "farms" have been divided into smaller estates.

[8] House, on the easterly side of Dunster Street, about midway between Harvard and Mount Auburn streets.

[9] House, fronting Harvard Street, between Plympton and Linden streets: long the residence of Dr. Sylvanus Plympton and Mrs. Elizabeth B. Manning.

[10] House, on Arrow Street, near Bow Street; for many years the residence of William Winthrop.

[11] "Mrs. Oliver was sister to Vassall; and Mrs. Vassall was sister to Oliver. The deceased father of Vassall and Mrs. Oliver was brother to Mrs. Ruggles, to Mrs. Borland, and to the deceased husband of the widow Vassall; and the deceased mother of Vassall and Mrs. Oliver was sister to Col. Phips, to Mrs. Lechmere, and to Mrs. Lee. The widow Vassall was also aunt to Mr. Oliver and to John Vassall's wife.

and the dance — living in prosperity, united and happy, until, alas ! this ruinous war severed them, and left all their houses desolate, except two, the proprietors of which were also soon obliged to flee." [1]

Of the loyalists before named, Judge Danforth retired soon after the outbreak in Sept., 1774, to the house of his son in Boston, where he died Oct. 27, 1777, aged about 81. Judge Lee is said to have dwelt in Boston during the siege, after which he returned to his estate, which he enjoyed unmolested until his death Dec. 5, 1802, at the age of 93. Capt. Ruggles sold his estate, Oct. 31, 1774, to Thomas Fayerweather, and removed from Cambridge ; his subsequent history is unknown to me. All the others were regarded as enemies to the movement in behalf of liberty ; they became " absentees," and their estates, together with the estates of Ralph Inman, Esq. [2] and Edward Stow, a mariner, [3] were seized for the public use, and were leased by the Committee of Correspondence. Their account current with said estates for the year 1776 is preserved in a manuscript now in my possession. I copy a specimen : —

" Dr. The estate of Thomas Oliver Esq. late of Cambridge, Absentee, to the Committee of Correspondence of the town, for the year 1776. For taking into possession and leasing out said estate, the sum of £2. Also for supporting a negro man belonging to said estate,   £3. 12 For collecting the personal estate,   £8.

Cr. By cash received as rent,   £69."

Similar charges are made for services, and credits given for rent, in regard to the estates of John Borland, Esq., deceased, £27 rent ; [4] Richard Lechmere, Esq., £36 rent, and £6 for wood and brush which was taken off said estate ; [5] Jonathan Sewall, Esq., £26 18 4 ; [6] John Vassall, Esq., £100 ; Widow Penelope Vassall, £15 ; William Brattle, Esq., £29 ; Ralph Inman, Esq.,

---

[1] *Letters*, Munsell's Ed., 1867, p. 140.

[2] House on Inman Street, opposite to the head of Austin Street.

[3] Resided on the south side of the river ; described as of Boston, 1778, in the Proscription Act.

[4] Borland died in Boston, June 5, 1775, aged 47. " His death was occasioned by the sudden breaking of a ladder, on which he stood, leading from the garret floor to the top of his house." — *N. E. Chronicle.*

[5] This property was three fifths of the "Phips Farm," in Ward Three, or East Cambridge, of which one fifth was inherited by Lechmere in the right of his wife, and the other two fifths had been purchased from Col. Phips and the Vassall heirs.

[6] The estate formerly owned by Lechmere, at the corner of Brattle and Sparks streets.

£40; Edward Stow, £10; David Phips, Esq., £40. Five of these estates were subsequently confiscated and sold by the Commonwealth; the estates of Lechmere (144 acres) and Oliver (96 acres), to Andrew Cabot, Esq., of Salem, Nov. 24, 1779; the estate of Sewall (44 acres) to Thomas Lee of Pomfret, Conn., Dec. 7, 1779;[1] the estate of Phips (50 acres) to Isaiah Doane of Boston, May 25, 1781; and the estate of Vassall (116 acres) to Nathaniel Tracy, Esq., of Newburyport, June 28, 1781. Inman returned soon, and his estate was restored to him. The heirs of Borland and the widow Vassall succeeded to the ownership of their estates in Cambridge; but several houses and stores in Boston, formerly belonging to Borland, were advertised by the agents of the Commonwealth to be leased at auction, March 1, 1780. General Brattle conveyed all his real estate in Cambridge, Dec. 18, 1774, to his only surviving son, Major Thomas Brattle, and died in Halifax, N. S., October, 1776. By the persevering efforts of Mrs. Katherine Wendell, the only surviving daughter of General Brattle, the estate was preserved from confiscation, and was recovered by Major Brattle after his return from Europe, — having been proscribed in 1778, and having subsequently exhibited satisfactory evidence of his friendship to his country and its political independence. Besides the persons already named, there were a few other loyalists, or tories, in Cambridge, but not holding such a prominent position: John Nutting, carpenter, was proscribed in 1778; Antill Gallop, a deputy sheriff, who had promised conformity in September, 1774, is said by Sabine[2] to have gone with the British troops to Halifax, in 1776; also George Inman (H. C. 1772, died 1789) and John Inman, sons of Ralph Inman, Esq.

After the close of the war, it was proposed to permit the proscribed loyalists to return, — not indeed to share in the administration of the government, but to reclaim their confiscated estates. This proposition did not meet the approval of the inhabitants of Cambridge. At a town meeting, May 5, 1783, instructions to their representative, reported by a committee consisting of James Winthrop, Samuel Thatcher, and Abraham Watson, Esquires, were unanimously adopted: —

"Sir, The choice that this town has made of you, to represent

---

[1] Sometimes called "English Thomas," to distinguish him from another Thomas Lee, his nearest neighbor. He was a rich merchant, honored and beloved for his generosity to the poor. He died May 2[?] 1797, in the 60th year of his age.

[2] *American Loyalists*, pp. 308, 381.

us in the General Court sufficiently proves the confidence we place in your integrity and abilities: and though we have no doubt of your attachment to the interest of the town and the welfare of the commonwealth, yet we think it expedient, in the present situation of affairs, to express our sentiments to you for the regulation of your conduct, that you may be enabled to act decisively and with vigor, whenever you shall be called upon to give your voice in the General Court upon the following subjects.

" The long and severe conflict which the United States have maintained with the King of Great Britain and his auxiliaries is now brought to a conclusion by a treaty in which our independence is fully recognized. But while with pleasure we anticipate the blessings of peace, it gives us no small uneasiness to observe an article in the treaty, which, in its consequences, may lessen the value and shorten the duration of it. The Congress are there bound earnestly to recommend it to the different States to provide for the restitution of the property of the absentees; and that they may return to America, and remain there twelve months in endeavoring to regain possession of their lost estates. This article, if the States should comply with it, will, we apprehend, be productive of as great if not greater calamities than any we have yet experienced. It is, however, some consolation, that the final ratification of that article depends upon the voice of the people, through the medium of their Representatives. Their conduct, upon this occasion, will determine whether it is to be a lasting peace or only a temporary cessation of hostilities. Whether Great Britain had the right they claimed of making laws binding on the then Colonies in all cases whatsoever, was a question that for a long time was fully discussed in numberless publications, previous to the connection being dissolved between that country and these States. By this means it was hardly possible there could be one person who had not considered the subject with attention, and was not prepared to give his voice on the question. At length the time arrived, when it became necessary to decide it by the sword. Then it became the duty of every man to declare his sentiments, and to make his conduct conform to his declarations. Happily for us, by far the greater part determined never to submit to the exercise of so unreasonable a claim; and in support of their determination have resolutely carried on a war, in which our enemies have practiced a degree of cruelty and destruction that has scarcely been equalled among civilized nations. A few, however, attentive to their own emolument, or influenced by some other cause not more justifiable, abandoned their country, and sought for protection under the forces which invaded it, and with them united their efforts to subjugate their fellow-citizens, and in many instances have distinguished themselves by their cruelties and barbarities. Having thus taken their side of the question, they ought surely to abide the consequence. It is hardly conceivable that persons, who have discovered such an enmity to their country, and who have exerted every effort to overturn our government, will ever make peaceable subjects of it. Without spending time to particularize every objection that may be offered against the return of those persons who are described by the laws of this Commonwealth as Conspirators and Absentees, and being convinced as we trust you are, of the dangerous consequences that will attend the admitting them again to reside among us, — we instruct you to use your influence and endeavors, by all proper means to prevent any persons of the foregoing description from ever returning, or regaining their justly forfeited estates: and if any such persons have already crept in, that the most speedy and effectual measures may be adopted for their removal."

CHAPTER XII.

CIVIL HISTORY.

FOR more than a century and a half after the settlement of Cambridge, with slight exceptions, that part of the town lying eastwardly from Quincy and Bow streets, generally denominated the "Neck," consisted of woodland, pasturage, swamps, and salt marsh. In chapter ii. an account is given of the first division of land on the northerly side of Main Street, into small lots in "the old field" and "small lot hill," and larger lots, varying in size from six to one hundred and thirty acres. Gradually these lots passed into fewer hands, until at length the larger portion of the whole was embraced in three and subsequently four farms.

The "old field" early became the property of Edward Goffe [1] and John Gay; by sundry conveyances the larger portion became vested in Chief Justice Francis Dana, who subsequently purchased the whole tract formerly called "small lot hill" (except, perhaps, a few acres in the northeasterly corner), and several other lots of land on both sides of the highway now called Main Street. Judge Dana erected a spacious mansion on the westerly side of "the highway to the common pales," [2] now called Dana Street, about midway between Main and Centre streets, which house was destroyed by fire Jan. 19, 1839. The Judge fully appreciated the beauty of the scenery visible from his residence, as is manifest from his care to prevent any obstruction to the view in one particular direction; in an agreement with Leonard Jarvis, concerning an exchange of lands, Jan. 3, 1797, it was stipulated that said Jarvis should "forever hereafter keep open the way [3] of forty feet wide, lately laid out by the said Jarvis over and across Pelham's Island (so called) to the canal cut by him through his marsh, for the mutual benefit of both parties

---

[1] He erected a house a few rods eastwardly from the junction of Main and Bow streets. A very old house, perhaps the original structure, standing on this spot, is said to have been taken down in 1774.

[2] The highway which separated the "old field" from "small lot hill."

[3] Now called Front Street.

their heirs and assigns, ... so as to leave open an uninter
rupted view from the said Dana's present dwelling-house of such
part of Cambridge Bay and of Boston as may fall in the course
of the same way, so far as the said Jarvis's land, lately Inman's
extends." Judge Dana also owned much land on the southerl
side of Main Street, both marsh and upland, including the "Soder
Farm," so called, bounded northerly on Main Street and easterl
on Pleasant Street, and a large tract, bounded northerly on Mai
Street and westerly on Putnam Avenue. His estate bordere
on the southerly side of Main Street, from Putnam Avenue t
Bay Street, from Vernon Street to Pearl Street; and from Brook
line Street to Front Street; also on the northerly side of Mai
Street, from a point about two hundred feet westerly from Rem
ington Street to a point about midway between Hancock and Le
streets. The Judge had therefore a strong personal interest ir
the improvement of this part of the town.

Of the large lots lying eastwardly from "small lot hill," th
first two were owned by Governor Thomas Dudley and his so
Samuel Dudley. When Dudley left Cambridge his real estat
was purchased by Roger Harlakenden, who died in 1638, an
his widow married Herbert Pelham. In 1642, Pelham appear
to have owned the above mentioned lots, together with the nex
two, formerly owned by Richard Goodman and William Wes
wood; the whole containing 118 acres,[1] and extending fro
Main Street to Somerville line. Pelham also became the own
of the real estate of Simon Bradstreet, one portion of which w
a lot of upland and marsh, long known as "Pelham's Island;
its boundaries very nearly coincided with Columbia Street on t
west, School Street on the north, and Moore Street on the eas
the east and west lines being extended across Main Street, b
yond Goffe's Cove, so far as to embrace sixty acres in the who
lot. These two large lots passed, by several conveyances,
Ralph Inman, who became the owner in 1756; his executor co
veyed the same to Leonard Jarvis, Aug. 21, 1792, except t
acres, south of Goffe's Cove, previously sold to Judge Dan
Subsequently Jarvis purchased the land between these two lo
extending from Norfolk Street to Columbia Street, and norther
from one hundred to two hundred feet beyond Austin Street;
that he then owned all the land bordering on the northerly si
of Main Street from the point about midway between Hanco

[1] After 1719, "Mr. Pelham's great lot" is generally described as contain
104 acres.

and Lee streets to Moore Street, and about fifty acres on the southerly side of Main Street, easterly from its junction with Front Street.

The lot of Atherton Hough (or Haugh) "in Graves his neck," containing 130 acres in 1635, and embracing all the upland in East Cambridge, was enlarged, by the addition of the lots originally assigned to John Talcott, Matthew Allen, and Mrs. Mussey, before 1642, when it was described as containing 267 acres. Subsequently the 63 acre lot of Governor Haynes was added, and when the estate was purchased, Aug. 15, 1706, by Spencer Phips (afterwards Lieut.-governor), it was said to contain "300 acres more or less;" but it actually contained 326 acres, when measured for division after his decease. In his inventory, this tract is called two farms, with a house and barn on each. The whole was bounded on the west by a line commencing at a point thirty feet south of School Street, and about one hundred feet east of Columbia Street, and thence running northerly, nearly parallel with Columbia Street to Somerville; on the north by Somerville and Miller's River; on the east by Charles River; on the south by School Street, from the point of beginning, to Moore Street, then on the east by a straight line extended to a point about fifty feet south of Plymouth Street, and about one hundred and fifty feet west of Portland Street; then turning at a right angle, the boundary line extended in the direction of the Great Dam, which is still visible, to Charles River, crossing Third Street near its intersection with Munroe Street. (See the Plan.) This estate was divided in 1759 between the children and grandchildren of Lieut.-gov. Phips, namely, Col. David Phips; Sarah, wife of Andrew Bordman; Mary, wife of Richard Lechmere; Rebecca, wife of Judge Joseph Lee; and the children of Elizabeth, the deceased wife of Col. John Vassall. Lechmere soon afterwards purchased the shares of Col. Phips and the Vassall heirs, and became the owner of all the upland and a large portion of the marsh in East Cambridge, which was confiscated by the State and sold to Andrew Cabot, of Salem, Nov. 24, 1779. Judge Lee had the northwesterly portion of the "Phips' Farm," and Andrew Bordman had the southwesterly portion, extending from School Street to a point nine feet northerly from the intersection of the easterly lines of Windsor Street and Webster Avenue, and bounded south on the Jarvis estate, west on the Jarvis, Wyeth, and Foxcroft estates, and extending so far east as to include somewhat more than thirteen acres of marsh on the easterly side of North Canal.

Such was the unimproved condition of the easterly and now most populous section of Cambridge, before West Boston Bridge was opened for public travel, Nov. 23, 1793. At that time, Rev. Dr. Holmes says:[1] "Below the seat of the late Chief Justice Dana, there were but four dwelling-houses; one on the Inman place,[2] now belonging to Jonathan L. Austin, Esq.; one[3] nearly opposite, on a farm of Judge Dana, formerly the Soden farm, south of the main road; one on the Phips' farm, lately owned by Mr. Andrew Bordman;[4] and one at Lechmere's Point."[5] A new impulse towards improvement manifested itself immediately after the opening of the bridge. Building lots for houses and stores were laid out by Jarvis and Dana, which were soon occupied. Dr. Holmes further says that, during the month next after the opening of the bridge, "a store[6] was erected and opened near the west end of the causeway[7] by Messrs. Vose & Makepeace,[8]

---

[1] "Memoir of Cambridgeport," appended to a sermon at the ordination of Rev. Thomas B. Gannett, Jan. 19, 1814.

[2] On Inman Street, at the head of Austin Street. The mansion house, with a part of the farm, was purchased by the Austins when the Jarvis estate was sold in 1801. The house was removed in 1873 to the corner of Brookline and Auburn streets.

[3] This farm-house stood until about 1840, on the westerly side of Pleasant Street, near its intersection with River Street.

[4] Andrew Bordman, grandson of Lieut.-gov. Phips, inherited this estate on the death of his parents. The house stood on the northerly side of Plymouth Street, between Webster Avenue and Berkshire Street, and was wantonly destroyed about thirty years ago.

[5] On the northerly side of Spring Street, between Third and Fourth streets; it was demolished about the year 1820.

[6] This store remains standing on the northerly side of Main Street, directly opposite to Osborn Street.

[7] The causeway extended from the river to the junction of Main and Front streets, passing near the northerly side of Pelham's Island.

[8] Among those who were actively engaged in promoting the settlement of Cambridgeport, the name of Royal Makepeace is very conspicuous. Born March 29, 1772, at the age of twenty-one years, or earlier, he left his native town (Western, now Warren, Mass.), and came to Boston, in company with Robert Vose, his townsman, each having borrowed for that purpose the sum of twenty-five dollars. After a short mercantile apprenticeship, they entered into partnership, and commenced business in Boston at the South End. They soon afterwards removed to Cambridgeport, where, as heretofore stated, they erected the first store after the completion of the bridge in 1793. In addition to their regular business as grocers, they commenced buying and selling real estate. This partnership was dissolved in 1803, by the death of Mr. Vose. In the business of the store John Cook became a partner; but Rufus Davenport, a Boston merchant, was the principal associate of Mr. Makepeace in his subsequent transactions in real estate in which it would seem that Mr. Davenport contributed the larger part of the cash capital, which was offset by the skill and judgment of Mr. Makepeace, who was the leading spirit in nearly all the scheme projected for public improvement. He also rendered faithful and useful service in various town offices, and as Representative in the General Court. After the ruin of his financial enterprises, he removed to Baltimore, in 1832, to superintend the "Canton Company Improv

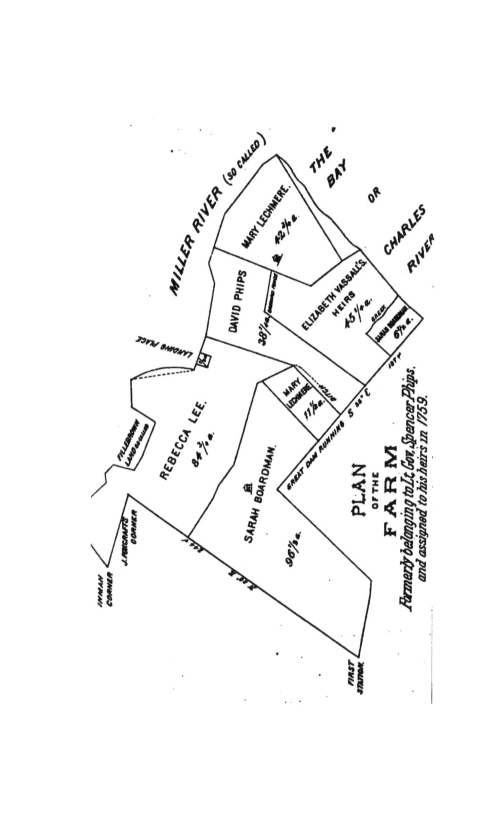

MILLER RIVER (SO CALLED)

THE BAY OR CHARLES RIVER

MARY LECHMERE. 42 3/4 a.

DAVID PHIPS

38 1/4 a.

ELIZABETH VASSALL'S HEIRS 45 1/4 a.

CREEK

SARAH BOARDMAN 6 3/4 a.

LANDING PLACE

FILLEBROWN LAND & C. LATE

REBECCA LEE. 84 3/4 a.

MARY LECHMERE 11 1/4 a.

GREAT DAM RUNNING S 55° C

SARAH BOARDMAN.

96 3/4 a.

J. MARCRAFTS CORNER

INMAN CORNER

FIRST STATION

PLAN OF THE FARM

Formerly belonging to Lt. Gov. Spencer Phips.
and assigned to his heirs in 1759.

which, after the opening of the great road, was the first framed
building set up between Boston and Old Cambridge. The following year, a large house designed for a tavern [1] was built by
Leonard Jarvis, Esq., and soon after were erected six other houses
and stores." [2] Of these six houses and stores, some may be identified with tolerable accuracy. Vose & Makepeace erected the
dwelling-house, which remains standing on the westerly corner
of Main and Osborn streets, opposite to their store, before Dec.
17, 1795. Jonathan Brooks erected a store between Cherry and
Windsor Streets, on the northerly side of Main Street, before
June 5, 1795, — perhaps the same building so long occupied by
Eliphalet Davis, and now by his son Thomas M. Davis, for the
manufacture of fancy soap. Scott & Hayden erected a store
on the lot next westerly from the store-lot of Vose & Makepeace, before 1800. Besides these, Stanton Parker erected a store
and shed on the northerly side of Main Street, the precise location not known, before Nov. 11, 1794. Asaph Harlow purchased
a lot on the northerly side of Main Street, Jan. 15, 1798, most
of which was used in 1873 for the construction of Portland Street;
and the house which he erected was then removed a few feet eastwardly to the easterly corner of Portland and Main streets.
Richard Thayer bought a lot, Sept. 1, 1802, and erected the
house now standing on the westerly corner of Main and Portland
streets. Next westerly from the Thayer estate was a lot, with
a currier's shop thereon,[3] which was sold by Daniel Mason to Oliver Blake, Sept. 28, 1797. William Watson sold to Josiah and
Phinehas B. Hovey a large lot, two hundred feet in width, on
the westerly corner of Main and Brookline streets, Oct. 14,
1799, on which was very soon erected the store which was occupied more than half a century by the late Phinehas B. Hovey,
who died April 17, 1852, and was succeeded by his son Josiah
Dana Hovey, the present occupant. On the adjoining lot, at the
easterly corner of Main and Pearl streets, a tavern was erected
before April 10, 1802, and was then occupied by James Adams;
but the land was not sold, and it now remains in possession of
the Watson family. Judge Dana sold the lots fronting on Main
Street, between Pearl and Magazine streets, in Jan., 1800, and

---

ments," so called, and died in a green
old age, his eye not having lost its bril-
liancy, June 6, 1855. — See *Makepeace
Genealogy*, by William Makepeace.

[1] The tavern stood on the lot next
eastwardly from the store of Vose &

Makepeace. It was destroyed by fire,
Dec. 22, 1851.

[2] *Ordination Sermon, ut sup.*

[3] This lot was described in the deed as
being "a few rods east of Pelham's
Island."

March, 1801. Arrangements were made for other improvements,
by laying out, on paper at least, several streets. Moreover,
Judge Dana and Mr. Jarvis, for the exclusion of salt water from
their marsh lands lying south of Pelham's Island and east of
Brookline Street, constructed before 1797 a substantial dike,
which yet remains, on the outer side of Sidney and Auburn
streets. In connection with this dike, Judge Dana opened the
Canal which now extends from the head of Goffe's Cove to
Brookline Street, about a hundred feet southerly from Auburn
Street. Mr. Jarvis laid out Front Street, as far as to the bend
near Village Street, and opened a canal from that point southerly
to Goffe's Cove, before 1797.

The prosperity of this incipient village early received a severe
check. In less than five years after the bridge was opened, and
before much had been accomplished in the work of reclaiming
marshes and swamps, Mr. Jarvis became indebted to the United
States in a large sum, and his real estate was seized by the government. In the subsequent conveyances of this estate by the
United States Marshal, it is recited that, at a "Circuit Court for
the District of Massachusetts," June 1, 1798, the United States
"obtained judgment against Leonard Jarvis of Cambridge, in said
District, Esquire, for the sum of thirty-nine thousand six hundred and ninety-two dollars and twenty-one cents, and fourteen
dollars and twenty cents costs of suit;" and that an execution,
issued July 6, 1798, was "levied on certain real estate situated
in Cambridge aforesaid, . . . said estate being two hundred and
forty-five acres of land, more or less, consisting of upland and
marsh, with sundry buildings," etc. From this time for nearly
three years this estate was entirely withdrawn from the market,
including both sides of Main Street from Moore Street to Front
Street, and extending on the northerly side to a point midway
between Lee and Hancock streets. But what at first seemed
utterly disastrous, proved in the end to be beneficial. In January, 1801, this estate, having been divided into fifty-four lots,
varying in size from a few thousand square feet to forty-seven
acres[1] was sold at public auction. "From this time," says Dr.
Holmes, "commenced a rapid settlement. Several large stores
were erected the next year, and soon after dwelling-houses. . . . .
In the space of about five years, upwards of a hundred families
have settled on this spot; and the number of inhabitants is esti-

[1] Delineated on a plan drawn by Peter   the Middlesex Registry of Deeds, Book
Tufts, Jr., Aug. 22, 1800, and recorded in   164, p. 545.

mated at more than one thousand." [1] The principal land-holders
had not hitherto manifested a very strong desire to transfer their
lands to new owners. Perhaps each waited for the others to sell,
hoping to share the benefit of augmented prices without parting
with their own property at a low rate. Mr. Watson sold very
few lots before 1801; Judge Dana bought more than he sold;
and Mr. Bordman seems not to have sold a single lot, or even to
have made preparation for sales by obtaining access to the Main
Street. Indeed Judge Dana and Mr. Watson did not afterwards
sell freely; but much the larger portion of their lands descended
to their posterity. Mr. Bordman, on the contrary, in 1801,
united with others in laying out Windsor Street; giving all the
land through his own estate, from School Street to Webster
Avenue, and in the same year he sold that portion of his estate
lying east of Windsor Street and south of Harvard Street, somewhat more than six acres, to Charles Clark and Daniel Mason,
who immediately divided it into small lots and brought it into
the market. In 1808, he laid out into building-lots all his lands
west of Windsor Street and south of Harvard Street; and in
1804 he sold all which remained of his farm on the east side of
Windsor Street, sixty-five acres, to Rufus Davenport and Royal
Makepeace, who offered it for sale in small lots, but were disappointed in the result. Mr. Austin, who purchased the Jarvis
Mansion-house, with forty-seven acres of land, laid out several
lots on Main Street between Temple and Inman streets, and
opened Austin Street through its whole length, with building-
lots on both sides, in 1801: he also sold a section east of Norfolk
Street between Washington and Harvard Streets, to Davenport
& Makepeace, who prepared it at once for the market. From
this time there was no lack of accommodations for all comers;
the supply was fully equal to the demand.

In addition to the efforts of individuals to increase the market
value of their own lands, by means of dikes and streets, other
improvements of a more public character were projected for the
general advantage of the community. Expensive avenues into
the country were constructed to attract travel and business. The
"Cambridge and Concord Turnpike Corporation" was established
March 8, 1808, with authority to make a turnpike-road from the
westerly side of Cambridge Common to Concord; [2] and two years
afterwards, March 8, 1805, the corporation was authorized to

[1] *Ordination Sermon, ut sup.*　　[2] The Cambridge portion of this turnpike is now called Concord Avenue.

extend the turnpike to the Causeway near West Boston Bridge.[1] The "Middlesex Turnpike Corporation" was established June 15, 1805, with authority to make a turnpike-road from Tyngsborough through Chelmsford, Billerica, and Bedford, to Cambridge, uniting with the Cambridge and Concord Turnpike near West Boston Bridge.[2] Other avenues were subsequently opened, which will receive notice in another place.

By an Act of Congress, approved Jan. 11, 1805, it was enacted "that the town or landing-place of Cambridge in the State of Massachusetts shall be a port of delivery, to be annexed to the district of Boston and Charlestown, and shall be subject to the same regulations as other ports of delivery in the United States." Accordingly this part of Cambridge has, since that time, been designated Cambridgeport. To make the place available as a "port of delivery," canals were constructed from Charles River through the Great Marsh, giving an extensive water-front. These canals are described in an agreement, dated July 8, 1806,[3] and recorded in the Middlesex Registry of Deeds, Book 172, page 496. The land devoted to this purpose is said to be a part of the "hundred share estate, so called by said owners by articles under seal."[4] The description of the canals may be briefly condensed as follows: —

BROAD CANAL, 80 feet wide, from low-water mark in Charles River to Portland Street, parallel with Broadway and Hampshire Street, at the distance of 186 feet, northerly, from the former, and 154 feet from the latter.

WEST DOCK, bounded by a line commencing at a point in the westerly line of Portland Street, 154 feet northerly from Hampshire Street, thence running parallel with Hampshire Street to a point 100 feet from Medford Street (now Webster Avenue); thence parallel with Medford Street, to a point 100 feet from Bristol Street; thence parallel with Bristol Street, to a point 100 feet from Portland Street; thence "parallel with Portland Street 210 feet to the southerly line of land late of Walter Frost;" thence in "a straight line to a point which is on the

---

[1] This extension is now known as Broadway.

[2] The Cambridge portion of this turnpike is now called Hampshire Street.

[3] Broad Canal, at least, was projected as early as May 19, 1802, when Voss & Makepeace conveyed to Josiah Mason, Jr., a right to use the "Canal which is to be made," where Broad Canal now is.

[4] The "hundred share estate" was owned thus: Rufus Davenport, fifty-five shares; Royal Makepeace, twenty-five shares; Henry Hill, ten shares; Josiah Mason, Jr., four shares; Daniel Mason, three shares; Charles Clark, three shares.

westerly line of Portland Street, 20 feet southerly and westerly of the northeasterly line of land late of Timothy and Eunice Swan; then turning and running southerly and westerly on Portland Street, to the bounds of West Dock begun at;" with the "right of a water-communication, or passage-way, 25 feet wide, through Portland Street under a bridge, from the main part of Broad Canal to that part called West Dock."[1]

NORTH CANAL, 60 feet wide, 180 feet easterly from Portland Street, and extending from Broad Canal to a point near the northerly line of the Bordman Farm. This canal was subsequently extended to Miller's River. According to an agreement, June 14, 1811, between the Lechmere Point Corporation and Davenport & Makepeace, the latter were to have perpetual right to pass with boats and rafts "through Miller's Creek or North River, so called, to North Canal and Broad Canal," and to extend North Canal, through land owned by the Corporation, to Miller's River; and the Corporation was to have the right to pass through the said canals to Charles River, so long as the canals should remain open.

CROSS CANAL, " bounded by two straight lines, 30 feet apart, and running at a right angle with Broadway from Broad Canal, between lots 279 and 280, through Broadway, and between lots 263 and 264 to South Dock."

SOUTH DOCK, bounded by a line commencing at the southeast corner of Cross Canal, thence running southeasterly 53 feet; thence southwesterly, parallel with the line of Cross Canal to a point 10 feet distant from land of the Proprietors of West Boston Bridge; thence westerly, at the same distance from said Proprietors' land, to lot 215 : thence northerly, at a right angle with the causeway of West Boston Bridge, 81 feet; thence northwesterly, 98 feet, to the easterly corner of lot 214; thence, in a straight line, to the southerly corner of lot 262 ; thence, on said lot 262, 67 feet, to lot 263; thence southerly and easterly on said lot 263, 54 feet, and on Cross Canal, 30 feet, to the point of beginning. This dock was connected with Charles River by a creek, over which was the bridge, long known as " Little Bridge," at the junction of Main and Harvard streets.[2]

---

[1] Although scarcely a vestige of this dock now remains, it was plainly visible a quarter of a century ago. It seems to have been designed as the head of navigation and a central point of business. Lots fronting on the dock were laid out, twenty feet wide, apparently designed for stores and warehouses, some of which were sold at a high price; but it does not appear that any such buildings were erected.

[2] Little Bridge was superseded by a

SOUTH CANAL, 60 feet wide, about midway between Harvard Street and Broadway, from South Dock to a point 113 feet easterly from Davis Street.

"In 1802, a school house was built on a piece of land [1] presented by Mr. Andrew Bordman to the town for that purpose. It cost about six hundred dollars; upwards of three hundred dollars were paid by the town of Cambridge, and the remainder contributed by individuals." "In 1803, a Fire Society was formed, which, at an expense of upwards of five hundred dollars, procured an excellent engine; and a company was raised to take charge of it." [2]

By an act passed June 15, 1805, Royal Makepeace, John Cook, Josiah Mason, Jr., Daniel Mason, and Andrew Bordman, were "constituted and made a corporation and body-politic, by the name of the Cambridgeport Meeting-house Corporation, . . . for the purpose of building a meeting-house and supporting public worship therein, in the easterly part of Cambridge." Of the hundred shares of stock in this Corporation, Rufus Davenport was the owner of twenty, and Royal Makepeace of seventeen. A spacious brick meeting-house was erected on the westerly side of the square bounded by Broadway, and Boardman, Harvard, and Columbia streets. The easterly half of the square was given by Andrew Bordman, and the westerly half by the owners of the "hundred share estate." [3] This house was dedicated Jan. 1, 1807. By an Act passed March 1, 1808, the proprietors of the meeting-house, together with all the inhabitants and estates in the Fifth School District, in Cambridge, east of Dana Street and a line extended in the same direction northerly to Charlestown (now Somerville), and southerly to the river, were incorporated

solid roadway about thirty years ago. By the raising of the grade between Broadway and Main Street, and the extension of Sixth Street, in 1873, the South Dock and Cross Canal were effectually obliterated.

[1] At the northwesterly corner of Windsor and School streets, where a large brick school-house now stands.

[2] Dr. Holmes' *Ordination Sermon*, ut sup.

[3] A portion of this square was offered to the County of Middlesex, for the accommodation of a court-house and other County buildings; but the offer was not accepted. The meeting-house was occupied until Nov. 10, 1833, when it was so much damaged by the wind that it was abandoned, and a new house was erected, in 1834, on the northerly side of Austin Street, between Norfolk and Essex streets. The lot, having ceased to be used for a meeting-house, was forfeited, and reverted to the heirs and assigns of the donors. It is worthy of note, as indicating the expectations indulged at that period, that when the meeting-house was erected, there was not a single dwelling-house on Columbia Street; this fact was assigned by the Selectmen, Nov. 3, 1806, as a reason for not establishing that street as a public highway.

as the Cambridgeport Parish; and Feb. 2, 1809, the proprietors (reserving private ownership of pews) conveyed to the Parish the meeting-house and lot, containing two acres, together with a parsonage lot at the northeasterly corner of Harvard and Prospect streets.

By an Act passed March 4, 1809, Rufus Davenport, Henry Hill, Samuel May, Elijah Davenport, Pliny Cutler, and their associates, were incorporated as the "Cambridgeport manufactory, for the purpose of manufacturing cotton and sea-salt;" and they were further authorized, Feb. 27, 1813, to manufacture "printing-types and other articles usually manufactured in chemical laboratories." I find no trace, however, of the establishment of such a manufactory.

While the measures adopted for the improvement of Cambridgeport were in the "full tide of successful experiment," a similar enterprise was undertaken at Lechmere Point in which the prime mover was Andrew Craigie.[1] The earliest transactions were conducted by Mr. Craigie with much skill and secrecy. His name does not appear on the records until the whole scheme was accomplished; indeed he took no deed of land in his own name until Feb. 14, 1803, when he purchased of Abraham Biglow nearly forty acres of land, formerly the northwesterly part of the Inman or Jarvis Farm. But other purchases, manifestly in his interest, had been made at an earlier period. It has heretofore been stated that the estate of Richard Lechmere was confiscated by the State, and sold to Andrew Cabot in 1779. This estate, together with the share of the Phips Farm assigned to Judge Lee and his wife, and subsequently bought by Cabot, was sold for £3,300 to Seth Johnson of New York, Jan. 31, 1795, and mortgaged by him to John Cabot for £2,200: and on the 18th of December, 1797, Johnson, for a nominal consideration, quitclaimed all his interest in the estate to Bossenger Foster of Cambridge (brother-in-law to Mr. Craigie), who, by an agreement dated six months later, engaged to convey the estate to Craigie, on the performance of certain conditions. The next step was to secure the reversionary rights of Mrs. Lechmere and her children in the confiscated estate of her husband, or in so much thereof as was held in her right by inheritance from her father. These

---

[1] Mr. Craigie was apothecary-general of the Northern Department of the Revolutionary Army, Sept. 5, 1777, when the Council of Massachusetts granted him supplies for the General Hospital. He purchased the Vassall House, or Washington Headquarters, Jan. 1, 1792, and resided there until Sept. 19, 1819, when he closed an active life, checkered by many vicissitudes.

rights were conveyed, Oct. 14, 1799, by Lechmere and his wife
to Samuel Haven of Dedham, whose wife was daughter of. Mr.
Foster and niece of Mr. Craigie.   Mr. Cabot took possession of
the estate under the mortgage from Johnson, having obtained judgment therefor in 1800, and sold the same to Samuel Parkman of
Boston, Aug. 26, 1803.   Parkman conveyed to Craigie all his
rights in the whole estate, by deed dated June 8, 1806, and on the
26th of January, 1807, the widow and administratrix of Bossenger
Foster conveyed to Mr. Craigie (her brother) the Johnson title,
pursuant to the beforementioned agreement.   Having thus secured a complete title to the whole of the Phips Farm, except the
share assigned to Andrew Bordman and his wife, Mr. Craigie
bought of Jonas Wyeth, 3d, Feb. 11, 1807, about forty acres,
formerly the northerly part of the Inman or Jarvis estate, and
May 5, 1807, of the heirs of Ebenezer Shed, about five acres,
lying partly in Somerville, and adjoining the land purchased of
Wyeth, so that he now owned about three hundred acres of land,
in two parcels nearly adjoining each other ; the easterly parcel
included almost the whole of East Cambridge, and extended
westerly to a point near the intersection of Webster Avenue with
Cambridge Street, bounded southerly by a line passing near the
intersection of Windsor Street with Webster Avenue; the westerly parcel extended from Elm Street to a line about midway between Fayette Street and Maple Avenue ; its southerly boundary
was an old lane, long ago discontinued, commencing on Inman
Street, one hundred and seventy-six feet south of Broadway, and
crossing Broadway near its intersection with Elm Street ; on the
west side of Inman Street, the south boundary was a line varying from four hundred to three hundred feet north of Broadway.
Although Mr. Craigie's title to this whole property was substantially complete, inasmuch as it was within his control, yet he had
not, up to this time, received a release of the reversionary rights
of Mrs. Lechmere and her children ; for obvious reasons he preferred to let this part of the title remain in the hands of his relative, Mr. Haven.   As early as June 21, 1806, he seems to have
submitted a claim against the Commonwealth for damages on
account of " a breach of the covenants of warranty," in the deed
of the Lechmere estate to Cabot ; for when he sought, at that
date, to improve his property, by " building a dam from Prison
Point in Charlestown to Lechmere's Point in Cambridge and
erecting mills on the same," the General Court inserted in the
act of incorporation a provision that it should " be of no avail or

effect . . . . until a release and discharge of all the covenants
of warranty made by this Commonwealth of any of the lands
conveyed by said Commonwealth, lying at or near Lechmere's
Point mentioned in this Act, shall be obtained from the person
or persons who are legally authorized to make such release or
discharge." So also when John C. Jones, Loammi Baldwin,
Aaron Dexter, Benjamin Weld, Joseph Coolidge, Jr., Benjamin
Joy, Gorham Parsons, Jonathan Ingersoll, John Beach, Abijah
Cheever, William B. Hutchins, Stephen Howard, and Andrew
Craigie, with their associates, were incorporated, Feb. 27, 1807,
with authority to erect Canal Bridge, familiarly called Craigie's
Bridge, from " the northwesterly end of Leverett street " in Boston " to the east end of Lechmere's Point," a similar provision
was inserted that the act should be of no effect " until a release
and discharge of all the covenants of warranty contained in the
deed of James Prescott, Joseph Hosmer, and Samuel Thatcher,
Esqs., unto Andrew Cabot and his assigns shall be made and obtained from Andrew Craigie or the person or persons who are
legally authorized to make such release and discharge."   The
memorial setting forth this claim of damage is mentioned in the
Records of the Executive Council, Feb. 9, 1807, while the petition for leave to erect Canal Bridge was pending in the General
Court : " The Committee to whom was referred the memorial
of Andrew Craigie, praying that some measures might be adopted
to ascertain the terms on which his claim to damages for a breach
of the covenant of warranty contained in a deed made by this
Commonwealth to Andrew Cabot of land lying at or near Lechmere's Point, so called, and on which the same claim may be adjusted, beg leave to report : that on the 24th of November, 1779,
this Commonwealth by its Committee conveyed to Andrew
Cabot the fifty-four acres and one quarter of land as stated in the
said memorial, in which deed of conveyance there was a general
warranty against the lawful claims and demands of all persons ;
that the said Andrew Craigie by sundry successive conveyances
duly executed is the assignee of the said Cabot, and is by law
entitled to the benefits of the said warranty and capable of dis-
charging the same ; that the said fifty-four acres and one quarter
of an acre, on the death of Richard Lechmere, will by law revert
to Mary Lechmere his wife, or to her heirs, in whose right the
said Richard possessed the same at the time of its confiscation ;
that the land in question, from its local situation, appears to be
capable of important improvements, but from various connecting

circumstances it is very difficult to ascertain its value to the proprietor; that he has mentioned no sum of money for which he would discharge the Commonwealth from the warranty," etc. The Committee thus reported the facts, without any specific recommendation. It would seem that Mr. Craigie did not succeed in obtaining any further compensation, and that he preferred to abandon all claim for it, rather than to forfeit the privilege of erecting the dam and bridge before mentioned; for on the 9th of May, 1808, he executed a deed releasing all such claims for damage, in consideration of the right granted to him by two Acts of the General Court, in 1807 and 1808, to erect a bridge from Lechmere Point to Boston; which release was accepted and approved by the Governor, May 12, 1808.

Having thus released the Commonwealth from liability to damage for breach of warranty, Mr. Craigie completed his record-title by receiving, for the nominal consideration of one dollar, a conveyance, dated Sept. 20, 1808, of the reversionary right to "all the estate which was set off to Mary Lechmere," which had been held for him since Oct. 14, 1799, by his friend and kinsman, Mr. Haven. The actual value of the property was much enhanced by the privilege to erect a bridge, and to make the other improvements authorized by the General Court. But the apparent inflation of value was scarcely exceeded by the more recent and almost fabulous transactions in coal-fields and oil-wells. As nearly as can be ascertained from the records, Mr. Craigie paid less than twenty thousand dollars for the whole estate. Reserving sufficient land and flats for the construction of the bridge and the location of a toll-house, he put the remainder on the market at the price of three hundred and sixty thousand dollars, in sixty shares of six thousand dollars each. At this price, three shares were conveyed to Harrison G. Otis, three to Israel Thorndike, and one, each, to Ebenezer Francis, William Payne, Thomas H. Perkins, and John Callender, by deeds dated Nov. 30, 1808. The bridge was completed in 1809, and roads were opened to Cambridge Common, to Medford, and elsewhere, to attract travel from the country to Boston over this avenue. To enable the proprietors to manage and dispose of their valuable real estate, which had hitherto remained apparently undivided and uninhabited (except by a single family in the old Phips farm-house), the General Court, by an Act approved March 3, 1810, incorporated "Thomas Handasyde Perkins, James Perkins, William Payne, Ebenezer Francis, and Andrew Craigie, being tenants in common " of lands at and near Lechmere Point, with their associates, as " the Lechmere Point Corporation." Within the next two months the several proprietors conveyed their shares to the Corporation at the nominal price of five dollars. Streets and lots of suitable size were laid out; but the records indicate that the sales of land were few. The first deed of a house-lot, entered on record, is dated Aug. 20, 1810, and conveys to Samuel S. Green the lot on the northeasterly corner of Cambridge and Second streets, where he resided more than three-score years, and where he died, Sept. 8, 1872. One store-lot, on Bridge Street, had previously been sold to Aaron Bigelow, but the deed was not placed on record so early as the other. The records exhibit only ten deeds of lots given by the Corporation, until Sept. 20, 1813, when a sale was made to Jesse Putnam, which contributed materially to the prosperity of the new village; this lot was bounded on East Street 400 feet, on North Street 400 feet, on Water Street 300 feet, and " on land covered with water " about 400 feet, and was conveyed by Putnam, March 16, 1814, to the " Boston Porcelain and Glass Company." But the " crowning mercy " to the whole enterprise was the agreement, approved by the Corporation Nov. 1, 1813, and by the Court of Sessions at the next December Term; namely, that the Corporation would give to the County of Middlesex the square bounded by Otis, Second, Thorndike, and Third streets, and a lot, seventy-five feet in width, across the westerly side of the square [1] bounded by Thorndike, Second, Spring, and Third streets, and would erect thereon a court-house and jail, satisfactory to the Court, at an expense to the Corporation not exceeding twenty-four thousand dollars, on condition that as soon as the edifices were completed, they should be used for the purposes designed. The town protested most earnestly against the removal of the courts and records from Harvard Square, but in vain. At the March Term of the Court, 1816, a committee reported that the court-house and jail were satisfactorily completed, and it was ordered that they be immediately devoted to their intended use. It was also ordered that the sum of $4,190.78 be paid to the Corporation, being the amount expended in excess of $24,000. From this time, the success of the enterprise was assured.

During the period embraced in this chapter, while two new villages were established, which, after many vicissitudes, became more populous than the older settlements, the town was sadly

---

[1] The County has since purchased the other portions of the square.

shorn of its already diminished proportions by the incorporation of its second and third parishes into separate towns. Dr. Holmes, writing in 1800, says,[1]—

	ACRES.	RODS.
" The First Parish in Cambridge contains,	2,851	60
The Second Parish in Cambridge contains,	4,845	118
The Third Parish in Cambridge contains,	2,660	81".

The original organization of these parishes will be mentioned elsewhere. Their separation from the parent trunk occurred almost simultaneously. The third parish was incorporated as the town of Brighton, Feb. 24, 1807, and became a part of the city of Boston, Jan. 1, 1874. The second parish was incorporated as the town of West Cambridge, by an Act passed Feb. 27, 1807, but not to take effect until June 1, 1807; its corporate name was changed to Arlington, April 30, 1867. By the incorporation of these two towns, Cambridge lost nearly three quarters of its territory, but probably somewhat less than half of its population.

The political disturbances in the country, at the commencement of the present century, were disastrous to its commercial prosperity. The Embargo, proclaimed in December 1807, followed by other hostile measures, culminating in a declaration of war against Great Britain, in June 1812, paralyzed the commerce of the whole country. Grass grew in the streets of the seaports, and ships rotted at the wharves. Cambridge felt this calamity the more keenly, because it involved so many of her citizens in distress. Merchants, mechanics, and laborers, mutually dependent on each other, were thrown out of business, and some were reduced to absolute want. A general and rapid depreciation in the value of real estate followed, particularly in Cambridgeport;[2] the owners ceased to erect houses and stores; those who had purchased on speculation were unable to effect sales, and some of them were financially ruined. General stagnation ensued, from which the new village did not fully recover for many years, and the hope of making it a great commercial centre seems to have been utterly and forever abandoned.

In common with many towns in New England, Cambridge earnestly protested against the Embargo. At a town-meeting, Aug. 25, 1808, an address, reported by a committee consisting of

---

[1] *Mass. Hist. Soc. Coll.*, vii. 6.

[2] Lands, which had been worth in the market more than twenty cents per square foot, were afterwards sold for less than one cent per foot. The settlement of East Cambridge had not been commenced when the Embargo was declared; but its growth was retarded by the hostilities which followed.

Royal Makepeace, Francis Dana, and Samuel P. P. Fay, was adopted, to wit: —

"To the President of the United States of America: The inhabitants of Cambridge, in the Commonwealth of Massachusetts, in legal town-meeting assembled, respectfully represent: That we are sensibly impressed with our obligation to submit to and support the laws of our country; and we flatter ourselves that we have been and ever shall be forward to manifest our patriotism, and make any sacrifice, and submit to any privation, that the interest and honor of our country shall require. But in times of great public calamity and distress, we deem it no less our duty than our privilege, 'peaceably to assemble and petition the government for a redress of grievances.' Under these impressions, we feel constrained to confess to your Excellency that we, in common with our fellow citizens of the Eastern States, suffer a severe and increasing distress from the operation of the laws 'laying an embargo on all ships and vessels in the ports and harbors of the United States.' Could we see a termination of our sufferings, we would submit in silence. But with consternation we observe that this is not a temporary measure, but imposed by perpetual laws. We admit the power of Congress to regulate commerce; but laws to abolish it, and raise a perpetual barrier to foreign intercourse, we believe was never contemplated by our national compact.

"Your petitioners inhabit a district of the Union which does not abound with all the conveniences of life. The fisheries and commerce have contributed in an eminent degree to give us whatever of wealth, happiness, and importance, we enjoy. We can never, therefore, subscribe to the opinion, 'that it would be unwise evermore to recur to distant countries for the comforts and conveniences of life.' Situated as we are on the shores of the Atlantic, we have occasion to remark and bitterly realize many distressing consequences of the embargo laws, which fall not under the immediate eye of Government, the recital of which, we are confident, will excite all your excellency's philanthropy, and induce you to exercise the power with which you are invested, for the relief of your fellow-citizens. The laws which shut us out from the ocean, the better part of our inheritance, palsied all our enterprise. The farmer gathers his harvest with a heavy heart, while he has no hope of vending his surplus, and the mechanic, sailor, and fisherman, find that their willing industry will no longer enable them to supply their daily wants. Many, very

many, who, by a long course of persevering industry, supposed
they had reached the desired point of independence, find their
property so fallen in value, that it must be wholly sacrificed for
the payment of their debts. Their endeavors to extricate themselves avail them nothing; and they can only weep over the ruin
that overwhelms them and reduces their families to beggary.
Our distress is rendered the more severe and intolerable by a
conviction that the neighboring British Provinces, by the very
measures that embarrass us, are acquiring a consequence which
their natural advantages could never have given them.

"We apprehend that the benefits expected by your Excellency
and Congress from the Embargo have been but partially experienced. It is a notorious fact that great numbers of our native
seamen, disheartened by their situation, have resorted to the
British Provinces to obtain the means of subsistence, and entered
voluntarily into the service of that very nation from which the
hand of government has been extended to protect them. Our
hope and expectation now rests in the laws authorizing your excellency, in the event of important changes in the measures of
the belligerent powers affecting neutral commerce, during the
recess of Congress, to suspend, in whole or in part, the acts laying an embargo. The existing Revolution in Spain is a change
indeed important to the world, and cannot fail to awaken the
sympathy of every friend of mankind. The trade of Spain and
Portugal and their colonies is now open and offers a golden harvest to the first nation who shall show themselves wise enough to
gather it. We therefore request your Excellency to suspend the
operation of the embargo laws, so far at least as they relate to
Spain and Portugal and their dependencies; or, should your Excellency doubt that you have such power, that you will call Congress together for that purpose."

This address, says the record, was adopted "almost unanimously"; and the selectmen were directed to forward it to the
President. Very soon a reply was received, — apparently an
autograph of the President, — which is still preserved in the office of the city clerk : —

"To the inhabitants of the town of Cambridge, in legal town-
meeting assembled. Your representation and request were received on the 8th inst., and have been considered with the attention due to every expression of the sentiments and feelings
of so respectable a body of my fellow-citizens.[1] No person has

---

[1] In the original, as usual in Jefferson's manuscripts, capital letters are generally
omitted at the beginning of sentences.

seen, with more concern than myself, the inconveniences brought on our country in general by the circumstances of the times in which we happen to live; times to which the history of nations presents no parallel. For years we have been looking as spectators on our brethren of Europe, afflicted by all those evils which necessarily follow an abandonment of the moral rules which bind men and nations together. Connected with them in friendship and commerce we have happily so far kept aloof from their calamitous conflicts, by a steady observance of justice towards all, by much forbearance and multiplied sacrifices. At length, however, all regard to the rights of others having been thrown aside, the belligerent powers have beset the highway of commercial intercourse with edicts which, taken together, expose our commerce and mariners, under almost every destination, a prey to their fleets and armies. Each party, indeed, would admit our commerce with themselves, with the view of associating us in their war against the other. But we have wished war with neither. Under these circumstances were passed the laws of which you complain, by those delegated to exercise the powers of legislation for you, with every sympathy of a common interest in exercising them faithfully. In reviewing these measures, therefore, we should advert to the difficulties out of which a choice was of necessity to be made. To have submitted our rightful commerce to prohibitions and tributary exactions from others would have been to surrender our independence. To resist them by arms was war, without consulting the state of things or the choice of the nation. The alternative preferred by the Legislature, of suspending a commerce placed under such unexampled difficulties, besides saving to our citizens their property and our mariners to their country, has the peculiar advantage of giving time to the belligerent nations to revise a conduct as contrary to their interests as it is to our rights. 'In the event of such peace or suspension of hostilities between the belligerent Powers of Europe, or of such a change in their measures affecting neutral commerce as may render that of the United States sufficiently safe in the judgment of the President,' he is authorized to suspend the Embargo. But no peace or suspension of hostilities, no change of measures affecting neutral commerce, is known to have taken place. The Orders of England and the Decrees of France and Spain, existing at the date of these laws, are still unrepealed, so far as we know. In Spain, indeed, a contest for the government appears to have arisen; but of its course or prospects we have no information on which prudence would undertake a hasty change in our policy, even were the authority of the Executive competent to such a decision. You desire that, in defect of such power, Congress may be specially convened. It is unnecessary to examine the evidence or the character of the facts which are supposed to dictate such a call; because you will be sensible, on an attention to dates, that the legal period of their meeting is as early as, in this extensive country, they could be fully convened by a special call. I should with great willingness have executed the wishes of the inhabitants of Cambridge, had peace, or a repeal of the obnoxious Edicts, or other changes, produced the case, in which alone the laws have given me that authority; and so many motives of justice and interest lead to such changes that we ought continually to expect them. But while these Edicts remain, the Legislature alone can prescribe the course to be pursued. TH: JEFFERSON. Sept. 10, 1808."

The appeal of the people to the President was fruitless. Equally vain was an address by the General Court to the members of Congress. A spirit of hostility to England was predominant in the national government; the Embargo was made more stringent, and enforced by regulations which were here considered unreasonable and unconstitutional; and the general condition of the people, both present and prospective, " was nothing bettered, but rather grew worse." Under such circumstances, at a town meeting, Jan. 27, 1809, " The act lately passed by Congress for enforcing the Embargo was read and submitted to the town for their consideration; and after maturely considering the same, and also considering the present alarming situation of our country," a vigorous protest against the hostile measures of the general government was adopted by a very large majority of the inhabitants.

This protestation, and hundreds of similar character by the people of New England, were in vain. In Congress, the influence of France was in the ascendant, and the Embargo was followed, in June, 1812, by an open declaration of war against Great Britain. For the next two or three years, Cambridge suffered its full proportion in the general stagnation of business. Cambridgeport did not recover from the blight which had fallen upon it; and the growth of East Cambridge was sadly retarded. —

With a very decided majority of voters politically opposed to the war, and smarting under the losses and inconveniences resulting from it, the town could not be expected to enter with

enthusiasm into its support, or voluntarily to assume a dispropor-
tionate share of its burdens. In fact, no reference to the war,
during its continuance, is found on the Town Records. A few
months after its close, May 8, 1815, the town " Voted, that the
report of the Committee appointed to determine what compensation, if any, should be allowed by the town to the militia-men
drafted and called out for the defence of the State, be accepted :
— the report allows four dollars to each person for every thirty
days service." The Cambridge Light Infantry was called into
service by the Governor, for the defence of the State, and readily
responded to the call. There may have been some voluntary en-
listments into the regular army of the United States : but any
evidence of such a fact is not found.

One of the most eminent citizens of Cambridge, ELBRIDGE
GERRY, was Governor of Massachusetts from May 1810, to May
1812, and Vice-president of the United States from March 4, 1818,
until Nov. 23, 1814, when he suddenly expired, as he was about to
enter the Senate Chamber in Washington for the performance of
his official duties. However bittterly his politics were denounced,
Mr. Gerry enjoyed the personal respect and esteem of his townsmen ; yet neither their affection for the man, nor their regard for
his high political position, could overcome their detestation of the
war, of which he was an advocate and defender, nor induce them
to volunteer their persons or their property in its behalf. Hence
the dignified silence of the Town Records.

When the news of Peace arrived, in February, 1815, there was
a general outburst of joy in Massachusetts. In many towns,
public meetings of prayer, and praise, and mutual congratulation,
were held. There was such a meeting in Cambridge, Feb. 23,
1815, and an address was delivered by President Kirkland.
Among the papers presented by Hon. John Davis to the Massachusetts Historical Society is a handbill, or broadside, announcing
the approaching festivity, as follows : —

CELEBRATION

OF THE RATIFICATION OF THE

TREATY OF PEACE

between the United States of America and the U-
nited Kingdom of Great Britain & Ireland,
at Cambridge, Feb. 23, 1815.

ORDER OF PROCESSION.

The procession will be formed at University Hall, and move
at 11 o'clock A. M. in the following order, to
the Rev. Dr. Holmes's meeting-house.
Military Escort.
Musick.
Marshal.   Chief Marshal.   *Marshal.*
The President of the University and the other Gentlemen, who officiate.
Government of Harvard College.
Selectmen of Cambridge.
Marshal.   Committee of Arrangements.   *Marshal.*
Strangers.
Marshal.
Resident Graduates.
Students.
Marshal.
Citizens of Cambridge.
Marshal.

ORDER OF EXERCISES.

1. Anthem — *By Stephenson.*
   "I was glad when they said unto me," &c.
2. Prayer, by the Rev. Dr. Ware.
3. Reading of select portions of the Holy Scripture, by the Rev. Mr. Gannett.
4. Hymn, written for the occasion.

Almighty God, to thee we bow,
To thee the voice of gladness raise;
Thy mercy, that hath blessed us now,
In loud and grateful songs we praise.

But light from Heaven has shone at last,
And PEACE is beaming from above,
The storm of doubt and fear has past,
And hope returns, and joy, and love.

Long hast Thou stretched the avenging
hand
And smote thy people in thy wrath;
Hast frowned upon a guilty land,
While storms and darkness veiled thy
path.

Then praise to that Eternal Power,
Who bids our wars and tumults cease,
And hymn, in this auspicious hour,
The God of mercy — God of Peace.

5. Address, by the President of the University.
6. Poem, by Mr. Henry Ware.
7. Prayer, by the Rev. Dr. Holmes.
8. Anthem, from Handel's "Grand Dettingen Te
   Deum,"
   "We praise thee, O God," &c.
9. Benediction.

CHAPTER XIII.

CIVIL HISTORY.

IT has already been stated in chapter v., that a ferry was established in 1635 across Charles River (at the foot of Dunster Street), from which there was a road through Brookline and Roxbury to Boston. The only other feasible route to Boston was through Charlestown, and across a ferry near Copp's Hill. Desiring to avoid the inconvenience and peril of a ferry, the inhabitants of Cambridge consented, Nov. 10, 1656, "to pay each one their proportion of a rate to the sum of 200*l.* towards the building a bridge over Charles River, upon condition the same may be effected without further charge to the town." A place for the bridge was selected, at the foot of Brighton Street ; but the work was too great to be accomplished at once. Three years afterwards, Feb. 4, 1659–60, " the former propositions and votes that had passed, for the building of a bridge over Charles River, were again considered and debated ; and the question being propounded, whether the town did agree and consent that the said work should be yet further prosecuted, and that 200*l.* should be levied on the inhabitants of this town towards the effecting thereof, the vote passed on the affirmative." The structure was probably completed before March 23, 1662–3, when it was ordered, " that the bridge be laid in oil and lead, provided that it exceed not 40*l.* charge to the town." This bridge was much larger than any which had previously been erected in the colony. From the first it was called the " Great Bridge ; " and such is still its legal designation. The cost of maintaining such a bridge, together with a long causeway, was very great, compared with the means of defraying it, and many methods were devised to relieve the town of some portion of the burden. Under date of Oct. 12, 1670, the action of the General Court is recorded : " Whereas, the Bridge over Charles River, which was first erected at the cost of that town, together with the free contribution of several public spirited persons in some neighbor towns, which bridge being now decayed, and by reason of the danger is presented to the county of Middlesex, and the town of Cambridge, as they allege in their petition, being not able to repair it, so that of necessity it must be pulled up and slighted, and the passage there must be secured by a ferry as heretofore, which is not so safe, convenient, or useful, as a bridge, for a ferry is altogether useless in the winter, and very inconvenient to transport horses, and not at all accommodable for carts or droves of cattle : The premises considered, it is ordered by this Court and the authority thereof, for the encouragement either of the town of Cambridge or any particular persons that shall repair the bridge, or erect a sufficient cart-bridge over the River at Cambridge, and maintain the same for the safety of the passengers, they are hereby empowered to take toll at the rates following, viz., one penny for every person ; three pence a head for every horse and man ; six pence for every cart ; two pence a head for every horse or other neat cattle ; one half penny a head for sheep, goats, or swine : and if any refuse to pay the toll aforesaid, it shall be at the liberty of such as maintain the said bridge to stop their passage. And this order to continue in [force] so long as the said bridge is maintained serviceable and safe for passage." [1] The tolls, thus authorized, seem not to have been long continued, if ever exacted ; for when Newton was incorporated as a separate town, Jan. 11, 1687–8, it was ordered that the expense of maintaining the bridge " be defrayed and borne as followeth : (that is to say) two sixth parts thereof by the town of Cambridge, one sixth part by the said Village,[2] and three sixth parts at the public charge of the county of Middlesex." Newton continued to pay its proportion of the expense until May 4, 1781, when it was exempted from further liability by the General Court.[3] In like manner, when Lexington was incorporated, March 20, 1712-13, and West Cambridge, Feb. 27, 1807, they were required to share with Cambridge the expense of maintaining the bridge, in proportion to the respective valuation of the several towns, which they continued to do until they were released from that obligation, March 24, 1860, by the General Court.[4] In the meantime, various expedients were adopted by the Court to aid Cambridge in sustaining what was considered, and what actually was, a grievous burden. Thus, in June, 1694, it was " resolved, that

[1] Mass. Col. Rec., iv. (ii.) 470.
[2] Newton was at first called Cambridge Village.
[3] Mass. Rec., xiii. 98.
[4] Mass. Spec. Laws, xi. 56.

the town of Newton pay one third part of the charge of said
bridge."[1] And in June, 1700, it was "resolved, that the Great
Bridge in Cambridge, over Charles River, be repaired from time
to time, one half at the charge of the town of Cambridge, and
the other half at the charge of the county of Middlesex."[2]
Again, Oct. 25, 1733, the bridge having been "very thoroughly
and effectually repaired," after a large portion of it had been
carried away by the ice, the Court granted to Cambridge, £117
16s., to Newton, £100, and to Lexington, £82 4s., in all £300,[3]
in consideration of their extraordinary expense; and on the 22d
of June, 1784, "Voted, that three thousand acres of the unappropriated lands of the Province be and hereby are granted to
the towns of Cambridge, Newton, and Lexington, to enable
them forever hereafter at their own cost and charge, to keep,
amend, and repair, the Great Bridge over Charles River in Cambridge; the land to be laid out in three several parts, in equal
proportion to each of the said towns."[4] A "plat" of the thousand acres allotted to Cambridge, lying west of Lunenburg, was
exhibited and confirmed, Sept. 18, 1784.[5] All other corporations
having been released from liability, the General Court made a
final disposition of the matter by an act passed March 11, 1862,
by which the city of Cambridge and the town of Brighton were
"authorized and required to rebuild the Great Bridge over
Charles River," the expense to be borne "in proportion to the
respective valuations of said city and town;" and it was provided that a draw, not less than thirty-two feet wide, should be
constructed "at an equal distance from each abutment," that
"the opening in the middle of said draw" should be "the dividing line between Cambridge and Brighton at that point," and
that thereafter each corporation should maintain its half part of
the whole structure at its own expense.[6]

In June, 1738, a petition of Edmund Goffe, William Brattle,
and others of Cambridge, for liberty to establish a ferry between

[1] Mass. Prov. Rec., vi. 348.
[2] Ibid., vii. 92. This tax on the county may not seem unreasonable, when it is considered that a large portion of the travel to and from Boston passed over the bridge in preference to the Charlestown Ferry. If Newton was exempted from its former obligation, it was manifestly only for a short time.
[3] Mass. Rec., xv.4 53. On the 28th of the following January the town voted thanks to the General Court for the aid rendered; and also "to Col. Jacob Wen-dell Esq. and Mr. Craddock for their kindness to us in procuring and collecting a very bountiful subscription for us, to en-courage and enable us to go through the charge of the repair of our Great Bridge."
[4] Mass. Rec., xvi. 32.
[5] Ibid., xvi. 54.
[6] Mass. Spec. Laws, xi. 280.

Cambridge and Boston, of which the profits should be paid to Harvard College, also a similar petition of Hugh Hall and others of Boston, and a petition of John Staniford of Boston for liberty to construct a bridge from a point near the copper works in Boston to Col. Phips' farm (now East Cambridge) were severally referred to the next General Court,[1] and both enterprises were abandoned. Nearly fifty years afterwards, Feb. 11, 1785, the town appointed a committee "to support in behalf of the inhabitants of this town the petition of Mr. Andrew Cabot to the General Court, now sitting, praying leave to erect at his own expense, a bridge over Charles River, from Lechmere's Point in this town to Barton's Point, or such other place in West Boston as shall be thought most expedient;" and to demonstrate that such a bridge would be more important than one at the ferryway, as petitioned for by some of the inhabitants of Charlestown. This effort to secure a direct route to Boston failed; the Charlestown petition was granted, March 9, 1785; and Charles River Bridge was opened with imposing ceremonies on the 17th of June, 1786. The desired accommodation for Cambridge, however, was not long postponed. In the "Columbian Centinel," Jan. 7, 1792, appeared this advertisement:—

"WEST BOSTON BRIDGE. As *all* citizens of the United States have an *equal* right to propose a measure that may be beneficial to the public or advantageous to themselves, and as no body of men have an *exclusive* right to take to themselves such a privilege, a number of gentlemen have proposed to open a new subscription for the purpose of building a bridge from West Boston to Cambridge, at such place as the General Court may be pleased to direct. A subscription for two hundred shares in the proposed bridge will this day be opened at Samuel Cooper's office, north side of the State House."

This subscription "was filled up in three hours."[2] A petition was immediately presented to the General Court, and on the 9th of March, 1792, Francis Dana and his associates were incorporated as "The Proprietors of the West Boston Bridge," with authority to construct a bridge "from the westerly part of Boston, near the Pest House (so called), to Pelham's Island in the town of Cambridge," with a "good road from Pelham's Island aforesaid, in the most direct and practicable line, to the nearest part of the Cambridge road," and to take certain specified tolls "for and during the term of forty years;" and they were required to "pay

---

[1] *Printed Journal House of Representatives.*   [2] *Centinel*, Jan. 11, 1792.

annually to Harvard College or University the sum of three hundred pounds during the said term of forty years."[1] On the 22d of March, twelve Directors were chosen, and preparations made for immediately commencing the work. Its completion was announced in the "Centinel," Wednesday, Nov. 27, 1793: "The Bridge at West Boston was opened for passengers &c., on Saturday last. The elegance of the workmanship and the magnitude of the undertaking are perhaps unequalled in the history of enterprises. We hope the Proprietors will not suffer pecuniary loss from their public spirit. They have claims on the liberality and patronage of the government; and to these claims government will not be inattentive." Dr. Holmes, who witnessed the building of the bridge, and who may be supposed to have been familiar with the details, describes it as "a magnificent structure. It was erected at the expense of a company incorporated for that purpose, and cost 76,700 dollars. The causeway, on the Cambridge side, was begun July 15, 1792; the wood-work, April 8, 1793. The bridge was opened for passengers, Nov. 23, 1793, seven months and an half from the time of laying the first pier. It is very handsomely constructed; and, when lighted by its two rows of lamps, extending a mile and a quarter, presents a vista which has a fine effect.

"It stands on 180 piers, and is	3483	feet long.
Bridge over the Gore, 14 do.	275	do.
Abutment, Boston side,	87½	
Causeway,	3344	
Distance from the end of the causeway to the first church in Cambridge,	7810	
Width of the Bridge,	40	

"It is railed on each side, for foot passengers. The sides of the causeway are stoned, capstand and railed; and on each side there is a canal, about 30 feet wide."[2]

The peculiar circumstances connected with the construction of Canal (or Craigie's) Bridge are related in chapter xii. The sharp rivalry between the proprietors of West Boston and Canal

[1] *Mass. Spec. Laws*, i. 361–364. The corporators were Francis Dana, Oliver Wendell, James Sullivan, Henry Jackson, Mungo Mackay, and William Wetmore. By a subsequent Act, June 30, 1792 (i. 394) the franchise was extended to seventy years, and the annuity to Harvard College was reduced to two hundred pounds. The franchise was further extended, Feb. 27, 1807 (iv. 76–81), to seventy years from the completion of Canal (or Craigie's) Bridge; and the proprietors of that bridge, by its charter then granted, were required to contribute one half of the annuity payable to Harvard College.

[2] *Coll. Mass. Hist. Soc.*, vii. 3, 4.

Bridges, and between land-owners especially benefited by the one or the other, resulted in the erection of other bridges and the opening of several new streets.

PRISON POINT BRIDGE is said to have been erected by virtue of a charter, granted June 21, 1806, to Samuel H. Flagg and others, as " Proprietors of the Prison Point Dam Corporation," for "building a dam from Prison Point in Charlestown to Lechmere's Point in Cambridge, and erecting mills on the same." No dam was constructed nor mill erected: but in 1815, Prison Point Bridge was built for the benefit of Canal Bridge ; and this is presumed to have been done under authority of the charter for a dam granted in 1806, partly because that charter authorized the proprietors to construct a travelling path across the dam, not less than thirty feet in width, and partly because in an act relative to the Boston and Lowell Railroad Corporation, March 5, 1832, Prison Point Bridge is repeatedly called " the Branch or Prison Point Dam Bridge."[1] This bridge was laid out as a county road in January, 1839.

RIVER STREET BRIDGE was built for the advantage of the West Boston Bridge Proprietors and the owners of real estate in Cambridgeport. Jonathan L. Austin and others were incorporated March 2, 1808, for the purpose of building this bridge and what is now called River Street, to be completed within two years; which term of limitation was extended. one year, by an act passed Feb. 13, 1810.[2] The bridge and road were soon afterwards completed, and were maintained by the proprietors until Nov. 12, 1832, when the town assumed the care of the bridge, and since that time it has had charge of both bridge and roadway.

THE WESTERN AVENUE BRIDGE was built by the proprietors of West Boston Bridge, under authority granted by an act passed June 12, 1824,[3] empowering them to build a turnpike from Central Square to Watertown; and it was maintained by the said proprietors, until they sold their whole franchise to the Hancock Free Bridge Corporation.

THE BROOKLINE BRIDGE had no immediate connection with either of the rival bridges, but was erected for the benefit and at the expense of persons owning real estate in its immediate vicinity. By an act passed April 25, 1850,[4] Sidney Willard,— Edmund T. Hastings, Columbus Tyler, David R. Griggs, and

[1] Mass. Spec. Laws, vii. 222.
[2] Ibid., iv. 147, 248.
[3] Ibid., vi. 204.
[4] Ibid., ix. 218.

their associates were " empowered to erect a pile bridge over the Charles River between the city of Cambridge and the town of Brookline, from points at or near the old wharf or embankment, which is near where the Boston and Worcester Railroad passes under a bridge on the Western Avenue (so called) to the opposite bank of the river in Cambridge," and to receive certain rates of toll for the term of fifty years. By mutual agreement, however, and by permission of the General Court, it was transferred to the city, and became a free bridge, in 1869 ; and since that date Cambridge has not been burdened by toll bridges.

West Boston and Canal Bridges had already become free, long before the expiration of their respective charters. In 1828, the General Court discussed the propriety of purchasing both these bridges and making them free at an early day ; and a company was incorporated April 16, 1836, for the accomplishment of the same purpose; but the financial disturbances in that year defeated the project. A new charter was granted March 26, 1846,[1] to Isaac Livermore, Charles Valentine, William Reed, and their associates, as proprietors of the Hancock Free Bridge, empowering them to build a bridge across Charles River, between West Boston and Canal Bridges, but requiring them to purchase both those bridges if their proprietors would sell them at a price to be determined by three disinterested appraisers. They were also authorized to receive the established rates of toll, until the outlay with legal interest should be refunded, over and above all expenses, and a fund of $150,000 should be secured for the future maintenance of the bridges ; after which they should become the property of the Commonwealth. The purchase was made ; and not long afterwards both bridges were thoroughly rebuilt, and a considerable portion of the west end of West Boston Bridge was converted into a solid roadway. By an act passed May 30, 1857,[2] the proprietors were authorized to convey both bridges to the City of Cambridge, to be forever maintained by said city as free bridges, whenever the accumulated fund should amount to $100,000. This desirable event occurred on the 30th of January, 1858, when the legal forms of transfer and acceptance were completed, and notices were posted throughout the city, to wit: —

" FREE BRIDGES. From and after this day, Saturday, Jan-

---

[1] *Mass. Spec. Laws,* viii. 602.
[2] *Ibid.,* x. 751. By a subsequent Act (xii. 1020), it was provided that the fund should be equitably divided between Cambridge and Boston, and that the Bridges should thereafter be perpetually maintained by the two cities, at a like equitable proportion of expense.

uary 30, 1858, the West Boston and Canal Bridges will become
free public avenues forever. The Directors of the Hancock Free
Bridge Corporation and the City Government of Cambridge will
assemble at the Athenæum[1] on Monday next, February 1, 1858,
at eleven o'clock A. M., and, preceded by the Brigade Band, will
proceed in carriages to the two Bridges, which will be surrendered to the City of Cambridge by the Bridge Corporation.
The bells in the City will be rung, and a salute fired. All persons desirous to join the procession are requested to assemble at
the Athenæum at eleven o'clock A. M. on Monday next."

The citizens responded to this invitation in great numbers.
A procession, more than a mile in length, and escorted by the Na-
tional Lancers, moved from the City Hall through Main Street,
over West Boston Bridge, through Cambridge Street, Bowdoin
Square, Green and Seventh streets, over Canal Bridge, through
Bridge, Cambridge, Fifth, Otis, and Third streets, Broadway,
North Avenue, and Waterhouse, Garden, Harvard, and Main
Streets, to the City Hall, where a collation was served, and con-
gratulations were exchanged. In the procession was the venerable
Moses Hadley, who had been toll-gatherer on West Boston Bridge
more than fifty-four years. The procession was saluted with
hearty cheers at many places; and it did not forget to halt at the
Washington Elm, while the Band gave enthusiastic expression to
Washington's Grand March.

Not only the River Street and Western Avenue bridges, but
most of the thoroughfares through the city, which were opened
during many years, were constructed for the benefit of West
Boston or Canal Bridge. Main Street, eastward from Columbia
Street, was originally a causeway, built in connection with West
Boston Bridge;[2] and River Street and Western Avenue were
built in connection with the bridges bearing the same names, as
already described. Concord Avenue was originally the easterly
end of the Cambridge and Concord Turnpike, for which a charter was granted March 8, 1808;[3] it was laid out as a free highway
in May, 1829. By an act passed March 8, 1805, the Cambridge
and Concord Turnpike Corporation was authorized to extend
their road from its eastern termination, "near to the house of
Jonas Wyeth in Cambridge, to the causeway of West Boston
Bridge, near the house of Royal Makepeace."[4] This portion —

---

[1] The same building which is now
called the City Hall.

[2] Main Street, westward from Pleasant
Street, Kirkland Street, North Avenue,
and Brattle Street, were among the earli-

est highways, and their location has been
described in chapter ii.

[3] *Mass. Spec. Laws*, iii. 161.

[4] *Ibid.*, iii. 514.

of the turnpike was also laid out as a public highway in May, 1829, and it is now known as Broadway. Hampshire Street was the easterly end of the Middlesex Turnpike, whose charter was granted June 15, 1805;[1] so much of that turnpike as was situated in Cambridge became a public highway in September, 1842. All these, as well as Webster Avenue (which was opened before 1809, and was until 1860 called Medford Street), were constructed as avenues to West Boston Bridge, without material aid or opposition from the town. The turnpikes were made at the expense of their stockholders and others interested in West Boston Bridge and Cambridgeport lands; and Webster Avenue, by the parties specially interested, and at their own expense.

But when Andrew Craigie had completed his purchase of the Lechmere or Phips estate, and was ready to bring it into the market by building Canal Bridge to connect it with Boston, a sharp rivalry between him and his associates on the one hand, and the proprietors of West Boston Bridge and the Cambridgeport residents and land-owners on the other, for several years kept the town in constant excitement and turmoil. Whenever either party desired to open a new avenue to its bridge, it was resolutely opposed by the other party, as adverse to its own interest. The majority of voters sometimes favored one party, sometimes the other. All, or nearly all, the desired avenues were at last obtained, but through much tribulation.

The severest contest between the two parties was in regard to Mount Auburn Street and Cambridge Street. It has already been stated that the road from Cambridge to Watertown for many years substantially coincided with the present Brattle Street, Elmwood Avenue, and Mount Auburn Street. To shorten the distance between Watertown and West Boston Bridge, the Town appointed a committee, Dec. 26, 1805, to present a petition to the Court of Sessions "to establish the road as now laid out from the garden of the Hon. Elbridge Gerry to the garden of the late Thomas Brattle, Esq."[2] At a subsequent meeting, Feb. 17, 1806, the other party triumphed, and the committee was discharged. The subject was again discussed, Nov. 17, 1806, Mr. Craigie having offered to give the land and make the road so far as it crossed his farm, if the town would establish a new road from Gerry's corner to a point on Brattle Street, nearly opposite to his house;[3] the town voted in favor of establishing such a road,

---

[1] *Mass. Spec. Laws.*, iii. 611.

[2] That is, the present Mount Auburn

Street, between Elmwood Avenue and Brattle Square.

[3] Such a road would continue the con-

and appointed a Committee to procure the discontinuance of the
road from Gerry's corner to Brattle's garden. On the 27th of
May, 1807, the Selectmen laid out the road, as desired by Mr.
Craigie; but it does not appear that the town accepted it. A
year later, May 2, 1808, the West Boston Bridge interest was
again in the ascendant, and the town voted (104 against 65) to
lay out Mount Auburn Street (west of Brattle Square), appropriated $3,000 to defray the expense, and directed the Selectmen
to construct the road immediately. On the 16th of May, Andrew Craigie and thirty-five others protested against the making
of the road; and it would seem that violent measures were
adopted to prevent it, for on the 7th of June following, the town,
by a majority of 116 against 71, approved what the Selectmen
had done, directed them to complete the work, and appointed
them as a committee " for the purpose of prosecuting Andrew
Craigie and others, for trespasses committed, or which may hereafter be committed by him or others upon the road " before described. In continuation of this road, and to complete a nearly
straight avenue from the Watertown line to West Boston Bridge,
the town voted, Sept. 6, 1808, to lay out Mount Auburn Street,
from Holyoke Street to Main Street. Meanwhile, Mr. Craigie
made several efforts to have Brattle Street laid out from Fayerweather Street to " Wyeth's sign-post," which stood near the
present junction of Brattle and Mount Auburn streets, to counteract the effect of opening the new Mount Auburn Street ; this
object was not accomplished until September, 1812, when that
portion of Brattle Street was very properly laid out, — not by
the town, however, but by the county, as a county road.

What is now known as Cambridge Street was constructed in
the interest of Mr. Craigie and his associates, the owners of Canal
Bridge, almost the whole of East Cambridge, and a portion of
Cambridgeport. In connection with William Winthrop and the
heirs of Francis Foxcroft, they opened and graded the road from
Canal Bridge to the Common, except about an eighth of a mile
next eastward from Elm Street, where the land was owned by
parties having an adverse interest.[1] After other ineffectual efforts to have the road completed and established as a public
highway, a petition was presented by Thomas H. Perkins and

nection with Mason Street, over which
and Cambridge Street, already projected,
it was designed to conduct the travel
toward Lechmere's Point.

[1] The owners were Henry Hill, Rufus
Davenport, and Royal Makepeace, all
largely interested in Cambridgeport lands.

fifty-two others to the General Court, June 6, 1809, setting forth,
"that the Canal Bridge across Charles River, between the west
end of Leverett Street, in Boston, and Lechmere's Point, so called,
in Cambridge, was begun during the last season, and great progress was made therein, that the work has been again resumed
this spring, and is now pursued with great spirit and alacrity, so
that the Bridge will probably be completed and ready for the
accommodation of passengers by the middle of July next; that
there is not now any public highway leading to the west end of
said Bridge;" and that the Court of Sessions, for lack of a quorum of disinterested Justices, had failed to establish such a public
way. " Wherefore your petitioners pray, that you will take
their peculiar case into your consideration, and provide for their
relief, either by appointing a committee in such a way as to you
may seem most fit, to explore, view, and mark out new highways
from the westerly end of said Bridge to communicate with the
great roads into the country at such places as will best comport
with common convenience and the public good, or in such other
way as you in your wisdom may appoint; which Committee shall
be further authorized and instructed to notify all persons and corporations who may be in any wise interested and affected by their
proceedings, of the time and places, when and where they shall
report; and who shall make their report to the Court of Sessions
for said County of Middlesex, or to some other tribunal which
may be authorized finally to hear all persons and parties, and establish such new highways as the public convenience may require." An order of notice was issued, and at a meeting held on
the 12th day of June, " the following order was taken thereupon
by the town: Whereas a road has been laid out and made by
Andrew Craigie and others, from the west end of Canal Bridge
(so called), to the road near the Colleges, called Cambridge and
Concord Turnpike, or Concord Street, leading to Cambridge
Common, excepting over a small piece of land belonging to
Henry Hill and others, which prevents a communication from
said Bridge to said Common; therefore voted, that the Selectmen be authorized and directed to lay out a road or way over
the land aforesaid of the said Hill and others, of the same width
of the road made by said Craigie, so that all obstructions may
be removed to the opening of the said road from Canal Bridge
to Cambridge Common. Voted, that a committee of five be
appointed to prepare and present a petition and remonstrance
against the petition of Thomas H. Perkins and others to the Hon.

Legislature of this Commonwealth now in session, and to state
such facts and to petition for such measures in regard to this
matter as they may judge proper. Voted, that the Committee
consist of the following gentlemen: Hon. Francis Dana, Esq.,
Hon. Elbridge Gerry, Esq., Hon. Jonathan L. Austin, Esq.,
Messrs. Royal Makepeace and John Hayden."

The Committee, thus appointed, presented to the General
Court a long and very energetic remonstrance, a copy of which
remains on file in the office of the City Clerk. They commence
by alleging " that the inhabitants of Cambridge and Cambridgeport are deeply afflicted by the incessant machinations and in-
trigues of Mr. Andrew Craigie, in regard to roads ; " in proof of
which they refer to the fact that, at the last session of the General Court, Mr. Craigie caused two petitions to be presented for
the appointment of a committee with extraordinary powers to
lay out roads in Cambridge ; that these petitions " seemed by
their tenor to proceed from disinterested persons, whereas some
of the petitioners were proprietors of the Canal Bridge, and
others deeply interested in lands connected with the proposed
roads ; and Mr. Craigie, who was not a petitioner, supported
them in person and with two lawyers, in the absence of all the
petitioners; these two petitions being manifestly, as the remonstrants had stated, a continuation of a plan of him and his coad-
jutors, commenced in 1797, and invariably pursued to 1809, to
turn the travel to that quarter; and the same game he is evidently now playing, by the petition signed by T. H. Perkins and
others."   " That such a petition, viz. to lay out roads without
number, with courses undefined, by a committee of the Legislature, your remonstrants conceive, never was before offered to
any Court, Legislative or Judicial, of Massachusetts ; " that a
Bill reported in accordance with these petitions, was rejected ;
" that the principal object of all these petitions, viz. to open a
road from Mr. Wyeth's sign-post to Mr. Fayerweather's corner,[1]
has been three times before the Court of Sessions of Middlesex,
has been as often rejected by it, and has been once suppressed
after it had obtained by intrigue and surprise the sanction of that
honorable Court ; and it is now a fifth time pending in the existing Court of Sessions of that County ; that the petition of T. H.
Perkins and others prays for a committee to explore, view, and
mark out new highways from the westerly end of the Canal
Bridge to communicate with the great roads into the country,"

---

[1] Namely, Brattle Street, from Fresh Pond Lane to Fayerweather Street.

etc. ; " that this petition is predicated on the feeble pretence that
there is not any public highway leading to the west end of said
Bridge, — an highway which Mr. Craigie has ever had it in his
power, by a petition to the town, to attain, and which is now
ordered by a vote of the town, by removing every obstacle to be
laid out and established." This remonstrance was effectual ; the
committee, to whom the petition was referred, reported that " it
is inexpedient for the Legislature to appoint any Committee to
view or mark out any of the highways aforesaid ; " and the report was accepted.

Agreeably to the vote of the town, before recited, the Selectmen laid out a road over the lands of Hill and others, so as to
make a continuous avenue from Canal Bridge to Cambridge
Common ; and the road was accepted by the town July 10, 1809.
But this was not satisfactory to Mr. Craigie ;[1] and on the following day (July 11) he presented a petition to the Court of
Sessions, that a road might be " laid out from the west end of
the Canal Bridge in a straight line through the lands of Andrew
Craigie, Henry Hill, Aaron Hill,[2] Rufus Davenport, Royal Makepeace, William Winthrop, Harvard College, and John Phillips,
over what is called Foxcroft Street, to the Common in said Cambridge, and over and across said Common to or near the house of
Deacon Josiah Moore," which "road is already made over the
whole of it, except a few rods only." This petition was referred
to a committee, who reported in its favor, Aug. 1, 1809 ; whereupon another committee was appointed, who reported Sept. 11,
the laying out of the road, with a schedule of land damages
amounting to $2,055 ; whereof the sum of $1,327 was awarded
to Andrew Craigie, and $292 to William Winthrop.

The town, considering it to be unreasonable that Mr. Craigie
should claim and receive damages for land used in the construction of a road which he so much desired, and for which he had
so long been earnestly striving, petitioned the Court of Sessions
in December, 1809, for the appointment of a jury, " to determine
whether any and what damages said Craigie has sustained by
means of said road," alleging " that in fact said Craigie sustained
no damages." At the next term of the Court, in March, 1810,
it was ordered that a jury be empanelled, and at the next term
in June, Edward Wade, Coroner, returned the verdict of the

---

[1] The road, as laid out by the town, did not include the portion already con- structed by Mr. Craigie, and no damages were awarded.

[2] No land of Aaron Hill was taken.

jury, and the case was continued to December, when the verdict
was set aside by the Court, and it was ordered that another jury
be empanelled. The case was then continued to March, and
again to June, 1811, when Nathan Fiske, Coroner, returned the
verdict of the jury, which the Court set aside, and continued the
case to the next September, when neither party appeared.

On petition of the town of Cambridge, setting forth that two
cases in which said town was petitioner for a jury to assess the
damages, if any, suffered by Andrew Craigie and William Winthrop for "land taken for the highway from the Canal Bridge to
Cambridge Common," had accidentally been dropped from the
docket of the Court of Sessions, and praying relief, the General
Court, June 22, 1812, ordered the Court of Sessions "to restore
said cases to the docket," and to proceed "as if they had never
been dismissed therefrom." Accordingly, on the records of the
Court of Sessions, Jan. 5, 1813, the former proceedings are recited,
together with the action of the General Court, and a mandamus
from the Supreme Judicial Court, requiring the Court of Sessions
at this January Term, to "accept and cause to be recorded the
verdict aforesaid, according to the law in such case made and provided, or signify to us cause to the contrary." The record
proceeds thus: "And on a full hearing of the parties in the
premises, the Court here do accept said verdict, and do order that
it be recorded; which verdict is as follows: We, David Townsend jr., Thomas Biglow, Thomas Sanderson, Nathaniel Brown,
William Wellington jr., Jonas Brown, Ephraim Peirce, Jacob
Gale, Moses Fuller, Thadeus Peirce, Arthur Train, and Gregory
Clark, having been summoned, empanelled, and as a jury sworn
to hear and determine on the complaint of the town of Cambridge
against Andrew Craigie, have heard the parties, duly considered
their several allegations, and on our oaths do say, that, by the
laying out and establishing of the highway from Cambridge Common to Canal Bridge, and by the passage of the same highway
over lands of Andrew Craigie, the said Craigie has sustained no
damage." It may be added, that the same proceedings were
had in regard to the damage awarded to William Winthrop; and
the jury, in like manner, determined that "the said Winthrop
has sustained no damage."

Thus ended the exciting contest concerning Mount Auburn
and Cambridge streets. I have entered so fully into the details,
partly because they illustrate the character of the long-continued
rivalry between the two bridges, but chiefly because I have been

assured by the late Abraham Hilliard, Esq., that in the trial of
the Cambridge Street case, the principle of law was first announced
and established in the courts of this Commonwealth, that the
damage which a land owner sustains by the taking of his land for
a highway, and the benefit which he derives from its construction,
shall be equitably adjusted, and offset against each other; and
if the benefit be equal to the damage, he shall receive nothing
more.

14

CHAPTER XIV.

CIVIL HISTORY.

ALTHOUGH Cambridge was early abandoned as the seat of government, it maintained from the beginning a prominent rank among the towns in the Colony. It was designated, before the establishment of counties, as one of the four towns in which Judicial Courts should be held. Having until that time exercised the whole power of the Colony, both legislative and judicial, the General Court ordered, March 3, 1635–6, " That there shall be four courts kept every quarter ; 1. at Ipswich, to which Neweberry shall belong ; 2. at Salem, to which Saugus shall belong ; 3. at Newe Towne, to which Charlton, Concord, Meadford, and Waterton shall belong ; 4th, at Boston, to which Rocksbury, Dorchester, Weymothe, and Hingham shall belong. Every of these Courts shall be kept by such magistrates as shall be dwelling in or near the said towns, and by such other persons of worth as shall from time to time be appointed by the General Court, so as no court shall be kept without one magistrate at the least and that none of the magistrates be excluded, who can and will intend the same." [1] And when the Colony was divided into counties, May 10, 1643,[2] the courts continued to be held in Cambridge, as the shire-town of Middlesex. As " the business of the courts there is much increased," it was ordered, Oct. 19, 1652, that two additional sessions should be held for that county in each year, both at Charlestown. These courts were continued for many years, and a court house and jail were erected in that town. At a later date, courts were established and similar buildings erected in Concord, and also, at a comparatively recent day, at Lowell. All these places were regarded as " half-shires " ; but the County Records were never removed from Cambridge, as the principal shire, except as follows : During the usurpation of Sir Edmund Andros, he appointed Capt. Laurence Hammond of Charlestown to be Clerk of the Courts and Register of Probate

---

[1] *Mass. Col. Rec.*, I. 169.   [2] *Ibid.*, II. 38.

and Deeds, who removed the records to Charlestown. After the revolution and the resumption of government under the forms of the old Charter, Captain Hammond denied that the existing courts had any legal authority, and refused to surrender the records which were in his possession. The General Court therefore ordered, Feb. 18, 1689–90, " that Capt. Laurence Hammond deliver to the order of the County Court for Middlesex the records of that county ; that is to say, all books and files by him formerly received from Mr. Danforth, sometime Recorder of that County, as also all other books of record, and files belonging to said county in his custody."[1] A year afterwards, Feb. 4, 1690–1, the Marshal General was directed to summon Captain Hammond to appear and show cause why he had not surrendered the Middlesex Records ; and on the next day, he " peremptorily denying to appear," the General Court ordered the Marshal General to arrest him forthwith, with power to break open his house if necessary.[2] The records were at length surrendered. Again, at a town meeting, May 11, 1716, an attempt was made to reclaim missing records: " Whereas the Register's office in the County of Middlesex is not kept in our town of Cambridge, which is a grievance unto us, Voted, that our Representative be desired to represent said grievance to the honorable General Court, and intreat an Act of said Court that said office may forthwith be removed into our town, according to law, it being the shire-town in said county."[3] By the records of the General Court it appears that on the 8th of June, 1716, Colonel Goffe complained that no office for the registry of deeds was open in Cambridge, being the shire-town of Middlesex ; the Representative of Charlestown insisted that his town was the shire ; and a hearing was ordered.[4] A week afterwards, June 15, " upon hearing of the towns of Cambridge and Charlestown as to their respective claims of being the shire-town of the County of Middlesex, resolved that Cambridge is the shire-town of said County. Read and non-concurred by the Representatives."[5] The case between the two towns being again heard, June 18, 1717, it was resolved by the whole court, that " Cambridge is the shire-town of the said county ; "[6] and on the following day it was voted in concurrence " that the public office for registering of deeds and conveyances of lands for the County

---

[1] Mass. Prov. Rec., vi. 117.
[2] Ibid., vi. 172.
[3] Samuel Phipps, Esq., of Charlestown, succeeded Captain Hammond as Register

of Deeds, and kept his office and the records in Charlestown up to this time.
[4] Mass. Prov. Rec., x. 68.
[5] Ibid., p. 68.
[6] Ibid., p. 145.

of Middlesex be forthwith opened and kept at the shire-town of Cambridge."[1] This order was immediately obeyed.

I have not ascertained when or where the house was erected in which the judicial courts were first held in Cambridge. It seems to have been burned in 1671. In the Court Files of that year, is a document commencing thus: "At a County Court held at Cambridge, 4 (8) 1671. After the burning of the Court House, wherein was also burnt the Court Book of Records for trials, and several deeds, wills and inventories, that have been delivered into Court before the fire was kindled," etc.[2] The Court afterwards passed this order: "Upon information that several Records belonging to this County were casually burnt in the burning of the house where the Court was usually kept, this Court doth order that the Recorder take care that out of the foul copies and other scripts in his custody he fairly draw forth the said Records into a Book, and present the same to the County Court, when finished: and that the Treasurer of the County do allow him for the same."[3] The first Court House of which we have any definite knowledge, was erected, about 1708, in Harvard Square, nearly in front of the present Lyceum Hall.[4] It appears by the Proprietors' Records that "at a meeting of the Proprietors of Cambridge, orderly convened, the 26 day of January 1707-8, — Voted, That the land where Mr. John Bunker's shop now stands, with so much more as will be sufficient to erect the Court House upon (to be built in this town), be granted for that end, in case a Committee appointed by the Proprietors do agree with Andrew Bordman and John Bunker for building a lower story under it . . . . Deac. Nathaniel Hancock, Jason Russell, and Lieut. Amos Marrett, were chosen a committee to agree with said Bunker and Bordman about building under the said house."

The Committee reported, Feb. 9, 1607-8: "Pursuant to the aforesaid appointment, we, the subscribers above mentioned, have agreed with and granted liberty unto the said John Bunker and Andrew Bordman to make a lower room under the said

[1] *Mass. Prov. Rec.*, x. 147.
[2] The volume which was burned contained the Records after October, 1663, up to October 4, 1671.
[3] *County Court Rec.*, iii. 172.
[4] This Court House stood where the Market House was erected more than a century later. Its position is indicated

on a pen and ink plan drawn about 1750, and here reproduced by permission of its owner, Henry Wheatland, M. D., of Salem. The Court House (called Town-house on the plan) stood further south than is here represented, — its northerly end being several feet south of the southerly front of the meeting-house.

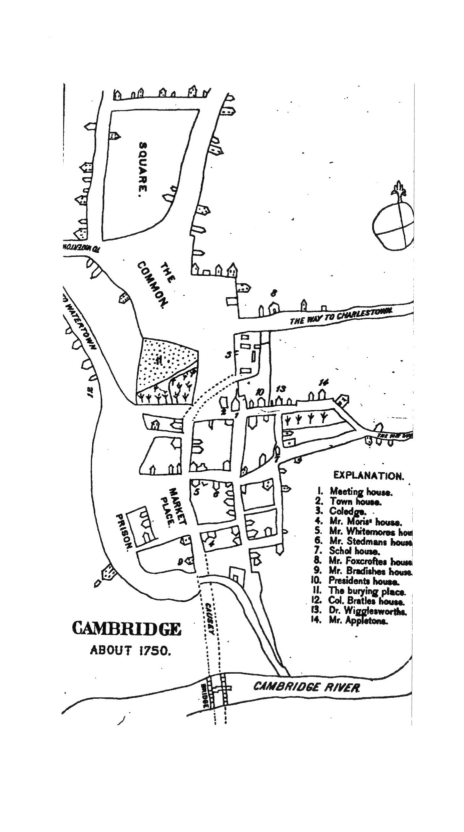

EXPLANATION.

1. Meeting house.
2. Town house.
3. Coledge.
4. Mr. Moris' house.
5. Mr. Whitemores house.
6. Mr. Stedmans house.
7. Schol house.
8. Mr. Foxcroftes house.
9. Mr. Bradishes house.
10. Presidents house.
11. The burying place.
12. Col. Bratles house.
13. Dr. Wigglesworths.
14. Mr. Appletons.

CAMBRIDGE

ABOUT 1750.

house (which we apprehend will be about thirty foot in length and twenty-four foot in width), the said lower room to be about seven or eight foot stud, betwixt joints, with a cellar under the whole of the said house; the aforesaid lower room and cellar to be for the use of the said John Bunker and Andrew Bordman, their heirs and assigns forever, excepting an entry through the middle of the said lower room, of about six foot wide, and a stairway for passage into the said Court House, or chamber, as the committee for building the same shall see meet; the remainder of the said lower room and the whole of the said cellar to be for the use and benefit of the said John Bunker and Andrew Bordman, their heirs and assigns, forever, as aforesaid. It is the true intent and meaning of this agreement, that the said John Bunker and Andrew Bordman shall, at their own cost and charge, build the cellar and lower room aforesaid, and finish the same up to the girts, and keep so much of the said buildings as appertains to them the said Bunker and Bordman, viz., up to the girts aforesaid, in good repair, at all times, on penalty of paying treble damage that the upper room may sustain by reason of the said Bunker and Bordman's neglect in causing their part of said building to be kept in good repair," etc. The County Court had previously " Ordered, that there be allowed out of the County Treasury towards the erecting a suitable Court House for the use of the County in the town of Cambridge, thirty pounds, the one half thereof to be paid at the raising and covering, and the other half at the finishing of the same; the said house to be not less than four and twenty foot wide and eight and twenty foot long, and of height proportionable." [1] This house, diminutive as its proportions now appear, was used by the courts for about half a century. But in 1756 the Court of Sessions appointed a committee to provide better accommodations, either by enlarging and repairing the old house or erecting a new one. Whereupon the town, Nov. 2, 1756, declared by vote its willingness to pay its customary proportion of the cost of a " new Court House, to be erected, of such model and dimensions, and in such place in the town, as the Committee of said Court shall judge most suitable and commodious: provided the materials of the old meeting-house now about to be taken down, be given and applied (so far as they shall be wanted) to that use, together with the town's proportion of the present Court House." On the 29th of the same month, the Proprietors voted to grant land, " not exceeding one

[1] *Sessions Records,* April 28, 1707.

quarter of an acre, whereon to erect a new Court House," the
place to be determined by a joint committee of the proprietors,
of the town, and of the Court of Sessions.   At length a lot of
land, where Lyceum Hall now stands, was purchased of Caleb
Prentice, who conveyed the same Nov. 5, 1757, to William Brattle, Andrew Bordman, and Edmund Trowbridge, for the use of
the town of Cambridge, and county of Middlesex, "for erecting
and continuing a Court House upon forever hereafter."   On this
lot a house was erected, more spacious than the former, and was
occupied by the courts more than half a century.   An attempt
was afterwards made to erect another edifice in the centre of Harvard Square; and the Proprietors voted, June 14, 1784, "to give
and grant to the town of Cambridge, for ever, so much land adjoining to the land on which the old Court House stood (which
was nearly opposite to where the present Court House stands),
as shall be sufficient to make up a piece forty six feet square;
. . . . including and surrounding the land on which the old
Court House stood (which was thirty feet by twenty-four feet),
for the purpose of erecting a building to keep the County Records
and hold the Probate Courts in." [1]   It does not appear, however, that any such building was erected.   An ineffectual attempt
was also made in 1806 by prominent men in Cambridgeport to
induce the County to erect a court house on the easterly side of
what was long called the "meeting-house lot," bounded by
Broadway, and Bordman, Harvard, and Columbia streets.
Andrew Craigie and his associates were more successful. Having
given ample grounds, and erected a court house and jail at an
expense of $24,000, as related in chapter xiii., they were re-
warded by the removal of the courts and records in 1816 to the
edifices prepared for them, where they remain to this day.   The
old Court House having been abandoned by the County was
used for town and parish purposes until April 19, 1841, when the
town quitclaimed all its right and interest in the house and the
lot (containing about ten perches) of land on which it stood for the
nominal consideration of one dollar, to Omen S. Keith and others,
in trust for the use of the proprietors of the Lyceum Hall to be
erected on the premises; provided, nevertheless, that the grantees
"do and shall forever grant and secure to the town the right of
the inhabitants of the first Ward in said Cambridge to the use of
the Hall for all necessary meetings of the voters in said Ward."
The old Court House was soon afterwards removed to Palmer
Street; it still remains, being occupied for secular purposes.

[1] *Proprietors' Records.*

The earliest notice which I have found of a place of imprisonment in Cambridge is contained in the following report, preserved in the Middlesex Court Files: —

"January the 7th 1655. Wee, whose names are underwritten, being appoynted by the County Cort of Middlesex to provide a house of Correction, with a fit person to keep the same, do make our return to the honored Court as followeth : Impr. Wee have bargained and bought of Andrew Stevenson of Cambridge his dwelling house with about half a rood of land adjoyning to the same, being bounded with Mr. Collines on the north and east, and the highway on west and south,[1] with all the appurtenances and privileges thereoff ; the said Andrew hereby covenanting and promising, for him and his heyres to make legal conveyance thereoff to the County when thereunto demanded. In consideration whereoff we do covenant with the said Andrew Stevenson, his heyres and assignes to pay and satisfie to him or his assignes sixteen pounds in cattle or 18li in corne, at or before the first of May next; and at the same time the said Andrew to deliver his house in as good repaire as now it is for the use of the County. Also wee have agreed with our brother Edward Goffe to errect an addition thereunto, in length 26 foote and in proportion to the other house, and a stack of chimneys in the midle, and to finish the same as may be most sutable for the work and end proposed. Also, wee do desire the honored Court to allow unto our brother Andrew Stevenson (who hath willingly at our request yelded himselfe to the service of the County in that place) such an annual stipend as may be due incouragement to continue the same with all diligence and faithfulnes, according as need shall require.

EPHRAIM CHILD,
EDWARD JACKSON,
RALPH MOUSELL,
EDWARD GOFFE."

On the other side is endorsed, — "This witnesseth that I, Andrew Stevenson, do consent to the within named propositions and covenant, as witnes my hand this 7th. 11mo. 1655.[2]

ANDREW A. S. STEVENSON."

---

[1] The House of Correction stood on the easterly side of Holyoke Street, about two hundred feet northerly from the present location of Mount Auburn Street. After the erection of a jail, this estate was reconveyed to Stevenson, whose heirs sold it to Jonathan Nutting, March 25, 1695.

[2] By the Court Records and Files, it appears that the House of Correction or

In October, 1660, the County Court ordered, that the House
of Correction, or Bridewell, should be used as a prison for the
County, until further provision be made. Such provision was
made by the erection of a jail [1] before Aug. 26, 1692, when it
was ordered by the Court, "that the County Treasurer take care
that their majesties Goal at Cambridge be repaired, for the comfortable being of what persons may be committed forthwith." [2]
It was also ordered, Dec. 14, 1703, "that an addition be made to
the prison at the west end thereof, of eighteen foot square, with
studs conformable to the old house." A dozen years later, the
old part of the prison became so unsatisfactory, that the Court
appointed "a committee to agree with carpenters and other
workmen to erect and build a good well-timbered house in Cambridge for a Prison, for the accommodation of a keeper, to be
thirty-six foot long, and for width agreeable to the foundation
of the old Goal or Prison, two storeys high, fifteen foot stud, with
a stack of chymneys in the middle, to be done and finished work-
manlike, as soon as may be conveniently effected. . . . . Further
ordered, that Coll. Edmund Goffe, the present Sheriff, repairs

---

Bridewell was erected in 1656. Andrew
Stevenson was the prison keeper from
1656 to 1672; William Healy, from 1672
to 1682, when he was removed from office; Daniel Cheever, from 1682 until he
was succeeded in office by his son Israel
Cheever about 1693. In 1691, the prison-
keeper presented a petition for relief,
which is inserted, as characteristic of that
period: —

"To the honored Court for the County
of Middlesex, holden in Cambridge by
adjournment this 11th day of May 1691,
the petition of Daniel Cheever, keeper of
the Prison in Cambridge humbly sheweth,
That your poor petitioner is in great
straits and want at present, by reason
that his salary hath not been paid him
for some considerable time past, and having a considerable family depending on
him for maintenance, he is compelled to
make his complaint to this honored Court,
hoping to find relief, begging some order
may be taken speedily for his supply,
which otherwise cannot be done without
great loss and damage to your petitioner;
and he would further inform this Court,
that George Newbe, who is under bond to
pay a fine imposed on him by this Court,

hath a pair of young oxen which he
would part with, in order to said payment; which oxen your petitioner desires
he may have, and then would put off his
old oxen to help supply him with necessaries for his family. Also he further
desires to add that Sylvester Hayes hath
lain upon him this many months, without
any consideration from Charlestown,
which your petitioner is not able to
bear, therefore desires redress of this
honored Court in this particular also.
But not further to be troublesome, your
petitioner earnestly requests your serious
consideration of what is premised, and
remains your Honors' most humble servant." — *Court Files.*

[1] The jail stood on the northerly side
of Winthrop Street, between Winthrop
Square and Eliot Street; and this continued to be the place for imprisonment
until the new county buildings were
erected at East Cambridge.

[2] This was when the witchcraft excitement was at its extreme height, and the
prisons in several counties were put in
requisition to confine the unhappy victims
who were accused in Essex.

the chymneys in the new Goal, and what also may be needfull for the reception of and securing of criminals."

Until 1720, the "Common" extended to Linnæan Street, and included also a few acres, lying in a nearly square form, at the northwesterly corner of Linnæan Street and North Avenue.[1] This extreme point of the Common was set apart as a "Place of Execution," or "Gallows Lot," as it was more familiarly called. And after the Common was reduced to its present size, and the lots in this square fronting on the streets, had been granted to individuals, about one acre in its extreme northwesterly corner was reserved for its former use, until trials, and imprisonments, and executions were transferred to East Cambridge.[2] It was entered from North Avenue through a bridleway or passage, between Lancaster Place and Arlington Street, now called Stone Court.

The names and the number of the wretched convicts who suffered the extreme penalty of the law at this "Place of Execution," are unknown to me. One horrible example, however, was recorded by Professor Winthrop, in his interleaved Almanac, under date of Sept. 18, 1755: "A terrible spectacle in Cambridge : two negroes belonging to Capt. Codman of Charlestown, executed for petit treason, for murdering their said master by poison. They were drawn upon a sled to the place of execution ; and Mark, a fellow about 30, was hanged ; and Phillis, an old creature, was *burnt to death*." The "Boston Evening Post," of Sept. 22, states more particularly, that "the fellow was hanged, and the woman burned at a stake about ten yards distant from the gallows. They both confessed themselves guilty of the crime for which they suffered, acknowledged the justice of their sentence, and died very penitent. After execution, the body of Mark was brought down to Charlestown Common, and hanged in chains on a gibbet erected there for that purpose." Dr. Increase Mather, in his diary, printed in the first volume of the "Proceedings of the Massachusetts Historical Society," page 320, says that on the 22d of September, 1681, "there were three persons executed in Boston,—an Englishman for a rape ; a negro

---

[1] Delineated on an old plan in the City Hall.

[2] This lot was described in the *Proprietors' Records*, April 3, 1836, as "about one acre of land, called the Gallows Lot, in front of the house of James Rule, and separated from his real estate by a bridleway leading from the county road to said land," etc. It was sold on the 24th of the same month to William Frost, and described as bounded "easterly, southerly, and westerly, by his own land, northerly and northeasterly by a bridle-way, leading from the county road to land belonging to Mary Stone and Susanna Jarvis," etc.

man for burning a house at Northampton; and a negro woman
who burnt two houses at Roxbury, July 12, in one of which a
child was burnt to death. The negro woman was burnt to death,
— the first that has suffered such a death in New England." It
is devoutly to be hoped that the woman who thus expiated her
crime at Cambridge, in 1755, was the *last* "that has suffered
such a death in New England."

"Ye have the poor with you always;" and the judicious relief of their wants is an important but often a very perplexing
duty. For several years, as will be related in chapter xv., the
church assumed this duty, and made suitable provision for the
destitute and distressed. It does not distinctly appear at what
time the management of this charity passed into the hands of
the town. The earliest reference to this subject which I find on
the Town Records is under date of June 29, 1663: "Jane
Bourne [or Bowen] making her complaint to the selectmen, that
she can find none in the town that is willing to entertain her to
their service, and craving their favor that she may have liberty
to provide for herself in some other town, with security to such
as shall so entertain her, — the Townsmen do grant her request
in manner following, viz., so as that she place herself in some
honest family; and in case she stand in need of supply, or the
town whither she shall resort do see reason to return her again
upon the town, she shall be still accepted as one of the poor of
this place; and this is to be understood and taken as binding to
the town for one year next after the date hereof, any law, usage,
or custom, to the contrary, notwithstanding." Again, under date
of April 8, 1672: "The terms of agreement of the selectmen
with Thomas Longhorne for the keeping of William Healyes
child, as followeth: That the said Thomas Longhorne is to bring
up Hanna Hely, daughter of William Healy, born in the year
1671, providing all necessaries for her of food and clothing in the
time of her minority and suitable education meet for one of her
sex and degree; and for his satisfaction, he is to be allowed out
of the Town Rate five pounds a year for five years; and if she
should die before those five years be expired, or it should be provided for by any of its friends before that time, then he is to
have no more than for the time he keep it, after five pounds per
annum; only forty shillings of said pay is to be made in cash, —
or, if not, then so much in other pay at money price." In like
manner, for more than a hundred years after this date, provision
appears to have been made for the poor, in private families,

under the supervision of the selectmen. At length it was determined, March 15, 1779, to purchase a house in which they might be gathered together, and their wants be more systematically supplied. Accordingly, " the committee who were chosen at the last Town Meeting, March 1, 1779, to purchase a workhouse for the poor of the town, reported that they could purchase of Deac. Samuel Whittemore a suitable house for that purpose. Voted, That said Committee purchase the house and land belonging to said Whittemore, take a deed for the same for the town, and that the Treasurer be directed to give security for the same, or hire the money to pay for it. Voted, that the Selectmen take care of the said house, and appoint some discreet person as Overseer." The estate consisted of a dwelling house and twenty-five square rods of land on the northeasterly corner of Brighton and South streets, and was conveyed to the town by deed dated March 29, 1779. For some reason this estate proved unsatisfactory; and the town voted, March 1, 1785, " that Mr. Caleb Gannett, Stephen Dana, Esq., Capt. John Walton, Deac. Aaron Hill, and William Winthrop, Esq., be a committee to inquire whether there is any person who is desirous to purchase the house and land belonging to the town, situate near the causeway, which was bought for a workhouse and almshouse, and what price it will fetch ; and they are also to inquire whether another place can be purchased in the town that will answer for said purposes, and upon what terms it can be had." The committee having been authorized so to do, reported, March 6, 1786, that " they sold the house at public auction for £19, 10s.; they afterwards sold the land for £37, 10s., both amounting to £57." They had also received an offer from the heirs of Abraham Watson of a house and about five acres of land for the sum of £60. This estate [1] was on the southwesterly corner of North Avenue and Cedar Street, and was conveyed to the town by deed dated March 9, 1786. The committee reported, June 12, 1786, " that an house is nearly finished and will be ready within a few days for the reception of the poor," and recommended that it " be called the Poor's House; " also that there " be chosen and appointed, as soon as may be, five persons, distinct from the Selectmen, to be Overseers of the Poor," who should have the general charge of the house, and provide all necessary " food, fuel, clothing, and medicine, proper for " the occupants, and tools and materials necessary to their proper em-

[1] Formerly owned by Matthew Cox.

ployment; that the Overseers should "appoint a suitable person
to be Warden of the Poor's House," who should "cause his family to lead their lives and behave at all times soberly, quietly,
decently, orderly, and regularly; particularly he shall cause them
to attend the public worship on Sundays as often and generally
as conveniently may be;" and he "shall endeavor to form the
paupers under his care to habits of economy, frugality, temper-
ance, sobriety, and industry; particularly he shall keep them employed in such useful and profitable labors as they may be respectively able to perform, within doors or without doors, having
regard to their different sexes, ages, bodily strength, former
habits of life, and all other circumstances, with the approbation
of the Overseers;" and that they should also appoint a suitable
physician, and employ all necessary servants. The Warden
should be required to pay all the earnings of the paupers,
monthly, to the Overseers, who should pay the same, half yearly,
to the Treasurer, drawing on him for the funds necessary to defray all charges; and the Treasurer should keep a separate account of all such receipts and payments. Finally, "the Overseers
of the Poor shall from time to time make such regulations, not
inconsistent with these general regulations, the laws of the Commonwealth, or the principles of humanity and benevolence, as
they may judge fit for the better ordering of the Poor's House
and the affairs of it; which regulations so by them made shall be
binding until the expiration of the year for which such Overseers
shall be chosen, or until they shall be by them revoked." This
report was accepted; and Dr. William Kneeland, Mr. Jeduthun
Wellington, Deac. Aaron Hill, Mr. Ebenezer Stedman, and Mr.
Edward Jackson, were thereupon elected as the first "Overseers
of the Poor, distinct from the Selectmen."

In this house, and under such regulations, the pauper establishment was admininistered until 1818, when a new Almshouse
was erected in Cambridgeport. By deed dated April 2, 1818,
Jonathan L. Austin and Benjamin Austin conveyed to the town
about eleven acres of land, being the whole square bounded by
Harvard, Norfolk, Austin, and Prospect streets, except one house
lot, previously sold, at the corner of Norfolk and Austin streets,
"measuring 100 feet on each of said streets, 100 feet on the
westerly side, and 78 feet on the northerly side." The Overseers reported to the town, Nov. 2, 1818, that they had sold the
old Almshouse to Jonathan Fowle, for $454.50, and had erected

on the lot purchased of the Austins a brick house [1] 55 feet long, 36 feet wide, about half three stories high, and the other half two stories high, with accommodations for sixty persons, and had removed the paupers into it. A code of Rules and Regulations, an Address by Royal Makepeace, on behalf of the Overseers, and a Sermon delivered in the Almshouse by Rev. Dr. Holmes, in September, 1818, are entered at full length on the Records of the Overseers of the Poor.

The new location of the Almshouse did not prove satisfactory; and a desire for further change was soon manifested. As early as Nov. 14, 1831, a Town-house having been erected on the north-easterly corner of the square, a committee was appointed by the town " to cause the Almshouse lands to be surveyed and laid out into proper streets and building-lots, and to ascertain what the same may be sold for; also to ascertain for what sum a suitable spot of ground for an Almshouse may be purchased, and a proper and suitable Almshouse erected thereon." During the night preceding July 30, 1836, the Almshouse, together with the out-buildings, was utterly consumed by fire, and one of its wretched inmates perished. The order for surveying the Almshouse lands was renewed, Aug. 22, 1836; and it was further ordered, that the building-lots be offered for sale at auction. Meantime, the town voted, Aug. 8, 1836, " that the Overseers of the Poor be authorised to make such temporary provision for the support of the Town's Poor, and such of the State's Poor as are not of competent health to labor, by hiring a building, or otherwise, as they may consider for the interest of the town." The Overseers accordingly hired a spacious house, originally designed for a tavern, on the northerly side of Main Street, nearly opposite to Osborn Street, which was occupied until a new Almshouse was erected at Riverside.

The town purchased, Dec. 9, 1836, of Amos Hazeltine, for $5,600, eleven and a quarter acres of land, bordering on Charles River, and extending from Western Avenue nearly to River Street, together with two acres and three quarters on the opposite side of Western Avenue, extending from the river to Putnam Street. A committee reported in April, 1838, that a

---

[1] This house stood on the westerly side of Norfolk Street, opposite to Worcester Street. It contained " a kitchen, 30×15 feet, a bathing room, and three cells, in the basement story; a work-room 30×15 feet, and six other sizable rooms, in the first story; and ten chambers in the second story; a large garret, 55×24 feet, and a cellar, 34×24 feet." Connected with the house were a wood-house, 30×15 feet, and a barn 35×25 feet. The land cost $1,750; the buildings, $4,851.77; total, $6,601.77.

brick Almshouse had been constructed on the first mentioned lot, at an expense of $7,490.90; and the paupers were again placed in a comfortable habitation.

Within a few years afterwards, a desire was manifested to abandon this pleasant spot, which had attained a greatly increased marketable value, and to try the experiment of farming on a larger scale. Accordingly the city purchased, Aug. 7, 1849, of Samuel Smith and Spencer Cook, for $12,000, about thirty-two acres of land, situated partly in the northwesterly corner of Cambridge and partly in the southwesterly corner of Somerville, and erected a stone Almshouse of the size and fashion then prevalent. The cost of the whole establishment was reported by a committee to be, — for the land, $12,000; for the house, $32,970.69; for fences, furniture, etc., $3,000; total, $47,970.69. The house was formally placed in the custody of the Overseers of the Poor, April 8, 1851, with much congratulatory speech-making, in presence of a large assembly of citizens, and the paupers were transferred to their new home. When this house was erected, its magnificent proportions were considered necessary for the accommodation of the large number of State paupers then under the charge of the city. Shortly afterwards, the Commonwealth adopted a new policy, erected State Almshouses, and withdrew its paupers from the care of cities and towns. Complaints were uttered, that the erection of so large a house for so few inmates was unnecessary, and involved an extravagant outlay of money. But such complaints are no longer heard; partly, because the increase of city paupers has kept pace with the rapidly increasing population, until the house is nearly if not altogether filled; and partly, because the citizens have become accustomed to expenditures so much more unnecessary and extravagant, that this has dwindled into comparative insignificance. The old Almshouse (together with the land) was sold, May 22, 1851, to Little & Brown, publishers and booksellers, for $24,000; they converted it into an establishment for the manufacture of books, and erected many additional buildings. Subsequently the larger part of the estate became the property of H. O. Houghton & Co., by whom it was further embellished and rendered famous as the seat of the Riverside Press.

Ordinaries, or houses of public entertainment, were established at a very early period. The General Court ordered, March 4, 1634-5, " that no persons whatsoever shall keep a common victualling house, without license from the Court, under the penalty of xx*. a week."[1] The power of granting licenses " to keep houses of common entertainment, and to retail wine, beer, &c." was transferred to the County Courts, May 26, 1647, " so as this Court may not be thereby hindered in their more weighty affairs."[2] Various laws were enacted, regulating such houses, notably in 1645 ;[3] yet so necessary were they considered, that the town of Concord was presented by the grand jury, June 19, 1660, " for not having a common house of entertainment," and was " enjoined to presént a meet person to be allowed at the next Court at Cambridge for that employment, on penalty of 5l., and to pay costs of Court, 2* and 6ᵈ."

Great caution was manifested in the appointment of grave and respectable citizens to keep ordinaries and to sell intoxicating drinks. The first person licensed by the General Court, Sept. 8, 1636, " to keepe a house of intertainment at Newe Towne," was Thomas Chesholme[4] a deacon of the church, and afterwards Steward of Harvard College. He was also licensed " to draw wine at Cambridge," May 18, 1640.[5] His dwelling-house was on a lot at the northwest corner of Dunster and Winthrop streets, adjoining the lot on which the first meeting-house was erected; so that the first church edifice and the first tavern in Cambridge stood side by side; and from all which is known of Deacon Chesholme's character, it may be confidently believed that he permitted nothing to be done in the one which could bring disgrace upon the other. The first person " allowed to sell wine and strong water " in Cambridge, March 12, 1637-8,[6] was Mr. Nicholas Danforth, a selectman, a representative in the General Court, and one of the most active and honored citizens. He resided on the northerly side of Bow Street, near Plympton Street, but died about a month after the date of his license. The next year, May 22, 1639, " Mr. Nathaniell Sparhawke was permitted to drawe wine and strong water for Cambridge.[7] He also was

[1] Mass. Col. Rec., l. 140.
[2] Ibid., ii. 188.
[3] It was then forbidden to " suffer any to be drunk or drink excessively, or continue tippling above the space of half an hour, in any of their said houses, under penalty of 5s. for every such offence suffered; and every person found drunk in the said houses or elsewhere shall forfeit 10s., and for every excessive drinking he shall forfeit 3s. 4d.; for sitting idle and continuing drinking above half an hour, 2s. 6d.; and it is declared to be excessive drinking of

wine when above half a pint of wine is allowed at one time to one person to drink : provided that it shall be lawful for any strangers, or lodgers, or any person or persons, in an orderly way, to continue in such houses of common entertainment during meal times, or upon lawful business, what time their occasions shall require." — Mass. Col. Rec., ii. 100.
[4] Mass. Col. Rec., l. 186.
[5] Ibid., l. 292.
[6] Ibid., l. 221.
[7] Mass. Col. Rec., l. 259.

a deacon of the church, and resided on the easterly side of Brighton Street, about midway between Harvard Square and Mount Auburn Street, in the house formerly owned and occupied by the Reverend Samuel Stone.

We come next to the establishment of an ordinary which was long known as the "Blue Anchor Tavern." Dec. 27, 1652, " The Townsmen do grant liberty to Andrew Belcher to sell beer and bread, for entertainment of strangers and the good of the town;"[1] and the County Court granted him a license, June 20, 1654, " to keep a house of public entertainment at Cambridge." Mr. Belcher was a trustworthy man, occasionally employed by the General Court to perform important duties. He was respectably connected; his wife was daughter of Mr. Nicholas Danforth and sister of Deputy Governor Thomas Danforth; their son, Andrew Belcher, Jr., was a member of the Council, and his son, Jonathan Belcher, was Governor of Massachusetts and of New Jersey. It does not appear where he first opened a " beer and bread " shop, or a " house of public entertainment; " but on the first of October, 1671, his son Andrew, then residing in Hartford, Conn., purchased of Sarah Beal, widow of Deacon Thomas Beal, an estate at the northeast corner of Brighton and Mount Auburn streets, where the sign of the Blue Anchor was soon afterwards displayed. Mr. Belcher was licensed for the last time in April, 1673, in which year he probably died. In April, 1674, license was granted to his widow Elizabeth Belcher, and afterwards from year to year until she died, June 26, 1680. She was succeeded by her son Andrew Belcher, who was licensed in 1681 and 1682.[2] In September, 1682, Capt. Belcher sold the estate to his brother-in-law Jonathan Remington, who performed the duties of host until April 21, 1700, when he died, and was succeeded by his widow, Martha Remington, daughter of the first Andrew Belcher. The Belcher family ceased to be inn-holders May 12, 1705, when the widow and children of Captain Remington sold to Joseph Hovey the estate " near the market-place, commonly called and known by the sign of the Blue Anchor." Joseph Hovey retained the house only four years, and then sold it to his brother John Hovey, who died in 1715. His widow Abiel Hovey

[1] Although this was not, as Rev. Dr. Holmes supposed, "the first license for an inn, in Cambridge" (*Coll. Mass. Hist. Soc.*, vii. 28), it may be regarded as the most important, in respect to its character and permanency.

[2] Capt. Belcher's son Jonathan, afterwards Governor of Massachusetts, was born Jan. 8, 1681-2, and probably in this house.

received license for two years, and then married Edmund Angier, who conducted the business until April 4, 1724, when he died and his widow Abiel again assumed charge of the house; she married Isaac Watson, Aug. 27, 1725, in whose name business was transacted about four years, when it passed into the hands of John Hovey, son of the former owner. In November, 1731, the General Court authorized the Court of Sessions to grant (out of the usual season) to Joseph Bean, late of Boston, "a license to keep a Tavern in Cambridge, in the house of Mr. John Hovey, which he hath lately hired, and has for many years past been used as a house of public entertainment." On the 23d of April, 1737, Mr. Bean bought of Nathaniel Hancock an estate on the westerly side of Brighton Street, about midway between Harvard Square and Mount Auburn Street, to which he transferred the sign of the Blue Anchor; and for nearly a century afterwards it was a famous Tavern. Mr. Bean sold the estate, Jan. 26, 1749, to Ebenezer Bradish; Mr. Bradish died in 1785, and his son sold it, Feb. 29, 1796, to Israel Porter, who is well remembered by many now living, and who died May 30, 1837, aged 99, according to the town record. A part of the tavern-house remains stand-ing, though much changed in appearance.[1]

John Jackson kept a public house near the northwesterly angle of Brattle Street and Brattle Square, probably from about 1672 until 1695, when he was succeeded by Capt. Josiah Parker, who purchased the estate in 1699, and was an inn-holder as late as 1725, and perhaps until he died in July or August, 1731.[2]

---

[1] At this house the Selectmen met for the transaction of public business, and probably paid for the use of rooms by their patronage of the bar. Among the paid bills remaining on file is the follow-ing:—

"The Selectmen of the town of Cambridge to Eben'. Bradish,   Dr.

		£0.	17.	8
March, 1769, To dinners and drink,		£0.	17.	8
April, "	To flip and punch,	0.	2.	0
May 1, "	To wine and eating,	0.	4.	3
May, "	To dinners, drink and suppers,	0.	13.	0
	To flip and cheese,	0.	1.	3
	To wine and flip,	0.	4.	0
June, "	To punch,	0.	2.	3
July, "	To punch and eating,	0.	4.	0
August, "	To punch and cheese,	0.	3.	7
Oct., "	To punch and flip,	0.	4.	3
	To dinners and drink,	0.	13.	8
Dec., Jan., 1770, & Feb., Sundries,		0.	12.	0

£4. 16. 7 "

[2] It does not distinctly appear whether Samuel Gibson was an inholder; but in 1672 he was punished for unlawfully en-tertaining students. The following depo-

15

Another tavern, somewhat famous for many years, stood on the southerly side of Mount Auburn Street, about midway between Brighton and Dunster Streets. It seems to have been first opened in 1726, by John Stedman, grandson of Robert Stedman, the former owner of the same estate. He was succeeded, in 1728, by his widow, Sarah Stedman, and she, in 1734, by her son Ebenezer Stedman, who died Sept. 18, 1785, aged 76.

Time would fail me should I attempt to enumerate and describe all the inn-holders who have flourished in Cambridge. During the first century after the foundation of the town, licenses were granted to the following named persons (and perhaps others) besides those who have already been mentioned: —

Daniel Champney, 1691.	James Cutler, 1718–1735.
William Russell, 1696–1715.	Thomas Thompson, 1721–1724.
Samuel Phipps, 1707–1709.	Elizabeth Thompson, 1725.
Elizabeth Phipps, 1710–1712.	Thomas Brown, 1721.
Edward Marrett, 1709.	William Bond, 1722–1724.
Susanna Stacey, 1709, 1713–1715.	Peter Oliver, 1727–1729.
Hannah Stacey, 1712, 1716–1724.	Joshua Gamage, 1729–1731.
Ruth Child, 1713–1715.	Daniel Champney, Jr., 1730–1733.
Samuel Robinson, 1714–1720.	Thomas Holt, 1730–1731.
John Smith, 1715–1717.	Thomas Dana, 1731–1735.
James Ingham, 1716–1720.	William Bowen, 1732.
Samuel Smith, 1716–1735.	Jonathan Starr, 1735.

During the early part of the present century, the Davenport Tavern, at the westerly corner of North Avenue and Beech Street, was widely celebrated for the concoction of flip; and in

sition and confessions are preserved in the files of the County Court: "Urian Oakes, aged 14 yeares and upward do testifie that about 10 dayes since he and Percifall Greene being gathering up fruits in the Marshals orchard, Mr. Edw; Pelham came to them with a fowling peece in his hand and desired him to shoot a foule of G[m]. Farlengs, and when he was disapoynted there, he brought him to y[e] fence between y[e] Marshals yard and Capt. Gookins, where sat a turkie, and desired him to shoot y[t], w[ch] he accordingly did, and y[e] fowle being killed y[e] s[d] Pelham took y[e] coate of y[e] s[d] Urian and wrapt up the turkie in it, and sent it by Percifall Greene to Samuel Gibsons and bid him, leave it at y[e] said Gibsons house." "Samuel Gibson being examined do con-

fesse y[t] about 10 dayes sence Percifall Greene came to his house and brought a turkie wrapt up in a coate and left it there, and was dressed by his wife, and baked in the oven, and in the night following it was eaten by Mr. Pelham, John Wise, and Russell, stud[ts]." etc. "Goodwife Gibson his wife do confesse y[t] w[d] is above related is y[e] truth, and y[t] she suspected it not to be stoalen, but that Mr. Pelham said he came by it honestly, and was frequently at their house. 23 (7) 1672." The result appears on the Court Records, Oct. 1, 1672. "Samuel Gibson, being convicted of entertayneing some of the stud[ts]. contrary to law, is sentenced to be admonished and to pay a fine of forty shillings in money. And he stands committed until it be p[d]."

the easterly sections of the town the hostelries at the easterly corner of Main and Pearl streets, the westerly corner of Main and Douglass streets, near the westerly corner of Main and Moore streets, at the junction of Main Street and Broadway (and another a few rods farther eastward), at the junction of Cambridge and Bridge streets, and at the junction of Bridge and Gore streets, besides a generous local patronage, reaped an abundant harvest from the country teams engaged in transporting merchandise to and from Boston; which teams almost entirely disappeared immediately after the construction of railroads, and the inns did not long afterwards flourish.

Besides innkeepers, the County Court licensed others to sell intoxicating liquors by retail. Among the names of such retailers, in addition to those who have already been mentioned, the following appear during the first century : —

John Stedman, 1653–1686.	Jonathan Remington, 1713–1735.
William Manning, 1654–1686.	Nathaniel Hancock, Jr., 1707–1709.
Edmund Angier, 1674–1686.	Mary Bordman, 1708–1714.
Samuel Andrew, 1684–1691.	John Stedman, 1717–1734.
William Andrew, 1701.	Sarah Fessenden, 1720–1735.
Mrs. Seeth Andrew, 1702–1703.	Mary Oliver, 1731–1732.
Zachariah Hicks, 1704–1717.	Edward Marrett, 1733–1735.
Martha Remington, 1705–1712.	

Two of these retailers in their old age found it necessary to appeal to the County Court for relief; their petitions are still preserved on file, to wit : —

" To the honored Court assembled at Cambridge, all prosperity wished. Thease are to informe you that I wase brought up in an honest collinge in ould England, where we sould all sortes of goodes and strong waters, withought offence. I have bine now in this land forty-nine yeres and upwards in this towne, and have payd to the magistre and ministre, and to towne charges, and all willingly; that I have helped to beare the burthen and heate of the daye; and now I am 74 yers and upward, yet I can abide in my shope and attend my collinge, though litell is to be gotten by anye thinge I can by; that my trad will not maintayne my ffamily and other charges of towne and countrey and ministrye. There being so many sellers that never served for a trade, I desire that it might be no offence to aney that I continue in that collinge I was brought up to, and may have yo[r] leave to sell rome, it being a commodity sallabell and allowed to be brought into the countrey; and many that was

formerly a commodity is not now. Hopeing you will grant me
my request, I rest y' servant,   EDMUND ANGIER."
April 7, 1686.

"To the honored County Court sitting by adjournment at
Charlestown, 24, 8ᵐ., 1690. The petition of John Stedman of
Cambridge, aged 88, sheweth, That your petitioner, as is well
known, hath had a license to sell Rum for many years past,
which never was discontinued till the Revolution, since which he
would have sought for the renewal of it, had he had the least
notice when or where he ought to apply himself for it, or that
any others renewed theirs: That your petitioner wonders that
his daughter Sharp should be summoned to this Court for selling
Rum without license, she never having sold any at Cambridg on
her own or her husband's account, but upon the sole and proper
account and by the order of your petitioner, who is well assured
that he hath never given cause to be dealt with in extremity, he
having never bin behindhand in paying for his draft, or in serv-
ing the country to his power. Your petitioner therefore praies
that his said daughter Sharp may no further be molested or discouraged from her dutiful and charitable assistance of your petitioner for his support and comfort in his extream old age, and
that a license may be granted him as formerly. So praies your
humble servant,   JOHN STEDMAN."

In addition to innholders and retailers, venders of beer and
bread were licensed, one of whom, Andrew Belcher, has already
been mentioned. Another was Mrs. Bradish, probably the wife
of Robert Bradish,[1] who resided on the westerly corner of Harvard and Holyoke streets, where the Holyoke House now stands.
The following appeal to the County Court, without date, is in
the handwriting of President Dunster, and is preserved in the
files for 1654 : —

"Honored Gentlemen, as far as it may stand with the wholesome orders and prudential laws of the country for the publick
weal, I can very freely speak with and write in the behalf of
sister Bradish, that shee might be encouraged and countenanced
in her present calling for baking of bread and brewing and selling
of penny bear, without which shee cañot continue to bake : In
both which callings such is her art, way and skill, that shee doth
vend such comfortable penniworths for the reliefe of all that send

---

[1] The license may have been granted to her husband; but she seems to have
been the active manager of the business.

unto her as elsewhere they can seldom meet with. Shee was complained of unto me for harboring students unseasonably spending there their time and parents' estate; but upon examination I found it a misinformation, and that shee was most desirous that I should limit or absolutely prohibit any ;that in case of sickness or want of comfortable bread or bear in the College only they should thither resort and then not to spend above a penny a man, nor above two shillings in a quarter of a year; which order shee carefully observed in all ordinary cases. How far she had publick allowance by the townsmen hertofore I leave to Br. Goff or any of our townsmen that are with you to shew: and how good effects for the promoting of the weal publick and how christian a thing in itself godly emulation is, as your historical knowledge informs you so your experience abundantly demonstrates, as contrarywise the undoing measures of monopolyes. The Lord to guide and prosper all your administrations shall bee the prayer of yours in what he can.   H. DUNSTER."

From time to time the Court established a scale of prices for ordinaries: —

"At a meeting of the magistrates and committee to take the Treasurer's account, Dec. 30, 1679; For the regulating of expenses at the County Courts, it is ordered that henceforth, for the juries, there shall be allowed in money,

For their breakfast, one man,		£0. 0. 4.
For their dinner, " "		0. 1. 3.
For their supper, " "		0. 1. 0.
for the magistrates,		
For dinner, " "		0. 2. 0.
For supper, " "		0. 1. 6.
for the marshall and constables, one meal,		0. 1. 0.

"And wine and beer, &c., to be included in the abovesaid sums; and if any ordinary shall exceed the abovesaid order, it shall be at their own peril."

In the Proprietors' Records, 1635, it is stated that a large lot, originally designed for Richard Saltonstall, "is now to be entered the Market Place." It was bounded northerly on Mount Auburn Street, easterly on Brighton Street, and southerly on Winthrop Street. This lot retained the name of Market Place more than two hundred years; but there is no evidence that any

¹ *Middlesex Co. Rec.*

market house was ever erected thereon.[1] It may have been used, long ago, as an open mart for the interchange of goods between producers and consumers; but even of this, no proof remains. Again, when Davenport & Makepeace, in 1805, laid out streets in the Phips Farm, a Market Place was reserved at the junction of Market Street and Broadway; but the time has not yet arrived for appropriating it to its intended use. In July, 1812, the first effectual movement was made for securing the long-desired accommodation. Premising that "a convenient market-stall, sufficiently capacious to admit meat and other articles to be exposed for sale, protected by a roof or covering from the rains and the sun, erected near the town pump in Cambridge, will be of general benefit," twenty-four persons subscribed an agreement for the accomplishment of that purpose. The "town pump" stood near the centre of Harvard Square; and the Square was then much smaller than it now is, having since that period been enlarged on the northeasterly and westerly sides. On the westerly portion of this Square a building was erected, about thirty-four feet long and twenty-five feet wide, with posts, and rails around it, probably encumbering nearly the whole space granted for that use by the proprietors of common lands; namely, "a square piece, measuring forty-six feet on each side." John Bowers engaged to erect the building for such price as should be determined by Deac. Josiah Moore, Deac. John Watson, and Mr. Thomas Mason. The referees reported, Nov. 5, 1812, that Mr. Bowers was entitled to $210.55, for labor and materials, and that materials had been furnished by subscribers, amounting to $38.89. They also estimated that it would cost $81.00 additional "to complete the coving, furnish posts and railings around the house, steps to each door,[2] raising the earth around it, providing benches, cleaver, block, and additional hooks, painting the building, and procuring Dearborn's patent Balance, with a scale attached thereto, that will weigh from half a pound to five hundred and forty weight."[3]

[1] The Market Place is now generally called Winthrop Square. After remaining open and common for two centuries, on petition of Levi Farwell and others, April 7, 1834, the Selectmen were authorized "to permit Market Place, so called, to be enclosed as they shall judge for the ornament and benefit of the town and the petitioners; provided that the enclosure shall be of a permanent nature and without expense to the town; and provided also that the town shall have a right to remove the enclosure, if they shall hereafter see fit."

[2] One door was at the south end, and one on the east side.

[3] To defray the whole cost, amounting to $329.94, and to provide "a fund for repairs," a joint stock was established of forty shares, valued at ten dollars, each, which were immediately taken as follows: Oliver Wendell, three shares; Caleb Gan-

At their meeting, Jan. 11, 1813, the proprietors established several Regulations, the first three of which were as follows: — "1. No person occupying said market house shall be permitted to use or vend spirituous liquors therein, except on such public occasions, and under such restrictions, as the committee may hereafter agree to and direct. 2. That no fire be carried into or kept in the market house, and that no cigars or pipes be allowed to be smoked therein. 3. That no shell or other fish be permitted to be kept in said market house, at any season of the year."[1]

The first occupant of the market house seems to have been Joel Wellington, who paid rent for the quarter ending March 31, 1813; he also occupied it several years after April 1, 1814. The second occupant was Henry Greenwood, under a lease dated March 31, 1813, in which lease the committee of the proprietors reserved "one quarter part of said house, — viz., next to the balance and scale, for the purpose of accommodating those who may bring into the market, butter, eggs, or fowls, or any kinds of sauce; but no person shall be admitted to vend therein such articles of provision as are usually supplied by butchers." The committee also reserved "the right of letting said market house on Wednesday and Thursday of Commencement week, without any deduction from the rent thereof." And it is worthy of note, that, according to the Treasurer's account current, Israel Porter paid for the use of the market house on those two days and the intervening night, the sum of twenty dollars, while the whole rent of the house for the year, exclusive of those days, was only forty dollars. Afterwards, this reservation of two days was discontinued, and the rent was gradually increased to eighty dollars per annum, and taxes.

A lease of the ground under and around the market house had been granted by the Proprietors of Common Lands, extending to

nett, two; John Mellen, two; Josiah Moore, two; Samuel Bartlett, two; Israel Porter, two; Sidney Willard, one; Henry Ware, one; William Hilliard, two; Thomas Warland, one; Artemas Moore, one; Richard Bordman, two; Eliab W. Metcalf, one; John Farrar, one; John T. Kirkland, two; Levi Hedge, including Joseph McKean's subscription, one; James Read, Jr., two; Joseph S. Read, for himself and William Brown, one; James Munroe, for himself and Torrey Hancock, one; John Warland, for him-

self and William Warland, one; Samuel Child, one; Samuel Child, Jr., one; Jonas Wyeth, 3d one; Thomas Austin, one; Joseph Holmes, one; Royal Morse, one; John Walton, for himself and Ebenezer Stedman, Jr., one; Jacob H. Bates, one; William Gamage, one.

[1] A cellar was constructed in 1816, and was rented for fifteen dollars per annum to Zenas C. Atwood, "to keep for sale oysters; no kind of gambling, tippling, or riotous behaviour, to be suffered in said cellar."

April 1, 1833. But at a town meeting, April 8, 1826, a Committee, of which Abraham Hilliard was chairman, submitted an elaborate Report concerning the respective rights of the Town and the Proprietors of Common Lands in and to several lots therein described, and concerning sundry encroachments on the public highways. The report recited the history of the lot on which the Market House stood, showing that, after it had been occupied about fifty years by a court house, it had remained open for public travel during a still longer period, from about 1760 to 1812, and that the town had thus acquired the right of passage over it as a public highway; which report was accepted, and arrangements were made to secure the immediate or future removal of all encroachments on any of the public highways in the town. At a meeting of the Proprietors of the Market House, March 5, 1827, "a deed was presented by a committee of the town of Cambridge, for the Proprietors to sign, thereby acknowledging that they have no right or title to the land whereon the market house now stands; the proprietors refused to sign said deed, and voted, that William Hilliard, Levi Farwell, and Joseph Holmes be a committee for the purpose of ascertaining whether a suitable lot of land can be procured upon which to remove the market house, and upon what terms. After an ineffectual negotiation, lasting more than two years, resort was had to legal process. At the September term of the Court of Common Pleas, 1829, an indictment was presented by the Grand Jury against the Proprietors of the Market House, for keeping up and maintaining "a certain wooden building, extending in length thirty-four feet and in breadth twenty-five feet, with a cellar under the same, and with posts and railing on the sides thereof extending in length forty feet, standing upon the common and public highway in the town of Cambridge." The case was continued from term to term until June, 1830, when the result is thus recorded: "And now, Asahel Stearns, Esq., Attorney for the Commonwealth in this behalf, says, the within named defendants having paid the costs of prosecution, and given satisfactory security for the removal of the nuisance within forty days from this seventeenth of June, 1830, he will no further prosecute this indictment." In due time the building was removed, and the Square has since remained open and unobstructed.   —

The enclosure at the corner of North Avenue and Garden Street is generally supposed to be the most ancient burial-place in Cambridge. It was used for that purpose as early as January, 4, 1635–6, when it was "ordered, that the burying-place shall be paled in; whereof John Tayloot is to do 2 rod, Georg Steele 8 rod and a gate, Thomas Hosmer 8 rod, Mathew Allen 1 rod, and Andrew Warner appointed to get the remainder done at a public charge; and he is to have iiis. a rod." But at an earlier date, April 7, 1634, we find this record: "Granted John Pratt two acres by the old burying-place, without the common pales." This evidently refers to some spot devoted to the burial of the dead, earlier than the one then in use. Its location is not certainly known, yet it is indicated with some degree of probability by two circumstances: (1.) The lot owned by John Pratt in 1635, was situated on the southerly side of Brattle Street, and on both sides of Hilliard Street. (2.) The "common pales" are supposed to denote the stockade which was erected in 1632, nearly, if not precisely in the line of the present Ash Street, and of which Dr. Holmes says traces existed when he wrote his History in 1800. It is not unreasonable then to suppose that "the old burying-place without the common pales" may have been at or near the westerly corner of Brattle and Ash streets, in the grounds now owned by Samuel Batchelder, Esq.

A hundred years after the second burial-place was ordered to be "paled in," the town enclosed it by a substantial stone wall, instead of the old wooden fence, or pales. The corporation of Harvard College contributed one sixth part of the expense, as appears by their Records under date of Oct. 20, 1735: "Whereas there is a good stone wall erected and erecting round the burying-place in Cambridge, which will come to about £150, and whereas there has been a considerable regard had to the College in building so good and handsome a wall in the front; and the College has used, and expects to make use of the burying-place as Providence gives occasion for it; therefore, Voted, that as soon as the said stone wall shall be completed, the Treasurer pay the sum of twenty-five pounds to Samuel Danforth, William Brattle and Andrew Bordman, Esq., a committee for the town to take care of the said fence." After another hundred years, in his Preface to "Epitaphs from the old Burying-ground in Cambridge," 1845, Mr. William Thaddeus Harris says, "It is rather surprising, that, in this age of improvement, Cambridge should fall behind her neighbors, and suffer her ancient graveyard to lie neglected. Interesting as it is from containing within its limits the 'tombs of the prophets,' the spot is often visited by the curious stranger; but it is to be feared that he as often leaves it with feelings of regret at its desolate appearance." It should be added, that this "desolate appearance" has been almost entirely removed within the last thirty years, and, though not profusely ornamented, an air of quiet neatness now marks the spot.

This ground, however, was of such limited dimensions, that in the course of nearly two hundred years the mouldering remains of some must have been disturbed, to give place to others. The increasing population of the two new villages in the easterly part of the town made the necessity urgent for additional room. Accordingly, at a Town-meeting, May 27, 1811, a committee was appointed " to contract for a piece of land in the most eligible situation, for a new burial-ground in Cambridgeport." The Committee reported, August 5, that they had selected a spot, and they were empowered to purchase it. On the first day of January, 1812, Jonathan L. and Benjamin Austin, for $791.67, conveyed to the town two acres one quarter and twenty rods of land, bounded north by Broadway and east by Norfolk Street, with a right of way to Harvard Street by a passage forty feet wide. For more than half a century this ground was used as a public burying-place, chiefly by the inhabitants of Cambridgeport and East Cambridge. Meantime the beautiful cemetery at Mount Auburn was consecrated by solemn religious services, Sept. 24, 1831, and the less extensive but scarcely less beautiful and attractive Cambridge Cemetery was in like manner consecrated, Nov. 1, 1854. In one or the other of these cemeteries many of the inhabitants purchased lots, and reverently removed to a more quiet and secluded resting place the remains of their deceased friends. The ground, being comparatively disused for new burials, and divested of many treasures formerly deposited therein, gradually assumed a desolate and forlorn appearance, until a general desire was expressed to discontinue entirely its former use and to convert it into a public park. Application was accordingly made to the General Court for permission to effect the desired change; and on the 29th of April, 1865, it was "Resolved, that the city council of the city of Cambridge is hereby authorized, at the expense of said city, to remove the remains of the dead from the burial ground between Broadway and Harvard Street in Ward Number Two, in said Cambridge, to the Cambridge Cemetery, or such other burial place in the vicinity of Cambridge as the relatives and friends of the deceased may designate and provide. . . . . Said ground shall be surrounded by suitable enclosures, and shall forever remain unused for a public street, unoccupied by any building, and open as a public park. In due time the work was accomplished; a suitable fence was erected, the ground properly graded, walks constructed, and trees planted, so that the park has already become ornamental to the city.[1]

Cambridge Common originally extended northwestwardly as far as to Linnæan Street, including all the land thus far between Garden Street and North Avenue. It was used for military parades and other public purposes, but especially for the safe keeping of the herd of cows, through the nights of the summer season, and was therefore called the Cow-common. In April, 1720, a survey was made for the purpose of division; but the work was not completed until 1724, when that portion lying northerly of Waterhouse Street was laid out into lots, which were assigned to individuals. The Common was thus reduced substantially to its present dimensions. It continued to be the property of the "Proprietors of Common Lands," until Nov. 20, 1769, when they "Voted, that all the common lands belonging to the Proprietors, fronting the college, commonly called the Town Commons, not heretofore granted or allotted to any particular person or persons, or for any special or particular use, be and the same is hereby granted to the town of Cambridge, to be used as a training-field, to lie undivided, and to remain for that use forever; provided nevertheless, that if the said town should dispose of, grant, or appropriate the same, or any part thereof, at any time hereafter, to or for any other use than that aforementioned, that then and in such case the whole of the premises hereby granted to said town shall revert to the Proprietors granting the same, and the present grant shall thereupon be deemed null and void, to all

---

[1] Across the westerly end of this burial place a large lot was reserved for the burial of paupers and strangers, generally called the "Strangers' Lot." In the Cambridge Chronicle, Aug. 20, 1846, the late Mr. Daniel Stone, who had long been Superintendent of the ground, published some reminiscences, among which was the following: "Remarkable Coincidence. In February, 1826, Lemuel Johns, an Indian aged fifty-nine years, from the tribe that once owned Grafton, ... was buried in the Strangers' Lot, as his turn came in rotation. From two to three feet from the top of the ground, the diggers came upon an ancient Indian fireplace, and had to remove nearly a ton of stones from the spot. That part of the town being, according to appearance, formerly a great place for Indian resort, we expected to come across other relics of the Red men; but before and since that time, there have been more than 2500 burials in all parts of the lot, and this is the only discovery we have made. This was the only Indian buried in the ground, and it would seem that he had been providentially brought into the improvements of perhaps some of his ancestors."

intents and purposes, as if the same had never been made." At
a town meeting, March 3, 1828, the Selectmen reported that
they had purchased for the town all the remaining rights of the
Proprietors in the common lands, and had taken "a good and
sufficient deed thereof, and caused the same to be recorded."

Before the Common was fully released to the town, a desire was
manifested to embellish it and convert it into a pleasant park.
At a town meeting, April 7, 1823, a petition was presented by
William Hilliard and others for liberty, at their own expense,
"to make certain improvements on the Common in said town, by
setting out trees, fencing in certain parts, etc., not incompatible
with the original grant to said town." The petition was referred
to a Committee, who having "matured nothing" were discharged
at the next meeting. The matter seems then to have rested
until June 5, 1830, when it was enacted by the General Court,
"that Israel Porter, Stephen Higginson, Asahel Stearns, Joseph
Holmes, and Francis Dana, with their associates, be and they
are hereby authorized and empowered, at their own expense, and
under the direction of two commissioners, to be appointed by the
governor, with the advice of the council, to enclose such part or
parts of the Common in Cambridge, in the County of Middlesex,
as the said commissioners shall determine, due regard being had
to the public convenience and necessity. And the said commissioners, after giving due notice to all persons interested, shall
have power to make such alterations with respect to the direction
of the roads by which the said common is traversed, as they shall
see fit, and shall designate the portion or portions of the said
common to be enclosed, by metes and bounds, and shall make
report of their doings, under their hands and seals, and file the
same in the Secretary's office as soon as may be convenient after
the said service shall have been performed. And they are further
authorized and empowered to level the surface of the ground, to
plant trees, and lay out and make walks within said enclosure,
in such manner as, with the approbation of the selectmen of the
said town, they may think proper, leaving suitable and convenient avenues for the accommodation of persons who may have occasion to enter or pass over any part of said enclosure on foot.
Be it further enacted, that the said enclosure shall be forever
kept and appropriated to public use only, as a public park,
promenade, and place for military parade; and no part thereof
shall, on any pretence, be appropriated to any purpose of private
use or emolument." [1] The work was accomplished in due time,

1 *Mass. Spec. Laws*, vii. 7.

and the expenses were defrayed by the petitioners and their associates. Meantime, a determined opposition to any enclosure of the Common was manifested by many persons in East Cambridge, and by certain market-men and others residing in Arlington and elsewhere, among whom Col. Jeduthun Wellington was especially prominent, notwithstanding the weight of more than fourscore years. On their petition a town meeting was held, Oct. 8, 1830. The people assembled in the old Court House, — the usual place of meeting; but so great was the concourse that they immediately adjourned to the meeting-house of the First Parish. After an angry and stormy debate, it was voted, by a majority of 169 against 119, to postpone indefinitely the further consideration of the first and second articles in the warrant, to wit: "Art. 1. To take into consideration the expediency of petitioning the Legislature, at their next session, so far to repeal the Act passed in June last, authorizing certain persons therein named to inclose Cambridge Common, as to secure to the public the right to travel over the said Common by the roads heretofore laid out by competent authority. Art. 2. To see if the town will take any measures in relation to the proposed inclosure of Cambridge Common." Another meeting was held, Nov. 1, 1830, when it was voted by a majority of 299 against 211, to postpone indefinitely the further consideration of the question, whether the town will petition the Legislature so far to repeal the act authorizing the enclosure of the Common, as to " secure to the public the right to travel over said Common by the road passing by Dr. Hill's and the late Deacon Moore's [1] to the road leading to Canal Bridge,[2] and also the right to travel over said Common by the road heretofore called the Cambridge and Concord Turnpike." Although the town thus declined to ask for even a partial repeal of the obnoxious act, it appears that individuals presented a petition to the General Court; for at a meeting of " the subscribers for enclosing and ornamenting Cambridge Common," Jan. 11, 1832, it was voted, " to request the Hon. Judge Fay and Prof. Ashmun to attend before the Committee of the Legislature to defend the interests of the subscribers." The appeal to the General Court being ineffectual, as a last resort a petition was presented to the County Commissioners; whereupon the town, voting by ballot, and by a majority of 343 against 111, appointed Judge Story, Judge Fay, and William J. Whipple, " to oppose before the County Commissioners, and otherwise, the petition of

[1] Mason Street.   [2] Cambridge Street.

Jeduthun Wellington and others, for a highway to be laid out over Cambridge Common." The history and result of this petition appear on the records of the Commissioners, January Term, 1835: "A petition of Jeduthun Wellington and others for a new highway across Cambridge Common was presented to the County Commissioners" at the May Term, 1832, and an order of notice was issued. The case was heard at the September Term, 1832, when after argument and due deliberation, the Commissioners "did adjudge and determine that they had no jurisdiction in the premises, and could not by law lay out and establish a public highway over and across said Common, as prayed for," etc. "Whereupon the said petitioners applied to the Supreme Judicial Court of this Commonwealth for a mandamus upon said Commissioners, requiring them to exercise jurisdiction in the premises; and the said Supreme Judicial Court having refused to grant such writ of mandamus, it is now ordered, that said petition, which has been continued from term to term, to await the determination of the said Supreme Judicial Court, to this time, be dismissed." Costs of Court were assessed upon the petitioners, who pursued this litigation no further. This result was highly gratifying and advantageous to the inhabitants of Old Cambridge, who thus secured in perpetuity, for themselves and their successors, a spacious and pleasant park, rich in historical recollections. It was here that Washington assumed the command of the American army; and here still flourishes the venerable elm, under which tradition says he stood, while his commission was read and proclaimed. Long may that monumental tree escape the ravages of the rampant vandalism which disgraces the present age.

But the benefit thus derived was not without its drawback. The old proverb, that "every rose has its thorn," was verified in this case. The fierce and angry contest, which gave to Old Cambridge its beautiful Common, indirectly transferred to Cambridgeport the public meetings of the town and the offices for the transaction of municipal affairs. The old Court House [1] would not contain the multitude assembled on the 8th of October, 1830, and the meeting, according to a former custom, adjourned to the

---

[1] It was agreed, Dec. 24, 1632, "that every person undersubscribed shall meet every first Monday in every month within the meeting-house." Probably the town meetings were uniformly held in the meeting-house, or church edifice, until about 1708, when a house was erected at the joint expense of the town and county, to be used for both court house and town-house. A similar concert of action was had in 1756, when the town agreed to share the expense of erecting a new court house, which was also used as a town-house until 1831.

meeting-house of the First Parish. It is understood that some members of that Parish expressed a natural unwillingness to have their house of worship used for the transaction of secular business, and especially for the indulgence and expression of angry passions. After the close of this unpleasant meeting, some of the citizens discussed the propriety of erecting a house sufficiently large to accommodate the voters, so that there might be no further occasion to use the church; and it very naturally occurred to them that if such a house should be erected, it would be well to place it where it would best accommodate the whole town.[1] The result was the insertion of an article in the Warrant for the next town-meeting, Nov. 1, 1830, " to see if the town will erect a Town-house on the Almshouse lot, or some other suitable spot, as prayed for by John Cook and others." This article was referred to a committee consisting of three prominent citizens in each section of the town, to wit: Samuel P. P. Fay, Royal Makepeace, John Cook, Stephen Higginson, Asahel Stearns, Levi Farwell, William Parmenter, Samuel S. Green, and Ephraim Buttrick. This committee reported, March 7, 1831, " that, having considered the subject, it is, in their opinion, expedient that a town-house should be erected on the easterly part of the almshouse lot in the parish of Cambridgeport, as more central to the population of the town than the present house, and that a house sufficient to accommodate the town may be built for a sum not exceeding $2,000 : that when such house shall be finished, all town meetings should be held therein from and after that time." The report was accepted; and Levi Farwell, Luther S. Cushing, and William Parmenter were appointed as a committee " to report a suitable location, prepare plans, and report estimates for a town-house." At the next town meeting, April 4, 1831, the committee recommended that the town-house be erected at the northeasterly corner of the Almshouse lot,[2] and presented a plan of an edifice, drawn by Asher Benjamin, and estimated to cost $2,505. The town accepted the report, elected a building committee, consisting of John Chamberlin, Luther S. Cushing, and William Parmenter, and authorized the Treasurer to pay the bills therefor, not exceeding the sum of $3,000. Subsequently an additional appropriation of $1,300 was made. The total expense, including $296.09 for furniture and $145.13 for fencing the lot, was $4,351.19. In asking for estimates, the

---

[1] Some of these facts are stated on the authority of the late Samuel S. Green, Esq., as within his personal knowledge.

[2] At the corner of Harvard and Norfolk streets, where the Catholic Church now stands.

building committee inserted this specification: " The house is to
be of wood, forty-six feet in front or breadth, and seventy-six
feet long, with posts twenty feet and four inches high, and the
roof one fourth of its base in height; on each end of the building,
in addition to the aforesaid length, will be a portico, of six feet in
width, consisting of six fluted Doric columns, with an entablature
and pediment." Internally, there was one principal hall, fifty-
nine feet long, of the whole width and height of the building.
At the rear, or west end, were two rooms, half the full height,
each eighteen feet long and fifteen feet wide, with an entry between them: over which was another room extending across the
whole, to which access was had by two flights of stairs from the
principal hall.   The town held its first meeting in the new house
March 5, 1832, and all subsequent town-meetings were held in
the same place.   After Cambridge became a city in 1846, the
Mayor and Aldermen assembled in the southerly small room,[1]
and the Common Council in the larger room above, until the
evening of Dec. 29, 1853, when, in the midst of a furious snow-
storm, the whole building was utterly consumed by fire.   Fortu-
nately, all the Records and other books and public papers were
preserved, the larger and more valuable portion being removed
while the flames were raging, and the remainder being afterwards
found in the safe uninjured, except that they were discolored by
smoke.   After the destruction of this edifice, rooms for the accommodation of the City Government were obtained in the Cambridge Athenæum, at the easterly corner of Main and Pleasant
streets.   This edifice was subsequently purchased and converted
into the present City Hall.

For the space of forty years after the erection of West Boston
Bridge, Cambridgeport was an isolated village, separated from
Old Cambridge by a belt of land half a mile in width, almost
wholly unoccupied by buildings.   East Cambridge was even more
completely separated from the other two villages by the Great
Marsh.   In 1835, the heirs of Chief Justice Dana sold the tract
of land now called "Dana Hill," having laid it out into streets
and lots; and they sold other portions of the same estate, in
1840, extending, on the northerly side of Harvard Street, as far
westerly as Remington Street.   Buildings were soon erected on
this territory, so that, within a few years, Old Cambridge and
Cambridgeport became one continuous village, and the original

---

[1] The northerly room was the office of the City Treasurer.

parish line would not be observed by a stranger. East Cambridge also, though more slowly, approached Cambridgeport, especially on Cambridge Street; and an extensive system of improvement has been recently commenced, which promises to convert the northerly portion of the Great Marsh into dry land, and at no distant day to unite the inhabited portions of the two villages "along the whole line." Meanwhile, it was natural, in the early days when the two new villages were struggling into existence, that a spirit of rivalry, sometimes attended by jealousy, should become manifest between each other and between both and the ancient town. Their interests were sometimes adverse. Sharp contests between Cambridgeport and East Cambridge, or rather between the large landholders in the two places, in regard to streets and bridges, have been mentioned elsewhere. The removal of the courts and the public offices to East Cambridge, by the authority of the County Court, was a sore grievance to the people of Old Cambridge, and by no means agreeable to the inhabitants of Cambridgeport, whose access to the Court was easier before than after the removal. It was another grievance to Old Cambridge, that the municipal government should be removed from its time-honored seat to Cambridgeport; but this was approved by East Cambridge, because the new place was easier of access. On the other side, the new villages had long standing grievances, growing out of a real or supposed unwillingness of Old Cambridge to give them their full share of schools, streets, and other public conveniences. Especially in regard to streets, they frequently complained that they were required to pay their proportionate share of the expense of keeping all the old streets in repair, and at the same time to pay the whole expense of making and repairing the streets necessary for their own convenience, including those which were constantly used by Old Cambridge in passing to Boston. At the expiration of half a century after the erection of the bridge, many of those sources of mutual jealousy had disappeared, and time had at least partially healed the wounds occasioned by events which were beyond remedy. The new villages had become sufficiently strong to protect their own interests and to secure for themselves a fair and equitable proportion of public conveniences. At the same time, no one section was able to control or oppress the two others; and it does not appear that any desire to do so was cherished. Many of those who had been active in the early struggles had passed off the stage; a great majority of the inhabitants had become such since those struggles ended; and although each may have had a natural desire to make his own particular dwelling-place pleasant and convenient, and may have cherished a generous spirit of rivalry, yet all had a common pride in the reputation of the whole town, and desired the prosperity of all its institutions.

In the midst of this general harmony and peace, a desire for a division of the town was unexpectedly manifested by a portion of the residents in Old Cambridge, who presented to the General Court a petition, dated Dec. 15, 1842, as follows: —

" To the Honorable Senate and House of Representatives of the Commonwealth of Massachusetts.

" The undersigned inhabitants of the westerly part of Cambridge, being that part of the town usually called Old Cambridge, respectfully represent, —

" That, in consequence of the rapid increase of population in those parts of the town being nearest to Boston, and called Cambridgeport and East Cambridge, the town in fact consists of three distinct and separate communities, which are generally known to the public by those names, and each of which has a Post Office recognized in the United States Laws by the said names of Cambridge, Cambridgeport, and East Cambridge; That the time cannot be far distant, when a division of the town, for the convenience of elections and other municipal purposes, will be deemed as necessary as it ever has been at any former period of its history, when the towns of Newton, Lexington, Brighton and West Cambridge were successively separated from the parent town of Cambridge. Your petitioners believe that the present is a favorable time for an amicable division of the town, and they therefore respectfully pray that the town of Cambridge may be divided, and that that part thereof lying westerly of Lee Street and a line drawn in the direction of said street northerly to the boundary line of Somerville, and southerly to Watertown Turnpike, and by said Turnpike to Charles River, may be incorporated as a distinct town, by the name of Cambridge."

Legislative action was postponed until the next General Court, when a supplementary petition was presented, identical with the former, with slight verbal changes, except that the name " Old Cambridge " was proposed instead of " Cambridge." The customary order of notice on both petitions was issued, requiring the town to show cause why it should not be divided, and the inhabitants assembled Jan. 22, 1844: at which meeting it is recorded, that " The subject of the second article in the warrant being under consideration, the following Preamble and Resolutions were adopted, — 312 voting in the affirmative, and 73 in the negative: Whereas, it is understood that there are now pending before the honorable Legislature two petitions, ... praying for a division of this town; and whereas an order of notice . . . . has been issued and duly served on this town; . . . . and whereas the inhabitants of the town, in pursuance of a warrant issued by the selectmen, are now in town meeting assembled, to take into consideration the subject of the division of the town; and whereas, after full inquiry made and full discussion had, no person on behalf of the petitioners being able to show any good and sufficient reason for such division: therefore

"Resolved, that the division of this town, as prayed for in either of said petitions, or in any other manner, would be not only inexpedient, but greatly and permanently prejudicial to the true interests and the legitimate weight and influence of the town."

A committee was thereupon appointed, representing the several principal villages, "to appear before the Legislature and oppose any such division of the town." The case was earnestly contested, but the opposition was successful. The General Court, in the absence of any good reason for division, granted leave to withdraw the petition; and the town had rest for two years.

At the March meeting[1] succeeding this attempt to divide the town, for the purpose of obviating one of the difficulties in the administration of municipal affairs, a committee was "appointed to consider the expediency of combining the duties of sundry Boards of town-officers, imposing said duties upon a single Board, and paying to the persons performing said duties a reasonable compensation for their services." This committee submitted a report, May 12, 1845, recommending "that the Boards of Assessors, Overseers of the Poor, and Surveyors of Highways be abolished, and the duties heretofore performed by those Boards be in future discharged by the Board of Selectmen; that the duties of Auditor of Accounts be transferred to the Town Clerk, who shall *ex-officio* be clerk of the Board of Selectmen; that the chairman of the Board of Selectmen be *ex-officio* a member of the School Committee; that the Selectmen be authorized and required annually to appoint some member of their Board to be Chief Engineer; and that the Selectmen and Town Clerk be reasonably paid for their services." The report was recommitted,

[1] March 11, 1844.

with authority to revise and print. It came up for final action, Jan. 5, 1846, and its further consideration was indefinitely postponed.

After the defeat of this measure, several citizens, before leaving the Town-house, being confident that some change in the method of conducting the public business was highly desirable, if not indeed imperatively necessary, signed a petition requesting the Selectmen to appoint a legal meeting, to see if the town would ask for a City Charter. Accordingly the inhabitants of the town met, Jan. 14, 1846, and " voted, that the Selectmen be instructed to petition the Legislature for the grant of a City Charter. Voted, that the Selectmen, together with Simon Greenleaf, Omen S. Keith, Abraham Edwards, Sidney Willard, Thomas Whittemore, Isaac Livermore, William Parmenter, Ephraim Buttrick, Thomas F. Norris, and the Town Clerk, be a Committee to draft a Bill in conformity to the preceding vote, and to use all proper means to procure its passage."

A renewed effort was made for a division of the town, while action on the petition for a City Charter was pending; but now, as before, a large majority of the whole town opposed the division. At a town meeting, Feb. 18, 1846, by the votes of 246 in the affirmative against 50 in the negative, it was " Resolved, that, in the judgement of this meeting, the true interest and glory of the town of Cambridge require that it remain undivided. Resolved, that we will oppose the division of the town, as prayed for, ... by all fair means. Resolved, that the Selectmen be requested to appear before the Committee of the Legislature to whom said petition has been committed, and to oppose the prayer of said petition, and to employ counsel, if they shall deem it expedient." After a full hearing, the petitioners, as in the former case, had leave to withdraw their petition, and the town again escaped dismemberment.

Before narrating the result of the petition for a City Charter, one more effort for a division may be mentioned. In January, 1855, a petition was presented to the General Court, short, but expressive and very remarkable: " To the Honorable the Senate and House of Representatives in General Court assembled : Your petitioners pray that a portion of the westerly part of the City of Cambridge comprising Ward One [1] be set off and incorporated into a town by the name of Cambridge, and that the

---

[1] Ward One then embraced all the territory lying westerly of the line of Dana Street.

remaining portion of the territory of said City be called Cambridgeport, or such other name as may seem fit." This was followed by a petition from certain inhabitants of the Third Ward, asking to be incorporated as a distinct town, but more modestly requesting that the new town might be called East Cambridge. On the 21st of February, 1855, orders of notice on these petitions having been read, it was ordered, by concurrent vote of the City Council, "That the Mayor be authorized to adopt such measures in opposition to the prayer of said petitions as he shall judge expedient ; and that he be also authorized to employ counsel, if he shall deem it expedient." It is proper to mention the fact, that when this vote to resist a division of the City was passed, the First and Third Wards, in which the petitions originated, had a clear majority of members both in the Board of Aldermen and in the Common Council. The petition from East Cambridge was not urgently pressed ; but upon that from Old Cambridge an earnest struggle ensued.[1] The opposition was again successful, and Cambridge remained undivided. Whatever excitement attended this contest speedily abated, and those who were most prominently active on either side cherished a spirit of mutual friendship and respect as aforetime. And now, after an interval of more than twenty years, it is not known that a desire for division is entertained in any section of the city.

The petition for a City Charter was opposed by the citizens who desired a division of the town ; but its advocates presented such satisfactory arguments in its favor that it was granted, and "An Act to establish the City of Cambridge" was approved March 17, 1846, containing a provision that it "shall be void, unless the inhabitants of the town of Cambridge, at a legal town meeting, called for that purpose, shall, by a majority of the voters present and voting thereon by ballot, determine to adopt the same, within twenty days after its passage." Such a meeting was held March 30, 1846, when, according to the Record, "the polls having been opened at twenty minutes past ten o'clock, A. M., for the reception of ballots on the question whether the town will adopt the Act of the Legislature, passed on the 17th of March instant, entitled ' An Act to establish the City of

---

[1] In his argument against division, the principal speaker made effective use of the extraordinary fact, that the petitioners, like their predecessors in 1844, did not ask to be set off *from* Cambridge, but to be incorporated as Cambridge, — an un-precedented request; and that their suggestion was altogether gratuitous, that "the remaining portion of the territory of said city be called Cambridgeport, or such other name as may seem fit."

Cambridge,' and closed, agreeably to vote, at six o'clock, P. M., the result was ascertained to be as follows; whole number of ballots, 869; in the affirmative, 645; in the negative, 224; the majority in favor of adopting said Act being 421. Whereupon said result was announced by the Moderator, and proclamation made, that the Town of Cambridge, having accepted its Charter by the requisite majority of votes, as therein prescribed, had become a City."

CHAPTER XV.

As stated more at large in chapter ii., Cambridge was originally designed to be a fortified town, the seat of government, and the residence of the rulers. It was agreed, Dec. 28, 1630, that all the Assistants, except two, should build there "the next spring, and to winter there the next year." Dudley and his son-in-law, Bradstreet, were the only Assistants who fully performed what was promised. Apparently there were very few inhabitants in the town for a year and a half, until Aug. 14, 1632, when "the Braintree Company," otherwise called "Mr. Hooker's Company," were directed by the Court to remove thither. Under such circumstances, it is not surprising, that, contrary to the usual custom, a church was not immediately organized, and a house erected and dedicated to the service of God. There is no evidence within my knowledge that meetings were held in Cambridge for religious worship, before the arrival of "Mr. Hooker's company;" and for a whole year afterwards, until Mr. Hooker himself arrived, this flock probably had no pastor nor stated teacher. Meantime, Prince says,[1] on authority of a manuscript letter, that in "this year (1632) is built the first house for public worship at Newtown (after called Cambridge) with a bell upon it." No notice of the erection of such a house is found on the records of the town; yet the fact that it had been erected seems to be recognized in an agreement made Dec. 24, 1632, "that every person undersubscribed shall meet every first Monday in every month, within the meeting-house [2] in the afternoon, within half an hour after the ringing of the bell." The connection between Mr. Hooker and the "Braintree Company" is related by Mather, and more concisely by Dr. Holmes: "The recent settlers of Newtown had, while in England, attended the ministry of the Reverend Thomas Hooker, who, to escape fines

---

[1] *Annals*, ii. 73.
[2] The house first erected for public worship, was on the southwesterly corner of Dunster and Mount Auburn streets.

and imprisonment, for his nonconformity, had now fled into Holland. To enjoy the privilege of such a pastor, they were willing to migrate to any part of the world. No sooner, therefore, was he driven from them, than they turned their eyes towards New England. They hoped that, if comfortable settlements could be made in this part of America, they might obtain him for their pastor. Immediately after their settlement at Newtown, they expressed their earnest desires to Mr. Hooker, that he would come over into New England, and take the pastoral charge of them. At their desire, he left Holland; and, having obtained Mr. Samuel Stone, a lecturer at Torcester, in Northamptonshire, for an assistant in the ministry, took his passage for America, and arrived at Boston September 4, 1633. . . . . Mr. Hooker, on his arrival at Boston, proceeded to Newtown, where he was received with open arms by an affectionate and pious people. He was now chosen pastor, and Mr. Stone teacher, of the people at Newtown ; and on the 11th of October, 1633, after solemn fasting and prayer, they were ordained to their respective offices." [1] Under this date, Winthrop says, — " A fast at Newtown, where Mr. Hooker was chosen pastor, and Mr. Stone teacher, in such manner as before at Boston." [2] As he says nothing concerning the organization of the Church at that time, it would seem probable that it had been constituted previously, but at what precise date does not appear. From the same authority we learn the name of the Ruling Elder of this church, in September, 1634 : " At this court, Mr. Goodwin, a very reverend and godly man, being the elder of the congregation of Newtown, having in heat of argument, used some unreverend speech to one of the assistants, and being reproved for the same in the open court, did gravely and humbly acknowledge his fault, &c." [3] In 1636, the Church with its officers removed to Hartford, Connecticut, as related in chapter iv., and thenceforth ceased all visible connection with Cambridge. [4]

Meantime a new company arrived from England, under the leadership of Rev. Thomas Shepard, who purchased the houses and lands of their predecessors, and organized a new church even

1 *Coll. Mass. Hist. Soc.*, vii. 12.
2 Savage's *Winthrop*, i. 115.
3 *Ibid.*, i. 142. Elder William Goodwin, eminent in the State as well as in the Church, died at Farmington, Conn., March 11, 1672-3.
4 Mr. Hooker, that " bright and shining light," died July 7, 1647. Though renowned " in both Englands " for his gifts and graces, his Christian humility was conspicuous at the hour of death. As related by Mather, " when one that stood weeping by the bed side said unto him, 'Sir, you are going to receive the reward of all your labors,' he replied, 'Brother, I am going to receive mercy.'" The pious, learned, and witty Mr. Stone died July 20, 1663.

before the actual removal of the former, embracing probably a very few of its members who remained here. Winthrop, who undoubtedly was present, describes with much particularity the organization of this Church, under date of Feb. 1, 1635–6 : —

" Mr. Shepherd, a godly minister, came lately out of England, and divers other good Christians, intending to raise a church body, came and acquainted the magistrates therewith, who gave their approbation. They also sent to all the neighboring churches, for their elders to give their assistance, at a certain day, at New-town, when they should constitute their body. Accordingly, at this day, there met a great assembly, where the proceeding was as followeth : — Mr. Shepherd and two others (who were after to be chosen to office) sate together in the elder's seat. Then the elder of them began with prayer. After this, Mr. Shepherd prayed with deep confession of sin, etc., and exercised out of Eph. v. — that he might make it to himself a holy, etc. ; and also opened the cause of their meeting, etc. Then the elder desired to know of the churches assembled, what number were needful to make a church, and how they ought to proceed in this action. Whereupon some of the ancient ministers, conferring shortly together, gave answer, that the Scripture did not set down any certain rule for the number. Three (they thought) were too few, because by Matt. xviii., an appeal was allowed from three ; but that seven might be a fit number. And, for their proceeding, they advised, that such as were to join should make confession of their faith, and declare what work of grace the Lord had wrought in them ; which accordingly they did, Mr. Shepherd first, then four others, then the elder, and one who was to be deacon, (who had also prayed,) and another member. Then the covenant was read, and they all gave a solemn assent to it. Then the elder desired of the churches, that, if they did approve them to be a church, they would give them the right hand of fellowship. Whereupon Mr. Cotton, (upon short speech with some others near him,) in the name of their churches, gave his hand to the elder, with a short speech of their assent, and desired the peace of the Lord Jesus to be with them. Then Mr. Shepherd made an exhortation to the rest of his body, about the nature of their covenant, and to stand firm to it, and commended them to the Lord in a most heavenly prayer. Then the elder told the assembly, that they were intended to choose Mr. Shepherd for their pastor, (by the name of the brother who had exercised,) and desired the churches, that, if they had any thing to except against him, they would impart it to them before the day of ordination. Then he gave the churches thanks for their assistance, and so left them to the Lord." [1]

The relations previously existing between Mr. Shepard and many of the early members of this Church are mentioned by himself in his autobiography. Born Nov. 5, 1605, at Towcester, Northamptonshire, and educated at Emanuel College in Cambridge, A. B. 1623, A. M. 1627, he took orders in the English Church; but as he could not conscientiously conform to all its ceremonies, he was constantly harassed by its rulers, and prevented from the exercise of his ministry in peace. After preaching at Earles Colne somewhat more than three years (where he secured the lasting friendship of Roger Harlakenden), and about a year at Buttercrambe, Yorkshire (where he married his first wife), and another year in sundry places in Northumberland, he sought refuge from constant persecution, by a removal to New England. He failed in his first attempt, however, being driven back by stress of weather; but his second attempt was successful, and he arrived at Boston Oct. 3, 1635, with his "wife, child, brother Samuel, Mr. Harlakenden, Mr. Cooke, &c." [2] Two days afterwards, he came to Cambridge and took lodgings at the house of Mr. Stone. "The reasons," says he in his Autobiography, "which swayed me to come to New England, were many. 1. I saw no call to any other place in Old England nor way of subsistence in peace and comfort to me and my family. 2. Diverse people in Old England of my dear friends desired me to go to New England, there to live together, and some went before and

---

[1] Savage's *Winthrop*, i. 180. The organization of this Church is commemorated in *A Discourse on the Cambridge Church Gathering* in 1636, *delivered* in *the First Church on Sunday, February 22, 1846, by William Newell, Pastor of the First Church in Cambridge*. See also *Lectures on the History of the First Church in Cambridge, by Alexander McKenzie, Pastor of the First Church in Cambridge and Shepard Congregational Society*, in which not only is the gathering of the church described, but its subsequent history traced to 1872. The *Discourse* relates the facts, embellished with the charms of a highly poetic imagination; the *Lectures* exhibit the fruits of careful and patient investigation, and a loyal adherence to the truth of history;

together, they may supply what this present work lacks in the graces of description and fullness of detail. A general reference is now made, once for all, to those *Lectures* for a particular account of the doctrines taught and the books written by Mr. Shepard and by his successors in the ministry.

[2] Besides these, he mentions among the brethren who shared his unsuccessful attempt to cross the ocean, and who afterwards became members of his church, "brothers Champney, Frost," subsequently Ruling Elders, "Goffe, and diverse others, most dear saints." He also acknowledges special acts of kindness rendered to him in England by Mr. Russell, Mr. Collins, and Mrs. Sherborne,— names afterwards familiar in Cambridge.

writ to me of providing a place for a company of us, one of which was John Bridge,[1] and I saw diverse families of my Christian friends, who were resolved thither to go with me. 3. I saw the Lord departed from England when Mr. Hooker and Mr. Cotton were gone, and I saw the hearts of most of the godly set and bent that way, and I did think I should feel many miseries if I stayed behind. 4. My judgment was then convinced not only of the evil of ceremonies, but of mixed communion, and joining with such in sacraments, though I ever judged it lawful to join with them in preaching. 5. I saw it my duty to desire the fruition of all God's ordinances, which I could not enjoy in Old England. 6. My dear wife did much long to see me settled there in peace, and so put me on to it.[2] 7. Although it was true I should stay and suffer for Christ, yet I saw no rule for it now the Lord had opened a door for escape ; otherwise I did incline much to stay and suffer, especially after our sea storms. 8. Though my ends were mixed, and I looked much to my own quiet, yet the Lord let me see the glory of those liberties in New England, and made me purpose, if ever I come over, to live among God's people as one come out from the dead, to his praise."

Actuated by such motives, Mr. Shepard entered upon the work of the ministry here. His ordination doubtless soon followed the organization of the church, but the precise date is not re-

[1] John Bridge became a deacon of the church here.

[2] Mrs. Shepard lived only a fortnight after this " settlement in peace " seemed to be secured by the organization of the church. She was doubtless the first female admitted as a member of the newly constituted body. Her husband left on record an affecting account of her admission and her "unspeakable joy," which was quoted and preserved by Rev. Cotton Mather, in a Sermon entitled *The Temple Opening* (1709), pp. 30, 31: "Another passage must be from our celebrated Shepard, who in a manuscript which I have in my hands relates the gathering of the church at Cambridge quickly after his coming into New England, and the condition of his own virtuous consort, at that time very near her death of consumption. The relation has these words in it: 'It pleased the Lord to join us into church-fellowship. After the day was ended, we came to her cham-

ber, she being unable to come unto us. And because we feared her end was not far off we did solemnly ask her if she was desirous to be a member with us; which she expressing, and so entering into covenant with us, we thereupon all took her by the hand and received her as become one with us, having had full trial and experience of her faith and life before. At this time and by this means the Lord did not only show us the worth of this ordinance, but gave us a seal of his accepting of us and of his presence with us that day ; for the Lord hereby filled her heart with such unspeakable joy and assurance of God's love, that she said to us she had now enough; and we were afraid her feeble body would have at that time fallen under the weight of her joy. . . . . And thus, a fortnight almost before her death unto her departure, in the midst of most bitter afflictions and anguishes, her peace continued.'"

corded. From the concurrent testimony of his contemporaries, during his short ministry his praise was in all the churches. No record of admissions to the church is known to have been made by Mr. Shepard, except a small manuscript volume in the library of the New England Historic Genealogical Society, entitled, " The Confessions of Diverse propounded to be received and were entertained as Members."[1] It contains fifty confessions, all in the handwriting of Mr. Shepard, varying in length from a quarter of one page,[2] to eight pages.[3] Only two bear any date, namely, the forty-first,[4] Jan. 8, 1640, and the forty-seventh,[5] Jan. 7, 1644. The first in the series, though one of the shortest, may serve as a specimen of their character : —

" Edward Hall's Confession. The first means of his good was Mr. Glover's ministry, whereby he saw his misery from Jer. 7, the temple of the Lord, and that he was without Christ. But he went from thence to another place, under the sense of an undone condition ; but in that place he was deprived of the ordinances of God, and hence the Scripture came oft to mind, what if a man win the world, and lose his soul ? Hence he desired to come to that place again ; but the minister was gone. But Mr. Jenner came, and by him he saw more evil in himself ; but Mr. S.[6] came, and then the Lord did more clearly manifest himself to him from John 3, concerning the new birth. And here he saw more of his misery, and that he had followed examples and duties, and made them his Christ, and lived without Christ. Hereby the Lord let him see he was Christless, and built upon false foundations, and by this text he saw himself no new creature, but only a mended man. Now when the Lord did humble him under this, he saw the want of Christ, and that without him he must perish. And afterwards John 5. 40 was opened, you will not come to me to have life ; and here he saw how freely Christ was offered, and hereby the Lord did stay and comfort his spirit, and so was stirred up with more vehemency to seek Christ. And· then that promise was opened, the Son of man came to seek that which was lost ; and he did not know but the Lord might seek him. And out of that text, 1 Pet. 2. 8, that unto you that believe he is precious ; and here he saw his unbelief in cleaving to Christ by fits and starts. And since the Lord

---

[1] See N. E. Hist. Gen. Register, xxiii. 289.
[2] "Mrs. Greene."
[3] "Mr. Dunster."
[4] "Goodman Sherington."
[5] "Goodman With."
[6] Rev. Thomas Shepard, probably.

brought him to this place, he found his worldliness; and this bred many fears whether ever any work of Christ in him was in truth, and that he was one that might fall short of Christ, and that he was humbled ; but his heart was not deep enough, and hence he was put to more search whether ever he was humbled. Yet the Lord made it more clear from Ephraim's condition, Jer. 31. 18, that the Lord had made him loathe himself, and this made him loathe him[self] ; and here he hath found more enmity of his heart against the Lord than ever before. But hearing the Lord was willing to take away his enmity, he, by Rev. 22. 14, was brought nearer to the Lord."

Besides these fifty persons, the names of others may be gathered from the lists of Freemen in the Colony, during that period; for as none were then admitted to political freedom except members of churches, it may safely be supposed that all the Cambridge men thus made free were members of the Church. Moreover, Mr. Shepard's successor, the "matchless Mitchell," prepared in 1658 a manuscript account of " The Church of Christ at Cambridge in N. E., or, the names of all the members thereof that are in full communion," etc., which, after having long been lost, was discovered in 1815, by Rev. Dr. Holmes, among the Prince manuscripts, and was published by Rev. Dr. Newell, in the Appendix to his " Discourse on the Cambridge Church-gathering." It must be remembered, however, that this list contains the names of those who were admitted to membership between 1649, when Mr. Shepard died, and 1658, when the record was made, as well as of those who were previously members; also, that the names of some deceased members may have been omitted.

There are still preserved two folio volumes, which may be styled Church Books, chiefly devoted to financial affairs, containing a particular account of receipts and disbursements by the Deacons, together with some historical notices. From these books something may be gleaned concerning the condition and work of the Church.

On the inside of the cover of one volume is the following memorandum : —

" Goodman Hayes departinge this natural life 1639 hee disposed of his children as followeth commending them to the Lord and the care of these friends following : unto Mr. Goodyn of Harford his daughter Anna ; unto Goodman Lewis his sonn

Jeames; unto Goodman Taylcoat his daughter Elizabeth; unto
Goodman Clark his daughter Sarah; his eldest son to Mr. Hook-
ers and Mr. Goodyns dispose; and the youngest child he committed to the mother. The congregation of Harford did give
toward satisfying of some here that he did owe money unto 25ᴸ.
which hath been thus paid out to that end.

	£	s.	d.
" Imprimis pd to Mr. Hill for Goodman Stanley 30ˢ.	1.	10.	0
Item alsoe pd to Mr. Cullott in full of his det 17ᴸ. I say per me John Cullock.	17.	00.	0
Item alsoe pd Mr. Robert Payne of Ipswich for Good- man [ ]	3.	10.	0
Item more a month's diet of the 4 children is owing me for "			

On a fly-leaf of the same volume, we find the disposition of a
benefaction: —

" Item, Mr. Harlakingdon gave the Church a legacye of 20ᴸ.[1],
wᶜʰ wee received a young cow for it of Mr. Pellam[2] in the beginning of the year 1640. Wee gave the summers milk of the
cow to brother Towne and brother John French; the first calfe
dyed. The winteringe cost to John Stone 25ˢ. wᶜʰ some the
second calfe was sold for. The second summers milke wee gave
to sister Manninge and brother John French. The 3d summers
milke was yelded Elder Frost and alsoe all the winteringe of it.
The beginning of the year 1643 wee yeelded it Elder Frost for
his owne; at that time it was worth but 5ᴸ."[3]

The first entry in the Record proper is somewhat mutilated.
What is supposed to be lost is here supplied, but enclosed in
brackets.

" [An account] of the moneys by contri[bution] upon the
first day of [the week for] the supply of the wants of the Church
of Christ and the needy people of Cambridge since the second
day of the tenth month in the year of Christ 1638.

---

[1] In the will of Roger Harlakenden, 1638, is this bequest: "I give to Mr. Shepard our pastor forty pounds, and to our Elders that wᶜʰ is in their hands, and to the pore brethren of our congregation twentye pounds to be ordered by Mr. Shepard."

[2] Herbert Pelham, Esq., married the widow of Harlakenden.

[3] Winthrop says that in 1640 "cattle and all commodities grew very cheap." (ii. 7.) And Hutchinson says, "the price of a milch cow had kept from 25 to 30l., but fell this year to 5 or 6l." — Hist. Mass., i. 93.

"Imprimis was contributed the first day of the week being the second day of the 10th month, 1638 (part of it was in papers, namely 8ᵈ.) } £. s. d. 0. 19. 5

"Item was contributed the second sabbath in the 10th month 25ˢ. 4ᵈ. (whereof was in papers 3ˢ. 4ᵈ.) } 1. 5. 4"

Then follow on the first page the weekly contributions until the last Sabbath in the sixth month, or August, amounting, in the nine months, to nearly fifty pounds, including two which are specially recorded thus: —

"Item Mrs Sara Sims the 7th of Feb. brought for herselfe   0. 10. 0

Item [1ᵐᵒ. 1639] was on a day of thanksgiving (at Mr. Eatons) given forty-nine shillings and six pence. } 2. 9. 6"

On the other side of the account we find ₍ —

" What the layinges (out ha[ve been   ] as on the other side appears [   ] were contrybuted on severall occasions for the supply of manyfold nessessyties.

£. s. d.

" Imprimis for eleven quartes of red wine for the use of the Lords tabell upon the 9th day of the tenth month[1] at 15ᵈ. a quart. } 0. 13. 9

And for bread for the Lords tabell at that time 8ᵈ. For a messenger to goe for the wine 12ᵈ. } 0. 1. 8

Lent my brother Towne   5. 0. 0

Payᵈ for this booke (to keepe accounts in)   0. 4. 6

Given to Elder Frost the 18 of January [2] 20ˢ.   1. 0. 0

Pᵈ for a lether pillow to put in the cushin to the desk 5ˢ; it wayᵉd 5ᵇ. } 0. 5. 0

Payd for sendinge a messenger (goodman Crackbone) to Charlestowne and Roxbery to atayne helpe for preachinge in our pastors weaknes 2ˢ. } 0. 2. 0

Payd to goodman Line for 5 quarts and ½ pint of wine   0. 6. 6

Payd my brother Towne for his half yeﬀrs alowance   1. 5. 0

and payd him for 5 times goinge with messages to the church 0. 3. 4

Given to Elder Frost the 22 of the 3ᵈ month 20ˢ.   1. 0. 0

Given my brother John French 8ˢ.   3. 0. 0

Given to our brother Hall the 11th of the 4th month toward the rearing of his house that was blown down. } 1. 0. 0

For the refreshing my brother Sill in time of fayntnes sent him 4 pints of sack, 2ˢ. 4ᵈ. } 0. 2. 4

Pd to my brother Cane for goinge to Salem with a message to Mr. Philips when he was about to come to us. } 5. 0. 0 / 0. 5. 0

[1] 1638.   [2] 1638-9.

Given to Elder·Frost toward his buildinge 40*.	2. 0. 0
Lent our brother Bealle the 9th of the 5th month, 5*.	5. 0. 0
Payd the hyman [1] that brought Mr. Philips and for his goods bringing from Salem when he removed to us.	0. 0. 0 "

Thus far the account is copied entire. The last charge is erased in the account, and underneath is written, " we [
] this and took it out of that received for officers maintenance." Shortly afterwards the following disbursements are recorded : —

" Payd my brother Cane for helpinge Mr. Philips at his first coming to set up his goods, 5*.	0. 5. 0.
Payd my brother Cane for carying a leter to Salem (concerninge clearing about Mr. Philips) to Mr. Hawthorne.	0. 5. 0
Payd my brother Cane for his helpe in Mr. Philips removinge to Mr. Pellams house for 1 day and ½.	0. 3. 0
Pd for a help of another to mend Mr. Pelams house for Mr. Philips.	0. 1. 6 "

These several disbursements on account of Rev. John Phillips furnish the only evidence to be found in the Church Record concerning the attempt which was evidently made to secure him as a teacher of the church of which Mr. Shepard was pastor. Savage describes [2] him as of " Dedham, 1638, a famous minister of Wrentham (which is about 30 miles N. E. from Ipswich, England), where he obtained his living as rector 1609, and married 6 Jan. 1612 Elizabeth a sister of famous Dr. Ames, which gave him favor in the eyes of puritans, was desired to accept office here in several places, especially Cambridge, perhaps in connection with the newly begun College, but preferred to go home in the autumn of 1641." From Lamson's " History of the First Church and Parish in Dedham," pp. 77–82, it would seem that Mr. Phillips did not "take office" in Dedham until 1640, "the Lord ordering things so by a special providence that he no where settled" until that time. It is certain from our old Church Record, that he came here from Salem in 1639; and it is probable that he removed from this town to Dedham in 1640, without completing the contemplated arrangement for a permanent settlement here. His residence in Cambridge was in the old ox-pasture, on the northwesterly side of Kirkland Street, near Oxford Street. It was afterwards the homestead of Deputy-governor Danforth, as appears by the Town Record: " At a meeting of the

[1] Hoyman, or boatman.   [2] Geneal. Dictionary.

inhabitants of this town in May 1650, it was voted and consented
unto by the Town, that the house which Mr. Philips built anent
Charlestowne lane, with the land adjoining and woodlot, should
be sold to Thomas Danforth for fifty pounds, to be paid by him
to Mr. Philips or his assigns in current country pay upon demand
at the said house; the said Thomas Danforth to enjoy the said
house and land to him and his heirs and assigns forever." It does
not appear by what authority the town thus disposed of Mr.
Phillips' estate; but a subsequent record, under date of Feb. 12,
1655-6, confirms the sale, notwithstanding the purchase-money
had not yet been demanded by Mr. Phillips, then residing at
Wrentham, to which place he seems to have returned when he
left New England. Deputy-governor Danforth resided on this
estate nearly half a century, having very much enlarged it by
subsequent purchases, and at his death in 1699 bequeathed it
to his daughter, the wife of Francis Foxcroft, Esq., whose descendants owned it more than a whole century afterwards.

Among the disbursements up to 1645 (at which point there
occurs a hiatus of more than twenty years in the account), are
many for the relief of the poor as well as for provisions for the
"Lord's table," and for other necessaries : —

[1639.] " To Elder Frost we sent the 15 of the 5th month
in beefe, chese candle and money to bhy corne in
all 20'.   1. 0. 0

Given my brother John French the 5th of the 11th
month   2. 0. 0

Given my brother Towne toward his expense in
a sicknesse   1. 0. 0

Our brother Syll being deeply indebted and that to
Mr. Ting 22¹. 12'. we did give of the churches
stock half soe much to Mr. Ting if he wold frely
forgive the other and give it to our brother Syll
wᶜʰ God moved him to do soe pd.   11. 6. 0

Payd my brother Towne his half years allowance 30'.   1. 10. 0

Payd him for paynes taken more than ordinary in
making cleane the meetinge house in the time of
its repayrpinge. 12'.   0. 12. 0

Payd for 9 times going to call the church together at
8ᵈ. a time 6'.   0. 6. 0

[1640.] To our Elder Frost the 20 of the 3ᵈ month 30'.   1. 10. 0
To our sister Albon 1 pk of malt 18ᵈ.   0. 1. 6

[1641.] Given our sister Francis More (to supply them
in there need) 5'.   0. 5. 0

17

Given our sister Grissell in a hard time 5ˢ.	0. 5. 0
Sent our sister Maning a leg of mutton 13ᵈ.	0. 1. 1
Sent our sister Banbrick being sick a brest of mutton	0. 0. 10
Sent our sister Albone the 27 of the 9 month 1641 } 7ˡ of venison	0. 1. 2
[1643.] Payd our brother Manninge for a belrope [1]	0. 1. 6
Item payd Elder Frost for a years allowance wᶜʰ was } due at midsomer in the yeare 1643, I say pᵈ him } by 10ˡ.	10. 0. 0
Payd on for looking to goody Alborne 4 weeks (she } found herself)	0. 12. 0
Sent our sister Albone 1 bottell sack ·11ᵈ.	0. 0. 11 "
[" Elder Frost," "brother Banbrick," "brother Syll," "sister Maninge" and "sister Stephenson," each received a similar benefaction during this year.]	
[1644.] " Payd Mr. Palsgrave for physic for our sister Albone	0. 2. 6
For 4 years rent for our sister Albone (besides 5 } months time allowed her for about 7ˢ. charge in } repayer wᶜʰ she did) I say 4 years	4. 0. 0
[1645.] For cloth for Ben. Eaton for 2 shirts 3ˢ. 4ᵈ.	0. 3. 4
1 pr shoes for Ben Eaton cost 22ᵈ. 1 pr cost 14ᵈ.	0. 3. 0
Payd our brother Briggam for something for cloth- } inge for his sone	0. 7. 6
Payd brother Chesholme for nessessaryes he layd out } for Ben. Eatons clothes	0. 6. 6
Payd for a goat for goody Albone to goodman Prentiss	0. 11. 0 "

The close of Mr. Shepard's ministry is ·described by Mather,[2] after his usual quaint manner: "Returning home from a council at Rowly, he fell into a quinsie, with a symptomatical fever, which suddenly stopped a silver trumpet, from whence the people of God had often heard the joyful sound. Among other passages uttered by him, when he lay a dying, he addressed those that were about him with these words: 'Oh love the Lord Jesus very dearly ; that little part that I have in him is no small comfort to me now.' He died August 25, 1649, when he was forty-three years and nine months old, and left behind him, of three wives, which he successively married, three sons who have since been the shepherds of three several churches in this country." [3]   And

---

[1] A similar purchase was made in 1640.

[2] *Magnalia*, Book iii., ch. v., § 13.

[3] His first wife was Margaret Touteville, who was mother of Thomas (H. C. 1653), minister at Charlestown ; the second was Joanna, daughter of Rev. Thomas Hooker, and mother of Samuel (H. C. 1658), minister at Rowley ; the third was Margaret Boradell, who survived him and was mother of Jeremiah (H. C. 1669), minister at Lynn and elsewhere. Besides these, John, a son of the second wife, survived the father, but died young.

Savage, who surely will not be considered a partial judge, says, "So well employed had been his short life, that no loss of a public man in our country was more lamented, except that of Gov. Winthrop a few months before."[1] It is much to be regretted that no monument marks his grave.

Almost a year elapsed between the death of Mr. Shepard and the ordination of his successor. In the mean time, a new meeting-house was erected. Of the style and dimensions of the old meeting-house we know nothing. Doubtless it was very plain and humble; yet it was rendered glorious by the manifestation of divine power in the preaching of Hooker and Shepard, two of the most brilliant lights of that age, insomuch that to the congregation of worshippers it became as "the house of God" and "the gate of heaven."[2] It was built, however, of perishable materials, and although it had stood less than twenty years, it had fallen into decay; it would seem also that it was not sufficiently large. At first, it was proposed to repair the house "with a four-square roof and covered with shingle," and Edward Goffe, Thomas Marrett, John Stedman, Robert Holmes, and Thomas Danforth, were appointed, Feb. 18, 1649–50, to superintend the repairs. But shortly afterwards, March 11, 1649–50, "At a general meeting of the whole town, it was voted and agreed, that the five men chosen by the town to repair the meeting-house shall desist from the same, and agree with workmen for the building of a new house, about forty foot square and covered as was formerly agreed for the other, and levy a charge of their engagements upon the inhabitants of the town. It was also then voted and generally agreed, that the new meeting-house shall stand on the watch-house hill."[3] The new house was erected immediately, as appears by the following extracts from the Town Records: Jan. 13, 1650–51: "The Townsmen do consent that one of the

[1] Geneol. Dict.

[2] In this house also were probably gathered the whole body of reverend and learned divines in New England at the first two Synods for the determination of vitally important questions both of doctrine and of church polity: 1. In 1637, when through the prophesyings of Mrs. Hutchinson and others, the religious community was violently agitated, and the two parties, styling each other Antinomians and Legalists, were on the brink of civil war, a Synod, composed of all the teaching elders in the country and delegates from the several churches, assembled at Cambridge, and condemned eighty-two opinions adjudged erroneous. 2. In 1646, a second General Synod assembled at Cambridge, and after sundry adjournments was dissolved in 1648, having adopted a system of church discipline called "The Cambridge Platform."

[3] The watch-house hill was in the southwesterly corner of the present College yard, and extended several feet into Harvard Square, which has been enlarged since that meeting-house was erected.

Elders and two of the Deacons, at the request of John Betts, shall determine whether in equity any satisfaction ought to be rendered by the town to the said John Betts for the land on which the new meeting-house standeth; and with their determination the said John Betts promiseth to set down satisfied." [1] Feb. 26, 1651-2. Ordered, " That the Townsmen shall make sale of the land whereon the old meeting-house stood."

The Reverend Jonathan Mitchell, described by Mather as the " matchless Mitchell," was born at Halifax, in Yorkshire, England, about 1624, and was brought by his father to New England in 1635. " Their first settlement," says Dr. Holmes, " was at Concord, in Massachusetts; whence, a year after, they removed to Saybrook, in Connecticut; and, not long after, to Wethersfield. Their next removal was to Stamford, where Mr. Mitchell, the father, died in 1645, ætat. LV. The classical studies of his son Jonathan were suspended for several years after his arrival in America; but, ' on the earnest advice of some that had observed his great capacity,' they were at length resumed in 1642. In 1645, at the age of twenty-one, he entered Harvard College. Here he became religiously impressed under Mr. Shepard's ministry, which he so highly estimated as afterward to observe, ' unless it had been four years living in heaven, I know not how I could have more cause to bless God with wonder, than for those four years' spent at the university. He was an indefatigable student, and made great acquirements in knowledge and virtue. His extraordinary learning, wisdom, gravity, and piety, occasioned an early application of several of the most considerable churches for his services in the ministry. The church at Hartford, in particular, sent for him with the intention of his becoming successor to the famous Mr. Hooker. He preached his first sermon at Hartford, June 24, 1649; and on the day following was invited to a settlement in the ministry in that respectable town. Having however been previously importuned by Mr. Shepard and the principal members of his society to return to Cambridge, free from any engagement, with a view to a settlement there, he declined an acceptance of the invitation at Hartford, and returned to Cambridge, where he preached for the first time, Aug. 12, 1649. Here a providential opening was soon made for his in-

---

[1] John Betts owned the lot adjoining the watch-house hill, and fronting on Harvard Square. It is described on the *Proprietors' Records* as " by the town, one acre of land, more or less; Edward Goffe, east; the watch-house hill, south; common, west; the land intended for the College, north."

duction into the ministry. Mr. Shepard died on the 25th of the same month; and by the unanimous desire of the people of Cambridge, Mr. Mitchell was now invited to become his successor. He accepted the invitation, and was ordained Aug. 21, 1650." [1] " Eighteen years," says Mather, " did he continue a pastor to the church of Cambridge. And as that which encouraged him to accept at first the pastoral charge of that flock, was his being able to write that character of them, that they were a gracious savoury-spirited people, principled by Mr. Shepard, liking an humbling, mourning, heart-breaking ministry and spirit, living in religion, praying men and women, ... so the continual prayers of such a people to the Lord Jesus Christ for him doubtless contributed more than a little unto his being furnished from heaven with such rich treasures of light and grace as made his ministry richly serviceable unto them all." [2] By the concurrent testimony of his contemporaries and subsequent writers he was remarkably distinguished for learning, eloquence, and piety, superadded to uncommon natural gifts. Morton testifies that " he was a person that held very near communion with God; eminent in wisdom, piety, humility, love, self-denial, and of a compassionate and tender heart; surpassing in public-spiritedness; a mighty man in prayer, and eminent at standing in the gap; he was zealous for order, and faithful in asserting the truth against all oppugners of it. In a word, he was a man whom God had richly furnished and eminently fitted for his work; lived desired, and died lamented, by all good Christians that knew him. It pleased God upon the ninth of July, 1668, in a hot and burning season, (but much more hot in the heat of God's anger to New England,) to take him to rest and glory." [3]

About eight years after his ordination, Mr. Mitchell commenced compiling an account of " the Church of Christ at Cambridge," etc., in which he rescued many interesting facts from oblivion. The financial records of the church, kept by the deacons, were not resumed until near the close of his ministry. A very few items may be reproduced: —

"20. 3. 67. to Mr. Michell in silver when he went to Rehoboth 0. 6. 0

---

[1] *Mass. Hist. Coll.*, vii. 48.
[2] *Magnalia*, iv., chap. iv., § 9.
[3] *New England's Memorial*, Davis's ed., pp. 336, 337. For a more full biography, see Mather's *Magnalia*, Book iv., chap. iv.; and Sibley's *Harvard Graduates*, i. 141–157; and for the character of his theological labors and writings, see Rev. Mr. McKenzie's *Historical Lectures*.

20. 3. 67 to bro. Okes [1] when he went to Rehoboth with Mr. Michell in silver	0. 4. 0
22. 4. 67 Payd to Daniell Cheavrs for veall to Mr. Chauncy when he was sick	0. 5. 0
3. 12. 67–8 Payd to Mrs. Danforth in her husband's absence in silver the sume of 25 shillings for wine sugar and spice at the buriall of Mrs. Chauncy who deseaced the 24 of the 11. 67	1. 5. 0
27. 4. 68 Paid to John Sheapheard for a fower gallon bottell to bring sack for the sacrament	0. 3. 0 "

The Town Records also afford some glimpses of the manner
of managing ecclesiastical affairs at this period: Nov. 9, 1657.
The town "Voted, affirmative, that the deacons, townsmen, Mr.
Jacson, Edw. Goffe, Mr. Stedman and Edw. Winship are appointed
to make a levy of two hundred and forty pounds for the maintenance this year, and for the payment of the debts of our reverend
pastor, Mr. Michell." 27, 1. 1665, The selectmen "Ordered,
that all persons that do contribute to the ministry of this place
do, upon the first second day [2] of May next, appear before the
deacons and selectmen, to clear the payment of their dues for
time past, or send in writing a receipt thereof under the hand
of our pastor or deacons, and that for the future every one do
annually attend the like order at the same time; the place of
meeting to be at the meeting-house, and the time by eight of the
clock in the morning." Feb. 18, 1658–9. "Voted, that the Elders,
Deacons, and Selectmen for the time being, shall be a constant
and settled power for regulating the seating of persons in the
meeting-house, from time to time, as need shall require." One
of the acts of this committee is recorded under date of Jan. 19,
1662–3.

"The committee for ordering the seating of people in the
meeting house, being met at the ordinary, appointed

Bro. Ri. Jackson's wife to sit there where sister Kempster was
wont to sit.

Mrs. Upham, with her mother.

Ester Sparhauke, in the place where Mrs. Upham is removed
from.

Daniel Champney, Ephraim Winship, on the south gallery.

Jno. Stedman, on the fore gallery on the south side.

Joanna Winship, in the place where Ester Sparhauke was
wont to sit.

---

[1] Edward Oakes, father of President Oakes.   [2] The first Monday.

Mary Lemon, where old sister Jackson was wont to sit.

Mr. Day, to sit in the 2d seat from the table.

Ens. Samuel Greene, to sit at the table.

Ri. Robbins, to sit in the place where Ens. Greene was wont to sit.

Jno. Gibson, where Mr. Day was wont to sit.

Richard Eccles, where John Gibson was wont to sit.

Benj. Crackbone, where Richard Eccles was wont to sit.

Justinian Holden, to sit in the foremost seats.

Robert Stedman, to sit in the second seats.

Goode Gates, at the end of the Deacons seats."

Almost all the congregation either walked to the meeting-house, or rode on horseback. For the accommodation of equestrians, in mounting, dismounting, and passing between their beasts and the house, Nov. 20, 1665, "The Townsmen do order the Constables to make a convenient horse-block at the meeting-house, and causeway to the door." And to secure order in the house and the comfort of the worshippers, Nov. 12, 1666, "Thomas Fox is ordered to look to the youth in time of public worship, until the next monthly meeting, and to inform against such as he find disorderly. . . . . The Constables are ordered to repair the glass about the meeting-house, and to get the pinning mended."

During his ministry, Mr. Mitchell encountered two special trials, namely, the division of his church, and the reputed heresy and open opposition of President Dunster. It has already been related in chapter viii., that as early as March, 1654–5, some of the inhabitants on the south side of the river requested "that they might have the ordinances of Christ amongst them, distinct from the town." Doubtless Mr. Mitchell shared the fears which were expressed by the townsmen, that "the fraction will prove destructive to the whole body." Upon the extreme urgency of the petitioners, the town consented, Jan. 23, 1659–60, "that the remote inhabitants on the south side of the River should annually be abated the one half of their proportion to the ministry's allowance, during the time that they were provided of an able minister according to law." And Jan. 15, 1661–2, all persons residing south of the river and more than four miles distant from the old meeting-house, were released from all ministerial charges, on condition that they should "give good security to the town for the payment of twenty pounds per annum forever to the use of the other part of the town belonging to the old meeting-house on the north side of the River." Although these propositions were not accepted, the agitation was continued for many years, until Newton became a separate town. Mr. Mitchell did not live long enough to witness the final catastrophe; but the church was effectually divided in his lifetime, and Rev. John Eliot, Jr., was ordained pastor of that portion which withdrew from the parent body, July 20, 1664. A still greater trial was the open opposition of President Dunster to an ordinance which Mr. Mitchell considered important and sacred. When Mr. Dunster became a member of Mr. Shepard's church, about 1640, he avowed his belief that the children of believers ought to be baptized, and his willingness that baptism should be administered by sprinkling.[1] Afterwards, he opposed both; he withheld his own infants from baptism, and publicly denounced such baptism as "not according to the institution of Christ," when administered to others. It is related by Mather that, besides his public advocacy of infant baptism, Mitchell labored privately with Dunster, though he felt "embarrassed in a controversy with so considerable a person, and with one who had been his tutor, and a worthy and a godly man."[2] His efforts to reclaim his former guide and instructor were unavailing. Dunster became more and more violent in opposition to what he regarded as error, until he both forfeited the office of President of the College and exposed himself to the penalty of a violated law. He was indicted by the grand jury, April 2, 1655, "for disturbance of the ordinances of Christ upon the Lord's day at Cambridge, July the 30th 1654, to the dishonor of the name of Christ, his truth, and minister."[3] It was testified

---

[1] "As prayer, so the Lord hath given 2 sacraments. 1. Baptism, by which we have our initiation; and concerning it, I believe that only believers and their seed ought to be received into the church by that sacrament; hence profane unbelievers are not to be received into the church. And that the seed are to be received, that of Paul is clear, — else your children were unholy; hence, if holy, let them be offered to God; let children come to me. And as children, so those that come to mature age ought to be received into the church by baptism. And concerning the outward elements, something there is concerning sprinkling in the Scripture; hence not offended when it is used." — Shepard's MS. Confessions.

[2] Magnalia, Book iv., ch. iv., § 10. To the lasting honor of Mitchell and Dun-

ster, it should be remembered that their personal friendship continued through life. In his will, Dunster styles Mitchell and President Chauncy (his successor in the presidency), his "trusty friends and brethren," and gave to each of them sundry books from his library. And Mather says, that "Mr. Mitchell continued such an esteem" for Mr. Dunster, "that although his removal from the government of the College, and from his dwelling-place in Cambridge, had been procured by these differences, yet when he died, he honored him with an elegy," which "very truly points out that generous, gracious, catholic spirit, which adorned that person who wrote it."

[3] Probably Mr. Mitchell was the "minister" then engaged in administering the ordinance of baptism.

that, on that day, " Mr. Dunster spake to the congregation in the time of the public ordinance, to the interruption thereof, without leave, which was also aggravated in that he being desired by the Elder to forbear and not to interrupt an ordinance of Christ, yet notwithstanding he proceeded in way of complaint to the congregation, saying I am forbidden to speak that in Christ's name which I would have testified. And in his following speeches, he asserted as his testimony in the name of Christ these things: 1. That the subjects of baptism were visible, penitent believers, and they only, by virtue of any rule, example or any other light in the new Testament. 2. That there was an action now to be done which was not according to the institution of Christ. 8. That the exposition, as it had been held forth, was not the mind of Christ. 4. That the covenant of Abraham is not a ground for baptism; no, not after the institution thereof. 5. That there were such corruptions stealing into the church, which every faithful Christian ought to bear witness against. The Court ordered that Mr. Henry Dunster, according to Eccleast. Law, page 19, at the next Lecture at Cambridge should (by such magistrates as should then be present) be publicly admonished, and give bond for his good behaviour.

" Mr. Henry Dunster acknowledged that he had spoken these particulars above named, and said that he owned them and that he would stand by them in the fear of God; and after farther debate he gave in his answer in writing as followeth: April 4th 1655. I answer to the presentment of the grand jury: — I answer, first, that I am not conscious that I did or said any thing contemptuously or in open contempt of God's word or messengers, and therefore I am not guilty of the breach of that Law, page 19, as I conceive. For the particulars that were charged against me, the terms, words, or expressions, wherein they are presented to the honored Court, I own not, being not accurately the same that were spoken, especially the 1st, 4th, and 5th; but the matter or purport of them I spake. I also acknowledged, and do, that for the manner they were not seasonably spoken; but for the matter, I conceived then, and so do still, that I spake the truth in the fear of God, and dare not deny the same or go from it, until the Lord otherwise teach me; and this I pray the honored Court to take for mine answer. As for any words or expressions that in mixed or broken conference, interrogations by sundry persons propounded and mine answers interrupted before they have been fully expressed, I heartily and humbly pray you, mine honored

Judges, as you desire to find mercy with our gracious Judge, the Lord Jesus Christ, that you will be pleased to give the most candid and christian construction, if any were amiss, seeing charity thinketh no evil, and seeing by interruptions they were not perfected, and especially since my sickness yesternight my mind and expressions are not in a capacity to be so clear and distinct as usually; that therefore no lapse in expression, proceeding from the aforesaid grounds or mere natural infirmity may be improved against your humble servant and afflicted brother,

HENRY DUNSTER."

It is reported by his biographers, that Mr. Mitchell was a Fellow of Harvard College, 1650, a member of the Synod which assembled at Boston in 1662, and very frequently employed on ecclesiastical councils and in resolving questions propounded by the General Court; and that, while he was much younger than many of his associates, great deference was paid to his skill and judgment. The famous Baxter is reported to have said, " If an Ecumenical Council could be obtained, Mr. Mitchell were worthy to be its moderator." But his labors, and trials, and enjoyments, in the work of the ministry, came to a sudden termination July 9, 1668, when a violent fever destroyed his life. Although, while living, his name was renowned in the church, it is not found inscribed on any monumental stone, to denote the spot where his body was laid. There are circumstances, however, which render it highly probable that the bones found under the slab which bears the name of President Dunster are in fact the bones of Mitchell. They are briefly as follows: About thirty years ago, a desire was entertained to erect some memorial of Dunster. The place of his sepulture was unknown, but it was assumed to be underneath an ancient slab from which the inscription had disappeared. This assumption is said to have been grounded on two facts, which were supposed to point more directly to Dunster than to any other person — 1. It was perceived that this slab was of a peculiar stone, probably imported, and unlike any others in the cemetery except two, which bore respectively the names of President Chauncy and President Oakes, who died during the same half century. 2. There were found, not very far from this slab, two headstones, inscribed with the names of President Dunster's great-grandchildren. The subsequent proceedings are related by Palfrey: —

" His grave, in the old ' God's Acre,' near the halls of Harvard

College, was opened July 1, 1846, when the President and Fellows renewed the tablet over it. The remains were found lying six feet below the surface, in a brick vault which was covered with irregularly shaped flag-stones of slate about three inches thick. The coarse cotton or linen shroud which enveloped them had apparently been saturated with some substance, probably resinous, which prevented it from closely fitting the body. Between it and the remains of the coffin was found a large quantity of common tansy, in seed, a portion of which had evidently been pulled up by the roots. The skeleton appeared to be that of a person of middle size; but it was not measured, as the extremities of the bones of the arms and thighs had perished, as well as portions of the cancellated structure of these and of some other bones. The configuration of the skull, which was in good preservation, was such as to the phrenologists indicates qualities, both moral and intellectual, of a superior order. The hair, which appeared to have retained its proper place, was long behind, covering thickly the whole head, and coming down upon the forehead. This, as well as the beard, which upon the upper lip and chin was about half an inch long, was of a light brown color. The eyebrows were thick, and nearly met each other.[1]

The foregoing description indicates the remains of some eminent person. But are they the remains of Dunster? or, are they not rather the remains of Mitchell? It is no disparagement to Dunster to assume that Mitchell was fully his equal, both intellectually and morally; so that the skull might seem as characteristic of the one as of the other. The character of the grave and memorial slab is more suitable to Mitchell than to Dunster, because, 1. Dunster left a small estate, deeply involved in debt, and there is no evidence that his widow was able, or that the corporation of the College was disposed, to provide for him such an expensive sepulchre; but, on the other hand, Mitchell died in the meridian of his fame, and left a plentiful estate, so that his widow was able thus to honor him, unless (which is more probable) his church insisted on defraying the expense.[2] 2. The peculiar slab, similar, it is said, only to those which cover the remains of Chauncy, who died in 1672, and Oakes, who died in 1681, would more probably be placed over the grave of Mitch-

---

[1] *Hist. New Eng.*, ii. 534.

[2] The church, which long made a generous allowance to the widow of their beloved pastor, and was able to send a special messenger to England, to invite his successor, (and another to accompany him hither,) surely would not grudge him an honorable burial and a conspicuous stone of remembrance.

ell, who died in 1668, than over that of Dunster, who died nine
years earlier, in 1659. But if the structure and adornments of
the grave point to Mitchell rather than to Dunster, much more
its contents. For what conceivable reason should the coffin of
Dunster have been stuffed with tansy, or his body wrapped in
cerecloth? He died in February, when the frost might reasonably be expected to arrest decomposition and prevent any nox-
ious or offensive effluvia from his body. Morton, indeed, says,
" his body was embalmed and removed unto Cambridge; " but
it may reasonably be doubted whether the process was very
thorough or complete at that season of the year. On the contrary, Mitchell died in midsummer, and under circumstances requiring the utmost precaution against discomfort and danger.
Mather says, " Mr. Mitchell had, from a principle of godliness,
used himself to bodily exercise; nevertheless he found it would
not wholly free him from an ill habit of body. Of extreme lean,
he grew extreme fat; and at last, in an extreme hot season, a
fever arrested him." [1] This was a case loudly calling for cerecloth and tansy; and the proof is preserved that such cloth was
actually used. In the old Financial Record of the Church is
found this memorandum of disbursement: " To goodman Orton
of Charlestown, for making a terpaluing [2] to wrap Mr. Michell,
and for doing something to his coffing that way 4ˢ." And what
would be more natural than to adopt the custom, which certainly prevailed in the country in the early part of even the
present century, of placing tansy in and around the coffin, to
counteract the effect of unpleasant odors? The contents of the
grave described by Palfrey were precisely what we might expect
to find in the grave of Mitchell, and what we should not expect
to find in the grave of Dunster; namely, the cerecloth or tarpauling, which was necessary, and is known to have been used in
the one case, but not known to have been either necessary or used
in the other, and the tansy, which was in season, fragrant, and
adapted to its purpose, in the one case, and out of season, comparatively unfragrant, and useless in the other. On the whole,
it seems highly probable that the monumental slab, on which is
inscribed the name of President Dunster, actually covers the remains of Rev. Jonathan Mitchell.[3] It may be added, if this be

[1] *Magnalia*, Book iv., ch. iv., § 16.
[2] Tarpauling, cloth smeared with tar.
[3] The name of this eminent man is
spelled Mitchel on the College Catalogue;
I write it Mitchell, because, in several au-
tographs which I have seen, it was uniformly so written by himself; and it was
written in the same form by his two sons,
Samuel (H. C. 1681), and Jonathan (H.
C. 1687).

really the grave of Mitchell, the remains of Shepard probably rest near it, because the widow of these two pastors, as well as their bereaved and grateful church, would naturally desire that their bodies should rest near each other. It may also be safely supposed that Dunster was buried near the same spot; for where could his friends desire to place his body rather than near that of his former pastor and beloved co-laborer, Mr. Shepard, the only clergyman who had previously been laid to his rest in that cemetery? This supposition is to some extent rendered more probable by the proximity of the graves of the great-grandchildren.

For three years after the death of Mr. Mitchell, the church remained destitute of a pastor; during which time President Chauncy appears to have partially performed the duties of that office. The committee appointed by the town for that purpose voted, Dec. 20, 1669, that "fifty pounds be paid to Mr. Chauncy and such as labor among us in preaching the word," and "thirty pounds to Mistris Mitchell," and Dec. 23, 1670, forty-five pounds were in like manner granted to Mr. Chauncy, and thirty pounds to Mrs. Mitchell.[1] In the mean time the town and church were not idle or inactive. Thus it is recorded, Feb. 8, 1668–9. "For catechising the youth of this town; Elder Champney, Mr. Oakes, are appointed for those on the south side the Bridge. Elder Wiswall, Mr. Jackson, and John Jackson, for those at the new church. Deacon Stone, and Deacon Chesholme, for those at the remote farms. Lt. Winship, William Dixon and Francis Whitmore for those on west side Winottime. Deacon Stone and Deacon Cooper, for those families on the west side the common, and for Watertowne lane, as far towards the town as Samuel Hastings.[2] Thomas Danforth and Thomas Fox, for those families on the east side the common. Richard Jackson and Mr. Stedman, for those families on the west side of the town: Captain Gookin and Elder Frost, for those families on the east side of the town; — Water Street, leading from the meeting-house to the waterside being the partition." Again, May 10, 1669, "The Selectmen, taking into consideration, upon the complaint of some of the idleness and carelessness of sundry persons in the time of public worship, upon the Sabbath day, by keeping without the meeting-house, and there unprofitably spending their

---

[1] Similar gratuities were granted to Mrs. Mitchell, from year to year, as late as 1687.

[2] That is, to Ash Street.

time, whereby God's name is dishonored, — they do order, for
the time being, that the Constable shall set a ward of one man
during the time of public worship, one in the forenoon and
another in the afternoon, to look unto such persons, that they do
attend upon the public worship of God, that God's name and
worship be not neglected nor profaned by the evil miscarriage of
such persons."

. Hitherto the pastors of the church had dwelt in their own
houses; but now it was determined to erect a house, at the public expense, as a parsonage. July 5, 1669, "Voted on the
affirmative, that the Selectmen and Deacons, and Richard Jackson, and Mr. Stedman, and Mr. Angier, are appointed a committee, to take present care to purchase or build a convenient house
for the entertainment of the minister that the Lord may please
to send us to make up the breach that his afflicting providence
hath made in this place; and that the charge thereof be levied
on the inhabitants as is usual in proportioning the maintenance
of the ministry." Afterwards a different method of payment
was adopted. Sept. 9, 1669, "At a church meeting, to consider
about the selling of the church's farm at Bilrica, for the building
of a house for the ministry, it was voted on the affirmative, that
the said farm should be sold and improvement made of it for the
building of a house for the ministry."[1] In the old Financial
Record of the Church a particular statement is made that "a
committee was chosen for that purpose, which `tooke care for the
same, and to that ende bought fower akers of land of widdow
Beale to set the house upon, and in the yeare 1670 theare was a
house earected upon the sayd land of 36 foote long and 30 foote
broad; this house to remayne the churchis and to be the dwelling place of such a minister and officer as the Lord shall be
pleased to supply us withall, during the time hee shall supply
that place amongst us.[2] The chargis layd out for the purchas
of the land and building of the house and barne, inclosing the
orchyard and other accommodations to it:

"The purchas of the land in cash	40ˡ. 0ˢ. 0ᵈ
The building and finishing the house	263. 5. 6
The building the barne,	42. 0. 0

[1] It was sold Nov. 12, 1669, to Richard Daniels, for £220.
[2] This house stood on the northerly side of Harvard Street, two or three hundred feet easterly from Plympton Street.

The inclosing the orchyard and yards, and re-
payering the fencis, building an office-house,
and planting the orchyard with trees, and
seeling some part of the house and laying a
duble floore on sume part of it,   27. 1. 10

" In the yeere 1676, the hall and hall-chamber were sealed,
and another floore of bords was layed upon the chichin chamber.
The perticular chargis : —

    " 20 bushells of lime and the feching it   1^l. 1^s. 8^d
    800 of larth, 6^s. 8^d. a bushel of hayer, 1^s 0. 7. 8
    3 peckes of shreds, 1^s. 6^d ; lamblack, 8^d 0. 2. 2
    3560 nailes, 8^s. 10½^d 0. 8. 10½
    The mason's worke   1. 4. 0
    For brickes, and sand, and help to brick the kichen   4. 6. 4½ "

Other disbursements at this period were : —

March 6. 1668–9. " To Deacon Stone by a pair of shooes
   and a pound of suger, because the deacon had silver   0^l. 3^s. 6^d.
   though they cost him 4^s 6^d, had but

Feb. 4, 1670. " Payd in silver, by the apoyntment of the
   commitee for the mynister house unto the deputie
   governor, Mr. Francis Willoughby, by Deacon Stone
   and Thomas Chesholm, as appears by his discharg wch   8^l. 13^s. 6^d
   Deacon Stone hath, for the discharg of Mr. Michells
   funarall the sum of eight pounds thirteen shillings six
   pence. I say the sum of

The events connected with the induction of Mr. Oakes to the
pastorate are minutely detailed in the ancient record : "An account of seaverall providencis of God to the Church of Cambrigd,
after the death of that reverant and eminent man Mr. Jonathan
Micthell pastor of the church of Cambrigd whoe departed this
life July th 9, 1668, and the actings of the church for supply in
the ministry. The church, sume time after gave Mr. William
Stoutton a call, but they were denied, but after sume time of seek-
inge God by prayer the Lord was pleased to guide the church to
make theare application to Mr. Urian Oakes in old England which
to further the same theare was a letter sent from the church with
a mesenger namly Mr. William Maning with a letter alsoe sent
by seaverall magistats and ministers to invite him to come over
and be an oficer amongst us which he after counsill and advice
did except but devine providence ded hinder him for that yeere by
reason of a sicknes the Lord was pleased to visit his wife withall

and afterward tooke her away by death which hindered him for
that yeere. The church the next yeere renewed againe thear.
call to him by another letter but then he was hindered by an
ague that he was long visited withall in the yeere 1670. Thease
providencis interposing the church was in doupt wheather to
waight any longer but after sume debate the church was willing to
waight till the spring in the yeere 1671 and then had an answer
early in the yeere of his purpose to come over that sumer which
was acomplished by the good providence of God hee ariving in
New England July th 3, 1671, and finding good acceptance both
by the church and towne and in the country and joined a member
with our church and was ordained pastur of our church November
the eight 1671."

Mr. Oakes was received with demonstrations of joy. "At a
meeting of the church and town July the 17th 1671. — 1. To
acknowledge thankfulness to Mr. Oakes for his great love and
self-denial in parting with his friends and concerns in England to
come over to us. 2. To manifest unto him the continuance of
the earnest and affectionate desires of the church and people
that, as soon as well may be, he would please to join in fellowship here, in order to his settlement and becoming a pastor to
this church. 3. To intreat him forthwith to consent to remove
himself and family into the house prepared for the ministry.
4. That the deacons be furnished and enabled to provide for his
accommodation at the charge of the church and town, and dis-
tribute the same seasonably for the comfort of him and his family.
5. That half a year's payment forthwith be made by every one,
according to their yearly payment to the ministry; and the one
half of it to be paid in money, and the other in such pay as is
suitable to the end intended. All these particulars were voted
on the affirmative." The church and town united in keeping
"the 17th day of January 1676 a day of thanksgiving" that the
loss sustained by Mr. Mitchell's death was thus supplied. The
expense attending the removal of Mr. Oakes, including the services of a special messenger sent to accompany him hither, was
defrayed by the church. "August the 9th 1671. Delivered to
William Manning sixty pounds in silver to pay Mr. Prout toward
the transportation of Mr. Urian Oakes his familie and goods,
and other disbursements and for John Taylor his passage, I say
payed him the just sume of 60ʳ. 0. 0. Let it be taken notice of
that Mr. Prout dos demaund thirteen pounds more due to him."
This balance was subsequently paid, as appears by the account:

" Disbursed for Mr. Oakes transportation from Old England with his family 73*l.*" Also a gratuity was given to the messenger. Out of the legacy of £20 bequeathed to the church by Hezekiah Usher, who died in 1676, there was given " to John Taylor five pound, hee being in sume streights by reason of a dept in England he goeing to accompany our pastor to New England it was the ocation of it."

An additional glimpse of the customs of that period is obtained from the following " Account of the disbursements for the ordination of Mr. Urian Oakes pastor of the church of Cambrigd, being the 8 of November, 1671.

" It. 3 bushells of wheate	0*l.* 15*s.* 0*d*
It. 2 bushells ½ of malt	0. 10. 0
It. 4 gallons of wine	0. 18. 0
It. for beefe	1. 10. 0
It. for mutton	1. 4. 0
It. for 30*l* of butter	0. 15. 0
It. for foules	0. 14. 9
It. for suger, spice, and frute, and other small things	1. 0. 0
It. for labour	1. 8. 6
It. for washing the table lining	0. 6. 0
It. for woode 7*s*	0. 7. 0
It. suit 7*lb*, 3*s* bread 6*s*	0. 9. 0
	9. 17. 3 "

" Gathered by contribution of the church the saboth before the ordination for the sayde occasion } 4*l*. 7*s*. 1*d*.

" And the remainder of the charge was defrayed out of the weekly contribution } 5. 10. 2

9. 17. 3 "

As a further illustration of the customs, the following items are inserted : —

" Eldar Frost liing a longe time weake with others of his familly alsoe having the ague at the same time the church see meete to make a contribution for his relefe upon June 16, 1672. The sume gathered was in cash 7. 4. 9 and in other pay 2. 5. 8."

1675. " For a new hour-glass for the meeting-house, 0. 1. 0 "

" October the 22, 1676. The contribution was for Ensigne Samuell Green in the time of his sicknes and his family alsoe being sicke there was contributed in cash 10. 5. 7 and in bills 8. 7. 6."

" November 2d 1679. The contribution upon the saboth day

18

was for the reliefe of the family of John Gibson they being in a
low condition they being visited with the small pox and under
many wants. The sum contributed in cash was six pound nine-
teen shillings and fower pence. This contribution was disposed
of as followeth:

" To doctor Oliver for fisicke	3'. 10'. 0ᵈ
To Mr. Angier for things in his sicknes	0. 4. 0
To Mr. Stedman for things in his sicknes	0. 7. 6
To sister Belsher for wine for his funerall	0. 7. 0
To two nurses that tended him in his sicknes	1. 4. 0
To Hana Arington for nursing	0. 10. 0
To Jeremiah Holman's daughter for nursing .	0. 6. 0
For bords for his coffin	0. 2. 6
To John Palfree for making of his coffin	0. 4. 0
To old goodman Gibson in cash	0. 4. 4
	6. 19. 4."

Like his predecessors, Mr. Oakes died when he was yet comparatively a young man. He had long been subject to a quartan
ague; but his life was terminated by fever July 25, 1681, in the
fiftieth year of his age. His death was as sudden and unexpected
as that of Mr. Mitchell. " He was arrested with a malignant
fever which presently put an end unto his days in this world.
. . . . When he had lain sick about a day or two, and not so
long as to give the people of God opportunity to pray for his re-
covery, his church coming together with expectation to have the
Lord's Supper on the Lord's day administered unto them, to their
horror found the pangs of death seizing their pastor that should
have broken to them the bread of life." [1] The last ten years of
his life were years of trial, mental excitement, and severe labor,
partly in the proper work of the ministry, and partly resulting
from his connection with the College.[2] Within a year after his
ordination as pastor of the church in Cambridge, he was elected
Fellow of Harvard College, which office he (together with three
of his associates, Thomas Shepard, Joseph Brown, and John
Richardson) very soon resigned, under somewhat questionable
circumstances. The overseers of the College requested them to
resume the office; but they declined, until March 15, 1674–5, the
day on which President Hoar sent in his resignation. " On the
same day, Oakes and Shepard took their seats as members of the

[1] Mather's *Magnalia*, Book iv., ch. v., Oakes, see Sibley's *Harvard Graduates*,
§ 8.   173–185, and McKenzie's *Lectures*, 120–
[2] For a more extended notice of Mr.   127.

Corporation, and the seat Dr. Hoar had quitted was given to the Rev. Mr. Oakes." He hesitated to accept the office, but at length consented to perform its duties as President *pro tem.*, which he continued to do for five years; when, having been again elected, he was installed into the office of President on Commencement Day, in August, 1680, less than a year before his death.[1]

Ancient writers uniformly represent Oakes as a skilful and diligent teacher. The college was in a disorganized condition when he assumed its management, and required the most cautious and judicious guidance. This, together with the labor of instruction, was sufficient, it would seem, to tax his mental energy to the utmost, especially in connection with his various duties to his church and parish. But in addition to all this, his mind was disturbed by the consciousness that his opposition to President Hoar was regarded by many as the result of disappointed ambition, it being suspected that he coveted the presidency when it was vacated by the death of Chauncy, that he was offended when it was given to Hoar, and that he hoped yet to obtain it if his rival could be displaced. Mr. Oakes had other trials, more closely connected with his pastoral office. Intense political excitement prevailed in regard to encroachments by the British Government on the Charter, which, not long after the death of Oakes, was utterly subverted and abrogated. Intense religious excitement also prevailed in consequence of the renewed activity of those dreaded disturbers of the public peace, the Anabaptists and Quakers, who were encouraged thereto by the British Government. To this excited state of the public mind Rev. Samuel Danforth alluded in a letter addressed to his brother, Thomas Danforth, March 31, 1670: "The truth is, matters are so circumstanced that a man can hardly come into any company and enter into any discourse, but before he is aware he finds himself in the like fan and sieve as that wherein Satan winnowed Peter in the high priest's hall."[2] On the same subject the "Freemen of Cambridge" addressed a long memorial to the General Court, dated June 8, 1671 (just one month before the arrival of Oakes from England), in which they say: —

"After the experience of the Lord's goodness in giving a good issue to many other temptations wherewith in his wisdom he hath seen meet to exercise his people and churches here, it is

---

[1] Quincy's *History of Harvard College,*   [2] *Mass. Hist. Sec. Proc.,* 1873-1875, p. i. 34-38, and Sibley's *Harvard Graduates,*   308. 180.

none of the least trials to the faith and patience of his poor se
vants that which at present is upon us, viz., the Lord's judici
hand is delivering up many among us to their own heart's lust
that they can boldly, with a presumptuous high hand, give def
ance to the Lord's holy institutions and ordinances, to his de
ministers, despising the word of the Lord in their mouths, an
refusing to obey them that have the rule over them in the Lor
us is more especially the practice of the Quakers, Anabaptist
and Familists, that are of late risen up among us, and in the
wicked practices do they continue notwithstanding all the mea
that have been used for their conviction, and wholesome laws
this jurisdiction prohibiting them therein.   And if, by their i
corrigible hardiness, they can at last weary out God's minister
casting dirt and reproach on their persons, doctrine, and holy a
ministrations, which they well know will soon stick and easil
prevail to cause the word of God by them dispensed to be unpro
itable, and also shall perceive that there are some, who, thoug
they declare not themselves to own their corrupt opinions and
allow their wicked practices, yet can plead for their liberty an
implicitly at least make their reflections to the reproach of th
godly zeal of the authority here established, (seeking to refor
such exorbitant practices), and thereby so weaken their hand
that they wax feeble in that great work of the Lord, they hop
then that the day shall be theirs; but sure it is, if it be the
day, it will be a black and dark night, as with the Lord's peopl
so also with his truth and holy institutions, (examples where
are not a few in Eccl. histories), the upholding whereof in purit
and power, and the conveying of the same in pure streams dow
to our posterity, as it was the main end of the first planters, as
before declared, so it cannot but be the earnest desire and e
deavor of every Christian soul.   Be pleased, therefore, honorabl
sirs, to accept our tender of humble thankfulness as to the Lor
so also to your honored selves, who, under God are the walls
this our Jerusalem, for all your pious endeavors and holy ze
(tempered with much tenderness, as well becometh christians
against those highhanded and presumptuous sinners.   And it
our humble petition to this honored Court, that the laws here e
tablished against the wicked practices of those obstinate offende
may be fully executed, all discontentments that may tend to gi
any discouragement thereto notwithstanding; we being well a
sured that the tolerating of them will add to the catalogue
those things that he whose eyes are as a flaming fire in the mid

of his churches will soon espy and be offended with us for, as is
by himself affirmed, Rev. ii. 14, 20; but on the contrary it is
very pleasing when his people do hate those things that his soul
doth hate, as appears in the 6th verse of that chapter."[1]

Mr. Oakes expressed his opinion concerning these exciting
subjects in an Election Sermon, May 7, 1673: "They that are
weary of and disaffected to this government that God hath established among us, and shall betray and give up the civil interest
of New England, will have more to answer for than they are
aware of. He is a madman that will hope for the continuance of
our spiritual liberties, if the wall of our civil government be once
broken down. Those beasts that break down the hedge of our
civil government do not design or do it merely because they are
angry with the hedge, but because they would break in and de-
vour all that is precious and dear to us. The change of our government will inevitably introduce a sad change in our churches.
To divide what God hath conjoined, viz., civil and ecclesiastical
liberties, to deliver up civil and yet hope to keep spiritual liberties, is folly in its exaltation." Again, "The loud outcry of some
is for liberty of conscience; that they may hold and practice
what they will in religion. This is the Diana of some men, and
great is the Diana of the Libertines of this age. I remember
Julian the Apostate, that malicious and implacable enemy to
Christianity have observed that the Christian religion prospered
the more for the severe persecution in Dioclesian's time, and that
the Christians grew up thicker and faster for being mowed down
with the scythe of bloody enemies. He did for a while abstain
from severities against the Christians, and suffered all men to use
what religion they would; and Austin saith of it, *Libertatem
perditionis permisit*, he gave men liberty to destroy themselves.
Such is that liberty of conscience, even a liberty of perdition,
that some men are so unconscionably clamorous for. But remember, that as long as you have liberty to walk in the faith and
order of the Gospel, and may lead quiet and peaceable lives in
all godliness and honesty, you have as much liberty of conscience
as Paul desired under any government. 1 Tim. ii. 1. 2. He
that is allowed without molestation to walk with God, and serve
him with all good conscience, hath liberty enough. Never complain when that is your condition, that you may be as good as
you will. Oh take heed in all societies, and in all respects, of an
inordinate and undue affectation of liberty. The latter end of it

---

[1] *Mass. Arch.*, x. 14.

will be bondage and slavery." "I look upon an unbounded toleration as the first born of all abominations. If this should be
once born and brought forth among us, you may call it Gad, and
give the same reason that she did of the name of her son, Gen.
xxx. 11, *Behold a troop cometh*, even a troop of all manner of
abominations. This would be not only to open the wicket, but
to. fling open the great gate for the ready admission and reception
of all abominable heresies." [1]

In the ancient Record-book, Deacon Cooper continues his " account of seaverall providencis of God to the church of Cambrigd "
as follows : " Mr. Oakes our pastor being chosen to be president of the Colegd about a yeere before his death it pleased the
Lord to guide our church to give Mr. Nathanill Gookin a call to
bee helpfull in the ministry in order to call him to office in time
convenient which sume time after our pasturs death our church
ded give hime a call to the office of pastor which call he ded except of and was ordained pastor of our church November 15th,
1682. Alsoe theare weare ordained the same day two Ruling
Elders of our church, namly, Deacon John Stone, and Mr. Jonas
Clarke to the ofice of Ruling Elders." By the same hand we
have an account of the expense attending Mr. Gookin's ordination, and the manner in which that expense was defrayed : —

" Provision for 80 persons	9^l. 10^s. 0^d
For burnt wine 1^l. sugar 2^s. brandy 6^d. before diner	1. 2. 6
Wine for the mesengers in the morning	0. 16. 2
The chargis for the cakes for the mesingers } wheate flower 7^s. 8^d rose-water 9^d	0. 8. 5
12^{lb} of currans 6^s 15^{lb} of suger 4^s. 8^d	0. 10. 8
A pound of lofe suger 1^s east 6^d	0. ⁻1. 6
Spice 5^s. 6^d milke 17^d	0. 6. 11
Ten pound of butter 5^s a cheese 4^s	0. 9. 0
6^l. of porke 1^s. 6^d	0. 1. 6
Hay for the horsis 5^s helpe to tende the horsis 2^s	0. 7. 0
Half an ounce of cloves 6^d	0. 0. 6
	13. 14. 2

" How it was produced the pay for the charge of Mr. Gookins
ordination in maner as followeth : —

" Payed to John Jackson by cash in his hand	5^l. 0^s. 0^d
Payed to John Jackson out of the contribution upon the saboth dayes 5^l 2^s a part of the saide contribution being otherwayes disposed of then to the minister before Mr. Gookins ordination by the order of the church.	} 5. 2. 0

            ·   [1] Pages 49–54.

More payed to John Jackson out of Thomas Beales } 1ˡ. 8ˢ. 0ᵈ
   legacy toward the ordination by Walter Hastins

More payed by Walter Hastins toward the ordina- } 1. 10. 6
   tion of widow Beales legacy

By John Cooper 11ˡ a cheese, 4ˢ   0. 15. 0

By butter and hay and milke this 15ˡ. was   13. 15. 6
   payed by money that was in my hand."

Little is known of Mr. Gookin's personal history. His ministry was short, but it extended over a troublous political period, embracing the abrogation of the charter, the usurpation of the government by Andros as the agent of arbitrary power, and the revolution which reinstated the old charter-magistrates. Although his father, Major-general Gookin, was one of the most sturdy defenders of popular rights against the encroachments of tyranny, and his brother, Capt. Samuel Gookin, was an active participant in the struggle, sometimes on the one side and sometimes on the other, Mr. Gookin is not known to have turned aside from his pastoral duties, or to have taken any part in the political conflict. He was a Fellow of Harvard College, but probably did not act as a tutor after taking the entire charge of the church. Short as was the life of his predecessors, his own was even more brief, — lacking two months of thirty-four years. His pastorate was almost precisely as long as that of Mr. Oakes, — nearly ten years.[1] The ancient record says, "Mr. Nathaniel Gookin, our pastor, departed this life 7 day of August 1692, being the Sabbath day at night, about nine or ten o'clock at night. Elder Clark departed this life 14 January 99 or 1700, being the Sabbath day. Our pastor Mr. Nathaniel Gookin's wife Hannah died 14 day of May 1702, and was buried 16 day of May at the town's charge."[2] During Mr. Gookin's ministry, the church continued to "remember the poor." Contributions were taken for Joseph Graves, in 1683, Moses Eyers, in 1684, and Thomas Gould, in 1685, severally in " Turkey Slavery;" for poor Frenchmen, in 1686, who fled here for shelter; and in 1692 for " York captives with the Indians." In 1686, seven pounds were contributed for the relief

[1] Dr. Holmes says: "The shortness of Mr. Gookin's ministry, and the imperfection of the early records of the church, leave us very deficient in the means of obtaining his history and character." *Coll. Mass. Hist. Soc.*, vii. 54. But we have this testimony of his worth by one of his contemporaries: Judge Sewall in his MS. Journal says, "Mr. Joseph Eliot comes in and tells me the amazing news of the Rev. Mr. Nathaniel Gookin's being dead : 'tis even as sudden to me as Mr. Oakes' death. He was one of our best ministers, and one of the best friends I had left."

[2] The orthography of this record is extraordinarily vicious, and is here corrected.

of John Parker at the "Village," whose house had been burned.
"June 3, 1688. The contribution upon the Saboth day was for
the releefe of widdow Crackbon and her sone, hee being distracted. The sume contributed in cash was 8^s. 13^s., and in other
pay, by Maior Gookin a bl. of rie and a bl. of malt, 7^s. 6^d.; by
Thomas Androwes, 2^s.; by Sharabiah Kibby, 2^s.; by Simond
Gates, 4^s." Again: "Jan. 12, 1689. Theare was a contribution
for widdow Arrington and her family they being under the
aflicting hand of God, her sonns weare taken away by death and
her daughter and a grandchilde. The sum in cash was 6^s. 18^s.
The sum in common pay was 1^s. 2^s. 6^d."

While Mr. Gookin was laboring as an assistant to Mr. Oakes,
the County Court required certain statistical returns from the
several towns in the county, concerning the number of families
and taxable polls, schools, tything-men, and the amount of compensation paid to the pastors of the several churches. The Cambridge Committee made report, March 30, 1380, as follows: —

"The number of our families, according to our nearest computation, is one hundred and twenty-one. The number of our
persons,[1] according to our nearest computation, is one hundred
and sixty-nine. The annual allowance to our reverend pastor in
money is about 51^s; in goods and provisions about 78^s, 13. Sum is
129^s 13^s 0^d; with his dwelling in the house built for the ministry,
with four acres of land adjoining thereunto; also about twenty
load of wood annually carried to his house." It was voted, June
28, 1680, "that the maintenance that is annually allowed to the
ministry, Mr. Nathanill Gookin shall have one hundred pounds
thereof for this present year, and the remainder to be paid to Mr.
Oakes." After Mr. Gookin's death, the town voted, May 13, 1695,
"to give to the next minister that the church and town shall settle
among them ninety pounds per annum, in money, so long as he
shall carry on the work of the ministry in Cambridge;" and,
Jan. 23, 1712–3, "voted, that the sum of ten pounds per annum
be added to the salary of the ministry in this part of the town,
instead of the annual custom of carting of wood; so that the
said salary is one hundred pounds per annum." The nominal
salary remained unchanged until the close of Dr. Appleton's long
ministry, more than seventy years afterwards; but it was the
custom, for many years, to give the pastor "a considerable quantity of wood gratis, some years between thirty and forty loads,

[1] Ratable polls, or males sixteen years of age.

sometimes above forty loads." [1] A reasonable allowance was made, also, for the depreciation of values, during the Revolutionary War. Provision was made which resulted in the creation of a fund for the maintenance of the ministry. June 28, 1680, "Voted and agreed, that five hundred acres of the remote lands, lying between Oburne, Concord, and our head-line, shall be laid out for the use and benefit of the ministry of this town and place, and to remain to that use forever." In 1718, this land was sold, and of the proceeds one hundred and thirty pounds were expended on the Parsonage, and the remainder was invested in a fund, whereof two thirds of the interest should be paid annually to the pastor of the church, and the remaining third part should be added to the principal. It is understood that this fund recently amounted to more than twenty thousand dollars.

It was Mr. Gookin's lot to witness another division of his parish. In 1682, the "Farmers," as those were called who dwelt in what is now the town of Lexington, petitioned to be set off as a separate parish, "in order to provide for themselves a person that may be meet and able to dispense unto them the word of God ; " representing that they were " seated at a great distance, the nearest of them above five miles (some of them six, some eight, some nine, if not ten miles), from the public place of meeting to worship God in the town that we appertain unto." This petition was opposed by Cambridge, and was not granted by the General Court. It was renewed in 1684, when it met a similar fate. The request was finally granted, Dec. 15, 1691 ; and although a church was not organized, separate from the mother church, until nearly five years later, Rev. Benjamin Estabrook was engaged to preach one year in the parish, commencing May 1, 1692. He was ordained Oct. 21, 1696, and died July 22, 1697.

After the death of Mr. Gookin, more than four years elapsed before the ordination of his successor. In the meantime more than thirty ministers preached in the Cambridge pulpit, of whom Samuel Angier, William Brattle, and Increase Mather, preached more frequently than any other. The compensation to the preachers was ten shillings for each sermon ; and generally one person preached in the forenoon, and another in the afternoon. The commendable generosity of one eminent preacher is recorded by Deacon Hastings: " Mr. Increase Mather preached

[1] *Church Record.*

much in the time of our vacancy ; and he gave his to Mrs. Hannah Gookin, widow, and it was paid her and for entertaining the minister that preached with us." [1] The generosity of the parish ought also to be held in remembrance. The expense of Mr. Mitchell's funeral was defrayed by the parish, and donations were made to his widow (who was also widow of the former pastor, Mr. Shepard), as long as she lived. Mr. Oakes left no widow, and the College assumed the charge of his funeral, as in the case of their former President, Mr. Chauncy. The town (which was the parish) voted, Nov. 14, 1692, "to pay the expense and defray the charge of our Pastor Gookin's funeral charges, which amounted to about eighteen pounds in money : " and the continuance of the same benevolence is indicated by a vote, March 10, 1700–1, "that Mrs. Hannah Gookin should be paid three pounds, to pay the rent of her house this present year." The account is fittingly closed by the record under date of May 15, 1702 : " Voted, that the selectmen take care that Mrs. Hannah Gookin be decently buried at the charge of the inhabitants belonging to this meeting-house, and the charge of said funeral be added to the town rate granted this year."

Rev. William Brattle, born at Boston, November, 1662, H. C. 1680, Tutor and Fellow of the College 1692, one of the first two on whom the College conferred the degree of Bachelor of Divinity, 1692, who had supplied the pulpit occasionally since Mr. Gookin's death and constantly since March 25, 1696, was ordained pastor of the church Nov. 25, 1696. From this time a regular church record was made, which has been preserved in good condition. At the commencement of this record, Mr. Brattle says he " succeeded the Rev. Mr. Nathaniel Gookin, and was ordained a minister of Jesus Christ and a pastor to the flock at Cambridge, Nov. 25, 1696, per the Rev. Mr. Inc. Mather. The Rev. Mr. Morton, Mr. Allin, and Mr. Willard laid on hands. The Rev. Mr. Sam¹. Willard gave the right hand of fellowship. . . . . Deo sit gloria. Amen." The proceedings at this ordination seem to have been misapprehended by some historians. President Quincy says that Brattle " gave immediate evidence of his disposition to set himself free from some customs of the established Congregational Church. He preached at his own ordination, and forbade an elder, because he was a layman, to lay his hand upon his head during the ceremony. Both were deviations from the established practice of the early Congregational Churches." [2]

[1] Church Record ; orthography revised.   [2] History of Harvard University, i. 88, 89.

And he quotes the remark of Judge Sewall: " It was, at first, ordered that Mr. Brattle should not preach. But many being troubled at it, 'twas afterward altered." [1] Instead of deviating from the established custom, Mr. Brattle, in fact, conformed to it by preaching at his own ordination, though he earnestly desired to be excused from that service. In proof that it was not unusual for a pastor to preach his own ordination sermon, it is sufficient to quote two examples, which occurred near the same time and in this immediate vicinity. Rev. Thomas Shepard, grandson of the first pastor of this church, was ordained at Charlestown, May 5, 1680. " Mr. Shepard was ordained by Mr. Sherman of Watertown, and received the right hand of fellowship from President Oakes. He preached his own Ordination Sermon, and took his text from Hebrews, xiii. 20, That great Shepherd of the sheep. Another sermon was preached on this occasion, from Ezekiel xxxiii. 7, Son of man, I have set thee a watchman." [2] Rev. Benjamin Estabrook was ordained at Lexington, Oct. 21, 1696, exactly five weeks before the ordination of Mr. Brattle. Judge Sewall describes the exercises thus: " A church is gathered at Cambridge North Farms. No relations made, but a covenant signed and voted by ten brethren, dismissed from the churches of Cambridge, Watertown, Woburn, Concord, for this work. Being declared to be a church, they chose Mr. Benjamin Estabrooks their pastor, who had made a good sermon from Jer. iii. 15. Mr. Estabrooks, the father, managed this, having prayed excellently. Mr. Willard gave the charge; Mr. Fox the right hand of Fellowship." [3] These examples are sufficient to show that Mr. Brattle did not depart from an established Congregational custom, by preaching at his own ordination. On the contrary, he conformed to the custom, not willingly, but in deference to the wishes of others. In the Library of the Massachusetts Historical Society is preserved a manuscript letter from Mr. Brattle to Rev. Rowland Cotton of Sandwich, dated Nov. 6, 1696, in which he says: " I wrote to your good father the last week, and therein acquainted him and yourself, &c., that the ordination at Cambridge is designed (God willing) 25 this instant. Shall be glad to see you and others my friends, and in the meantime entreat your good wishes. I trust the Reverend President will preach the ordination-sermon; it is my hearty desire,

[1] *History of Harvard University*, i. 489.   [2] Sewall's MS. Journal.
[3] Frothingham's *History of Charlestown*, p. 192.

and that which must be, otherwise I shall have great dissatisfaction in my own mind, it being, according to my best light, most proper that, when there is time but for one sermon on such days, some grave Divine, and not the young Candidate, should give the said sermon." As a compromise, Mr. Brattle preached to gratify those who adhered to the custom, and in compliance with his earnest desire Dr. Mather preached, as appears by the deacon's record of the services.

In one matter, Mr. Brattle early adopted a practice, then recently introduced, at variance with the established usage. He obtained a vote of the church that public relations of experience should not be required of candidates for admission to membership;[1] and that the question upon admission should no longer be taken by "manual vote," but silence should be considered assent. This gave dissatisfaction to Deputy-governor Danforth and others: whereupon, — "At a church meeting at Mr. Bordman's house, May 4, 1697, — (1) Then propounded to Mr. Danforth and the whole body of the brethren who had remonstrated as to the votes of the church passed March 11, '96-7, at the house of deacon Hastings, whether, if I would condescend so far as to let something be communicated to the church by myself, or the Elder, wherein I received satisfaction from those who ask communion with us, as to their spiritual fitness for it, and this to be done at some time before or when they are, to be admitted as I shall judge best, and this to remain so long as the peace of the church requires it, — they would then be satisfied, and give no further trouble: — This proposal was consented unto by them all, no one expressing his dissent. (2) Then propounded to them whether, if the way and manner of taking the Church's consent, whether by handy vote, or silence, or any other indifferent sign, be left to the discretion of the Elders, this would be to their satisfaction: — to this, likewise, their consent was given, and no one expressed his dissatisfaction. Upon which I promised that, so long as the peace of the Church called for it, I would observe what I had now propounded to them for the accommodating the differences which had been among us."[2]

The connection of Mr. Brattle with his church for more than twenty years was peaceful and successful. His connection with the college, as Tutor and Fellow was even longer, and equally.—

<hr />

[1] The same course had been pursued at the gathering of the church at Lexington, Oct. 21, 1696.

[2] *Church Record.*

pleasant and beneficial. After the death of his brother, Thomas Brattle, he skilfully performed the duties of Treasurer of the College, for about two years. At the election of President, Oct. 28, 1707, he had one vote.[1] His literary attainments were further recognized by his election as a member of the Royal Society, — an honor conferred on very few Americans. After "a languishing distemper which he bore with great patience and resignation," he "died with peace and an extraordinary serenity of mind," Feb. 15, 1716–17, in the fifty-fifth year of his age. An obituary appeared in the "Boston News Letter," dated Feb. 25, in which it is said that his "good name while he lived was better than precious ointment, and his memory, now being that of the just, will be always blessed. They that had the happiness to know Mr. Brattle, knew a very religious, good man, an able divine, a laborious, faithful minister, an excellent scholar, a great benefactor, a wise and prudent man, and one of the best of friends. The promoting of religion, learning, virtue, and peace, every where within his reach, was his very life and soul, the great business about which he was constantly employed, and in which he principally delighted. Like his great Lord and Master, he went (or sent) about doing good. His principles were sober, sound, moderate, being of a catholic and pacific spirit." In a preface to Dr. Sewall's sermon on the death of Rev. Ebenezer Pemberton, Dr. Mather fully corroborates the foregoing testimony ; "In the same week another faithful minister of God was taken away, viz. the Rev. Mr. William Brattle, pastor of the church in Cambridge, whom also I had reason to have an intimate acquaintance with, for that I presided over the College all the time of his being a Fellow and a Tutor there ; and I had much comfort in his conversation. Had I not known his abilities, I would not have advised the precious Church in Cambridge to have elected and

---

[1] It is not unlikely that this vote was given by Increase Mather, D.D. A MS. letter from Mr. Brattle to him, dated May 8, 1707, preserved in the Library of Harvard College, indicates their mutual respect and affection. After hearty thanks for a book which he had recently received, Mr. Brattle says : "As to the affairs of the College, I wish they were under better circumstances than they are : I do not hear but that the Commencement is like to be carry'd on as of late: If not, I would with all earnestness wish that yourself would once more honor that society and that day with your presence and managements. I know it would be very great condescension in yourself ; but because of the special service which would come thence, and for the sake of the public glory that would attend it, I cannot but wish it. I have deep resentments of your respects to my unworthy self : it is what I am most apt to be proud of, that I have in any measure your smiles. The argument you urge my compliance from in case and of your presence, &c., is without flattery the greatest temptation from the head of honor that could assault me."

ordained him their pastor, and at their and his desire performed
that office of respect and love on Nov. 25, 1696. He that holds
the stars in his right hand was pleased to uphold him in the
pastoral office some months above twenty years. I am glad to
see his character already published, and that it is done without
hyperbolizing, that which is there said of him being true, and
nothing but justice to his memory. Where shall there be found
a suitable successor? " This surely does not indicate such a
jealousy and antagonism between Dr. Mather and Mr. Brattle as
some historians have represented.

It would seem that hitherto, very few pews had been constructed in the meeting-house ; instead of which there were long
seats appropriated to individuals by the " seaters of the meeting-
house." But early in Mr. Brattle's ministry, March 14, 1697–8,
the town " voted, that there should be a pew made and set up
between Mr. Samuel Gookin's pew and the stairs on the southeast corner of the meeting-house for the family of the ministry."
Soon afterwards, July 11, 1698, " on the motion of Mr. John
Leverett and Doctor James Oliver, the Selectmen do grant that
they shall have convenient place in the meeting-house for the accommodation of their respective families ; the place or places to be
set out to them by the Selectmen, the Elders consenting thereto :
the places which they desire are on each side of the east door of
the meeting-house." This meeting-house, having stood somewhat more than fifty years, had become dilapidated, and the inhabitants of the town voted, July 12, 1703, " that they apprehend
it necessary at this time to proceed to the building of a new meeting-house, and in order thereunto, there was then chosen Capt.
Andrew Belcher, Esq., Thomas Brattle, Esq., John Leverett, Esq.,
Col. Francis Foxcroft, Esq., Deacon Walter Hastings, Capt.
Thomas Oliver, and Mr. William Russell, a committee to advise
and consider of the model and charge of building said meeting-
house, and to make report of the same to said inhabitants." Final
action was delayed until December 6, 1705, when it was " voted
that the sum of two hundred and eighty pounds be levied on said
inhabitants, toward the building a new meeting-house amongst
them." Thanks were voted by the town, March 8, 1707–8, to
" the Honble Andrew Belcher, Esq.," for his gift " toward building our new meeting-house." The same generous benefactor had
previously given a bell, as mentioned in a former chapter. On
the 28th of September, 1703, the College granted sixty pounds
" out of the College Treasury towards the building a new meet-

ing-house;" and, August 6, 1706, "voted that Mr. Leverett with the Treasurer take care for the building of a pew for the President's family in the meeting-house now a building, and about the students' seats in the said meeting-house; the charge of the pew to be defrayed out of the College Treasury." This third house stood on or very near the spot occupied by the second, and seems to have been opened for public worship, Oct. 13, 1706, as Mr. Brattle's record of Baptisms shows that on that day he first baptized a child in that house, having performed a similar service in the College Hall on the previous Sabbath.

As before stated, Mr. Brattle died Feb. 15, 1716-7. On the next day after his decease, the town "voted, that the charge of wine, scarves, and gloves, &c., for the bearers at the funeral of our late Pastor, the Rev. Mr. William Brattle, deceased, be defrayed by the town, and that the deacons and selectmen, by themselves, or any three of them that they may appoint, order the management thereof." An account of money thus disbursed, amounting to £23 17 10, was presented and allowed March 11, 1716-7. Mr. Brattle's remains were deposited under the same slab which marks the resting-place of Dr. James Oliver, who deceased April 8, 1703.[1]

[1] On the day of the funeral, Wednesday, Feb. 20, 1716-7, there was an extraordinary snow-storm. The *Boston News Letter*, dated Feb. 25, says: "Besides several snows, we had a great one on Monday the 18th current, and on Wednesday the 20th, it began to snow about noon and continued snowing till Friday the 22d, so that the snow lies in some parts of the streets about six foot high." A more vivid description is given in a letter from Rev. John Cotton, of Newton (who was present at the funeral) to his father, Rev. Rowland Cotton, of Sandwich, dated Wednesday, Feb. 27, 1716-7, and preserved in the Library of the Massachusetts Historical Society: "Hon⁴. Father, I left 3 letters at Savel's yᵉ & yᵉ last week, besides 1 I put into Ezra Bourne hand *last Wednesday night at Cambridge*, wᵉ night (as he went to Malden & there I suppose kept prisoner till now) so I went to Boston, & by reason of yᵉ late great & very deep snow I was detained there till yesterday. I got with difficulty to yᵉ ferry on Friday, but cdnt get over: went back to Mr. Belcher's where I lodgd. Try'd again yᵉ next day. Many of us went over yᵉ ferry — Majʳ Turner, Price, Lynde, Brattle, Sogersby, Holyoke, Sewall, &c., & held a council at Charlstown, & having heard of yᵉ gᵗ difficulty of a butcher going tow'd neck of land, who was founder'd, dug out, &c., yᵗ we were quite discoragᵈ: went back & lodg'd wᵗ abundance of heartiness at Mr. Belchers. Mr. White & I tradg'd thrᵒ up to yᵉ South, where I knew Mr. Cobman was to preach in yᵉ forenoon, when he design'd to give the separate character of Mr. Pemb., [Rev. Ebenezer Pemberton, who died Feb. 13, 1717] wᵒ yᵉ wasn't time for on yᵉ Lecture, wᵗ he did sweetly & well; telling how emulous he always was to excell; his candle envied, &c., yᵗ when we saw him stand up how our expectations wᵉ always rais'd & yᵗ he always exceeded 'em & never deceiv'd 'em. Mr. Sewal upon — we have yᵉ Treas. in earthen vessels &c. Mr. Sewal spake well, very well, of his ascended Master & father, concerning wᵐ he cdnt be wholly silent, & then gave a breif, full, & good character, together wᵗ his last words wᵉ Messr.

Immediately after the decease of Mr. Brattle the Church adopted measures to supply the vacancy thus occasioned. A meeting for that purpose was duly appointed, and its proceedings were minutely recorded by President Leverett, in his Diary, preserved in the Library of Harvard College. As the result was so important, securing the settlement of a pastor who fed the flock of Christ nearly sixty-seven years, almost as long as the combined ministry of his five predecessors, this record is worthy of publication: "Friday, April the 19th, 1717. At a meeting of the Church of Christ in Cambridge. 1. The President being desired by the deacons and brethren opened the meeting with prayer. 2. The deacons proposed that a moderator might be chosen for the ordering and directing the meeting. 3. Voted, that the President be moderator of this meeting. He submitted to the vote of the brethren of the Church, and, opening the design and intention of the meeting, earnestly desired that every body would freely discover their minds and declare what measures they thought proper, and what steps they would take in order to a settlement of the ministry in this place. After a due time of silence Mr. Justice Remington expressed himself, that the nomination of some suitable persons seemed to be the first step to be taken. Some other spake to the same effect. No opposition being expressed, a vote was called and it was voted. 4. Voted, that the brethren express their minds as to nomination in writing, and the three persons that shall have the most votes shall be the persons nominated, out of which an election shall be made of one, in order to be settled in the pastoral office in this

Williams writ down. They'll all be in print. On Monday I assay'd again for Newton; but 'twas now also in vain. Nobody had been from Cambr. & there was lodg'd there Mr. Gerrish, Rogers, Fitch, Blowers, Prescot, Whiting, Chevers, & some others. Mr. Gerrish preach'd 23 Numb. 10, Mr. Rge beg. with prayer. Mr. Fitch beg. in ye aft'n. Mr. Blow. preach'd 2 Ex. 5 ult. clause. At Boston wr lodg'd as prisoners Mr. Sheph. Loring, Barnard, Holyoke, Porter, &c.

"I ordered my horse over ye ferry to Bostn yesterday, designing to try Roxbury way — but was so discorag'd by gentlemen in town, especially by ye Govr. wt whom I din'd yt I was going to put up my horse and tarry till Thursd. & as I was going to do it I met Cap. Prentice, Sam. Jacks. [Samuel Jackson] Stowell, &c. come down on purpose to break ye way & conduct me home — we yy kindly did & thro favor safely, last night; but wt such difficulty yt I design not down tomorrow. Tho' ye Dr's mind, he told me yesterday run much on a thaw — his text tomorrow ∧ 47, 18. They were afraid of a sudden thaw, bec. of a mighty flood. Before Cutler's door, so great was ye bank that yy made a handsome arch in it & sat in chairs, wt yr bottles of wine, &c. Denison came over yest. upon sno shoes & designs back tomorrow. I suppose bec. of Conventions *last week*, yr County was generally w'out preaching. I believe ye like was never known as to ministers absence from yr parishes," etc.

church. Pursuant to this vote, the brethren were desired by the moderator to write and bring in their votes, which they did; and upon the view, numbering and declaring the vote, Mr. Henry Flint, Mr. Jabez Fitch, and Mr. Nathaniel Appleton were the three persons agreed to be nominated, out of which the brethren should proceed to an election. Accordingly the moderator desired the brethren of the Church to bring in their votes for the choice of a person to settle in the ministry in this place, viz. one of three before nominated persons. Pursuant hereto the church brought in their votes in writing. 5. Upon sorting and numbering the votes, Mr. Nathaniel Appleton was by the church elected to the work of the ministry, in order to the taking upon him the pastoral office as God shall open the way thereunto. This was by a great majority; the votes for Mr. Appleton being 88, and the votes for Mr. Flynt but 8. The moderator declared to the church their election of Mr. Appleton as aforesaid. 6. It was proposed that those that had not voted for Mr. Appleton in writing might have the opportunity to manifest their satisfaction with the vote that had passed, that the brethren would manifest that they chose him as aforesaid by lifting up their hands, which was complied with, and it is said that there were but two that had acted in the foregoing votes that did not hold up their hands." After appointing a committee to ask the concurrence of the town with the church in their choice, "the moderator concluded the meeting with returning thanks to God for the peaceable and comfortable management of the affairs of the church. Laus Deo." [1] The town concurred, and Mr. Appleton was ordained Oct. 9, 1717. Dr. Increase Mather preached and gave the charge; Dr. Cotton Mather gave the right hand of Fellowship; and they, together with Rev. Messrs. John Rogers, of Ipswich, and Samuel Angier, of Watertown, imposed hands. Ministers and delegates of eleven churches in Boston, Charlestown, Watertown, Ipswich, Newton, Lexington, and Medford, "were invited," says President Leverett, "and were all present except Mr. Gibbs, who could not attend by reason of indisposition. The solemnity was carried on with as great decency and good order throughout as has been ever remembered at any time in any place. Laus Deo."

The town, having concurred with the church in the invitation to Mr. Appleton, voted, May 27, 1717, that the sum of one hun-

[1] This election was the more gratifying to President Leverett, because Mr. Appleton was a nephew of the President's wife. Twenty years afterwards, Mr. Appleton was gratified in a similar manner by the election of his brother-in-law, Rev. Edward Holyoke, to the Presidency of Harvard College.

dred pounds, and the stranger's money, the improvement of the
parsonage, and all other perquisites which our late Rev^d. Pastor
. . . . enjoyed, be annually paid to and enjoyed by the Rev. Mr.
Nath. Appleton, he settling in the work of the ministry, amongst
us, during his continuance therein." The Parsonage erected in
1670 having become dilapidated, the town voted, Aug. 1, 1718,
"that the sum of two hundred and fifty pounds be granted for
the building a new Parsonage-house, provided the sum of one
hundred and thirty pounds of the said money be procured by the
sale of town, propriety, or ministry lands in said town, as may be
thought most proper to be disposed of for said use." Accordingly, the church farm in Lexington was sold, and so much as
was not appropriated for the Parsonage was invested in a permanent fund. The records do not distinctly indicate whether
the Parsonage was wholly or only partly rebuilt. But Dr.
Holmes, writing in 1800, says, "All the ministers, since Mr.
Mitchell, have resided at the Parsonage. The front part of the
present house, at the Parsonage, was built in 1720." [1] The whole
house was taken down in 1848.

The congregation seems to have soon increased, demanding
additional room; and it was voted, Aug. 1, 1718, "that a new
upper gallery in our meeting-house over the women, agreeable to
the gallery over the men, be erected and built, provided the corporation of Harvard College be at the charge of the same; which
the Rev. Mr. President Leverett, on behalf of the College, offered
to do; the whole of the gallery on the south side of our meeting-
house being then resigned for the use of the scholars, excepting
the two wings of the front seat, which are to be improved by the
town till such time as the scholars have occasion for the same,
and no longer." Notwithstanding this enlargement of the seating capacity of the house, the people on the westerly side of Menotomy River desired better accommodation, and as early as May
10, 1725, petitioned the town to consent that they might become
a separate precinct. The town withheld its consent, on the
ground that "near one half of said inhabitants" had not signed
the petition. The request was renewed in 1728, but was not
successful until four years later. The General Court having dismissed the petition of James Cutler and others for incorporation
as a religious precinct, Nov. 8, 1732, a new petition, slightly
differing in form, was presented soon afterwards; which was
granted Dec. 27, 1732, and Menotomy became a precinct, with

[1] Mass. Hist. Coll., vii. 30.

substantially the same bounds which were assigned to it when it was incorporated as a town in 1807. This separation appears to have been entirely amicable, and a spirit of Christian fellowship and love is indicated by an act of the church mentioned by Dr. Holmes in "Coll. Mass. Hist. Soc.," vii. 33: "On the Lord's day, September 9, 1739, a church was gathered in this precinct by the Rev. Mr. Hancock of Lexington; and on the 12th day of the same month, the Rev. Samuel Cooke was ordained its pastor. On this occasion, the First Church in Cambridge voted, that £25 be given out of the church stock to the Second Church in Cambridge, to furnish their communion table in a decent manner."

In 1753 the First Parish resolved to erect a new meeting-house, and desired the College to defray a part of the expense; whereupon the corporation voted, Dec. 3, 1753, to pay "one seventh part of the charge of said house," provided the students should have the use of the whole front gallery, and "at least the third or fourth pew as to the choice" be set apart for "the President for the time being and his family." The erection of the house was delayed about three years. It "was raised Nov. 17, 1756, and divine service was first performed in it July 24, 1757."[1] Meantime further negotiation was had with the College, and a proposition was made to place the new house farther from the street, which would "very much secure it from fire as well as render the appearance of it much more beautiful," and also would render it "absolutely necessary in order to a suitable accommodation of the Parish that they should be allowed the use of a part of the President's orchard behind their said new meeting-house, where when they come to attend on divine worship they might place their horses, chairs, chaises, &c." Desiring "to make the said situation of the new meeting-house as convenient as may be," the corporation voted, Sept. 6, 1756, to grant to the Parish the use of a strip of land one hundred and sixteen feet and four inches in length by thirty-two feet and ten inches in width, on certain conditions; viz., "(1.) That the scholars' gallery shall be in the front of the said meeting-house, and the fore part of the said gallery seventeen feet on a perpendicular line from the said front, and that they shall enjoy all that space of the said front gallery contained within the mitre lines drawn from the angles where the foreparts of the side gallerys meet with the forepart of the front gallery to the corner-posts of the house, saving what shall be cut off from the said mitre lines by a pew at each corner of

[1] *Coll. Mass. Hist. Soc.,* vii. 34.

said house of about seven feet square.[1] (2.) That the said new meeting-house shall front southerly down the street, in the manner the old one now doth. (3.) That the front of the said new meeting-house be two and an half or three feet behind the backside of the old meeting-house. (4.) That there be a liberty for the President of the College to cart into his back yard, viz., at the backside of the said new meeting-house, wood, hay, boards, &c., for his own or the College use, as there shall be occasion for it." These conditions were accepted by a Committee of the Parish. The amount paid by the College is stated at £213 6 8. If this was exactly "one seventh part of the charge," the whole cost of the new house was £1,493 6 8, and the sum payable by the Parish was £1,280.[2]

[1] By consent of the corporation, the width of the gallery was reduced to fifteen feet and seven inches. Also a portion of "the mitral part" of the gallery was relinquished, "provided, that the part we thus cede to the Parish shall not be occupied by the negroes." The pew selected for the President was "that on the left hand entering in at the front door, if it may be had, and if not, then the third pew on the east side of the pulpit." The corporation also paid "for erecting two pews in the scholars' gallery in the new meeting-house for the Tutors to sit in."

[2] A large portion of this amount was subscribed by individuals, as appears by a MS. in the Library of Harvard College, entitled, "List of the number of subscribers and sums subscribed for building the N. Meeting house in Cambridge.["]

Sam¹. Kent,	£13. 12. 0
Nath¹. Kidder,	13. 12. 0
Peter Tufts,	14. 2. 0
Isaac Watson,	9. 6. 8
Sam¹. Whittemore,	12. 0. 0
Jacob Watson,	7. 0. 0
John Wyeth,	10. 0. 0
Peleg Stearns,	13. 6. 8
John Warland,	7. 6. 8
Isaac Bradish,	8. 0. 0
W⁴. Manning,	10. 13. 4
John Winthrop,	21. 11. 7
Judah Monis,	13. 6. 8
Ebenʳ. Fessenden,	11. 6. 8
Richᵈ. Champney,	8. 0. 0
Eb. Stedman,	17. 3. 0
Z. Boardman,	9. 6. 8
Edm. Trowbridge,	20. 0. 0

Edwᵈ. Ruggles,	6. 13. 4
Sam¹. Danforth,	14. 5. 0
Saml. Sparhawk,	13. 6. 8
W. Brattle,	26. 0. 0
Edw. Manning,	7. 4. 0
Edw. Wigglesw[orth]	16. 2. 8
Thos. Soden,	10. 0. 0
Edwᵈ. Marrett,	11. 6. 8
Jnᵒ. Fessenden,	10. 0. 0
Owen Warland,	7. 6. 8
Wᵐ. How,	8. 0. 1
Henry Flynt,	9. 6. 8
John Hicks,	7. 10. 0
Wᵐ. Angier,	7. 1. 0
Jonᵃ. Sprague,	10. 14. 0
Moses Richardson,	8. 12. 0
Mr. Appleton,	13. 6. 8
Ebenʳ. Bradish,	14. 10. 0
Thomas Kidder,	10. 0. 0
Jonᵃ. Hastings,	20. 0. 0
Stephen Prentice,	10. 13. 4
James Read,	10. 3. 0
Fr. Foxcroft,	18. 13. 4
Caleb Prentice,	8. 10. 0
Sam¹. Hastings,	11. 15. 0
Deacon Prentice,	8. 0. 0
Eb. Wyeth,	8. 0. 0
John Stratton,	8. 0. 0
Seth Hastings,	10. 0. 0
S. Thatcher,	10. 3. 4
Widow Tufts,	13. 6. 8
Am. Marrett's heirs,	8. 0. 0
And. Boardman,	16. 10. 0
Chr. Grant,	8. 5. 0
Wid. Sar. Hastings,	15. 0. 0
Richᵈ. Gardner,	13. 3. 4
Stephen Palmer,	7. 0. 0
H. Vassall,	20. 0. 0

No. 6.	No. 5.	No. 4.	No. 3.	No. 2.	No. 1.	
Richardson	Mary Tufts.	Samuel Kent.	Foxcroft.	Peter Tufts.	Edm. Trowbridge.	

No. 7.					
R. Gardner.		No. 37.			
		Hancock.			
No. 8.		No. 38.			
Bradish.		Sam'l Whittemore.			
No. 9.		No. 39.			
Edm. Trowbridge. ASSIGNED FOR Wm. Fletcher.		Stephen Prentice.			
		No. 40.		No. 51.	No. 58.
		Wm. Manning.		Sam'l Thatcher.	R'd Dana.
No. 10.		No. 41.		No. 52.	No. 57.
Rich'd Champney.		Aaron Hill.		E. Wyeth.	Peleg Stearns.
No. 11.		No. 42.		No. 53.	No. 56.
Seth Hastings.		John Hicks.		Caleb Prentice.	William How.
No. 12.		No. 43.		No. 54.	No. 55.
John Fessenden.		Isaac Bradish.		Isaac Watson.	James Read.

No. 13.	No. 14.	No. 15.	No. 16.	No. 17.	No. 18.
Stephen Palmer, Jun'r	J. Warland.	Appleton.	Holyoke.	Vassall.	Phips.

PLAN OF THE MEETING-HOUSE.

No. 36.	No. 35.	No. 34.	No. 33.	No. 32.	No. 31.
Widow Sarah Hastings.	Jon⁴ Hastings.	Colledge.	Nathaniel Kidder.	Samuel Hasting.	Ebenezer Wyeth.

No. 67.	No. 68. Widow L. A. v FL. SSENDEN. [Jbr. or Eben⁴]	No. 69.	No. 50.	No. 30.
John Dickson.		Inman.	Mik. Gill.	Sprague.

No. 49.

Thomas Soden.

No. 29.

Caleb Dana.

No. 48.

Henry Prentice.

No. 28.

E. Ruggles.

No. 59.	No. 63.
S. Danforth.	Eben⁴ Stedman.

No. 47.

Mr. Marrits Heirs.

No. 60.	No. 64.
J. Morris.	Z. Bordman.

No. 46.

Owen Warland.

No. 27.

Bordman.

No. 61. Grant.	No. 65. William Angier.

No. 45.

Edw⁴ Manning.

No. 26.

Wigglesworth.

No. 62.	No. 66.
E. Marrett.	John Stratton.

No. 44.

Jacob Watson.

No. 25.

Eben⁴ Stedman.

No. 19.	No. 20.	No. 21.	No. 22.	No. 23.	No. 24.
Brattle.	Ministerial Pew.	Winthrop.	Sparhawke.	Oliver.	Josiah Morse.

ERECTED IN CAMBRIDGE 1756.

The house thus erected by the joint contributions of the College, the Parish, and individuals, served its purpose until 1833, when it was taken down, and the land on which it stood was sold to the corporation of Harvard College. "In this edifice all the public commencements and solemn inaugurations, during more than seventy years, were celebrated; and no building in Massachusetts can compare with it in the number of distinguished men, who at different times have been assembled within its walls. Washington and his brother patriots in arms there worshipped, during the investment of Boston by the Provincial army, in 1775. In 1779, the delegates from the towns of Massachusetts there met and framed the Constitution of the Commonwealth, which the people of that State ratified in 1780. There Lafayette, on his triumphal visit to the United States, in 1824, was eloquently welcomed, during the presidency of Dr. Kirkland."[1]

Long before the "triumphal visit" of Lafayette, and several years before the erection of this famous edifice, another distinguished foreigner, Rev. George Whitefield, visited America, creating nearly as much excitement as Lafayette himself; with this difference, however, that while all united to honor the one, the other was vehemently applauded by some and resolutely and sternly opposed by others. Without discussing the subject in controversy between him and his opposers, it is sufficient here to record the historical fact, that the Pastor of the Cambridge Church and the Faculty of Harvard College set their faces as a flint against Mr. Whitefield, who had denounced the College and the New England clergy, as teachers of an unsavory and unprofitable religion, and alleged that a large number of grave and learned divines, held in honor and reverence throughout the vicinity, were in fact unconverted and destitute of vital piety. Professor Wigglesworth and others published vigorous replies to Mr. Whitefield, who was finally induced to retract or essentially modify his accusations against the College. Mr. Appleton declined to admit Mr. Whitefield into his pulpit, in accord-

B. Hancock,	10. 0. 0	Jos^h. Morse,	6. 13. 6
Pr. Holyoke,	20. 0. 0	Aaron Hill,	5. 1. 0
John Dickson,	13. 6. 8		
Rich. Dana,	15. 0. 0	L. M.	836. 2. 0
Caleb Dana,	13. 6. 8	— in O. T.	6270. 1. 3
Mr. Fletcher,	14. 0. 0	The sum total is not precisely accurate.	
Lt. Govr. [Phips]	40. 0. 0	A copy of the original Plan of this meet-	
Mr. Inman,	10. 0. 0	ing-house is here reproduced.	

[1] Quincy's *Hist. Harv. Univ.*, ii. 468.

ance with the advice of his brethren, which was published in
the "Boston Evening Post," Jan. 7, 1745, as follows:—

"Cambridge Jan. 1, 1744-5. At a meeting of the Association
of this and the neighboring towns, present, the Reverend Mes-
sieurs John Hancock of Lexington, William Williams of Weston,
John Cotton of Newton, Nath[l]. Appleton of Cambridge, Warham
Williams of Waltham, Seth Storer of Watertown, Eben[r]. Turell
of Medford, Nicholas Bowes of Bedford, Samuel Cook of Cambridge. The Rev. Mr. Appleton having applied to his brethren
of said association for our advice, relating to a request which hath
been made to him by a number of his church and congregation,
that he would invite the Rev. Mr. George Whitefield to preach in
Cambridge; after supplications to God and mature consideration
of the case proposed, and the several pleas made in favor of said
request, and the state of the town, as also the many weighty objections which lie against the said Mr. Whitefield, with respect
to his principles, expressions, and conduct, which are not yet
answered, nor has any Christian satisfaction been given by him
for them; considering also how much the order, peace and edification of the churches of this land are endangered, together with
the unhappy, divided state of many of them;—It was unanimously voted, that it is not advisable, under the present situation
of things, that the Rev. Mr. Appleton should invite the Rev. Mr.
Whitefield to preach in Cambridge. And they accordingly declared, each of them for themselves respectively, that they would
not invite the said gentleman into their pulpits. ☞ The above
advice was signed by each member of the association.

"Attest,   •   JOHN HANCOCK, Moderator."

Another article relative to the same subject appeared in the
"Boston Weekly News Letter," June 27, 1745: "Whereas it is
reported in the Gazette or Journal of this week, that the Rev.
Mr. Whitefield preached last Saturday at Cambridge, to prevent
misapprehensions and some ill consequences which may arise
from thence, you are desired to give your readers notice that he
preached on the Common, and not in the Pulpit; and that he did
it, not only without the consent, but contrary to the mind, of the
Rev. Mr. Appleton the minister of the place."

As early as May, 1747, a petition was presented to the General Court that the inhabitants of that part of Cambridge which
afterwards became the town of Brighton might be incorporated
as a separate religious precinct. A protest was presented by
other persons residing on the same territory, and the petition

was dismissed. After a like unsuccessful attempt in April, 1748, the petition was renewed by a committee in December, 1749, in which it is said, " There is within the bounds of the proposed new parish on the south side of the river, ... 2660 acres and 81 rods of land, by the plan; 42 dwelling-houses; about 50 families; above 50 persons in full communion with the church; and this part of the town's proportion to the Province Tax in 1748 was £700. 11ˢ. 8ᵈ., old tenor, and 67 ratable polls, about 290 souls." It is also said : " We have supported the gospel among us some part of the year for fourteen years, during which time we set apart a house for divine worship that had been a dwelling-house : upon finding it too small for the congregation we erected a convenient house for the worship of God, ... and soon after we had winter-preaching in this house we concluded to have summer-preaching in it also : and we are now in the 5 year that we have had constant preaching." [1] This petition, like those which preceded it, was dismissed. It was followed by another in June, 1758, in which it is more definitely stated that it was " necessary for the inhabitants on this side the river, about twenty-seven years since, to procure preaching among ourselves during the winter season, which we for the space of fourteen years continued to support at our sole expense, paying our full proportion of the gospel in the old town ; but afterwards finding the house in which we met neither convenient nor large enough for the purpose, we did about thirteen years since erect a meeting-house of suitable dimensions in the most suitable place to accommodate the people on this side the river, and have ever since supported the public preaching of the gospel among us at our own charge (except about ten or eleven pounds per annum which has been allowed us by the First Parish for a few years last past)," etc. [2] So strong was the opposition, however, that this petition was dismissed ; and another which was presented Feb. 22, 1774, met the same fate. At last, nearly half a century after the commencement of regular religious services (for the winter), and about thirty-five years after the erection of a meeting-house in which public worship was offered throughout the year, the inhabitants on the south side of the river were incorporated by the General Court, April, 1779, as a separate precinct with authority to settle a minister, and to provide for his support by a parish tax, — " *excepting* Samuel Sparhawk, John Gardner, Joanna Gardner, and Moses Griggs, and their estates, who shall

[1] *Mass. Arch.*, xii. 368–371.   [2] *Mass. Arch.*, xiv. 73–76.

be exempted from all ministerial taxes to said precinct, so long as they shall live or reside within the same, or until they or either of them shall give their hands into the Secretary's Office of this State, desiring that they with their estates may be considered as part of said precinct." The subsequent proceedings are related by Dr. Holmes in "Coll. Mass. Hist. Soc.," vii., 86, 87: "In 1780, the church members on the south side of Charles River in Cambridge presented a petition to the church, signifying their desire to be dismissed and incorporated into a distinct church, for enjoying the special ordinances of the gospel more conveniently by themselves. The church voted a compliance with their petition; and they were incorporated on the 23d of February, 1783. The Reverend John Foster was ordained to their pastoral charge, November 4, 1784."

Besides the incorporation of the second and third precincts, resulting in the establishment of two more churches professing the same faith which had distinguished the parent church during the century and a half of its existence, Dr. Appleton witnessed yet another secession from his congregation, involving what he must have regarded as a departure from the faith and order of the churches. A subscription was commenced in 1759 for the erection of an edifice, which was opened Oct. 15, 1761, for the worship of God according to the forms prescribed by the Episcopal Church. The organization and history of Christ Church Parish will be more fully noticed elsewhere. It is sufficient to say here that it drew from Dr. Appleton's parish several of its richest and most aristocratic members. Socially and financially, he must have regarded their secession as a serious loss.

The ministry of this sixth pastor of the church was long and peaceful, — two thirds of a century in length, but not marked by any very extraordinary characteristics. "The written record of his labors as pastor comprises little more than long lists of persons received to the church, of adults and children who were baptized, and of persons married. The summing up is as follows: children baptized, 2,048; adults, 90; admissions to the fellowship of the church, 784. All through this long ministry the pastor was busy in the duties of his office, preaching the word, striving for the salvation of those under his care, and for the edifying of the body of Christ."[1] Among the methods adopted for the furtherance of this object, Dr. Holmes says that "in 1736, a committee, chosen by the church to consult with the

[1] McKenzie's *Hist. Lect.*, p. 147.

pastor respecting measures to promote a reformation, proposed and recommended to the church, as what they ' apprehended might be serviceable for reviving religion and suppressing growing disorders,' that there be a number of wise, prudent, and blameless Christians chosen among themselves, whose special care it should be to inspect and observe the manners of professing Christians, and such as were under the care and watch of the church. The proposal was adopted, and a committee was appointed, for the purpose expressed in the recommendation. This committee, which was a kind of privy council to the minister, though without authority, appears to have been very serviceable to the interests of religion ; and it was renewed annually, for the space of about fifty years." [1] It was provided that this committee should consist of " three in the body of the town, one upon the common, one in Charlestown End, two at Menotomy, and two on the south side of the River." The members first elected were Samuel Danforth, Esq., Andrew Bordman, Esq., John Bradish, Deacon Samuel Bowman, Benjamin Goddard, John Cutter, Ephraim Frost, Daniel Dana, and Deacon Samuel Sparhawk.

The faithful and useful services of Dr. Appleton were recognized by the College in the bestowment of a degree, which, however common it may have since become, had never before been conferred by that corporation, except upon Rev. Increase Mather in 1692, and which was therefore a notable mark of honor. The record bears date July 9, 1771 : " The Rev. Mr. Nathanael Appleton having been long an ornament to the pastoral character and eminently distinguished for his knowledge, wisdom, and sanctity of manners and usefulness to the churches, and having for more than fifty years exerted himself in promoting the interests of piety and learning in this society, both as a Minister and as a Fellow of the corporation, therefore, Voted, that the Degree of Doctor in Divinity be conferred on the said Rev. Mr. Nathanael Appleton, and that a Diploma for that purpose be presented to him."

The longest human life has an end. On the verge of ninety years Dr. Appleton on account of his " very advanced age and growing infirmities " requested that a colleague might aid him in the pastoral office. Accordingly, Rev. Timothy Hilliard was elected by the church and congregation and was duly installed. Dr. Appleton survived this event less than four months. " His public usefulness, though diminished, for a few of his last

---

[1] *Coll. Mass. Hist. Soc.,* vii. 33, 34.

years, by the infirmities of age, did not entirely cease but with his life. He died Feb. 9, 1784, in the ninety-first year of his age, and sixty-seventh of his ministry; and New England can furnish few, if any, instances of more useful talents, and of more exemplary piety, united with a ministry equally long and successful." [1] A memorial tablet marks the resting-place of his body in the old burial-ground.

The prolonged pastorate of Dr. Appleton was succeeded by the shortest which the church experienced, from its organization in 1636 to its division in 1829. Rev. Timothy Hilliard, born in Kensington, N. H., 1746, H. C. 1764, Tutor 1768–1771, Chaplain at Castle William, 1768, was ordained at Barnstable, April 10, 1771. The climate proving unfavorable to his health he resigned his charge at Barnstable, and was installed at Cambridge as colleague with Dr. Appleton, Oct. 27, 1783. His ministry here did not continue quite seven years, yet it was productive of good fruits. His immediate successor, Dr. Holmes, says of him: " Placed by Providence in this conspicuous station, his sphere of usefulness became much enlarged, his labors being now extended to the University. For this new sphere he was peculiarly qualified. ' His pulpit talents were excellent. He was pleasing in his elocution. In prayer he was exceeded by few, being ready in his utterance, pertinent on every occasion, and devotional in his manner. His discourses from the desk were never such as could be said to have cost him nothing, but were well studied, pure in the diction, replete with judicious sentiments, clearly and methodically arranged, instructive, serious, practical, and truly evangelical; so that his public services were useful and edifying to all ranks of men, both learned and unlearned.' He was ' ever viewed by the Governors of the University as an excellent model for the youth under their care who were designed for the desk; and they considered his introduction into this parish a most happy event.' . . . . Though firm in the maintenance of his own religious sentiments, he was ' eminently candid, and ready to embrace all good men.' In public and private life, he was exemplary for virtue and piety. . . . . ' There was no minister among us,' said President Willard, ' of his standing, who, perhaps, had a fairer prospect of becoming extensively useful to the churches of Christ in this Commonwealth.' . . . . In his last illness, which was very short, he was supported by the Christian hope, which gave him a religious su-

[1] *Coll. Mass. Hist. Soc.*, vii. 68.

periority to the fear of death. . . . . He died on the Lord's-day morning, May 9, 1790, in the forty-fourth year of his age."[1] His "bereaved, affectionate flock," erected a suitable monumental slab, in the old burial-place, over his mortal remains.

Mr. Hilliard was succeeded in the pastoral office by Rev. Abiel Holmes, who was born in Woodstock, Conn., Dec. 24, 1763, Y. C. 1783, and was ordained pastor of a church at Midway, Georgia, Sept. 15, 1785, which church removed thither bodily from Dorchester, Mass. He resigned his pastorship of this church in June, 1791, and was installed pastor of the church in Cambridge, Jan. 25, 1792. His ministry was long and eventful. His parish was much enlarged by the establishment and growth of villages at Cambridgeport and East Cambridge, and it was subsequently diminished by their incorporation as a separate parish,[2] and the organization of churches in both villages. A new church was organized, Nov. 6, 1814, under the auspices of the College, which withdrew many of the officers and students from his congregation. These changes were effected peacefully, and with the coöperation of Dr. Holmes. He preached at the dedication of the meeting-house of the Cambridgeport Parish, and at the ordination of their first minister. He also assisted in the organization of the College Church.

But another change occurred, which occasioned much grief and sadness, and which he resisted earnestly and steadfastly though unsuccessfully. About the year 1815, a difference in opinion, which had for several years existed between the Trinitarian and Unitarian Congregationalists, attained such prominence as to disturb the relations between pastors of churches, and to rend the churches themselves into fragments. Such was the sad effect here. The pastor felt it to be his duty to bear testimony against what he regarded as the errors of Unitarianism, and to prevent their dissemination from his pulpit. A majority of his church approved the measures which he adopted, and adhered to him with unswerving fidelity. A minority of the church, with a majority of the parish, disagreed with him in opinion, and insisted that, if he could not conscientiously teach such doctrines as they believed to be true, he should at least allow other clergymen to do so in his pulpit. A long and unhappy controversy en-

[1] *Coll. Mass. Hist. Soc.*, vii. 64–66. The quotations by Dr. Holmes are from President Willard's *Sermon* at the funeral of Mr. Hilliard.   [2] The Cambridgeport Parish, which included both Cambridgeport and East Cambridge.

sued, which resulted in a division of the church. For obvious reasons, the particular incidents of this controversy are not here repeated. Each party published its own version of the whole matter in 1829: one, in a pamphlet of 58 pages, entitled, "An Account of the Controversy in the First Parish in Cambridge; " the other, in a pamphlet of 103 pages, entitled "Controversy between the First Parish in Cambridge and the Rev. Dr. Holmes, their late Pastor." It may suffice to record the result. An ex-parte council, called by the First Parish, assembled May 19, 1829, and, after due deliberation, "Voted, That there is plenary evidence of the facts, that Dr. Holmes has materially varied in his ministerial and Christian intercourse from that of his two immediate predecessors, and from that of more than thirty years of his own ministry; that such change more essentially affects the peace, comfort, and edification of the Parish, than any mere change in speculation, or in points of dogmatical theology; that this change has been persisted in, contrary to the repeated remonstrances of a large majority of the Parish, consisting of about three-fourths of the legal voters, including several members of the church; that this course has greatly grieved them, and so far impaired their confidence in their pastor, as to preclude the possibility of continuing his ministerial relation to them, either with comfort to himself, or any prospect of advancing their religious interests. Voted, That the First Parish in Cambridge have sufficient cause to terminate the contract subsisting between them and the Rev. Dr. Holmes, as their minister, and this Council recommend the measure, as necessary to the existence and spiritual prosperity of the society. This Council wish it to be distinctly understood," it is added, " that the service, to which we have in Providence been called, is one of the most painful services of our life. We do not arraign or condemn the motives of the Rev. Dr. Holmes. We are happy to testify that all our impressions of his course, during the peaceful state of his society, are associated with the most interesting and honorable views of his ministerial character and the Christian spirit." [1] In accordance with this " Result," the Parish notified Dr. Holmes, June 11, 1829, that his " services will not be required or authorized in the public religious services in the meeting-house in said Parish hereafter." [2] And, as Dr. Holmes expressed the opinion that he was still the legal minister of the Parish, and professed a willingness to perform all his pastoral

[1] *Controversy*, etc., pp. 87, 88.　　　　　　[2] *Ibid.*, p. 87.

and ministerial duties, as heretofore, the Parish committee, on the succeeding day, closed the correspondence thus: "You do not owe any such duties as aforesaid to said Parish, and that said Parish refuses to accept from you any service, or services, as such minister, or pastor, thereof. Hereafter you cannot occupy nor use the pulpit of the meeting-house of said Parish, as it will be exclusively appropriated to such preacher, or preachers, as said Parish shall employ to supply it." [1] On the next Sabbath, Dr. Holmes and those who adhered to him held religious services in the old Court House. They also called an ex-parte council, which assembled June 17, 1829, and, after a full examination of the case, agreed in this result: "In view of all the facts and evidence presented to this council, they are unanimously of the opinion, that the Rev. Dr. Holmes has not in any way forfeited his office as pastor of the first church and parish in Cambridge; and that he is still, according to ecclesiastical usage, the pastor and minister of said church and parish." [2] As before stated, a majority of the church adhered to Dr. Holmes, and acknowledged him as their pastor; but the majority of the parish would never thereafter acknowledge such relationship, and the breach between the two has never been healed.

The minority of the parish organized a new society, and adopted the name of the "Shepard Congregational Society," with which the majority of the church, claiming to be the First Church, united to maintain public worship and the ordinances of the gospel. Dr. Holmes soon asked for a colleague, and his request was granted. Rev. Nehemiah Adams, Jr., was ordained Dec. 17, 1829. On account of physical debility, Dr. Holmes requested a dismission, which was granted by the church, and confirmed by a council. He preached his farewell sermon Oct. 2, 1831. He continued to preach occasionally until near the close of his life. He died, of paralysis, June 4, 1837, in the 74th year of his age. It is worthy of notice, that even during the unhappy controversy in the parish, no "railing accusation" is known to have been heard against the moral and Christian character of Dr. Holmes; even the council, which determined that he had forfeited his ministry by a steadfast persistence in what he regarded as his duty contrary to the desires of others whose opinions differed from his own, bear a frank and manly testimony to his worth and sincerity as a Christian. His present successor in the ministry has thus described his labors and his character: "The minis-

[1] *Controversy, etc.*, p. 96.   [2] *Account of the Controversy, etc.*, p. 35.

try of Dr. Holmes here was but a few months short of forty years. With a single exception, it was the longest which the church has known. For nearly the whole of the time he was the only pastor in this part of the town, and he stood at the centre of a large parish, making his influence felt in every direction. He preached the word with fidelity and diligence. He fulfilled the various offices of our holy religion. He instructed the children, and gave them books. He formed libraries for the use of the parish. He watched over the schools. He gave of his substance to the poor. He brought into the parish the aid of others whom he esteemed able to edify the people. He zealously followed every good work. . . . . Dr. Holmes left a large number of printed works, consisting chiefly of sermons preached on various occasions. . . . . He published a small ' History of Cambridge,' [1] which is invaluable to any one interested in the ancient town. His largest work was ' The Annals of America from the Discovery by Columbus in the year 1492 to the year 1826. . . . . He was connected with a number of societies. From 1798 he was a most devoted friend of the Massachusetts Historical Society, and for more than twenty years its corresponding secretary. He was one of the founders of the Society for promoting Christian Knowledge, and of the American Education Society. He was a member of the American Academy of Arts and Sciences, one of the Trustees of the Institution at Andover, and an Overseer of Harvard University. His degree of Doctor of Divinity was received from the University of Edinburgh about 1805, and he was made Doctor of Laws by Alleghany College, in 1822." [2]

Dr. Holmes was the last pastor of the whole church. Each of the two branches, into which it was divided in 1829, asserts its claim to be " The First Church in Cambridge." Without reference to the validity of their respective claims, in a brief sketch of their history after the division, it seems most natural and proper to speak first of that branch which adhered to Dr. Holmes, and with which he remained connected during the residue of his life.

Rev. Nehemiah Adams, H. C. 1826, D. D. Amherst, 1847, was ordained Dec. 17, 1829, as colleague pastor. During his ministry there were " large additions to the church upon confession of faith. The loss of members was soon more than made good." [3] Religious services were held in the old Court House,

---

[1] In Coll. Mass. Hist. Soc., vii. 1-67.   [2] Ibid., pp. 222, 223.
[3] McKenzie's Hist. Lect., pp. 210-213.

until a new edifice, erected at the northwest corner of Holyoke and Mount Auburn streets, was completed; the corner stone was laid Sept. 21, 1830, and the house was dedicated Feb. 28, 1831. The pastorate of Mr. Adams was short. He accepted an invitation to become pastor of the Essex Street Church in Boston, and his connection with the church here was dissolved by an ecclesiastical council, March 14, 1834.

Mr. Adams was succeeded by Rev. John Adams Albro, who was born at Newport, R. I., Aug. 13, 1799; studied law at Litchfield, Conn., and, after practising that profession about two years, entered the Theological Seminary at Andover, from which he graduated in 1827. He received from Yale College, the same year, the honorary degree of Master of Arts; and also received the degree of Doctor of Divinity from Bowdoin College, in 1848, and from Harvard College in 1851. He was ordained in Chelmsford in 1827, installed in Fitchburg, May 9, 1832, and again installed here on the 13th of April, 1835. After a faithful service of thirty years, Dr. Albro requested a release from pastoral duty, which was granted, and which took effect April 15, 1865. He continued to reside here, preaching occasionally in the neighborhood, until he departed this life, after a very short sickness, Dec. 20, 1866. His ministry was successful, and his memory is cherished by those among whom he labored so long and so diligently.

The successor of Dr. Albro was Rev. Alexander McKenzie, who was born at New Bedford, Dec. 14, 1830, H. C. 1859, and ordained at Augusta, Me., Aug. 28, 1861. He was installed here, Jan. 24, 1867, and thus far his labors have been rewarded by large accessions to the church, and by general peace and prosperity. A new and much more spacious meeting-house has been erected, during his ministry, at the northwesterly corner of Garden and Mason streets; the corner-stone was laid April 29, 1871, and the house was dedicated May 22, 1872. The old meeting-house, which had been in use for more than forty years, was sold, and, having been re-consecrated, is now a Catholic church.

The other branch of the original church, which retained its connection with a majority of the First Parish, held a meeting on the 12th of July, 1829, and, in consideration of the fact that the two Deacons, William Hilliard and James Munroe, had neglected to meet with the church in the meeting-house, but adhered to Dr. Holmes, and had acted as deacons at his administration of the

Lord's supper to the majority of the church in the Court House, " Voted, as said William Hilliard and James Munroe have separated themselves, as above stated, from said church, and abdicated or abandoned their offices as deacons therein, and left said church destitute of a deacon, that said Hilliard and Munroe severally be removed and dismissed from his office of deacon of said church, if the above stated facts do not amount, in law, to a legal abdication or abandonment of said office of deacon ; and that the office of deacon in said church is now vacant, and that it is expedient and necessary now to elect a deacon or deacons thereof. Voted, To elect by ballot. Voted, That Abel Whitney be a deacon of said church. Voted, That Sylvanus Plympton be the Clerk or Scribe of said Church."[1] Being thus reorganized, the church united with the parish in the settlement of a pastor. Rev. William Newell, born at Littleton, Feb. 25, 1804, H. C. 1824, D. D. 1853, accepted a call, and was ordained May 19, 1830. After a long and peaceful ministry, he resigned his pastoral office March, 1868. He still dwells among his people, universally respected and beloved, having, for several years after his resignation, performed most of the duties of a pastor (preaching excepted) as a labor of love. The First Parish erected a new meeting-house on the westerly side of Harvard Square, between the ancient burial-place and Church Street, which was dedicated Dec. 12, 1833. The College contributed a portion of the expense, and became entitled to certain rights in the new house, equivalent to its interest in the house erected in 1756, which was now removed, and the land on which it stood was sold to the College. For the space of forty years, up to 1873, the annual Commencements of Harvard College were celebrated in this new house, which is still standing ; and it is perhaps not extravagant to apply to it the language used by President Quincy concerning the former house ; namely, that no existing " building in Massachusetts can compare with it in the number of distinguished men who at different times have been assembled within its walls." After the resignation of Dr. Newell, the church remained destitute of a regular pastor until March 31, 1874, when Rev. Francis Greenwood Peabody was ordained and duly installed as shepherd of the flock. Mr. Peabody was born in Boston, graduated at H. C. 1869, and at the Theological School in Cambridge, 1872.

From the beginning, the First Church in Cambridge has had a regular succession of Deacons; and for the first two thirds of a

[1] *Controversy*, etc., p. 109.

century, it had also Ruling Elders. Until 1696, the Church Records are imperfect, so that the dates of early elections cannot be ascertained. The dates of death are obtained from other sources.

RULING ELDERS.

	Elected.	Died.	Age.
Richard Champney .	– –	Nov. 26, 1669	
Edmund Frost . . .	– –	July 12, 1672	
John Stone	Nov. 15, 1682	May 5, 1683	64
Jonas Clark	Nov. 15, 1682	Jan. 14, 1711	80

DEACONS.

	Elected.	Died.	Age.
Thomas Marrett . .	Before 1658	June 30, 1664	75
John Bridge . . .	Before 1658	1665	
Nath¹. Sparhawk . .	Before 1658	June 28, 1647	
Edward Collins . .	Before 1658	April 9, 1689	86
Gregory Stone . .	Before 1658	Nov. 30, 1672	82
Thomas Chesholm . .	After 1658	Aug. 18, 1671	
John Cooper . . .	After 1658	Aug. 22, 1691	73
Walter Hastings . .	After 1658	Aug. 5, 1705	74
Nath¹. Sparhawk . .	After 1658	1686–7	
Samuel Cooper . . .	March 22, 1705	Jan. 8, 1717–8	64
Nath¹. Hancock . .	June 7, 1705	April 12, 1719	80
Samuel Kidder . . .	Jan. 22, 1718	July 4, 1724	58
Joseph Coolidge . .	Jan. 22, 1718	Dec. 17, 1737	71
Nath¹. Sparhawk . .	Aug. 5, 1724	Nov. 8, 1734	67
Samuel Bowman . .	Aug. 5, 1724	1746	67
Samuel Sparhawk . .	April 12, 1734	April 4, 1774	75
John Bradish . . .	May 5, 1738	July 17, 1741	60
Sam¹. Whittemore . .	Nov. 24, 1741	1784	90
Henry Prentice ¹ . .	Nov. 24, 1741	Oct. 18, 1778	84
Aaron Hill	July 14, 1774	Oct. 16, 1792	62
Stephen Sewall . . .	May 18, 1777	July 23, 1804	71
Gideon Frost . . .	June 30, 1783	June 30, 1803	79
James Munroe . . .	June 30, 1783	Sept. 14, 1804	69
John Walton . . .	Nov. 19, 1792	Nov. 23, 1823	81
William Hilliard . .	April 5, 1804	April 27, 1836	57
Josiah Moore . . .	Jan. 4, 1805	May 1, 1814	67
James Munroe . . .	Aug. 2, 1818	May 31, 1848	73

¹ Resigned July 14, 1774.

At the division of the church in 1829, the two surviving Deacons, with a majority of the members, adhered to Dr. Holmes. Subsequently other Deacons were installed into office, as follows: —

	Elected.	Died.	Age.
Stephen T. Farwell .	April 30, 1837	Oct. 20, 1872	67
Charles W. Homer .	Jan. 4, 1849	Feb. 15, 1873	71
Charles T. Russell [1] .	July 2, 1869		
George S. Saunders .	July 2, 1869		
Francis Flint . . .	Feb. 27, 1874		
Charles W. Munroe [2].	Feb. 27, 1874		
James M. W. Hall .	Jan. 27, 1875		
Aaron H. Safford . .	Jan. 27, 1875		

The Deacons elected by the other branch of the church were as follows: —

	Elected.	Died.	Age.
Abel Whitney . . .	July 12, 1829	Feb. 22, 1853	70
Sidney Willard . .	Dec. 15, 1833	Dec. 6, 1856	76
Charles R. Metcalf .	May 1, 1853		
Augustus A. Whitney	May 1, 1853		

[1] Resigned Sept. 15, 1871.   [2] Resigned Jan. 27, 1875.

CHAPTER XVI.

ECCLESIASTICAL HISTORY.

CHRIST CHURCH. — A comprehensive and interesting "Historical Notice of Christ Church," is appended to a sermon by Rev. Nicholas Hoppin, D. D., on the reopening of the church, Nov. 22, 1857. This church was originally established as a missionary station by the "Society for the Propagation of the Gospel in Foreign Parts," under the charge of Rev. East Apthorp, who was born in Boston, 1733, and educated at Cambridge, England. "The original subscription for building the church is dated at Boston, April 25, 1759. The petition to the society was signed by Henry Vassal, Joseph Lee, John Vassal, Ralph Inman, Thomas Oliver, David Phips, Robert Temple, James Apthorp. At a meeting held at Boston, September 29, 1759, the six first named gentlemen, with the Rev. East Apthorp, were chosen as the building committee; Ralph Inman, Esq., was appointed Treasurer." [1] These "six first named gentlemen" resided in Cambridge, and were among the richest citizens, "each of whose income was judged to be adequate to the maintenance of a domestic chaplain." [2] The church edifice, which is still preserved in good condition, was erected on the southerly side of the common, between the old burial ground and Appian Way. "A piece of land, one hundred feet square, was bought of Mr. James Reed, for £16. 2s. 1½d., lawful money." . . . . "This with the same quantity bought of the Proprietors of the common and undivided lands of the Town of Cambridge and taken in from the Common, formed the church lot. The price paid to the Proprietors was £13. 6s. 8d. lawful money, the church also paying for the removal of the Pound. The line of the Common, which was originally curved, was thus straightened, the burying ground being also extended up to the church line." [3] At the meeting, Sept. 29, 1759, when the size and general plan of the edifice were

[1] *Hist. Notice, etc.*, p. 21.   [3] *Hist. Notice*, p. 22.
[2] *Coll. Mass. Hist. Soc.*, vii. 34.

determined, it was voted, "That the expense of executing the
whole building is not to exceed £500 sterling." [1]   But although
"the dimensions of the building proposed by the committee were
adopted by the architect without change, the whole cost of the
church, not including the land, was about £1800 sterling." [2]
"The church was opened for the performance of divine service,
Oct. 15, 1761."   Rev. Mr. Apthorp again visited England in
1765, where he received the degree of Doctor of Divinity, and
became successively Vicar of Croydon, Rector of St. Mary-le-
Bow, London, and a Prebendary of St. Paul's Cathedral.   He
died April 16, 1816, aged 88 years.

The next Rector of Christ Church was Rev. Winwood Sar-
jeant, supposed to be a native of England, who was ordained
Priest by Bishop Pearce, Dec. 19, 1756.   He commenced his
rectorship as a missionary in June, 1767, and continued to perform the duties of his office, until the commencement of the
Revolutionary War, when he retired to Kingston, N. H., and
afterwards to Newbury.   In 1777 he had an attack of paralysis,
and in 1778 went to England.   He died at Bath, Sept. 20, 1780.
"The congregation had almost entirely dispersed at the beginning of the war.   Perhaps no church in the country was more
completely broken up.   Of all the persons who took part in its
concerns, including the sixty-eight original subscribers for the
building (several of whom, however, were of Boston), and twenty
original purchasers of pews, not a name appears on the records
after the Revolution but those of John Pigeon, Esq., and Judge
Joseph Lee.   The former espoused the patriotic side; the latter
was a loyalist, but being a quiet man and moderate in his opinions, remained unmolested." [3]   Divine service is said to have
been had in the church a few times while the army remained in
Cambridge.   It was also occupied and much damaged by the
soldiers, who were destitute of proper barracks.   It "was left
for many years in a melancholy and desecrated condition, the
doors shattered and all the windows broken out, exposed to rain
and storms and every sort of depredation, its beauty gone, its

---

[1] *Hist. Notice*, p. 21.

[2] *Ibid.*, p. 23.   Possibly this enormous
excess over the estimated cost of the edifice occasioned some disaffection which
resulted in what seems to be an unaccount-
able delay of payment for the land on
which it was erected.   The land was
granted by the Proprietors of Common

Lands, May 9, 1760; they appointed a
committee, Nov. 20, 1769, to commence
a suit against the grantees; the purchase-
money was paid by Major John Vassall,
Jan. 6, 1670, but no interest was allowed,
though payment had been delayed nearly
ten years.

[3] *Hist. Notice*, p. 46.

sanctuary defiled, the wind howling through its deserted aisles and about its stained and decaying walls; the whole building being a disgrace instead of an ornament to the town. No effort appears to have been made for the renewal of divine worship till the beginning of the year 1790."[1] The edifice was then repaired, and an effort was made for the regular administration of religious services. Rev. Joseph Warren, Rev. William Montague, and others, officiated for short periods, but for nearly forty years the church was generally supplied with lay Readers, among whom were Theodore Dehon, afterwards Bishop of South Carolina, and Jonathan-Mayhew Wainwright,[2] afterwards Bishop of New York. The church was thoroughly repaired in 1825, and was again "opened for service July 30th, 1826, when the Rev. George Otis, M. A., then tutor in the University, preached a sermon, afterwards printed."[3] Mr. Otis was chosen Rector, but declined the office, as it was supposed to be inconsistent with his official engagements to the College; he "however continued to officiate for the church, and was virtually its minister, till his lamented and untimely death, at the age of thirty-two, February 25th, 1828."[4] Rev. Thomas W. Coit, D. D., was Rector from Easter, 1829, to Easter, 1835; Rev. M. A. D'W. Howe, D. D., for a few months in 1836 and 1837; and Rev. Thomas H. Vail from the spring of 1837 to Easter, 1839.

Rev. Nicholas Hoppin, a native of Providence, R. I., and a graduate of Brown University, 1831, commenced his labors as Rector in November, 1839, and ministered to the church longer than all his predecessors in that office. During his rectorship the congregation so increased that it became necessary to enlarge the church edifice, and twenty-three feet were added to its length in 1857. A subscription had been commenced, in 1855, to procure a chime of bells for the church; the design was now prosecuted more vigorously and with such success that thirteen bells, at a cost of about five thousand dollars, were placed in the belfry of the church, and were first chimed on Easter morning, April 8, 1860. After a faithful and successful ministry for more than thirty-four years, Dr. Hoppin resigned the rectorship April 20, 1874. His degree of Doctor of Divinity was conferred by Trinity College in 1859.

[1] *Hist. Notice*, p. 58.

[2] Grandson of Rev. Jonathan Mayhew of Boston, who, a half century earlier, was a most zealous and formidable adversary of Rev. Mr. Apthorp and of Episcopacy generally.

[3] *Hist. Notice*, p. 61.

[4] *Ibid.*, p. 62.

The present Rector, Rev. William-Chauncy Langdon, entered upon the discharge of his duties Jan. 2, 1876.

The Wardens of Christ Church have been as follows : —

1762,	David Phips,	John Vassall.
1763,	John Vassall,	Robert Temple.
1764–1765,	Robert Temple,	Richard Lechmere.
1766,	David Phips,	Thomas Oliver.
1767–1770,	Thomas Oliver,	John Vassall.
1771,	John Vassall,	Ezekiel Lewis.
1772,	Ezekiel Lewis,	John Fenton.
1773,	Joseph Lee,	Jonathan Sewall.
1774,	David Phips,	John Pigeon.
1791–1795,	Jonathan Simpson,	Nathaniel Bethune.
1796,	John T. Apthorp,	Andrew Craigie.
1797–1799,	Leonard Jarvis,	Samuel W. Pomeroy.
1800,	Samuel W. Pomeroy,	Abraham Biglow.
1801,	Abraham Biglow,	Richard Richardson.
1802–1803,	Richard Richardson,	Jonathan Bird.
1804–1809,	William Winthrop,	Ebenezer Stedman.
1810–1813,	William Winthrop,	Abraham Biglow.
1814–1815,	Abraham Biglow,	Samuel P. P. Fay.
1816–1819,	Abraham Biglow,	William D. Peck.
1820,	Abraham Biglow,	J. F. Dana.
1821–1825,	Abraham Biglow,	Jonathan Hearsey.
1826–1828,	Abraham Biglow,	Samuel P. P. Fay.
1829–1832,	Joseph Foster,	Abraham Biglow.
1833–1835,	Joseph Foster,	Samuel P. P. Fay.
1836–1840,	Samuel P. P. Fay,	Isaac Lum.
1841,	Charles C. Foster,	James Greenleaf.
1842,	James Greenleaf,	Isaac Lum.
1843,	Isaac Lum,	Luther Foote.
1844,	C. Gayton Pickman,	Charles Chase.
1845–1846,	C. Gayton Pickman,	William E. Carter.
1847–1851,	William C. Bond,	William E. Carter.
1852,	George P. Bond,	John M. Batchelder.
1853–1859,	George P. Bond,	Charles F. Foster.
1860,	Herbert H. Stimpson,	Luther Crane.
1861,	Luther Crane,	Samuel Batchelder, Jr.
1862–1863,	Herbert H. Stimpson,	Samuel Batchelder, Jr.
1864,	Abraham Edwards,	Samuel Batchelder, Jr.
1865–1871,	Samuel Batchelder, Jr.,	J. Gardner White.
1872,	Samuel Batchelder, Jr.,	Jos. Fay Greenough.
1873–1874,	Samuel Batchelder, Jr.,	Wm. A. Herrick.
1875–1876,	Samuel Batchelder, Jr.,	J. Gardner White.

CAMBRIDGEPORT PARISH. — A brief account has already been given (chapter xii.) of the establishment of the "Cambridgeport Meeting-house Corporation," in 1805, and of the "Cambridgeport Parish," in 1808; also of the erection, dedication, and destruction, of their brick meeting-house on Columbia Street, and the erection of the present meeting-house on Austin Street. The church connected with this parish was not organized until July 14, 1809. Its first pastor was Rev. Thomas Brattle Gannett, born in Cambridge, Feb. 20, 1789, H. C. 1809, and ordained Jan. 19, 1814. During his pastorate occurred that theological contest which rent the parish and church of Dr. Holmes asunder. The great majority of the Cambridgeport Parish, together with their pastor, adhered to what was styled the liberal party, and were thenceforth known as Unitarians. Mr. Gannett, however, did not take an active part in the contest, but devoted himself entirely to the inculcation of those moral duties and Christian graces which become the true disciples of Christ. Indeed, he is reported to have expressed the highest satisfaction, in his mature years, that he had never preached a doctrinal sermon. Early in 1833 he closed his labors with a flock which had abundant cause to regard him with profound respect and love. "A good man, — one like Nathaniel of old, without guile, — according to the gift that was in him, had gone in and out before the people, pure and godly in his conversation, charitable in his words and feelings as in his deeds, keeping peace with all men."[1] He remained in Cambridge about ten years after the close of his ministry, during which period he represented his fellow-citizens two years in the General Court, and served them faithfully three years in the office of Town Clerk. He afterwards took charge of the Unitarian Church in South Natick, to which place he removed in 1843, and died there April 19, 1851.

Rev. Artemas B. Muzzey, born in Lexington, Sept. 21, 1802, H. C. 1824, was ordained at Framingham, June 10, 1830, dismissed May 18, 1833, and installed here Jan. 1, 1834. He resigned May 4, 1846, and was succeeded by Rev. John F. W. Ware, H. C. 1838, who was installed Nov. 29, 1846, and resigned April 1, 1864. He is now pastor of the church in Arlington Street, Boston. Rev. Henry C. Badger was installed Jan. 15, 1865, resigned Oct. 1, 1865, and was succeeded by Rev. George W. Briggs, B. U. 1825, D. D. 1855, who was installed

[1] Sermon by Rev. John F. W. Ware, on the *Fiftieth Anniversary of the Settlement of Rev. Thomas B. Gannett*, p. 19.

April 3, 1867. The four successors of Mr. Gannett are still actively engaged in the ministry ; may it be long before judgment
shall be pronounced upon their completed labors.

DEACONS.

	Elected.	Died.	Age.
Nathaniel Livermore .	1809 [1]	Aug. 7, 1862	90
Ephraim Forbes . .	April, 1817	Nov. 1817	
Isaiah Bangs . . .	Feb. 21, 1842	Mar. 22, 1859	73
Nathaniel P. Hunt .	Feb. 21, 1842	Oct. 29, 1854	61

UNIVERSITY CHURCH. " Until 1812, the College government
and students had united in public worship with the inhabitants
of the First Parish in Cambridge ; but in that year the Overseers
expressed the opinion, that it would be for the advantage of the
students, should religious instruction on the Sabbath be given
within the walls of the University." [2] " On the morning of
Lord's-Day, 6th Nov. 1814, the Church was organized, in the
presence and by the assistance of the pastor and delegates of the
First Church in Cambridge." [3] " A distinct church being organized, public worship has since been conducted within the College Chapel by the Faculty of the Theological School." [4] Appleton Chapel subsequently became the stated place of worship,
and after about forty years the *ex-officio* service of the Theological Faculty ceased ; since which time the church has been under
the care of a pastor specially designated by the Corporation of
the College. The successive pastors and stated preachers have
been, —

Rev. Henry Ware, H. C. 1785, D. D. 1806, from 1814 to 1840.[5]
Rev. Henry Ware, Jr., H. C. 1812, D. D. 1834, from 1840 to 1842.
Rev. Convers Francis, H. C. 1815, D. D. 1837, from 1842 to 1855.
Rev. Frederick D. Huntington, A. C. 1842, D. D. 1855, from 1855
to 1860.
Rev. Andrew P. Peabody, H. C. 1826, D. D. 1852, LL. D. Roch. U.
1863, from 1860 to the present time.

[1] The date of election does not distinctly appear ; but Mr. Ware, in his Sermon before quoted, says : " The church
appears to have been fully organized on
the 14th July, 1809 ; Nathaniel Livermore
being its first deacon, as he was also its
last."

[2] Quincy's *Hist. H. U.*, ii. 309.
[3] McKenzie's *Hist. Lect.*, p. 184.
[4] Quincy's *Hist. H. U.*, ii. 310.
[5] Rev. Dr. Kirkland officiated as joint
pastor, until he resigned the Presidency
of the College in 1828.

FIRST BAPTIST. — The First Baptist Church was organized "at the house of Mr. Samuel Hancock" in Cambridgeport, Dec. 17, 1817, seventeen males and twenty-nine females then subscribing the "Articles of Faith and a Covenant."[1] The church was publicly recognized on the 25th day of the same month by a Council regularly convened; and on the same day the meeting-house, which had been erected at the junction of Magazine and River streets, was dedicated. This house was a wooden structure, which was enlarged in 1827 and twice afterwards; it was utterly consumed by fire Jan. 22, 1866. Preparations were immediately made for the erection of a much larger house on the same spot. The corner-stone was laid Aug. 17, 1866. The chapel was dedicated March 17, 1867, in which religious services were held until the completion of the main edifice, which was opened and dedicated Dec. 25, 1867, on "the fiftieth anniversary of the organization of the church, and of the dedication of the former house of worship." "The cost of the whole building was about $90,000." It is a spacious brick edifice, not only convenient to its occupants, but ornamental to the city. On the 8th of February, 1819, William Brown and twenty-one others (several of whom resided in Brighton) were "incorporated as a religious society, by the name of the Baptist Church in Cambridge."[2]

The first pastor of this church was Rev. Bela Jacobs, formerly pastor of the Baptist Church in Pawtucket, R. I. He was installed July 22, 1818, and served the church faithfully and successfully until May, 1833, when he resigned, and became Secretary of the Baptist Educational Association. He received the degree of A. M. from Brown University, 1822. A further notice of him will be found in connection with the Second Baptist Church, of which he was afterwards pastor. Rev. Stephen Lovell was installed March 24, 1834, and resigned May 15, 1836, "and immediately after his resignation united with the Methodist Church in Portland, Maine." He was afterwards associated with Rev. Thomas F. Norris, in the editorship of the "Olive Branch," and died in Boston, Sept. 29, 1858, aged 59 years. Rev. Joseph W. Parker, U. C. 1831, was ordained Dec. 11, 1836. The church enjoyed prosperity during his ministry, which continued until Jan. 1, 1854, when he resigned, and entered upon his duties as Secretary of the Northern Baptist Education Society and

[1] *Brief History of the First Baptist Church in Cambridge, etc.,* p. 3.　　[2] *Mass. Spec. Laws,* v. 282.

Financial Agent of the Trustees of the Newton Theological Institution. He received the degree of D. D. from Brown University, 1852. Rev. Sumner R. Mason, formerly pastor of the Baptist Church in Lockport, N. Y., entered upon his labors the first Sabbath in March," 1855, and "on the 25th of the same month he was publicly recognized by religious services." He received the degree of D. D. from Chicago University. His ministry was diligent and successful for somewhat more than sixteen years. It had an unexpected and tragical termination on Saturday evening, Aug. 26, 1871, when a disastrous collision of cars occurred on the Eastern Railroad, at Revere, Mass., by which about thirty persons were killed,[1] and a still larger number wounded, — some of them fatally. Among those who were killed outright was Dr. Mason. He died at his post, while engaged in his Master's service; for the object of his journey was to fulfil an engagement to preach the gospel. His mutilated body was identified on the next day, and was interred at Mount Auburn on the following Thursday, after appropriate funeral services in the presence of a great congregation, and in the house where he had so long been a living power.

The present pastor of the church, Rev. Hiram K. Pervear, B. U. 1855, had been pastor of the Second Baptist Church in Cambridge about seven years, and of the First Baptist Church in Worcester nearly eight years, before his public recognition here on the 5th of January, 1878.

The church has had nine Deacons, to wit : —

	Elected.	Died.	Age.
Levi Farwell . . .	Feb. 10, 1818	May 27, 1844	60
William Brown[2] . .	Feb. 10, 1818	June 25, 1861	75
Josiah Coolidge[2] . .	July 30, 1844	Sept. 13, 1874	87
George Cummings[3] .	Aug. 23, 1844		
Josiah W. Cook . .	Aug. 23, 1844		
William B. Hovey .	Jan. 29, 1849	July 4, 1871	75
Joseph A. Holmes .	Jan. 29, 1849		
Albert Vinal . . .	Feb. 19, 1850		
Joseph Goodnow . .	Oct. 13, 1871		

[1] Among the killed was Rev. Ezra Stiles Gannett, D. D., born in Cambridge, May 4, 1801, H. C. 1820, for many years colleague-pastor (with Rev. W. E. Channing, D. D.), and afterwards sole pastor of the church now in Arlington Street, Boston.

[2] Deacons Brown and Coolidge were "dismissed to the Church in Old Cambridge, Aug. 16, 1844."

[3] Removed to Lancaster in 1850.

FIRST UNIVERSALIST. — On the ninth day of February, 1822, Peter Tufts, Jr., and thirty-three others were "incorporated and made a body politic and religious society by the name of the First Universalist Society in Cambridge."[1] For some years previously, Rev. Hosea Ballou and others had occasionally preached in the school-house then standing on Franklin Street. Immediately after its incorporation the society commenced preparations for the erection of the meeting-house which now stands at the junction of Main and Front streets in Cambridgeport. The corner-stone was laid with masonic ceremonies by Amicable Lodge, June 24, 1822; and the house was dedicated to the worship of God on the 18th of the following December. The church was organized June 19, 1827.

The first pastor of this church was Rev. Thomas Whittemore, who was born in Boston, Jan. 1, 1800, ordained, June 13, 1821, and after preaching somewhat more than a year at Milford, commenced his labors here in April, 1822, but was not formally installed until April 23, 1823. He resigned the pastorate, and preached his farewell discourse May 29, 1831, but remained a citizen of Cambridge until the close of his life.

As early as June, 1828, he purchased the "Universalist Magazine" (which was established July 3, 1819), and changed its name to "Trumpet and Universalist Magazine." This paper he conducted with consummate skill and energy until Feb. 18, 1861, about a month before his death, when he was compelled, by sheer exhaustion, to relinquish the charge. He represented the town three years in the General Court, and served the city one year in the Board of Aldermen. For many years he was President of the Cambridge Bank, and also of the Fitchburg and the Vermont and Massachusetts Railroads. He continued to preach, almost every Sabbath, until near the close of life. In 1837, he published "Songs of Zion," a volume of sacred music, a portion of which was original. He was the author of "Notes and Illustrations of the Parables of the New Testament," 1834; "A Plain Guide to Universalism," 1840; "Memoir of Rev. Walter Balfour," 1852; "Life of Rev. Hosea Ballou," in four volumes, 1854, 1855; and "The Early Days of Thomas Whittemore, an Autobiography," 1859. His first and last literary work was "The Modern History of Universalism," of which the first edition was published in 1830. He made large collections for a second edition, and published the first volume in 1860; but the completion of the second

[1] *Mass. Spec. Laws*, v. 464.

volume was prevented by his death, which occurred March 21, 1861. Tufts College bestowed on him the degree of Doctor of Divinity in 1860.

Rev. Samuel P. Skinner commenced preaching here June 5, 1831, and was ordained on the nineteenth day of the same month. His ministry was very short. About the first of May, 1832, he removed to Baltimore, and was for a time engaged in teaching. He subsequently preached in several places, and at length settled in Chicago, Ill. He died August 12, 1858, aged 48.

Rev. Lucius R. Paige was born in Hardwick, March 8, 1802, commenced preaching June 1, 1823, and was ordained June 2, 1825. After laboring in several places, as an evangelist, more than two years, and performing the duties of a settled pastor nearly four years at Springfield, and about two years at Glouces-ter (now Rockport), he commenced his ministry here May 20, 1832, was installed July 8, 1832, and resigned July 1, 1839. He continued to preach, occasionally, nearly thirty years afterwards, until the precarious condition of his health compelled him to de-sist. During his pastorate he published "Selections from Emi-nent Commentators," in 1833, and "Questions on Select Portions of the Gospels, designed for the use of Sabbath Schools and Bible Classes," in 1838; also a Centennial Address at Hardwick, 1838. He subsequently wrote a "Commentary on the New Testament," in six volumes, of which the first was published in 1844 and the last in 1870. While engaged in this work, as a relaxation from severer studies, he gathered materials for this History of Cam-bridge. Meanwhile, his literary labors yielding scanty returns, he devoted the business hours of the day to the performance of secular duties. He was Town Clerk from March, 1839, to Janu-ary, 1840, and from March, 1843, to May, 1846; City Clerk from May, 1846, to October, 1855; Treasurer of the Cambridgeport Savings Bank, from April, 1855, to April, 1871, during the larger portion of which period he was also successively Cashier and President of the Cambridge Bank. He received the degree of A. M. from Harvard College, 1850, and that of D. D. from Tufts College, 1861.

Rev. Lemuel Willis was born at Windham, Vt., April 24, 1802, commenced preaching July 28, 1822, was ordained Oct. 2, 1823, and was installed here Oct. 1, 1842, having previously been settled at Troy, N. Y., Salem, Washington, N. H., and Lynn. He resigned Sept. 28, 1845, and was afterwards pastor at Claremont, N. H., South Orange, Mass., and Portsmouth,

N. H. Since 1856 he has generally resided at Warner, N. H. Though he has passed beyond the age of three-score years and ten, his eye is not yet dim, nor is his mind clouded ; and he continues to preach and perform other ministerial duties.

Rev. Luther J. Fletcher was ordained in 1843, commenced preaching here Jan. 4, 1846, and was installed on the 5th of the following April. He resigned April 14, 1848, and was afterwards settled at Lowell and at Buffalo, N. Y. He received the degree of D. D. from St. Lawr. Univ. 1876. Rev. Edwin A. Eaton, who had been previously settled at Newburyport, commenced preaching here Jan. 7, 1849, resigned April 25, 1852, and was afterwards settled in Providence for six years, and at South Reading for a similar period. He retired from the ministry about 1870, and is now an Insurance agent in Boston. Rev. Charles A. Skinner was ordained in 1848, labored a few years in western New York, and was installed here July 17, 1858. He retained the pastorship longer than any of his predecessors ; and after a peaceful and successful ministry he resigned Sept. 29, 1867, in order to become the pastor of the church in Hartford, Conn., which office he still sustains. Rev. Benjamin F. Bowles was ordained in 1848, and held the pastoral office successively at Salem, Southbridge, Natick, Melrose, Manchester, N. H., and Worcester. He was installed here Dec. 6, 1868, and resigned Jan. 31, 1873 ; since which time he has been pastor of the Second Church in Philadelphia. The present pastor of this church is Rev. Oscar F. Safford, a graduate of the Theological School, St. Lawrence University, 1862, who was ordained in 1862, and who was settled at Danvers, Charlestown, Chicago, and Springfield. He was installed here Jan. 1, 1874.

DEACONS.

	Elected.	Died.	Age.
Samuel Watson . .	July 12, 1827	Feb. 1855	87
Flavel Coolidge . .	July 12, 1827	Feb. 1, 1848	73
Isaac Kimball . . .	July 12, 1827	Oct. 14, 1831	74
Simon Ames . . .	Dec. 28, 1831	Oct. 28, 1841	51
Alvaro Blodgett [1] . .	July 28, 1843	May 14, 1874	58
Joseph P. Howlett :	July 28, 1843		
Ebenezer P. Holman .	Oct. 28, 1847	Dec. 17, 1859	47
Robert White . . .	May 29, 1874		

[1] Deac. Blodgett resigned Sept. 3, 1858, and was re-elected May 25, 1866.

SECOND UNIVERSALIST. — By an Act of the General Court, Feb. 11, 1823, Calvin Brooks and others[1] were incorporated as the "Second Society of Universalists in the town of Cambridge." They held meetings for a time in a school-house on Third Street, between Bridge and Gore streets, and afterwards worshipped with the Unitarian Society in their meeting-house on Third Street. In July, 1834, the Society hired what was then called "Berean Hall," on the northerly side of Cambridge Street, between Third and Fourth streets, and occupied it until the early part of 1843, when it was purchased, enlarged, converted into a meeting-house, and was dedicated on the 5th day of December. In 1865 this house was sold, and the Society erected the neat and commodious church now standing on the northerly side of Otis Street, between Third and Fourth streets, which was dedicated Sept. 26, 1866.

This parish had no settled pastor until 1834, when Rev. Henry Bacon commenced his labors in November, and was ordained on the 28th of December. He resigned in the spring of 1838, and was afterwards settled at Haverhill, Marblehead, Providence, and Philadelphia. He was born in Boston, June 12, 1818, and died in Philadelphia, March 19, 1856. His was a busy life. Besides faithfully performing his pastoral duties, he was a prolific writer in various periodicals, the author of some small volumes, and editor of the "Ladies' Repository" twenty years. Rev. Elbridge G. Brooks was ordained at West Amesbury, Oct. 19, 1837, and was installed here Sept. 16, 1838. He resigned early in 1845, and was subsequently settled in Bath, Me., Lynn, New York, and Philadelphia, where he is still actively engaged in the ministry. He has written much for various periodicals, and in 1873 published a volume entitled "Our New Departure." He received the degree of D. D. from Tufts College in 1867. Rev. William R. G. Mellen was ordained at Milford, May 17, 1843, and was installed here Oct. 26, 1845. He resigned in October, 1848, and was afterwards settled in Chicopee, Auburn, N. Y., and Gloucester; he served his country several years as a Consul in a foreign port; and has since had the pastoral charge of several Unitarian societies. Rev. Massena Goodrich was ordained at Haverhill Jan. 1, 1845, commenced his ministry here April 8, 1849, resigned in January, 1852, and was afterwards settled at Goff's Corner, Me., Waltham, and Pawtucket, R. I. In 1861 he became a Professor in the Theological School at Canton, N. Y.;

[1] *Mass. Spec. Laws*, vi. 78.

after two or three years he returned to Pawtucket, and resumed
his pastoral duties. He received the degree of A. M. from Tufts
College in 1863. Rev. Henry A. Eaton was born in South
Reading (now Wakefield) Nov. 27, 1825, ordained at Milford
Sept. 11, 1859, took charge of this parish on the first Sabbath
in May, 1855, and resigned at the end of September, 1857. His
health was broken down, yet he preached, more or less, for two
or three years at Waltham, and Meriden, Conn. He died at
Worcester, of consumption, May 26, 1861. Rev. Henry W.
Rugg was ordained in 1854, and having preached three or four
years on Cape Cod, commenced his pastorate here on the first of
March, 1858; resigned at the end of three years, and was after-
wards settled at Bath, Me., and Providence, R. I. Rev. S. L.
Roripaugh was ordained in 1856, was pastor of this flock from
January, 1862, to the end of the year, and has since beeen settled
at New Bedford, North Bridgewater, Joliet, Ill., Valhermosa
Springs, Ala., and Atlanta, Ga. Rev. James F. Powers, Tufts
College, 1861, was pastor from the first of December, 1863, until
April, 1866. He was afterwards settled in Malden, and about
1872 took orders in the Episcopal Church. Rev. Henry I. Cushman was ordained May 15, 1867, resigned May 31, 1868, and
was afterwards associate pastor of the Second Universalist Church
in Boston, and pastor of the First Universalist Church in Providence. His successor was Rev. Frank Maguire, a graduate of St.
Lawrence Theological School, 1863, whose pastorate extended
from Oct. 1, 1868, to Jan. 1, 1871, after which he was settled at
Fitchburg. He was ordained in 1868, and had previously
preached at Greenport, N. Y., and Waterville, Me. Rev. Sumner Ellis, ordained at Boston, Nov. 1851, and successively pastor
at Boston, Salem, Brighton, Lynn, Milwaukee, Chicago, and
Newark, had charge of this parish, as stated supply, from April
1, 1872, to Sept. 29, 1874, when he returned to Chicago. He
was succeeded, as " stated supply," by Rev. Henry I. Cushman,
Nov. 1, 1874, and by Rev. William A. Start of Melrose, Sept.
4, 1875. Mr. Start has recently been appointed Secretary of the
Massachusetts Convention of Universalists. A further notice of
him may be found in connection with the Third Universalist
Society.

The church was organized Jan. 1, 1836. Its Stewards or Deacons have been : —

	Elected.		Held office until
Ebenezer Tirrell . .	Jan. 1836	Died	Dec. 3, 1839
Victor Eaton . . .	March 2, 1838	Died	Nov. 20, 1847
Daniel Jewett . . .	Oct. 30, 1840	Resigned	Dec. 2, 1843
Marshall S. Boyer .	Dec. 2, 1843	Resigned	1859
Peter Shorfenburg .	Feb. 2, 1848	Died	June 18, 1854
Barnabas Binney .	Jan. 1856	Died	March 18, 1874
John B. Winslow .	March 2, 1860	Removed from the city.	
Jonas Woodard . .	March 2, 1860		
Otis H. Hendley . .	Jan. 1870	Died	April 25, 1871
John M. Hastings .	Jan. 1870		
John C. Burdakin .	Jan. 16, 1875		

FIRST METHODIST EPISCOPAL. — "From the first settling of Lechmere Point (or East Cambridge) the few inhabitants were obliged to attend church in Boston or Charlestown until the autumn of 1818, when the Methodist Society was formed by the following named persons, all of whom had been members of the church previous to their coming to the Point ; namely, William Granville,[1] Elizabeth Granville, Eliza Sargent, Lucinda Sargent, William Swindel, and Charles Elliot."[2] For a time they met in private houses ; and the first sermon to them was delivered by the Reverend Enoch Mudge in the house of Mr. William Granville. "Public worship was first regularly established in a school-house on North Third Street, where the Society worshipped until 1823, when Mr. Granville erected a small, convenient chapel on Gore Street, now occupied as a dwelling-house."[2] By an Act of the General Court, June 14, 1823, Amos Binney and others were incorporated as "Trustees of the Methodist Religious Society in Cambridge." "About this time a lot of land was donated to the society, on which a substantial brick church was erected, and dedicated in the autumn of 1825."[2] That house, on the southwesterly corner of Cambridge and Third streets, stood about forty-five years, when it was demolished, and a much larger brick edifice was erected on the same spot, at a cost of $45,000, which was dedicated December 12, 1872.

[1] Mr. Granville seems to have been a preacher or exhorter.   [2] MS. Letter from Mr. O. H. Darrell.

As nearly as can now be ascertained, the preachers in charge of this church were appointed as follows: —

1823,   Rev. Leonard Frost.
1824, 1825, Rev. D. Young. Died 12 March, 1826.
1826,   Rev. Ebenezer Blake.
1827, 1828, Rev. Enoch Mudge. Died 2 April, 1850.
1829,   Rev. Ephraim Wiley.
1830,   Rev. Bartholomew Otheman.
1831,   Rev. Ephraim Wiley.
1832,   Rev. Leonard B. Griffing.
1833,   Rev. George Pickering. Died 8 Dec., 1846.
1834,   Rev. James C. Bontecou.
1835,   Rev. Edward Otheman.
1836,   Rev. Elijah H. Denning.
1837,   Rev. Stephen G. Hiler, Jr.
1838, 1839, Rev. Henry B. Skinner.
1840, 1841, Rev. Edmund M. Beebe.
1842, 1843, Rev. Shipley W. Willson. Died 30 Dec., 1856.
1844, 1845, Rev. Samuel A. Cushing.
1846, 1847, Rev. Joseph A. Merrill. Died 22 July, 1849.
1848, 1849, Rev. James Shepard.
1850, 1851, Rev. John W. Merrill, W. U. 1834, D. D. (McK. C.) 1844.
1852, 1853, Rev. William H. Hatch.
1854, 1855, Rev. Converse L. McCurdy. Died 22 Nov. 1876.
1856,   Rev. Abraham D. Merrill.
1857, 1858, Rev. George Bowler.
1859, 1860, Rev. Moses A. Howe. Died 27 Jan. 1861.
1861, 1862, Rev. David K. Merrill.
1863,   Rev. Samuel Tupper. Died 11 Jan. 1869.
1864, 1865, Rev. William H. Hatch.
1866–1868, Rev. Isaac J. P. Collyer. Died 7 May, 1872.
1869, 1870, Rev. Pliny Wood. Died 1873.
1871–1873, Rev. William P. Ray.
1874, 1875, Rev. Charles T. Johnson, W. U. 1863.
1876,   Rev. George W. Mansfield, W. U. 1858.

THIRD CONGREGATIONAL (UNITARIAN). — The Third Congregational Society was incorporated June 16, 1827,[1] and in the course of the same year erected a substantial brick meeting-house, which is yet standing at the northwest corner of Thorndike and

[1] The corporators were eight citizens, named, "and all those persons who now have or hereafter may subscribe and pay the sum of fifty dollars towards the erection of a Congregational meeting-house at Lechmere Point in Cambridge." — Mass. Spec. Laws, vi. 373.

Third streets. The church was organized March 3, 1828. The first pastor was Rev. Warren Burton, H. C. 1821, who was born at Wilton, N. H., Nov. 23, 1800, and ordained here March 5, 1828. He resigned June 6, 1829, and after preaching for short periods in several places, and laboring abundantly in the cause of education, died in Salem, June 6, 1866. Rev. James D. Green, H. C. 1817, born in Malden, Sept. 8, 1798, was ordained at Lynn, Nov. 8, 1828, and installed here Jan. 6, 1830. He resigned the pastorate April 21, 1840, and soon afterwards retired from the ministry. Like other ex-pastors in Cambridge, he was called by his fellow citizens to the performance of various municipal duties. He was a Selectman, 1845, and Representative in the General Court six years, between 1841 and 1854. On the incorporation of the City in 1846, he was elected as its first Mayor, and was re-elected to the same office in 1847, 1858, 1860, and 1861. He was succeeded in the ministry by Rev. Henry Lambert, June 3, 1841, who resigned April 19, 1846. Rev. George G. Ingersoll, H. C. 1815, D. D. 1845, was installed Dec. 3, 1847, and resigned Oct. 14, 1849. He died in 1863. Rev. Frederick W. Holland, H. C. 1831, was installed Oct., 1851, and resigned June 3, 1859 ; he is actively engaged elsewhere in the work of the ministry. His successors, for short terms, were Rev. Frederick N. Knapp, H. C. 1843, from July, 1860, to July, 1861 ; Rev. William T. Clarke, from Oct. 1861 to Oct. 1862 ; Rev. Henry C. Badger, from Nov., 1862, to Nov., 1863 ; Rev. Rufus P. Stebbins, Amh. C. 1834, D. D. 1851, was a "stated supply" from Jan., 1864, to May, 1864. Rev. Stephen G. Bulfinch, Columbian, Wash. 1827, D. D. 1864, was pastor from Sept., 1865, to July, 1869, and died in 1870. He was succeeded by Rev. Samuel W. McDaniel, in Nov., 1869, who resigned, July, 1874. The parish is now destitute of a pastor.

DEACONS.

	Elected.		Held office until
Cornelius Clark . .	Jan. 27, 1830	Resigned	Jan. 3, 1833
Abraham P. Sherman	April 3, 1831	Resigned	Dec. 2, 1851
Robert Vinal . . .	Jan. 3, 1833	Resigned	Feb. 1846
George Newhall . .	Dec. 3, 1851	Died	May 24, 1869
John Palmer . . .	May 6, 1855		

SECOND BAPTIST. — As early as 1824, several persons residing in East Cambridge, being members of Baptist churches in Boston and elsewhere, established a Sabbath-school, and subsequently made arrangements " to have preaching one evening in a week, and to this end permission was asked to occupy one of the rooms in the Putnam School-house." In 1827 a meeting-house was erected on the northeasterly corner of Cambridge and Fourth streets, which was dedicated on the tenth of October in that year. This house was of wood, 66 feet in length, 46 feet in breadth, with a steeple about 100 feet in height, and cost, with its bell and furniture, about nine thousand dollars ; it was burned, with all its contents, April 14, 1837. With commendable spirit, the society erected a new house on the same spot, of brick, 70 feet in length, 54 feet in breadth, with a convenient vestry in the basement, which was dedicated Jan. 11, 1838. The church was formed Sept. 3, 1827, which was publicly recognized by a council convened for that purpose four days afterwards. The first pastor of the church was Rev. John E. Weston, who was ordained Oct. 10, 1827, having preached to the society for several months previously. He was a graduate of the Newton Theological Institution, and was a faithful minister of the church. He resigned April 4, 1831, and was invited to take charge of the Baptist Church in Nashua, N. H. ; but " in the month of July in the same year " he was unfortunately drowned at Wilmington, Mass. Rev. Jonathan Aldrich, B. U. 1826, a graduate of Newton Theological Institution, who had previously been pastor of a church in Beverly, entered upon his labors here June 2, 1833, resigned June 19, 1835, and took charge of the First Baptist Church in Worcester. Rev. Bela Jacobs, formerly pastor of the First Baptist Church in Cambridge, was installed here Aug. 23, 1835. His pastorate had a tragical termination on the morning of May 22, 1836, when, as he was about to leave his carriage, at the door of the meeting-house, his horse suddenly started, ran a few rods, dashed the carriage against the Univeralist Church, " at the same time throwing him against the corner with such force as to fracture his skull ; " he survived about an hour, and entered into rest. Mr. Jacobs had resided in Cambridge eighteen years, and was universally respected and beloved. His death was sincerely lamented, not only by the people of his charge, but by the whole community. Rev. Nathaniel Hervey, a graduate of Newton Theological Institution, who had been settled at Marblehead, was installed Sept. 18, 1836, and closed his ministry here Sept. 1, 1839. He was afterwards settled for a short time at Andover, and soon afterwards died, of consumption, at Worcester. Rev.

William Leverett, B. U. 1824, who had been pastor of the Dudley Street Baptist Church in Roxbury, was installed Oct. 4, 1840, and resigned at the end of the year 1849. After a short pastorate in New England Village, his health failed and he retired from the ministry. Rev. Amos F. Spalding, born in Boston, B. U. 1847, a graduate of Newton Theological Institution, who had been settled in Montreal, commenced his ministry here Aug. 1, 1852, and resigned Nov. 28, 1856. Rev. Hiram K. Pervear, B. U. 1855, a graduate of Newton Theological Institution, was ordained as an Evangelist Nov. 5, 1857, commenced preaching here in the previous summer, became the regular pastor April 30, 1858, resigned April 1, 1865, was installed over the First Baptist Church in Worcester, and on the 5th of January, 1873, took charge of the First Baptist Church in Cambridge. Rev. Frank R. Morse, D. C. 1861, a graduate of Newton Theological Institution, commenced his pastorate Sept. 3, 1865, and resigned Nov. 20, 1867. He was succeeded, Dec. 4, 1868, by Rev. George H. Miner, B. U. 1863, who resigned Aug. 21, 1872. Rev. Hugh C. Townley, who graduated at the University of Rochester, 1858, was called to office here April 1, 1873, having previously been settled at Peekskill, N. Y., and Woburn, Mass. He resigned April 1, 1875. The present pastor is Rev. George W. Holman, who was born in Somerville, 1841, educated and ordained in the State of New York, and had been pastor at Radnor, Pa., Fort Edward, N. Y., Lewiston, Me., and Holliston, Mass. He was installed Nov. 7, 1875.

DEACONS.

	Elected.		Held office until	Age.
Enos Reed	Oct. 17, 1827	Died	July 8, 1871	75
John Donallan . .	April 1, 1829	Died	May 18, 1867	69
Henry S. Hills . .	Sept. 15, 1854			
Daniel Grant . . .	Oct. 4, 1870	Resigned	Oct. 30, 1874	
William B. Savage .	Oct. 4, 1870			
Alonzo Stewart . .	July 2, 1875			
Ambrose H. Sanborn	July 2, 1875			

FIRST EVANGELICAL CONGREGATIONAL. — " The First Evangelical Congregational Church, formed in that part of the city of Cambridge usually called Cambridgeport, was gathered Sept. 20, 1827. It consisted originally of forty-five members, most of whom, being residents of this place, had been previously connected with the Hanover Street Church, Boston, then under the pastoral care of Rev. Lyman Beecher, D. D."[1] The society connected with this church consists of the pew-owners, by whom " all questions of taxation are decided." In the settlement of a pastor, " it is the right and privilege of the church to nominate, and of the pew-holders to concur or non-concur; and upon their non-concurrence, the church nominate anew, until the parties agree."[2] Their first meeting-house was dedicated Sept. 20, 1827; it stood on the southerly corner of Norfolk and Washington streets, and " was held by the Deacons in trust for the use of the religious society worshipping in it, but subject, with certain restrictions, to the ultimate and entire control of the church."[3] This house was of wood and was several times enlarged, but still proving too small, and not sufficiently convenient, it was sold,[4] and a much larger brick house was erected on the westerly side of Prospect Street between Harvard and Austin streets : the corner-stone was laid July 29, 1851, and the house was dedicated June 30, 1852.

The first pastor of the church was Rev. David Perry, D. C. 1824, who was ordained April 23, 1829, and resigned October 13, 1830. He was succeeded by Rev. William A. Stearns, who was born at Bedford, March 17, 1805, H. C. 1827, D. D. 1853, was ordained December 14, 1831, and resigned December 14, 1854. " The pastoral connection was dissolved, that he might accept the Presidency of Amherst College, to which he had been elected." His pastorate was distinguished for energy and success ; and it is understood that his presidency was equally energetic and successful. He died 8 June, 1876. Rev. Edward W. Gilman, Y. C. 1843, who had been settled at Lockport, N. Y., commenced preaching here in July, 1856, was installed on the 9th of the following September, resigned Oct. 22, 1858, and was succeeded by Rev. James O. Murray, B. U. 1850, who was installed May 1, 1861, resigned Feb. 6, 1865, and became pastor of a church in New York. He received the degree of D. D. from Princeton College, 1867. Rev. Kinsley Twining, Y. C. 1853, formerly settled at New Haven, Conn., was installed here Sept. 12, 1867, resigned April 28, 1872, and took charge of a church

---

[1] *Historical Sketch of the Church*, in its *Manual*, 1870.
[2] *Ibid.*
[3] *Ibid.*

[4] The house was used for a lecture-room, and for similar purposes, until it was consumed by fire, Nov. 7, 1854.

in Providence, R. I. Rev. William S. Karr, A. C. 1851, was
installed Jan. 15, 1873, and dismissed Nov. 22, 1875, to take a
professorship in the Hartford Theological Seminary. Rev. James
S. Hoyt, Y. C. 1851, D. D. Olivet College, 1876, commenced
his pastorate Sept. 3, 1876, and was installed on the 15th day of
the same month.

DEACONS.

	Elected.		Held office until	Age.
William Fisk . . .	Jan. 3, 1833	Died	April 18, 1864	80
Samuel Barrett . .	Jan. 3, 1833	Resigned	Oct. 2, 1846.	
William Adams . .	July 3, 1846	Resigned	May 5, 1853	
Thaddeus B. Bigelow	Feb. 28, 1851	Resigned	Dec. 19, 1856	
William Davis . .	Sept. 29, 1854	Removed to N. H.		
Caleb H. Warner .	Sept. 29, 1854	Resigned	Sept. 29, 1872	
Sumner Albee . .	March 5, 1858			
Lucas B. Grover . .	April 24, 1868			
Henry N. Tilton . .	April 24, 1868			

SECOND EVANGELICAL CONGREGATIONAL. — The Second
Evangelical Church was organized March 30, 1842, and erected
a commodious meeting-house on the easterly corner of Austin
and Temple streets, which was dedicated Jan. 3, 1844. Meetings had previously been held in a chapel, erected on the same
lot, and dedicated May 3, 1842. Generally speaking, the members of this church were zealous advocates of the immediate
abolition of slavery. Their first minister was Rev. Joseph C.
Lovejoy, Bowd. Coll. 1829, who was installed Jan. 26, 1843.
He resigned May 10, 1858, and was afterwards active in politics.
He died here, Oct. 19, 1871, aged 67. Rev. Charles Packard,
Bowd. Coll. 1842, was installed April 26, 1854, was dismissed
March 21, 1855, and was succeeded by Rev. Charles Jones, whose
ministry extended from May 25, 1855, to Oct. 16, 1857. Rev.
George E. Allen, B. U. 1850, was installed May 20, 1858, and
resigned July 12, 1861. After a series of discouragements, by advice of a council, the church was disbanded Oct. 3, 1865, and many
of its members united with the Pilgrim Church, then worshipping in Stearns Chapel on Harvard Street, to which church they
contributed more than twelve hundred dollars (the residue of their
funds), to aid in defraying the cost of the new meeting-house on
the northerly corner of Magazine and Cottage streets. The

church edifice which had been the scene of many joys and many
sorrows, was sold, and was soon afterwards utterly consumed by
fire, Sept. 6, 1865.

DEACONS.

	Elected.		Held office until
David McClure . .	Dec. 12, 1843	Died	Jan. 20, 1852
Dexter Fairbanks .	Dec. 12, 1843	Dismissed	Feb. 2, 1849
Enos H. Baxter . .	April 28, 1846	Dismissed	July 27, 1855
Francis Hunt . . .	Jan. 18, 1850	Dismissed	May 9, 1854
Josiah H. Rugg . .	Jan. 18, 1850	Removed from the city	
Willard Sears . . .	Jan. 8, 1855	Dismissed	1857
George W. Wyatt .	Sept. 18, 1857	Resigned	June 8, 1860
Lyman G. Case . .	Sept. 18, 1857		Oct. 3, 1865
Curtis C. Nichols. .	Sept. 18, 1857		Oct. 3, 1865
Baxter E. Perry . .	Feb. 6, 1860	Resigned	Jan. 14, 1861
Edward Kendall . .	Jan. 14, 1861		Oct. 3, 1865.

The four deacons who were "dismissed" had previously removed from the city.

EVANGELICAL, EAST CAMBRIDGE. — The Evangelical Church
at East Cambridge was organized Sept. 8, 1842. In the course
of the next year a meeting-house was erected at the northeasterly
corner of Second and Thorndike streets, which was dedicated
Sept. 13, 1843, and taken down for removal to Somerville in
1876. The first pastor of the church was Rev. Frederick T.
Perkins, Y. C. 1839, who was ordained Jan. 11, 1843, and, after
a longer pastorate than has hitherto been held by any of his
successors, resigned May 26, 1851. He was succeeded by Rev.
Joseph L. Bennett, A. C. 1845, who was installed July 1, 1852,
and resigned Feb. 18, 1857. Rev. Richard G. Green was installed
March 31, 1858, resigned Sept. 17, 1860, and was succeeded by
Rev. William W. Parker, who was installed April 3, 1861, and
resigned March 22, 1864. Rev. Nathaniel Mighill, A. C. 1860,
was ordained Sept. 29, 1864, and resigned Sept. 24, 1867. Rev.
H. R. Timlow was the acting pastor from Oct., 1867, to March
31, 1870; and was succeeded by Rev. Samuel Bell, who was in-
stalled Nov. 1, 1870, and resigned May 29, 1872. Rev. D. W.
Kilburn supplied the pulpit from Sept. 1, 1873, to Sept. 1, 1874.
The church is at present destitute of a pastor.

DEACONS.

	Elected.	Remarks.
John Whipple . . .	Oct. 7, 1842	Removed from the City.
L. T. Winchester . .	Feb. 29, 1848	Removed from the City.
Lyman Morse . . .	May 4, 1849	Removed from the City.
John B. Taylor . .	April 11, 1851	
George N. Bliss . .	April 24, 1857	Removed from the City .
Wm. H. Pettingell .	Sept. 2, 1869.	

SAINT PETER'S CHURCH (EPISCOPAL). — The Parish of St. Peter's Church was organized at a meeting held Oct. 27, 1842. Religious services were held in the Town Hall until the completion of the church, which was commenced in 1843, and consecrated Jan. 31, 1844. This church was erected on the easterly side of Prospect Street, between Harvard and Austin streets, and was constructed of wood, with seats for two hundred and twenty persons. It was afterwards converted into a block of two dwelling-houses. In 1864 the foundation was laid of a much larger church, at the westerly corner of Main and Vernon streets; services were held in the Sabbath-school room as early as Sept. 1, 1866; the whole house was completed in Dec. 1867, and was consecrated Oct. 2, 1873. The several Rectors of the Church have been as follows: Rev. Darius-Richmond Brewer, from Dec. 4, 1842, to June 9, 1844; Rev. Edmund-Farwell Slafter, D. C. 1840, from July 21, 1844, to Sept. 30, 1846; Rev. Moses-Payson Stickney, from June 1, 1847, to April 7, 1851; Rev. William-Putnam Page, from Aug. 1851, to April 26, 1863; Rev. Charles Seymour, from Sept. 23, 1863, to March 31, 1866; Rev. Edwin-Bailey Chase, from Aug. 1, 1866, to Oct. 1, 1874, who died May 6, 1875. Rev. Edward M. Gushee, B. U. 1858, became Rector at Easter, 1875.[1]

The Wardens have been as follows: —

1842,	Simon Greenleaf,	G. F. R. Wadleigh.
1843–1844,	Isaac Lum,	G. F. R. Wadleigh.
1845–1846,	Isaac Lum,	John Dallinger.
1847–1848,	Isaac Lum,	Charles S. Newell.
1849,	Isaac Lum,	John Dallinger.
1850,	Stephen P. Greenwood,	Benjamin H. Ordway.

[1] With the exception of the Reverend grade of the several Rectors is unknown Messrs. Slafter and Gushee, the College to the writer of this history.

1851,	Stephen P. Greenwood,	Bela F. Jacobs.
1852,	Isaac Lum,	Asa P. Morse.
1853,	Benjamin Woodward,	Asa P. Morse.
1854–1855,	Luther Crane,	Asa P. Morse.
1856,	Isaac Lum,	Ethan Earle.
1857,	Swain Winkley,	John K. Palmer, M. D.
1858,	Goodrich M. Dayton,	William Page.
1859,	Goodrich M. Dayton,	Asa P. Morse.
1860,	Goodrich M. Dayton,	Francis Dana, M. D.
1861,	Asa P. Morse,	Justin A. Jacobs.
1862,	William D. Robinson,	Humphrey P. Caldwell.
1863–1864,	James H. Hallett,	Humphrey P. Caldwell.
1865,	James H. Hallett,	William Whitman.
1866–1876,	Edward R. Cogswell, M. D.,	William W. Dallinger.

St. John's Church. — The parish of St. John's Church was organized by Rev. John B. Fitzpatrick; and the church on the easterly side of Fourth Street, between Otis and Cambridge streets, was erected in 1841, and dedicated in 1842. Mr. Fitzpatrick was the first pastor; he was afterwards Bishop of the diocese of Massachusetts. He received the degree of D. D. from Harvard College, 1861, and died in Boston Feb. 13, 1866, aged 53 years. He was succeeded in 1848 by Rev. Manasses P. Dougherty, who may be regarded as the Apostle of the Catholic Church in Cambridge, inasmuch as he has organized three parishes, in addition to that of which he was originally pastor. His successors in the pastorship of St. John's Church were Rev. George T. Riordan; Rev. Lawrence Carroll; Rev. Francis X. Brannagan, who died in office, June 25, 1861, aged 29 years; Rev. John W. Donahoe, who also died in office, March 5, 1873, aged 45 years; and Rev. John O'Brien, the present incumbent. All these clergymen are supposed to have been liberally educated; but the particulars are not ascertained.

Harvard Street Methodist Episcopal. — A class of six members was formed in 1831, whose leader was James Luke, who still survives. In 1835, this class, which had hitherto met in or near Harvard Square, and had lost some of its members, by removal from the town, was established in Cambridgeport, and by new accessions consisted of seven members, under the leadership of Samuel Stevens, who died July 2, 1876. From this small beginning, the Harvard Street Methodist Episcopal Church has become one of the most vigorous and active religious organizations in the city. Meetings for public worship were held first in the "Fisk Block," at the westerly corner of Main and Cherry streets, and afterwards in the Town House, on the southwesterly corner of Harvard and Norfolk streets, where St. Mary's Church now stands. "In 1842, a wooden church, 40 by 60 ft. was erected at an expense of about $6,000, which was lengthened in 1851, twenty feet, increasing its value to $9,000. This edifice was burnt Nov. 26, 1857. A new church of wood, 60 by 80 ft., was immediately erected at an expense of $17,000, and dedicated Oct. 13, 1858. This house was burnt March 15, 1861, and the present edifice, a brick structure 61½ by 96½ ft. extreme length, was dedicated Nov. 19, 1862."[1] This house, like its predecessors, was built on Harvard Street, opposite to Essex Street. It has a spacious and commodious vestry on the ground floor, the audience room being approached by an easy flight of stairs.

"The church appears in the Minutes for the first time in 1841, when the first appointment was made." The preachers in charge, according to the Discipline of the Methodist Episcopal Church, were appointed at the Conferences holden in the years hereunder named : —

1841, 1842, Rev. Leonard B. Griffing.
1843, 1844, Rev. Isaac A. Savage, W. U. 1841.   Died 16 Feb. 1854.
1845,   Rev. Mark Trafton.
1846,   Rev. John Clark.   Died 19 Oct. 1849.
1847, 1848, Rev. I. J. P. Collyer.   Died 7 May, 1872.
1849, 1850, Rev. A. D. Merrill.
1851, 1852, Rev. Charles Adams.
1853, 1854, Rev. I. J. P. Collyer.   Died 7 May, 1872.
1855,   Rev. C. S. McReading.   Died 11 April, 1866.
1856,   Rev. Moses A. Howe.   Died 27 Jan. 1861.

---

[1] The corner-stone of this church was laid in masonic form, June 12, 1861, by the Grand Lodge of Massachusetts. A very characteristic prayer was offered by Rev. Edward T. Taylor, who was clad in the appropriate costume of a Knight Templar. Kneeling on the foundation stone, and brushing away the carpet which had been spread to protect his knees from its hard and sharp protuberances, he poured forth his fervent thanks and supplications on behalf of Christianity and Freemasonry, Christians and Masons, the Church and the Grand Lodge, alternately, and in about equal proportions. Especially he prayed that the Masons present might be blessed for the respect which they were showing to Religion, and that the members of the church might receive an abundant spiritual reward for their steadfastness in the midst of trials as by fire, and for their generous contributions to defray the expense of erecting this third house of worship. "Two churches, O Lord," said he, "formerly standing on this spot, have been destroyed by the hand of the incendiary, or by carelessness, which is as bad as an incendiary."

1857, 1858, Rev. Isaac Smith. Died 16 July, 1860.
1859, 1860, Rev. Gilbert Haven, W. U. 1846. Elected Bishop, 1872.
1861, 1862, Rev. Edward Cooke, W. U. 1838, D. D. (H. C.) 1855.
1863, 1864, Rev. Lorenzo R. Thayer, W. U. 1841, D. D. 1863.
1865–1867, Rev. Henry W. Warren, W. U. 1853.
1868, 1869, Rev. Nelson Stutson. Died 16 April, 1871.
1870, 1871, Rev. Ira G. Bidwell.
1872, 1873, Rev. Andrew McKeown.
1874–1876, Rev. Melville B. Chapman.

[For most of the statistics concerning this church I am indebted to its Secretary, Mr. Samuel L. Ward.]

OLD CAMBRIDGE BAPTIST. — The Old Cambridge Baptist Church was organized Aug. 20, 1844, and was publicly recognized Oct. 23, 1845. Eighty-three members of the church were formerly members of the First Baptist Church, and a large number of the society and congregation had worshipped with them in Cambridgeport. Their first meeting-house was a wooden structure, which was erected on the corner of Kirkland Street and Holmes Place, and was dedicated Oct. 23, 1845. This house was sold, Oct. 23, 1866, to what is now known as the North Avenue Congregational Society, and was removed bodily, without even disturbing the steeple, to the southerly corner of North Avenue and Roseland Street, where it now stands. The congregation worshipped for the next few years, partly in the meeting-house of the Shepard Congregational Society, generously offered for their use, and partly in Lyceum Hall. Meantime arrangements were made, and contributions on a magnificent scale were offered, for the erection of a new meeting-house. The effort was successful, and the spacious stone edifice, extending from Main Street to Harvard Street, opposite to Prescott Street, was dedicated Sept. 29, 1870.

The first pastor was Rev. Ezekiel G. Robinson, B. U. 1838, D. D. 1853, LL. D. 1872, who was installed Oct. 23, 1845, the day on which the church was recognized and the first meeting-house was dedicated. He resigned Sept. 13, 1846, and became Professor of Theology at Rochester, N. Y., and afterwards President of Brown University. His successor was Rev. Benjamin I. Lane, who was installed Dec. 30, 1846, and resigned March 8, 1849. The next pastor was Rev. John Pryor, who had received the degree of D. D. at King's College, N. S., and was installed March 25, 1850. He resigned July 26, 1861, and was succeeded by Rev. Cortland W. Anable, who was installed June 21, 1863, and resigned Oct. 27, 1871, having received the degree of D. D. from Madison University during his ministry here. The present pastor is Rev. Franklin Johnson, D. D., who was installed Dec. 31, 1878.

DEACONS.

	Elected.	Died.	Age.
William Brown . . .	Sept. 2, 1844	June 24, 1861	75
Josiah Coolidge . . .	Sept. 2, 1844	Sept. 13, 1874	87
John B. Dana . . .	Sept. 2, 1844		
Wm. T. Richardson . .	March 30, 1862		

LEE STREET. — The Lee Street Society was organized in 1846. Most of its original members, together with its first pastor, had been connected with the Cambridgeport Parish. Their first meeting-house, on the westerly side of Lee Street, near Harvard Street, was dedicated March 25, 1847, and was consumed by fire May 20, 1855. A new edifice was immediately erected on the same lot, which was dedicated Jan. 23, 1856. The church was organized April 9, 1847. Its first pastor was Rev. Artemas B. Muzzey, who had for twelve years previously been pastor of the Cambridgeport Parish. His pastorate here commenced Sept. 7, 1846, and continued until Feb. 20, 1854, when his resignation was accepted. He was installed at Concord, N. H., March 29, 1854; but after a pastorate of several years returned to Cambridge, where he now resides, preaching statedly at Chestnut Hill. His successor was Rev. Henry R. Harrington, H. C., 1834, who was ordained 1842, installed here Feb. 11, 1855, and resigned April 1, 1865. He has since been a successful superintendent of public schools in New Bedford. He was succeeded by Rev. Abram W. Stevens, a graduate of the Meadville Divinity School, who was ordained 1862, preached three years in Manchester, N. H., was installed Nov. 26, 1865, and closed his ministry here Nov. 1, 1870. The present pastor, Rev. John P. Bland, a graduate of the Cambridge Divinity School, 1871, was ordained Sept. 6, 1871.

DEACONS.

	Elected.	Died.
Ezra Dean	April 9, 1847	Aug. 8, 1858
Peter Mackintosh . . .	April 9, 1847	July 28, 1848
Eben Snow	April 27, 1847	

ST. PETER'S CHURCH (CATHOLIC). — The Parish of St. Peter's Church was organized in January 1849, by Rev. Manasses P. Dougherty, who still remains its faithful and beloved pastor. For more than a quarter of a century he has done much to promote the growth and prosperity of his church. He has been actively engaged in the organization of all the Catholic parishes in the city, except St. John's; and of this he was the second pastor. St. Peter's Church edifice, on the southerly side of Concord Avenue, near the Observatory, was erected in 1848, and dedicated in May, 1849.

THIRD UNIVERSALIST. — A Unitarian Society was organized Oct. 8, 1851, in North Cambridge (including several families residing in Somerville), under the name of the "Allen Street Congregational Society." The corner-stone of a meeting-house for its use had been laid a fortnight previously, Sept. 25, 1851, on a lot furnished for that purpose by Mr. Walter M. Allen, at the southeast corner of Allen and Orchard streets. This edifice was constructed of wood, "was finished Feb. 2, 1853," and was totally destroyed, March 19, 1865, by a fire which also consumed many other buildings. Another meeting-house, also of wood, was immediately erected on the same spot; it "was completed Dec. 21, 1865," and was afterwards enlarged. The corner-stone of a more spacious edifice was laid Oct. 23, 1875, on the south-westerly side of North Avenue and fronting on Union Square; constructed of brick, 67 by 85 feet, and containing 154 pews; this house was dedicated Sept. 14, 1876.

At a meeting of the society, Oct. 17, 1869, it was voted, "that the Allen Street Congregational society be, and the same is, hereby united with the Religious Societies of the Universalist Denomination of Christians." The society voted, June 29, 1870, to ask the formal fellowship of the Massachusetts Convention of Universalists, which was granted; and by an Act of the General

Court, approved March 27, 1874, its corporate name was changed to the "Third Universalist Society in Cambridge."

The first pastor of this parish and church was Rev. James Thurston, H. C. 1829, who was installed June 14, 1853, and resigned July 5, 1854. Rev. Caleb Davis Bradlee, H. C. 1852, was ordained Dec. 11, 1854, resigned the pastorship June 28, 1857, and soon afterwards took charge of a parish in Boston. Rev. John M. Marsters, H. C. 1847, formerly of Woburn, was installed April 25, 1858, resigned April 7, 1862, and was succeeded, on the first of the next September, by Rev. Frederick W. Holland, H. C. 1831, formerly pastor of the Third Congregational Society at East Cambridge, who retained his charge somewhat more than two years, when he resigned, and Mr. Marsters resumed the pastorate Feb. 10, 1865, and held it until Sept. 26, 1867, after which time, for more than a year, the pulpit was "supplied by various and numerous preachers." Mr. Charles E. Fay, T. C. 1868, was invited, Dec. 10, 1868, to become pastor; he preached statedly about a year, when, not having been ordained, he accepted a professorship in Tufts College, and discontinued his ministry. Rev. William A. Start, T. C. 1862, was ordained at Groton Junction (now Ayer), Sept. 24, 1862, and was installed here, April 10, 1870, having previously been pastor of the societies at Ayer and at Marlborough. "Under his ministry, the church building was enlarged, and the society greatly increased in numbers and strength."[1] He resigned Jan. 1, 1874, and removed to Chicago, but returned before the end of the year and was installed pastor of the Universalist Church at Melrose, March 7, 1875. Rev. Isaac M. Atwood was ordained at Clifton Springs, N. Y., Aug. 15, 1860, and commenced his pastorship here on the first Sabbath in April, 1874, having previously held the like office at Clifton Springs, Portland, Me., North Bridgewater (now Brockton), and Chelsea. He received the degree of A. M. from St. Lawr. Univ., 1869.

NORTH CAMBRIDGE BAPTIST. — In 1846, a Sabbath-school was established in North Cambridge, under the auspices of the Baptists. For a time it had permission from the City Council to meet in the Winthrop School-house;[2] but in 1852 this privilege was

[1] MS. letter from Jabez A. Sawyer, Esq., from which are derived many statistics in this sketch.

[2] "Cambridge, Sept. 26, 1846. By the authority vested in me by a vote of the City Council, passed Sept. 22, 1846, I hereby grant the use of the lower room in the school-house in the north district of Ward One, for the purpose of holding a Sabbath School, until otherwise ordered. JAMES D. GREEN, Mayor."

suddenly and unceremoniously withdrawn by the School Committee.[1] The friends of the school thereupon hired a lot of the
city, near the school-house, and erected " a neat and commodious
chapel, — at a cost, including furnishing, of $1,411.81,"[2] which
was dedicated Oct. 31, 1852, and was called " Our Sabbath
Home." Religious meetings were held in the chapel on Thursday
evenings, through the winter. In May, 1853, regular sabbath
services were established, and Rev. Alexander M. Averill, a
graduate of the Newton Theological Institution, soon became the
"stated preacher." A meeting-house was erected in 1854, on the
northwesterly side of Coggswell Avenue, near North Avenue,
which was dedicated Feb. 15, 1855. The Sabbath-school chapel
was soon afterwards removed, and connected with the new meeting-house ; ten years later the house was greatly enlarged and
beautified, and was reopened on the nineteenth anniversary of
the school. The church was organized in March, 1854, and was
publicly recognized on the 6th of the following April. Rev. Mr.
Averill continued to hold the office of pastor until October, 1859.
Rev. Joseph A. Goodhue, D. C. 1848, was elected to the pastorate in July, 1862, which he resigned in July, 1864, and was succeeded by Rev. Joseph Colver Wightman, B. U. 1852, who was
elected in February, 1866, and resigned in March, 1868. The
present pastor is Rev. William S. Apsey, Madison Univ. 1861,
who commenced his pastoral duties here in October, 1868.

This church has no officers bearing the name of deacons ; but
the duties ordinarily performed by such officers are assigned to a
" standing committee," consisting of four members, elected annually. " Upon this committee brethren Henry R. Glover and
Chester W. Kingsley have regularly served since the organization of the church ; different members have completed the number."[3]

NORTH AVENUE CONGREGATIONAL. — In September, 1857, a
religious society was organized in North Cambridge, under the
name of the " Holmes Congregational Society," which name
was changed, about ten years afterwards, to " North Avenue
Congregational Society." Its first place of worship was an
edifice of moderate size, called " Holmes Chapel," which was

---

[1] "CAMBRIDGE, *Sunday, July* 18, 1852.
To the members of the Sabbath School
held in the Winthrop school-house : I
am directed to inform you that the room
now occupied by you will not be at your
service after this day. N. WILKINSON,
Sub-School Committee, Ward One."

[2] *Memorial of the North Avenue Sabbath School,* p. 21.

[3] MS. letter from Warren Sanger, Esq.

dedicated Sept. 17, 1857. After a few years this house was found
to be too small for the congregation, and was sold (it is now
owned and occupied by the Methodist Society on North Avenue).
The Holmes Society bought of the Baptists, Oct. 23, 1866, their
meeting-house which stood at the corner of Kirkland Street and
Holmes Place, which was removed bodily to its present location
on the southerly corner of North Avenue and Roseland Street,
and was dedicated Sept. 29, 1867. "The succeeding four years
found this house too small, when it was enlarged by adding chan-
cel and transepts, and otherwise remodelling the house, giving it
its present seating capacity of 1,040." The house, thus improved,
was rededicated Dec. 15, 1872.

The church, now known as the North Avenue Congregational
Church, was organized Sept. 23, 1857, under the auspices of an
ecclesiastical council duly convened; it consisted originally of
forty-three members. The first pastor of this church was Rev.
William Carruthers, Bowd. Coll. 1853, who was installed Jan.
2, 1861, and was dismissed Feb. 21, 1866. Rev. David O.
Mears, born in Essex, Feb. 22, 1842, A. C. 1865, was ordained
and installed Oct. 2, 1867, under whose ministry "the growth of
the church and congregation has been rapid and substantial."
The following named persons have served this church as Deacons: —

John Harmon,	Daniel Fobes,
Samuel Chadwick,	H. D. Sweetser,
F. E. Whitcomb,	Henry M. Bird,
James R. Morse,	Wm. Fox Richardson,
William P. Hayward,	Frank Foxcroft.

PILGRIM CONGREGATIONAL. — In 1852, a mission Sabbath-
school was established under the joint direction of the Baptist,
Methodist, and two Congregational Churches in Cambridge.
After a few years it was managed solely by the First Evangelical
Church. In 1863, a chapel was erected for the accommodation
of the school, and as a missionary station.[1] It was soon opened
for religious services two evenings in the week, and Rev. William
R. Stone, a Methodist clergyman, who was at that time city missionary, was employed to preach on Sabbath afternoons. In
1864, Rev. Edward Abbott, Univ. of the City of New York,
1860, was invited to take charge of this mission, with the hope

[1] This edifice, known as the "Stearns of Harvard Street, about two hundred
Chapel," still stands on the northerly side feet easterly from Windsor Street.

of organizing a permanent congregation and church, and commenced his labors Jan. 1, 1865. A church was organized Nov. 21, 1865, under the name of the Stearns Chapel Congregational Church, and Mr. Abbott was installed as its pastor. "Fifty-one persons constituted the church at its formation, of which 15 were males, and 36 females. Of the entire number, 12 made profession of their faith for the first time, and 39 brought letters from other churches. Of the latter, 18 came from the First Congregational Church, 17 from the Second Congregational Church (recently disbanded), and the remaining 4 from different and distant churches." [1] Mr. Abbott was dismissed, at his own request, in November, 1869; he became assistant editor of the "Congregationalist," published several books, and performed other literary work. After the change of name and removal of this church, Mr. Abbott returned to the scene of his former labors, and gathered a new congregation, out of which the present Chapel Church was organized in October, 1872. During the last few years, still residing here, and still retaining his connection with the "Congregationalist," he has been connected with a third missionary enterprise in Belmont and Watertown, near Mount Auburn, which has proved so successful that a chapel has been erected, and the organization of a church is anticipated.

Rev. George R. Leavitt, W. C. 1860, was installed as pastor of the Chapel Church, May 4, 1870. The chapel, though enlarged in 1867, was still too small for the congregation; and a much more spacious edifice was erected on the northwesterly corner of Magazine and Cottage streets, at a cost of nearly forty thousand dollars; the corner-stone was laid May 18, 1871, and the house was dedicated Jan. 4, 1872. In anticipation of removal to a new meeting-house, at the distance of about a mile from "Stearns Chapel," and in view of the fact that the original name would not properly designate the church after its removal, it assumed the name of "The Pilgrim Congregational Church," Feb. 27, 1871. The church has had only three Deacons: —

John N. Meriam, elected Nov. 29, 1865.
Edward Kendall, elected Nov. 29, 1865.
Lyman G. Case, elected 1875.

BROADWAY BAPTIST. — A Sabbath-school, consisting of twenty-eight scholars and fifteen teachers, was opened Dec. 16, 1860, in a room at the corner of Harvard and Clark streets, under the

[1] *Manual and Historical Sketch of Stearns Chapel Church.*

patronage of the First Baptist Church. In 1861, a small chapel was erected for the accommodation of the school, and for religious meetings, on the southerly side of Harvard Street, about two hundred feet easterly from Pine Street. The school held its first meeting in this chapel Jan. 12, 1862; and it was dedicated as a house of worship Feb. 9, 1862. This chapel was afterwards sold, and removed to the southeasterly corner of Harvard and Essex streets, where it was occupied by a school under the direction of the Catholic Church. A new house of worship, for the accommodation of the Sabbath-school and the congregation which had been gathered in connection with it, was erected in 1866, on the southwesterly corner of Broadway and Boardman Street, eighty-six feet in length and sixty-four in breadth, which was dedicated Nov. 22, 1866. Meantime, Rev. William Howe, Waterville College, 1838, formerly pastor of the Union Church in Boston, had been engaged by the First Baptist Church as a missionary at this station. He commenced his labors early in 1863, which were so successful that on the 9th of May, 1865, a church consisting of fifty members was constituted under the name of "The Broadway Baptist Church," and he was unanimously elected pastor. The public services of recognition were held in the First Baptist Church, June 25, 1865. Mr. Howe remained pastor until July, 1870, when he resigned; he continues to reside in Cambridge, and performs clerical duties, but without pastoral charge. The present pastor of the church, the Rev. Henry Hinckley, H. C. 1860, was installed Dec. 13, 1870; he had previously been settled at Winchester, and more recently at Groveland, Mass.

· DEACONS.

	Elected.		Held office until	Age.
Ebenezer Hovey .	May, 1865	Died	March 25, 1866	65
Josiah Sparrow .	May, 1865	Resigned	Nov. 1872	
Jacob Eaton . .	Dec. 1867			
Simeon Taylor . .	Dec. 1867	Resigned	Oct. 1869	
Charles L. Fessenden	Nov. 1872			

FREE CHURCH OF ST. JAMES. — The Parish of St. James, at North Cambridge, was organized on Christmas day, 1864, and from that time divine service was regularly continued under the charge of Rev. Andrew Croswell, B. U. 1843, who was elected Rector at Easter, 1865, and remained in that office until Easter,

1871, when the failure of health compelled him to resign. He was succeeded by Rev. William H. Fultz (since deposed), whose connection with the church ceased in the summer of 1873. Rev. Theodosius S. Tyng, a graduate of Kenyon College, 1869, and of the Episcopal Theological School, Cambridge, 1874, took charge of the church Oct. 1, 1873, and became its Rector June 15, 1874. At first, divine service was held in a building on North Avenue, which was erected for a bank, and altered into a chapel. " The present church building stands upon Beech Street, on a lot acquired by the parish during the Rev. Mr. Croswell's rectorship. It was presented to the parish by Mrs. Mary L. Greenleaf, and consecrated Dec. 21, 1871." [1] The following named persons have served the church as Wardens : —

1865–1870,	Joseph H. Rice,	George A. Meacham.
1871–1872,	Joseph H. Rice,	George Vincent.
1872,	George Viucent,[2]	James M. Barker.
1873–1875,	James M. Barker,	George H. Mullin.
1876,	James M. Barker,	Daniel McNamara.

METHODIST EPISCOPAL. — The Methodist Episcopal Church in Old Cambridge was organized June 3, 1868 ; and on the same day, their chapel on the easterly side of North Avenue, between Holmes Place and Waterhouse Street, was dedicated.[3] The preachers in charge of this church have been as follows : —

1868, 1869, Rev. Abraham D. Merrill and Rev. James Mudge, Wesl. Univ. 1865. The Rev. Mr. Mudge received the degree of B. D. from the Bost. Theol. Sem. 1870 ; was transferred to the India Conference and assigned to missionary work, in 1873, and now has "charge of the publishing interests of the M. E. Church " in India. 1870, 1871, Rev. Samuel Jackson, Wesl. Univ. 1859. 1872, Rev. Pliny Wood. In 1873, Rev. Mr. Wood was appointed a commissioner to the National Exposition at Vienna, and died there of cholera. 1873, Rev. James Lansing, who was transferred to Nashville, Tenn., before the expiration of his year, and his place here was supplied by Rev. Mr. Beiler. 1874, 1875, Rev. David K. Merrill, to whom I am indebted for some of the foregoing facts. 1876, Rev. Charles Young.

[1] MS. letter from Rev. T. S. Tyng.

[2] Mr. Rice died July 28, 1872, aged 71 ; and thereupon Mr. Vincent was elected Senior Warden, and Mr. Barker, Junior Warden.

[3] This edifice, formerly called " Holmes Chapel," had for several years been occupied by what was then called the " Holmes Congregational Society," now the " North Avenue Congregational Society." It was purchased and removed to its present locality early in 1868.

St. Mary's Church. — The parish of St. Mary's Church was organized in 1866 by Rev. Manasses P. Dougherty, who performed the duties of pastor, in connection with his charge of St. Peter's Church, until May, 1867, when he was succeeded by the present pastor, Rev. Thomas Scully, who had previously served his country as Chaplain of the Ninth Regiment, Massachusetts Volunteers, in the War of the Rebellion. The corner-stone of the spacious brick church, at the southwesterly corner of Harvard and Norfolk streets, was laid July 15, 1866, and the edifice was dedicated March 8, 1868. The congregation is larger than any other in Cambridgeport.

St. John's Memorial Chapel. — On the twenty-second day of January, 1867, Mr. Benjamin T. Reed, of Boston, by legal indenture, placed in the hands of trustees one hundred thousand dollars, towards the founding and endowing of an Episcopal Theological School in Cambridge, which school was opened in the autumn of the same year. " In the year 1869, Mr. Robert M. Mason [of Boston], completed and presented to the Trustees the beautiful edifice of St. John's Memorial Chapel, as a free church for the permanent use of the students of the school, and of the congregation which might be gathered there as worshippers. This building, with its fine organ and other furniture, cost its generous donor seventy-five thousand dollars." [1] The congregation is not organized as a parish, nor has it any Rector or Wardens ; but the Faculty of the School are required to maintain, permanently, public worship and preaching in the Chapel, under the direction of the Dean of the Faculty. Rev. John S. Stone, D. D. was elected Dean at the organization of the School in 1867.

Chapel Congregational. — After the removal of the Pilgrim Church, in January, 1872 (see page 337), a mission Sabbath-school and religious services on the Lord's day were continued at Stearns Chapel, by the Rev. Edward Abbott, the former pastor of the church. A new church was organized Oct. 16, 1872, under the name of " Chapel Congregational Church," and on the same day the Rev. John K. Browne, H. C. 1869, was ordained and installed as its pastor. At his request, he was dismissed from his charge, Sept. 16, 1875, that he might devote himself to the foreign missionary service. He is now stationed at Harpoot, in Eastern Turkey.

[1] A Statement by the Trustees, etc., p. the westerly corner of Brattle and Mason 14. This elegant stone edifice stands on streets. —

Rev. Robert Beales Hall, W. C. 1870, who had preached two years at Wolfborough, N. H., was installed here Dec. 28, 1875. His ministry was acceptable, and gave promise of abundant success; but it was terminated by what seemed to be a premature death, Nov. 2, 1876, before he had quite attained the age of thirty-one years.

DEACONS.

H. Porter Smith, elected January, 1873.
Henry C. Williams, elected January, 1873.

COTTAGE STREET METHODIST EPISCOPAL. — The Cottage Street Methodist Episcopal Church — the outgrowth of a Mission Sabbath-school enterprise started in 1870, in Williams Hall — was organized April 5, 1871. It consisted of seventeen members. The church and society at first worshipped in Williams Hall, and afterwards in Odd Fellows Hall. In 1872 a convenient chapel was erected, which was dedicated June 19th. By the erection of this chapel, the Society incurred a debt of four thousand dollars, in addition to its own free and generous contributions. One of its original members, Mr. Amos P. Rollins, who died March 9, 1873, bequeathed two thousand dollars toward the extinction of this debt, on condition that the society should raise an equal sum within three years of his death, — which condition was complied with; but the estate of Mr. Rollins yielded to the society little more than half the original bequest.

The several preachers in charge have been as follows : —

1871–1874, Rev. Isaac F. Row.
1874–1875, Rev. W. L. Lockwood.
1875–1877, Rev. Jarvis A. Ames.

ST. PAUL'S CHURCH. — A new parish was organized in 1874, by Rev. Manasses P. Dougherty, in old Cambridge, under the name of St. Paul's Church. The meeting-house at the northwesterly corner of Mount Auburn and Holyoke streets, erected in 1830 by the First Church in connection with the Shepard Congregational Society, was purchased for the use of this new parish, and after being repaired and fitted for its new use, was opened for Divine service Dec. 25, 1873. Rev. Mr. Dougherty retained the pastoral charge of St. Paul's Church, as well as of St. Peter's, until Oct. 1, 1875, when he was succeeded by Rev. William Orr, the present pastor.

CHURCH OF THE SACRED HEART. — On the fourth day of October, 1874, the corner-stone was laid of an edifice to be called the Church of the Sacred Heart, on the southerly side of Otis Street, between Sixth and Seventh streets. It is to be constructed of stone, 150 feet in length and 75 feet in width, at an estimated cost of $80,000. The church is designed to seat twelve hundred persons. The basement under the whole building is to be fitted for the use of the Sabbath-school and various societies.

ASCENSION CHURCH. — Several attempts had been made, at different times, to establish the Episcopal Church in East Cambridge, but without success. In May, 1875, Rev. William Warland, a native-born son of Cambridge, H. C. 1832, finding several Episcopal families in that part of the city, offered his services as a missionary. The use of the Unitarian meeting-house, on the northwesterly corner of Third and Thorndike streets, was obtained, and on Whitsunday, May 16, 1875, worship according to the ritual of the Episcopal Church was commenced, and it has continued thus far with encouraging prospect of success. At the close of the first year, however, in May, 1876, an arrangement was made with the Second Universalist Society for a joint occupation of their church on Otis Street; since which time the Mission has a morning and evening service in that edifice, and the Universalists hold their regular service in the afternoon. No Episcopal parish has yet been organized, nor have the customary church officers been elected.

CHARLES RIVER BAPTIST. — The history of this church is briefly given in the printed order of services at its recognition: " Meetings for prayer held in 1869 at private houses. Sunday-school commenced April 8, 1870, meeting in the chambers of house No. 8, Magazine Court. Chapel dedicated Nov. 29, 1870. Regular preaching services commenced in July, 1874, and continued to the present time in charge of J. P. Thoms, Theo. C. Gleason, and Rev. G. T. Raymond." The chapel is a neat and convenient edifice of wood, 78 feet in length by 88 feet in width, capable of seating 800 persons, and standing at the southeast corner of Magazine Street and Putnam Avenue; it was erected in 1870, at an expense of about $8,500. Until recently this was substantially a missionary station, under the patronage of the First Baptist Church; but on the 25th of April, 1876, a new church was organized, consisting of forty members, twenty-eight

of whom had previously been members of the First Church; and on the 8th day of the following June, it was publicly recognized, and received into the fellowship of the Baptist churches. Rev. Fenner B. Dickinson was installed as pastor of the new church Nov. 13, 1876, and commenced his ministry under very favorable auspices.

As in the "North Cambridge Baptist Church," the official duties, ordinarily assigned to Deacons, are performed by the "Standing Committee" of this church.

CPSIA information can be obtained
at www.ICGtesting.com
Printed in the USA
LVHW050952181020
669074LV00008B/439